Autobiographical Occasions and Original Acts

Autobiographical Occasions and Original Acts

Versions of American Identity from Henry Adams to Nate Shaw

Albert E. Stone

University of Pennsylvania Press
Philadelphia
1982

Design by Patricia Pennington

Library of Congress Cataloging in Publication Data

Stone, Albert E.
    Autobiographical occasions and original acts.

    Includes bibliographical references and index.
    1. American prose literature—20th century—History and
criticism. 2. Autobiography. 3. Authors, American—20th century—
Biography. 4. United States—History—20th century—Biography.
I. Title.
PS366.A88S8   818'.508'09   82–7016
ISBN 0–8122–7845–3   AACR2
ISBN 0–8122–1127–8 (pbk.)

Printed in the United States of America

For Grace

Contents

The deepest side of being an American is the sense of being like nothing before us in history—often enough like no one else around us who is not immediately recognized as one of our tradition, faith, culture, profession. *"What do you do, bud?"* is the poignant beginning of American conversation. "Who are *you?* What am I to expect from *you?"* put in history's language, means that I am alone in a world that was new to begin with and that still feels new to me because the experience of being so *much* a "self"—constantly explaining oneself and telling one's own story—is as traditional in the greatest American writing as it is in a barroom.

ALFRED KAZIN

The sense of "I," or the sense of self, means that I experience myself as the true center of my world, as the true originator of my acts. This is what it means to be original. Not primarily to discover something new, but to experience in such a way that the experiences originate in me.

ERICH FROMM

Preface

ALFRED KAZIN IS QUITE CORRECT: constantly explaining oneself by telling one's own history is both theme and motive in many enduring works of American literature. Less highbrow culture, too, has as a chief staple similar stories of the private self. *True Confessions,* like Woody Allen's later movies and "The Today Show," touches the same deep currents and curiosities which animate *Song of Myself, Roughing It, Long Day's Journey into Night,* or *Invisible Man.* A powerful need to listen to each others' personal histories (and thus to learn more about our own) runs throughout our mobile, polyglot culture. This helps explain the ubiquity and popularity of autobiographical acts, which in many variations of narrative mode have flourished since the early years of the republic, and even before. Certainly autobiography in its many forms is widely produced and enthusiastically consumed today. One finds personal histories everywhere one finds books: on library shelves and in the syllabi of college courses; at the checkout counters of drugstores and supermarkets; on best-seller lists, as book club selections, and in reviews (almost weekly, it seems) of the *New York Times;* in the knapsacks of high school students and hitchhikers. The paperback revolution has made it possible, on the one hand, for a poet's or movie star's memoir to rival the latest detective story and, on the other hand, for the account of a forgotten runaway slave's life to be relived in a class on Afro-American history. No longer is autobiography a minor and neglected branch of American prose (as it was a scant fifteen years ago), and its history cannot be summarized in a few familiar names and titles. As the 1980s open, the popular appreciation and critical assessment of autobiography are signal features of American studies.

The chapters which follow are my contribution to this ongoing concern and recent critical enterprise. During the past decade, I have been drawn by several developments to reading and writing about autobiographies. In the background, first of all, are the tempestuous events of the 1960s and after, in which the self's struggle against oppressive social custom and political power found expression in the passionately personal narratives of Malcolm X, Norman Mailer, Anne Moody, and others. I began teaching these powerful works shortly after my return in 1969 from a Fulbright year in Prague. There I had seen in my classes at Charles University the immediate relevance of Thoreau, Whitman, Richard Wright—indeed, of the whole tradition of the personal voice in our letters. Then at Emory and Atlanta Universities in the early and mid-1970s I encountered enthusiastic and informed students responding to autobiographical writings of all sorts. Similar reactions soon characterized other audiences as well—students and older scholars at other universities where I have lectured, Upward Bound teenagers, middle-aged Foreign Service officers home on furlough, Indian scholars and newspapermen in New Delhi and Hyderabad. Many of the arguments and aperçus in these pages owe their existence or refinement to these amateurs and experts of autobiography, whose help I hereby acknowledge even though I cannot recall all their names and faces.

A second source of stimulation has been the work of critics and journalists recently exploring the frontiers of "fact" and "fiction" in American writing. Autobiography is but one of several forms of prose which straddle this frontier. The historical dimensions of nonfictional narratives like personal history, documentary, and high journalism have awakened my interest in what J. H. Hexter calls "the rhetoric of history," what David Levin examines in the "literary criticism of history," and questions of "historicism" raised by Roy Harvey Pearce and Wesley Morris. Moreover, history-making merges inevitably with psychology in the new field of psychohistory, which I find practiced most responsibly and imaginatively by Erik Erikson, Bruce Mazlish, Cushing Strout, and Joel Kovel. Though these scholars and clinicians have not always set their sights on autobiography, I have tried to translate certain of their methods and assumptions. Since autobiography is a literary as well as historical activity which recreates psychic as well as social experience, I have also drawn freely on the work of psychoanalytically oriented critics and clinicians, in particular Norman N. Holland, Frederick C. Crews, Phyllis Greenacre, Stanley Leavy, and José Barchilon. Autobiography's complex nature as simultaneously history, art, confession, and testament makes such eclectic criticism necessary; these minds have in my case made it possible.

Yet autobiography resists being squeezed into the very disciplines to which it is clearly connected. Hence arises the specifically autobiographical criticism which has become such a notable feature of recent American studies and European literary studies. As the pages and notes of this book indicate, I have been profoundly influenced by particular books and essays. These include the by now classic works of Georges Gusdorf, Georg Misch, Roy Pascal, and Jean Starobinski. Challenging theoretical statements by younger critics and historians have opened other avenues of thought and investigation. I am particularly indebted to the work, and the friendship, of James M. Cox, Francis Russell Hart, Philippe Lejeune, James Olney, and Robert F. Sayre. I owe a special debt of gratitude to my colleagues Robert Sayre, Wayne Franklin, and John Raeburn, who generously read and gave cogent criticism of sections of this work. There are others whose support and friendship have made a demonstrable difference. I should like especially to remember, with gratitude, the following: Daniel Aaron, Timothy D. Adams, Liliane K. Arensberg, Houston A. Baker, Jr., the late Alan Bussel, Robert Detweiler, William B. Dillingham, Peter W. Dowell, John A. Hague, William Hoffa, Carol T. Holly, Richard P. Horwitz, Kathryn Hunter, J. Paul Hunter, Trudy Kretchman, Cynthia Larson, Judy Lensink, Barrett J. Mandel, Anne Mayeaux-Hines, Richard Noland, Sherman Paul, Roger J. Porter, Ellen C. Rose, William C. Spengemann, Robert B. Stepto, Floyd C. Watkins, Cynthia Griffin Wolff, and Fredrick Woodard. In addition, I would like to thank my Iowa graduate assistants who have faithfully struggled to improve this manuscript: Jeffrey Miller, Robert Slocum, JoAnn Castagna, Mary Ann Rasmussen, and Anne Schatz. Laird C. Addis, Sr. has been an intelligent, prompt, and meticulous typist.

Generous institutional support for research and writing has been provided me by the National Endowment for the Humanities, which awarded me a fellowship in 1976–77, by the Graduate School of Emory University, the Graduate College of the University of Iowa, and the Ossabaw Island Project of Georgia. Librarians at the following institutions gave generous and expert assistance at crucial stages in my work: Bowdoin College, Emory University, Howard University, the Library of Congress, the University of Iowa, and Yale University.

Sections of the book have appeared in altered or abbreviated form in several books and journals. I am grateful to the editors and publishers of the following for permission to reprint: *The American Autobiography: A Collection of Critical Essays* edited by Albert E. Stone (Englewood Cliffs, N.J.: Prentice-Hall, 1981); *American Character and Culture in a Changing World,* edited by John A. Hague (Westport, Conn.: Greenwood Press, 1979); *Phylon: The Atlanta University Re-*

view of Race and Culture, vol. 39 (March 1978); *Prospects: An Annual of American Cultural Studies,* vol. 3, edited by Jack Salzman (New York: Burt Franklin, 1977); *The Yearbook of Research in English and American Literature,* vol. 1, edited by Herbert Graber, H. J. Diller, and Hans Bungert (Berlin: Walter de Gruyter, 1982); *Revue Française d'Etudes Américaines,* vol. 14 (1982).

1

Individual Stories and Cultural Narratives: Autobiography in Modern America

IN THESE PAGES I propose to explore a significant and flourishing yet still hazily understood aspect of twentieth-century American culture, the nonfictional writing by and about the self which goes under the umbrella of autobiography. In this century, and particularly in the years since World War II, no other mode of American expression seems to have more widely or subtly reflected the diversities of American experience or the richness of American memories and imaginations. Most conventionally, autobiography is encountered as high culture. The sophisticated narratives of personal experience written by Henry Adams, Gertrude Stein, Richard Wright, Lillian Hellman, and some others are American prose classics, ranking with a handful of older autobiographies like *The Autobiography of Benjamin Franklin, Walden,* and the *Narrative of Frederick Douglass, an American Slave, Written by Himself.* These venerable life-stories, and their modern equivalents *The Education of Henry Adams, The Autobiography of Alice B. Toklas,* and *Black Boy* (to single out three familiar titles) are securely located in the curricula of our colleges and schools and on the shelves of libraries and bookstores, and they are often cited in reviews and discussed in scholarly essays. Autobiography on this level is newly but now firmly respectable. It possesses a canon worthy of comparison with the personal literature of any other modern Western country.

Yet to describe personal history in such elite terms is manifestly incomplete. Just as clearly, autobiography is a demotic or Low Rent art, as Tom Wolfe would say. Like true confessions or Harlequin romances, the paperback autobiographies of a Mae West or Muhammad Ali sell by the hundreds of thousands from the racks of drugstores and

1

supermarkets, right alongside Alex Haley's *Roots.* In bypassing the usual high-cultural institutions, American readers reveal a catholic craving for sharing the lives of their more famous (or notorious) fellows. They exhibit as well a monumental unconcern over a fact often bothersome to critics, namely, that many of these best-sellers are ghost-written or products of a confessed collaboration. How can an autobiography, which by definition is a story in which actor and author are taken to be the same person, be written by another? This contradiction, however, goes unchallenged in many quarters; not only the reading public but publishers, professional writers, and their subjects as well find two names on the cover of a paperback autobiography perfectly acceptable. If we are to understand autobiography not simply as a literary convention but more broadly as a cultural activity, then the present-day practice of collaboration autobiography must be taken seriously. Not only is collaboration more and more common, but it has already produced in *Black Elk Speaks* and *The Autobiography of Malcolm X* two recognized literary classics. Here as elsewhere, lines between popular and elite are difficult if not impossible to draw.

In this century, too, autobiography even leaps barriers of literacy itself to become a form of folk expression, thanks to the anthropologist's notebook and the oral historian's tape recorder. The WPA project of the 1930s to record the lives of ex-slaves is one instance of such enlargement of subject matter and historical awareness. Another is Nancy Lurie's *Mountain Wolf Woman, Sister of Crashing Thunder: The Autobiography of a Winnebago Indian.* Perhaps the most popular recent achievement in this direction is Theodore Rosengarten's *All God's Dangers: The Life of Nate Shaw,* the epic account of an obscure Alabama tenant farmer.[1] Surely William Dean Howells was a perceptive prophet in 1909 when he called autobiography "the most democratic province in the republic of letters."[2] It now seems that all corners of our diverse country, each era of its history and many hitherto hidden and uncommon lives, have been recreated—given personal shape and social meaning—in the prose literature stretching from *The Education of Henry Adams* to *All God's Dangers* and beyond. Many modes and intentions of autobiography are represented on these now crowded shelves. Memoir, reminiscence, apology and confession, testament, case-history and life-history, diary and journal, personal journalism, the nonfiction novel or mock autobiography are all descriptive terms—some traditional, some newly invented—for different kinds of storytelling acts and cultural occasions included in modern autobiography. The sweep of this characteristically American activity is aptly reflected in Alfred Kazin's comment: "the experience of being so much a 'self'—constantly explaining oneself and telling one's story—is as traditional in the greatest American literature as it is in a barroom."[3]

Howells and Kazin address each other across seven decades of writing about the American self. During this period the sheer number of published autobiographies has risen dramatically. Upwards of ten thousand personal histories of Americans may now have appeared, according to the bibliographies of Kaplan, Lillard, and Brignano.[4] If this is a reasonable guess (and there is as yet no comprehensive bibliography of American women's autobiographies),[5] the figure happily coincides with Howells's category of "the best ten thousand autobiographies" as a suitably capacious context for enjoying and evaluating this popular literature. Himself an autobiographer as well as a novelist and critic, Howells was an enthusiastic but not undiscriminating reader. Writing personal history, he points out, affords one a matchless opportunity to make "the sincere relation of what he has been and done and felt and thought." Moreover, he invites "some entirely unknown person to come out with his autobiography and try if it will not eclipse the fiction of the newest novelist." At the same time he boasts of Benjamin Franklin as the author of "one of the greatest autobiographies in literature" and hails the recent and quite different achievements of Ulysses S. Grant, Julia Ward Howe, and Booker T. Washington.[6] Such open-minded awareness of tradition and innovation, of autobiography as both elite and popular art, provides an admirable model for later readers. Sooner than any other American critic, Howells perceived the protean possibilities in twentieth-century autobiography as democratic expression.

Indeed, autobiography is firmly rooted in our culture—and, as I shall argue, not simply in high literary culture. Reading another's life story is, as Howells suggests, to immerse oneself in human experience in all its interconnections and manifestations. To be sure, what lies there on the table is a book and therefore is, in Jean Starobinski's term, "discourse." It is the translation into a pattern of words of many acts of memory, reflection, and imagination. The autobiographer's whole consciousness remodels the past into a narrative shape which necessarily resembles chronicle, fiction, fable, dream, and myth. But autobiography is also and simultaneously "history," as Starobinski also emphasizes.[7] It recreates a past shared with others, one assumed to have actually occurred and not simply imagined. For both writer and reader of autobiography, this priority of past social experience and the struggle to shape and repossess its meanings form basic conditions of an informal "pact" or implicit understanding between author and audience, about which Philippe Lejeune, among others, has perceptively written.[8] When such expectations are stretched (as, say, in the case of an experimental narrative like Norman Mailer's *The Armies of the Night*), this very fact serves to raise the reader's historical as well as aesthetic consciousness. Thus while the strategies of the novelist, poet, dramatist, and even photographer are available to the modern autobiographer, so too are virtually all the techniques of the historian. An autobiographical act, therefore, makes a writer at once the creator and the recreator of his or her personal identity. Individual experience and the consciousness through which it has been remembered are simultaneously presented in a distinctive narrative structure and through a pattern of verbal images and metaphors. The result is both deliberate artistry and a more or less trustworthy account of the past, a history. Though free to combine impressions and images of the past in order to express present needs and even future expectations, the autobiographer is bound to that past in ways the novelist (even the historical novelist) is not. Like other historians seeking adductively to formulate plausible explanations and descriptions of past events, an autobiographer offers an interpretation of the surviving records of his or her own past.[9] Even when these records are simply private memories they become in a true sense public property. The reader is invited to reality-test as well as participate in such recoveries. The process of reinventing a plausible and satisfying history is therefore very much a collective enterprise. Writer and readers tacitly conspire to reenter, revivify, and finally understand a singular past which has been consciously remembered and less consciously revised or "forgotten," faithfully reproduced in certain respects but extensively reimagined in others.

If these preliminary perceptions of the twentieth-century autobiographical situation hold generally true—and all have been questioned by one or another of the critics whose work in recent years has so signally helped to focus attention on the whole literature of the self—then all autobiographies possess permeable boundaries. They are indeed centrifugal cultural works. They resist closure and the non-referentiality of art, while remaining art. In choosing this mode or convention of communication, the writer deliberately eschews the aesthetic freedom and integrity his discourse might have possessed had it taken other narrative forms. In anchoring present consciousness firmly in shared cultural experiences of the past, in human life in its myriad and at times contradictory manifestations, and in the reader's cooperating consciousness, the autobiographer necessarily surrenders some of the potential harmony, unity, and autonomy of art. In doing so, the author places a special burden on himself and the reader. On one level autobiographical communication is direct and uncomplicated: a single voice speaks to other men and women of the discovered meanings of personal existence. As Richard Lillard points out, such expression has special significance, for "autobiography is as near as mankind gets to a unified, lasting, prima facie version of what happens in an individual's lifetime."[10] This gives all autobiographies intrinsic interest and value. Readers—at least in Western cultures but increasingly so in other cultures as well, such as India—derive deep satisfaction from sharing in the act of memory and imagination which connects a self to the "extensive totality" of the world.[11] Hence any critique of autobiography as cultural activity must first come to grips with individual texts as places where such exchanges of useful pleasures and secret profits can and do occur.

Nevertheless, despite the "pleasures of the text," autobiography is never as simple as it seems. Because of its several often subtle and submerged connections to different dimensions of public life and private consciousness, an autobiography is, in the language of psychoanalysis, an overdetermined document. Its statements and implications must be explained in more than a single set of terms. As an account of past actions and gestures, autobiography asks to be judged skeptically as a version of history. As a deliberate pattern of words and the imitation of a distinctive voice, it is a story which seeks a sympathetic ear. As the articulation of past and present motives, impulses, and ideals, autobiography becomes a kind of case-history as well as a spiritual confession, with the reader as invited priest-psychiatrist. Finally, as a more or less trustworthy linguistic bridge between one self or soul and others, autobiography recreates a model of literate culture itself and the social circumstances in which individual personality is discovered, asserted, and confirmed (or denied) and community potentially established.

Recognizing intuitively this thick web of text and context is what makes Howells such a shrewdly prophetic voice near the century's beginning. In his invitation, for example, to the "unknown autobiographer" to rival the "newest novelist" he anticipates later autobiographical occasions like the appearance in 1929 of Anne Ellis's *The Life of an Ordinary Woman* or, in 1965, Claude Brown's *Manchild in the Promised Land*. At the same time, he identifies an important and prophetic critical issue in linking autobiography to fiction—a connection probably less obvious to nineteenth-century readers of memoirs and confessions than to present-day readers. Having written autobiography himself, Howells had struggled with the knotty problem of the

nature of autobiographical truth which has subsequently stirred energetic controversy among critics.[12] Yet in acknowledging the often
shadowy distinctions between the two narrative modes, he emphasizes the fact that for most modern readers the novel is the basic model
of prose narrative. On the other hand, Howells accepts autobiography
as social history too, in speaking of the writer's obligation to reveal how
his life has actually been, in his words, "circumstanced."[13] Past events
and relationships, social movements and cultural institutions, possess
for him—as they most likely still do for most readers—a fundamental
significance in the formation of any recreated self. The struggle to see
and state one's "circumstanced" location in time and social space, and
thereby to discover one's historical self, marks the commonly accepted difference between autobiography and fiction. There is therefore a direct line from Howells to a later critic of autobiography, such
as Francis Russell Hart, who has enlarged Howells's perception thus:
"in understanding fiction one seeks an imaginative grasp of another's
meaning." Hart writes, "In understanding personal history one seeks
an imaginative comprehension of another's historic identity. 'Meaning' and 'identity' are not the same kind of reality and do not make
the same demands. One has no obligation to a fantasy."[14]

Whether as a simple set of "meanings," or as mysterious "identity," or both in some intricate interaction Hart does not acknowledge,
autobiography indeed affords a special kind of information about a culture and the individuals embedded in it. Through the study of personal histories, as Gordon Allport points out, one can identify the
presence and relative weight of many social processes or institutions
as these occur in historical development. All such information comes
to us, however, in the shape of interpreted personal experience; it is
never raw data. The past is re-presented by a reminiscing writer who
tries to show how certain events, relationships, ideas, and institutions
have become functionally and imaginatively interrelated in his or her
own life. Because by their nature autobiographies are subjective, one
of a kind, ultimately incomparable, it is always risky to formulate generalizations about human nature, social behavior, and cultural patterns on the basis of such evidence.[15] But if one begins with the aim
of trying to understand how a single life becomes at once distinctive
and representative as the result of narrative reconstruction, then only
one document may be needed. For such purposes, an autobiography
offers a coherent version of one historical and social process. This account is commonly so structured by the author as to provide grounds
for extrapolating from the unique to general experience. Even when
the autobiographer does not explicitly cast his or her life in shareable

or typical terms, readers inevitably make such translations—at least into the terms of their own lives. Hence autobiography is a rich cultural medium for exploring the necessary interplay between the particular and the general. As Allport has written, "acquaintance with the particular case, a sense of its patterned character and its individualized laws of action stand at the gateway of generalized knowledge and at its terminus at the point of application. Insight is a product of the interweaving of nomothetic and idiographic understanding."[16] This is, I believe, a powerful sociological insight whose implications I hope to illustrate in these pages.

Indeed, many cultural situations and issues can be understood only in Allport's terms. For history and the human sciences, as well as for literature and philosophy, the recorded perceptions of specifically located individuals of the meanings they themselves attach to past experiences may prove indispensable. Not what an event actually was (which may often prove impossible or extremely difficult to establish) but what it has since come to mean to a participant or observer looking back in light of accumulated experience and altered perspective—this is the special province and promise of autobiography as social document. "Autobiography is a second reading of experience," Georges Gusdorf writes in his epoch-making essay of 1956, "and it is truer than the first because it adds to experience itself consciousness of it."[17]

By following Allport's advice and directing attention first to the particular case, the reader of autobiography may discern patterns and laws of action which, because they are anchored in specific situations and individual acts of memory and imagination, will yield valid but probably low-level generalizations about personality and culture. Such hypotheses, since they are based on idiographic evidence, can never afford universal, replicable, or predictive results. Yet using autobiography to understand a culture's past can be "scientific" in another sense. Like other participant-observer sciences—anthropology, for instance, or psychoanalysis—autobiography is a complex cultural activity which involves an individual gathering data from a human subject. This is doubly true, for in endlessly different ways all autobiographers are anthropologists returned from sojourns in the countries of their own pasts. Readers, too, are fellow travelers and interviewers. Though this participant-observer role is more obviously the case with Margaret Mead's *Blackberry Winter* or Loren Eiseley's *All The Strange Hours* (both personal histories written by anthropologists) than with less conceptually oriented life-stories, all autobiographers stand *outside* as well as *within* their own experience. In moving, therefore,

7

from the particular to the general and back to the particular again, testing generalizations narrowly rather than broadly, we employ a methodology which Paul Diesing argues is widely appropriate to the human sciences.[18]

A complementary approach is also suggested by "scientific" common sense: in dealing with idiographic documents one would do well to proceed toward generalizations by means of specific comparisons of a fairly limited number of texts and contexts. "The essence of anthropological work," Mead writes in *Blackberry Winter,* "is comparison"; "contrast through comparison is necessary to complete a picture."[19] Thus when Franz Boas sends the eager young anthropologist off to Samoa he advises her to look for both pattern and individual variation in the lives and communities to be studied. Moreover, in moving from one culture to another she is always to be prepared for "some as yet unrecorded mode of behavior" (140). These practical guidelines serve as well as the larger Freudian hypotheses about personality development which Mead also brings to Samoa and New Guinea. All contribute to an important anthropological insight which aptly applies to the reading and writing of autobiography: the realization that patterns which the participant-observer both discovers in and imposes upon a personality or culture are not the only ones which might have been worked out. Mead's own temperament and imagination dictate the selection of data and govern the conclusions in her anthropological writing. Within her autobiography, as well, they naturally find a central place. In *Blackberry Winter* "contrast through comparison" describes not only Mead's treatment of the Mundugamor and Tchambuli but also of her three husbands and her daughter and granddaughter.

By adopting Mead's principled yet personal mode of inquiry into her own life, the critic of autobiography necessarily employs the ad hoc conceptualizing which Allport argues is the only proper way to understand and interpret personal documents. Even more radical a champion of the particular than Mead, he urges us to let "the case speak entirely for itself, tell its own laws, dictate its own explanations."[20] Allowing each autobiographical text to locate itself in time, tradition, and culture, and assisting this location with heuristic rather than universal hypotheses are, then, commonsensical yet "scientific" approaches to personal documents.

I

Yet few readers follow Allport's advice unreservedly. Most of us, like Mead, bring certain basic assumptions and expectations to the encounter with each life-history. Implicit, therefore, in the whole process of selection, interpretation, and comparison of life situations and autobiographical strategies of self-presentation to be reflected in this book are several assumptions about autobiography itself and the culture in which it flourishes. These cluster most obviously and simply around the concept and implications of individualism. As Howells perceived intuitively in 1909, the cultural value or ideological impulse animating the autobiographical act and creating conditions for the reader's response to it is belief in the validity and importance of every single life. Allport later put the same ideological point in these words: "the aspiration of democracy is to foster the integrity of each individual."[21] In historical contexts broader than Howells' Progressive era or Allport's late 1930s ethos, this same linkage of individualism, democratic pluralism, and autobiography seems amply justified. Since long before the time of Tocqueville, Thoreau, and Andrew Jackson, Americans have confirmed and celebrated the individual, as few other cultures in history have done, through their social, economic, and political institutions. Karl J. Weintraub, writing as both historian and astute critic of European autobiography, succinctly states this Western cultural ideal. "It then appears to be a precious aspect of the human existence that each and every individual is individually distinctive, that every person is unique and, therefore, incomparable, unrepeatable, and ultimately indescribable. The individual is ineffable."[22] This litany of adjectives expresses certain deeply held assumptions about human nature which move inevitably beyond history into the domain of philosophy and theology.

Despite glaring contradictions in social practice and historical reality—indeed, often *because* of such tensions and denials—the individualist ideal continues to inspire many twentieth-century Americans, especially when they participate in autobiographical occasions as authors and audiences. Many everyday phenomena reflect and reinforce this ideological network. Thus the bumper sticker on the Volkswagen at the traffic light announcing "I'm Irreplaceable!" is more than a cute plea not to be bumped. It states a classic American belief, typically packaged and displayed for a mass, mobile public. So, too, autobiographies, which might be read as extended bumper announcements to the same effect. Both reflect the tenacious social ideal whose persistence is all the more significant when found repeated in personal histories of Afro-Americans, immigrants, penitentiary prisoners, and others whose claims to full individuality have often been denied by our society. Such historically disparate works as *The Autobiography of Benjamin Franklin,* Alexander Berkman's *Prison Memoirs of an Anarchist,*

9

and *The Autobiography of Malcolm X* therefore exhibit their authors's shared belief not only in *individualism* as a common cultural value but also in *identity* as a vital personal achievement.

Constructing plausible identities through autobiography is, then, a characteristic manifestation of contemporary culture's "extreme curiosity about 'selves' and our radical interest in the life of particularized human individuation."[23] This urge, long encouraged and publicly prized, defines autobiography as truly an original act. The term is Erich Fromm's and comes from the essay "The Creative Attitude," in which he observes: "The sense of 'I,' or the sense of self, means that I experience myself as the true center of my world, as the true originator of my acts. This is what it means to be original. Not primarily to discover something new, but to experience in such a way that the experiences originate in me."[24] Autobiography precisely fulfills Fromm's sense of an original act. Discovering and asserting the self who has moved on the social stage (if not before the floodlights of public history) and writes under the complex stimuli of memory and imagination is the "original" achievement autobiography affords and our culture applauds. Remembered events and relationships are taken over, appropriated, made one's own, in this act of narration. Even as the autobiographer reconstructs the "circumstances" of his or her existence, this awareness becomes the new experience which places the self at the center of its world. This makes each autobiography an originating act of consciousness because it is the record of an unique experience and an original work of art.

Personal identity therefore becomes one synonym for Fromm's "original act." Furthermore, the activity of explaining oneself by telling one's story begins as historical consciousness. This impulse to find order and meaning in past experience is the initial motive behind autobiography, as it is for other modes of history-making. Moreover, if all human knowledge originates in particular human experience, as the German philosopher Wilhelm Dilthey has declared, then autobiography is both a basic historical document and a truly "original act." Dilthey's two or three seminal chapters in *Pattern and Meaning in History,* published around the time of Howells's 1909 essay, constitutes on this point the fountainhead of modern autobiographical theory. "Autobiography," he wrote about 1907, "is the highest and most instructive form in which the understanding of life confronts us. Here is the outward, phenomenal course of a life which forms the basis for understanding what has produced it within a certain environment. The man who understands it is the same as the one who created it. A particular intimacy of understanding results from this."[25] As a conscious act of historical understanding, autobiography becomes for Dilthey "the germinal cell of history, for here the specific historical categories arise."

> Because the sequence of a life is held together by the consciousness of identity, all the moments of that life have their foundation in the category of identity. The discrete is linked into continuity; by following the lines of memory from the small figure of childhood living for the moment, to the man who maintains his firm resolute inner life in the face of the world, we can relate the succession of influences and reactions to something which is shaping itself and which, thus, develops as something inwardly determined. The value of outer events which affect this self lies in the fact that they do so. (89)

As subsequently reflected in the historical studies of autobiography by Georg Misch and more indirectly exemplified in the essays of Howells, this attitude has shaped the criticism of autobiography during much of the twentieth century. A prime focus of autobiographical attention falls, then, on life as past social experience. In Dilthey's view, man knows himself in society and history, not by introspection, meditation, or imagination. Through autobiography, life is brought to language, not, as literary purists insist, the other way around. Therefore a fundamental "original act" occurs whenever "the self grasps the course of its own life in such a way as to bring to consciousness the basis of human life, namely the historical relations in which it is interwoven" (111).

"I am I because my little dog knows me," Gertrude Stein wittily and ironically observes in *Everybody's Autobiography*.[26] Moreover, these and other self-defining relationships reveal their interconnections and meanings only through the passage of time. Hence Dilthey's dictum: "the relationship between present, past, and future is characteristic of our lives" (99). Awareness of personal if not cultural continuity is essential to autobiography. Links (as well as gaps) between *then* and *now* are found because they are assumed to exist. Consequently, as Russell Hart points out, *narrative momentum* becomes the literary feature of autobiographical texts wherein the self-historicizing impulse most clearly expresses itself, just as *dramatic description* and *metaphor* are clearer clues to the autobiographer's artistic identity and characteristic psychic states.[27] However, grasping autobiography first as historical narrative does not simplify the problematic nature of its "truth." Because autobiography is both descriptive and inven-

11

tive, is capable of verification by historical methods, yet lays claim to the veracity of imaginative art, one cannot be sure whether, or to what extent, a statement about the self and its past is intended to be literal or symbolic. One must therefore reality-test each text. Since statements are being asserted about a real world, these will necessarily prove themselves outside the text as well as within it. Only by checking against other available sources (e.g., biography, letters, newspapers, photographs, other autobiographies) can one sometimes determine at what level of literalness or metaphoric utterance a given writer is operating. In the process, as Roy Pascal points out, errors, omissions, and distortions of testable fact often turn out to be surprisingly unimportant.[28] As readers, we don't want to know everything about a life. We frequently discover as much about a self from what is not said as from detailed descriptions and confessions. Yet to evaluate the meaning of such errors and omissions, the skeptical reader must be prepared to look beyond the text.

Personal history, then, is consciously lived history. However, putting oneself at its center is, as Kazin points out, "not of course to command it, or even one's fate in life. To live history is to express most memorably a relationship to the past, to a particular setting, to a moment, sometimes even to a particular set of buildings. . . ."[29] Moreover, continuity is by no means the only conceivable relationship discovered between one's past, present, and future. In the twentieth century such Diltheyan confidence in the power of consciousness to create connections gives way in many cases to a powerful sense of discontinuity and dislocation. "A world so different from that of my childhood or middle-life can't belong to the same scheme," Henry Adams writes a friend in 1904. "Out of a medieval, primitive, crawling infant of 1838, to find oneself a howling, steaming, exploding, Marconiing, radiumating, automobiling maniac of 1904 exceeds belief."[30] Sixty years later, Malcolm X echoes a similar complaint: "How is it possible to write one's autobiography in a world so fast-changing as this?"[31] Not only the bewildering pace of social change but also twentieth-century suppositions about the self (Freudian, say, or Eriksonian) often render connections between personal identity and public history much more problematic—if not frankly fragmented and discontinuous—than Dilthey once assumed.

Indeed, the existence of radical splits between past and present has always characterized one particular variety of personal history: spiritual autobiography or confession. Thus Thomas Merton, no less than John Woolman or Saint Augustine, is motivated to write *The Seven Storey Mountain* by awareness of decisive differences and dis-

12

junctions between his secular self and his grace-filled soul after conversion. This experience, in Starobinski's view, is not unique to religious converts. It applies to all autobiographers, for "one would hardly have sufficient motive to write an autobiography had not some radical change occurred in his life. . . . It is the internal transformation of the individual—and the exemplary character of this transformation—that furnishes a subject for a narrative discourse in which 'I' is both subject and object."[32] This kind of awareness, though essentially psychological, has literary consequences. It confers upon autobiography its special character as *discourse-history* by subordinating chronology and biographical data to their imaginative realization in a later, altered consciousness. Starobinski's emphasis upon past and present moments and selves allows autobiography to be seen as an "original act" in another light. Although historical re-creation remains central to each autobiographical project, what always realizes that reconstruction is an imaginative activity with words. A narrating self reinvents the historical actor. No matter how meticulously the past has been remembered, checked, and arranged into a coherent story, it remains true that autobiography as history always suffers from incompleteness as it does from conscious and unconscious falsification. Yet as verbal artifact an autobiography necessarily manifests by every word, image, episode, and chapter division the architectural presence and imaginative identity of its author. Style is indeed a self, if not the only self. Even if, as frequently occurs in American autobiography, the author is an amateur whose only foray into literary creation is this book, the reader realizes that the nearest, clearest, and (in one sense) most trustworthy self is this writer, rather than the historical actor who is always a manipulated character in the narrative. Furthermore, since our social selves, especially for women and blacks, are partly masks or imposed identities, both the autobiographer and her audience may feel further justified in playing around with historic identity. To stress the self as the creator of history—even, at times, as the fabricator of fantasies— maximizes one's freedom from circumstances and social stereotype. In this way, an ideal self always coexists with an actual—that is, a determined—historical identity.

Constructing this double self involves a special kind of original act. It issues in a nonfictional narrative which is simultaneously fiction or metaphor. "We assume the life *produces* the autobiography as an act produces its consequences," Paul de Man writes, "but can we not suggest, with equal justice, that the autobiographical project may itself produce and determine the life and that whatever the writer *does* is in fact governed by the technical demands of self-portraiture and thus determined in all its aspects, by the resources of its medium?"[33] Practitioners of surfiction, transfiction, faction, or the new nonfiction novel, as I will show in Chapter Eight, heartily agree: there is simply no clear line to be drawn between fantasy and real life. The only actual locale of any autobiographical self is in the text. For a Lacanian structuralist like Jeffrey Mehlman, as for Ronald Sukenick the surfictionist, there is no self, only linguistic structures.[34] "We conceive of our lives in the image of fiction," Mutlu Konuk Blasing bluntly declares of the American autobiographers she discusses in *The Art of Life*.[35] For her, autobiographical consciousness can only be the turning back of time in the imagination. She shows scant sympathy for neither the reader's expectations of verifiable history nor the backward and forward motions of the writer's memory as it responds to pressures from a surviving historical record. And she is not curious about equally systematic reflections of a self reimagining itself moving through the life cycle amid a series of historical moments. This is how a psychohistorian like Erik Erikson sees autobiography as a product of "the curious process by which selected portions of the past impose themselves on our renewed awareness and claim continued actuality in our contemporary commitments."[36] At best, for deconstructionists and nonfiction novelists, the self at the typewriter is the only "true" presence or trustworthy recreation, just as that writer's present context is the only temporal state recoverable in the act of reading. However compelling this aesthetic-linguistic argument is with respect to theories of imaginative literature, I feel its limitations when applied in practice to autobiography. What I see as the unique open-endedness and multidimensionality of autobiography, and its resistance to containment within purely linguistic structures, are effectively reduced or denied. So, too, are other social dimensions of the autobiographical occasion.

Nevertheless, the careful exploration of language is clearly vital for understanding the overdetermined self exhibited in autobiography. For as John Sturrock and others assert, words reflect an ordering of experience different from that of historical chronology. Through association and juxtaposition they point to the timeless realm of the unconscious. There, Sturrock writes, "the power of association, of bringing into the light mnemonic instead of temporal contiguities, has infinitely more to tell us about our permanent psychic organization than the power of chronology."[37] Behind historic identity, therefore, beneath even the discourse of the artful storyteller, lurks another "self" whose psychic structures and states reveal themselves symbolically through language. In fact, autobiography's coded imagery often speaks more truly than more literal renditions of experience, for it suggests patterns of deep continuity within personality. At a certain point, therefore, the reader of autobiography must be prepared to transcend both history and narrative art. When the social self disappears into language and language itself becomes a screen on which psychic structures and spiritual essences throw their shadow, then distinctions between "fact" and "fantasy" are erased. At this point, the reader comes face-to-face with those dimensions of individuality and private experience evoked by Weintraub's mysterious adjectives, "unique," "incomparable," "unrepeatable," "indescribable," "ineffable." Here the "original act" of autobiography goes beyond Fromm's assumption of a social self placing itself at the center of its world. The writer's task then becomes to see and somehow to communicate the soul within or beyond the self. "Inside me, I quickly come to the barrier, the limit of what I am," Thomas Merton declares in *The Sign of Jonas,* "beyond which I cannot go by myself. It is such a narrow limit and yet for years I thought it was the universe."[38]

How to express this transcendent essence of identity and the timeless dimensions of human experience is a challenge by no means confined to spiritual autobiographers and visionaries like Merton or Black Elk, the Oglala Sioux holy man. Dilthey's finite past, present, and future are not the only time zones modern autobiographers inhabit. Before sentience, beneath consciousness, and after death are vitally significant dimensions of personal experience and sources of identity. The soul speaks *through* and *to* the self as Thoreau casts his fishing line upward into the clouds above Walden Pond, when Anaïs Nin drums on her belly in the maternity hospital, and as Shirley MacLaine recalls lying warmly under a single blanket in the frigid mountain darkness of Bhutan. Yet we must remember that such moments of "depth" are still connected to culture by consciousness and language. The presence of transcendence in *Walden, Diary-I,* and *"Don't Fall Off the Mountain"* is defined—as well as rendered even more ineffable—by the more mundane realities of the beanfield, Nin's friendship with Henry and June Miller, and Shirley MacLaine's visit to the orphanage in Calcutta. Both sorts of experiences are expressed in autobiographical acts which, in Barrett Mandel's aptly borrowed phrase, are always "reflection trained on mystery."[39]

II

To summarize these assumptions and definitions: even eccentric or experimental autobiographies recreate a self-in-its-world. We must therefore devise ways to see beyond and around as well *into* each singular self. This challenge to the reader closely resembles the one Ronald Grele has set for oral history: "Our aim is to bring to conscious articulation the ideological problematic of the author, to reveal the cultural context in which information is being conveyed, and to transform an individual story into a cultural narrative, and so to understand more fully what happened in the past."[40] Transforming an individual story into cultural narrative need not, however, deny the writer's original act of self-construction. Autobiographers intend such uses of their private lives. Thus in identifying not simply the kinds of information being conveyed but the ideological implications of a life-story, Grele means for us to perceive what is most personal as well as what is public and perhaps political in the text. Ideology is therefore as basic as myth in defining autobiographical acts and placing them in cultural context. Myth, as William C. Spengemann and L. R. Lundquist assert, provides conveniently sharable forms for an individual life—patterning it typically for Americans as a successful journey toward secular and spiritual perfection.[41] But ideology is equally necessary and perhaps even more socially functional, for in addition to the timeless designs of cosmic, natural, and social meaning embodied in mythic stories, there are the more specific beliefs and programs of social action which motivate individuals within a culture to change and act toward these ultimate ends. Because myth and ideology, as Warren Susman has argued, are equally essential to history in general, their presence and weight must be traced in personal history as well.[42] Declaring one's ideology, moreover, often signals the dramatic event or decisive inner change which Starobinski says is essential to the making of autobiography. Therefore the cultural critic's task is to identify and connect the mythic and ideological components of an individual's story, noting the distinctive ways each author manipulates ideas to make bridges between public life and private experience, past and present, and between writer and reader.

In the present century such linkages between public and private history may prove easier to establish than in some earlier eras. While the eighteenth and nineteenth centuries contained periods of relative social calm during or about which, it can be argued, few significant autobiographies were written, after 1900 there is scarcely a year which has not been recreated in autobiography and endowed with larger than private significance.[43] Thus the turn of the century is not simply a conventionally convenient beginning point for this study. Not only did the new century's early years see the publication of a cluster of influential and highly ideological autobiographies—including Booker T. Washington's *Up from Slavery* (1901), Charles Eastman's

Indian Boyhood (1902), *The Education of Henry Adams* (1907), Jane Addams's *Twenty Years at Hull House* (1910), Mary Antin's *The Promised Land* (serialized in 1911), and Alexander Berkman's *Prison Memoirs of an Anarchist* (1912), to mention only a few—but as I have already pointed out, critical awareness of this new form of literature also blossomed in the books and essays not only of Dilthey and Howells, but also of Georg Misch and Anna Burr.[44] Since then, the publication of socially significant autobiographies by both women and men has continued virtually without interruption. All the major intellectual and political events and crises of the modern era are represented in this literature. Wars and other characteristic modes of American violence; immigration and the movement of Americans from country to city, from Southern farms to Northern ghettoes, abroad to Europe and Africa; the impact of science and technology upon all areas of life; the struggle against the color line and the emergence of the Third World; women's emancipation from male definition of their rights and roles; new movements in art, architecture, literature, and the mass media; the Roaring Twenties, the Depression decade, and the strife-ridden 1960s—all these and many other social phenomena have been recreated as someone's personal experience to be collectively shared by the curious audiences of autobiography.

However, precisely because they do reflect the diversity and complexity of a culture at the point where individual and group experiences interact, autobiographies resist being subsumed under broad historical or intellectual categories. There always remains the private agenda, the emotional inflection, to which the reader must be endlessly and variously attentive. Grele's program therefore presents a challenge to the student of autobiography that is somewhat different from the challenge to the oral historian. The oral historian usually composes and then poses a schedule of specific questions to a living respondent, just as the psychoanalyst has the analysand and the limits of the therapeutic situation to guide that storytelling occasion. The results are personal information already packaged for translation into knowledge. Autobiographical occasions, on the other hand, are defined more firmly yet more ambiguously by the absent author, who as both subject and object presents an elusive target. Although an autobiographer also communicates information and often expresses quite openly an ideology, the ultimate aim (if we are to go along with Hart and other critics) remains identity and not historical messages. Embedded, therefore, in conscious generalizations about historical experience will be preconscious utterances from the inner darkness of the psyche. To make matters even more ambiguous, many twentieth-century autobiographers are well schooled in this language of the psyche; many have read their Freud, George H. Mead, or Erikson. This self-conscious familiarity with process psychology is still another distinguishing feature of twentieth-century autobiography. Yet even the best-read autobiographers, like Conrad Aiken or Anaïs Nin, are aware of the dangers of abstract psychological explanations. Often the stubborn voice of the individual autobiographer is heard speaking against the very abstractions and hypotheses his or her own story suggests. Nin, the novelist, diarist, and lay analyst, represents others less informed than herself when she cries, "If psychoanalysis is going to divest me of all decoration, costume, adornment, flavor, characteristic, then what will be left?"[45] Her motives for writing and editing the *Diary* are various, but surely the central impulse has been to record particulars of her inner life and the emergence of a woman artist. She is the storyteller of her own dream life as well as of everyday experiences as a Rankean analyst. So she fights off the generalizing psychologist and historian. "There is not one big cosmic meaning for all," she declares, "there is only the meaning we each give to our life, an individual meaning, an individual plot, like an individual novel, a book for each person. To seek a total unity is wrong" (1:vii). How, then, to balance Grele and Nin and to understand autobiography as both representative cultural history and stubbornly singular story is the challenge this subject presents to American cultural studies.

III

My own response to this challenge is embodied in the following chapters, which constitute neither an inclusive literary history nor a survey of contemporary social history as seen through autobiography. Although the still untapped riches of Kaplan's and the other bibliographies invite such treatments, they likewise warn of the formidable dangers in embracing so large and diverse a body of cultural documents. All recent critical work on American autobiography with which I am familiar acknowledges this obstacle. For example, there is at present no comprehensive history of American autobiography. Even the four books in print on the black tradition in autobiographical writing are selective rather than inclusive.[46] So, too, are the recent, more general studies by Blasing, Cooley, and Couser.[47] These critics follow more or less closely the lead of Robert F. Sayre and James M. Cox in building generalizations about American autobiography and culture on the foundation of a relatively few classics, a single theme, rhetorical stance, or historical period.[48] In this process certain texts become elevated to the status of canonical works. This often occurs too exclusively on the basis of literary criteria: narrative symmetry, metaphoric richness, and psychological complexity in the authorial persona. There is in much of this criticism a tendency (inherited perhaps from the myth-and-symbol tradition of cultural analysis) to treat autobiographies as iconic works of art rather than as "contingent, imperfect expressions of social and mental forces."[49] While gratefully acknowledging a debt to these critics (and to the Europeans whose names also besprinkle these pages), I remain uneasy over the tendency to treat autobiography chiefly as a branch of imaginative literature and thus to stress artistic creation over the equally complex processes of historical re-creation, ideological argument, and psychological expression. *Life* is the more inclusive sign—not *Literature*—which deserves to be placed above the gateway to the house of autobiography. Hence we must not only look more closely at particular texts than some critics in pursuit of an overarching thesis have done, but also compare synchronically works which deal with similar themes, social situations, or strategies of self-construction. In the process we may be able to throw light on cultural contexts which both unite and separate one life-story and another. Often this approach will involve discussion of autobiographies which are widely popular and critically acclaimed, for these are more likely to be representative of widely shared cultural values than obscure or experimental texts. In other instances, however, we will mention less familiar works, whose presence shall be justified in terms of their own imaginative power as personal documents and the light they throw on other autobiographies. Throughout we shall pursue the critical goals Gene Wise asserts are the ones which have come to characterize American Studies scholarship in the 1970s and 1980s and which distinguish cultural analysis today from earlier holistic approaches.[50] This analysis of modern American autobiography is intended to be particular, pluralistic, proportioned, and comparative.

To be more specific, in the succeeding chapters we shall examine six or seven characteristic occasions or situations which a number of modern American autobiographers have found themselves in, to speak both metaphorically and literally. The first occasion is, if not the oldest in the history of Western autobiography, doubtless the most common in the American literature of the self: the situation of an old man looking back over a long career and significant stretch of history to recapture the personal past against the background of sweeping cultural change. My two exemplary personal historians were both historians. Hence the methodological or imaginative advantages mentioned earlier in connection with Margaret Mead's anthropological outlook as autobiographer may find an appropriate parallel in the memoirs or historical narratives of W. E. B. Du Bois and Henry Adams. Who better stands a chance of ordering modern chaos than a historian? In answering this loaded question, these two Massachusetts-born, Harvard-trained intellectuals embrace between them over a century of crucial American experiences. These they analyze from their positions on both sides of the color line. The historical epochs presented through the dual perspective of *The Education* and *The Autobiography* begin in the eighteenth-century Quincy world of Adams's grandfather and end in the post-Sputnik realities which Du Bois, at his ninetieth birthday party, presents to his little great-grandson as the agenda of the future. Both men feel themselves carried on the tide of turbulent social, political, and intellectual events. Both struggle to find a narrative form adequate to reflect their personal identities as shaped by and shaping these forces. While Du Bois writes as a very old man but a new convert to world communism, Adams declares his ideological allegiance to a party so elitist that it includes exactly three members. *The Education,* as every reader remembers, is the story of ostensible failure. It therefore runs counter to the predominant American tradition of success stories. *The Autobiography,* however, declares Du Bois's continuing faith in "lurch and stagger" progress toward the solution of the twentieth century's central problem and records the author's many roles in this racial struggle. Though both books have been extensively analyzed, their "comparison through contrast" here may throw into sharper relief the ways two reticent old men both talk about themselves and keep silence as they illustrate for later autobiographers the problems of recreating historical identity under the bewildering circumstances of modern American life.

The second autobiographical occasion examined in Chapter Three is equally traditional yet juxtaposes a more disparate pair of autobiographers. Their common situation, however, makes several grounds for comparison, for both are holy men who relate their soul's experience as travelers through the American wilderness. Black Elk's destination is Harney Mountain, from which the blind old man and his white collaborator, John G. Neihardt, look down on the landscape of the past, which is organized around the vision vouchsafed many years earlier to a nine-year-old Sioux boy. The social and personal character of this holy man's life is recaptured through a remarkable act of collaboration. *Black Elk Speaks* is thus a unique cultural document whose form, vocabulary, and vision appear to place it outside Wasichu boundaries of autobiographical confession. More traditional, yet still eccentric to current social norms and historical definitions of selfhood, is Thomas Merton's *The Seven Storey Mountain*. The Trappist monastery at Gethsemani is only metaphorically a mountain from whose slopes Merton surveys his past as a self and his progress as a soul. Yet both works, one written out of a non-Western point of view in which self, society, language, and autobiography are strange if not meaningless categories, the other composed within an ancient Catholic tradition of self-abnegation and spiritual introspection, contain cogent critiques of American values. Their continuing popularity with American readers and their influence on other spiritual chroniclers are important components of the occasions they exemplify.

Historical memoir and spiritual confession are conventional yet flexible ways to categorize, at least preliminarily, the personal histories of Adams and Du Bois, Black Elk and Merton. No such convenient tradition embraces, however, the autobiographies examined in Chapter Four. Here the retrospective gaze of the writer is fixed, even more exclusively and emotionally than is the case with Black Elk, upon the self as child and youth. Nevertheless, though there is no ready-made literary convention to guide readers and authors, preoccupation with one's earlier years is surely a distinctive emphasis in many American autobiographies. From Whitman to Maya Angelou, the history of American self-constructions is punctuated with such stories. Louis Sullivan's *The Autobiography of an Idea* and Richard Wright's *Black Boy* contribute to a recurring and characteristically American occasion. What makes these particular stories comparable and exemplary is not so much new literary forms or even representative social location but these authors' ideological themes and psychological motives, for both the aging Chicago architect in 1924 and the much younger black novelist two decades later are impelled to reenter their pasts in search of origins of their own creative genius. In looking for it here, they differ strikingly from that other twentieth-century "genius" Gertrude Stein. While Sullivan grounds his career as innovative architect in a little boy's earliest encounters with nature on a Massachusetts farm, Wright reinvents himself within the far harsher social circumstances of his Mississippi family and the surrounding black and white communities. Creativity—like the violence which also compels Wright's memory and energizes his fiery imagination—is a notoriously elusive process for the historian or literary critic to account for. But in this chapter it is appropriate to bring to bear certain psychological and ecological insights by Phyllis Greenacre and Edith Cobb. Their hypotheses may illuminate these texts and suggest avenues of approach to other autobiographies about the childhood of the artist.

Violent experiences have characterized the lives of so many

21

Americans, famous and obscure, that other writers like Wright have sought understanding and order for their turbulent memories in the act of autobiography. Public violence like war, for example, has occasioned important autobiographies of the past like Grant's *Personal Memoirs* and Whitman's *Specimen Days*. And this mode of coping with violence continues into the present in a powerfully bitter autobiography of the Vietnam War, Ron Kovic's *Born on the Fourth of July*. But, it can be argued, the American domestic scene and private life have produced even more autobiographical occasions for the confrontation with violence than have the battlefield and military hospital. If so, this helps to explain the number of modern autobiographies which powerfully recreate the identity-forming experiences of racial violence, crime and punishment, mental sickness. If American public violence is recorded first in Indian captivity and slave narratives and later in the strife-ridden lives of Black Elk, Alexander Berkman, Emma Goldman, and Malcolm X, then quieter careers have provoked life-histories nearly as violent, if less well publicized. Helen Keller, Maya Angelou, Clifford Beers, and Conrad Aiken are but four names in a long list of autobiographers who have witnessed or endured family and psychic violence. By recreating such experiences, they have sought to turn painful memories into something of value. In Chapter Five two such narratives are explored and contrasted. Alexander Berkman's *Prison Memoirs of an Anarchist* is not only the first major prison autobiography in our literature, it is also a defense of political terrorism and a dramatic revelation of a tormented, violent self. Berkman's book brilliantly explores American values from the vantage point of the prison cell within which, for fourteen years, a man lived out the consequences of his deep, anarchic desires to kill, to be killed, to kill himself. If the fruitful tensions between autobiography and ideology are displayed in *Prison Memoirs of an Anarchist*, an equally remarkable result of looking into the face of violence is Conrad Aiken's *Ushant*. Here is the recaptured life of a private poet and novelist who deliberately turned his back on public affairs during the decades between the two world wars. Aiken's artistic and autobiographical identity is defined instead by memories of the family tragedy which overtook the boy of eleven when his father and mother took their lives in a double suicide. *Ushant* filters these shattering memories of a Savannah childhood event through a poet's mature imagination clarified by wide reading in Freudian psychology. The result is a dreamlike narrative which, even more clearly than *Black Boy*, reveals the affinities between autobiography and the modern psychological novel.

Sharp contrasts and intimate connections between public and private spheres, which make works like *Prison Memoirs* easier to translate into cultural narratives than *Ushant* or even *Black Boy,* are also to be found with increasing frequency in modern women's autobiographies. As Richard Sennett and Peter Berger have both argued, the historical process loosely labeled "modernization" creates no more decisive divisions within personality than the one between public and private life.[51] This split in social experience, it can be argued, defines women's identities even more painfully—and creatively—than it does for other groups. In any case, tensions between old conventions and new circumstances, between rigid social stereotypes and the urge to define oneself in wider terms, have become so intimately part of modern women's lives that they inevitably affect the writing and reading of autobiography. The outpouring of personal histories by American women, and the recent critical attention devoted to them by feminist scholars and others, are notable aspects of culture studies generally and Women's Studies in particular. Because the stereotyped gender roles and career choices women encounter are established chiefly by men, it is difficult *not* to approach this literature ideologically. Hence my title and focus for Chapter Six, "Becoming a Woman in Male America." Here the problem of selection, both of approaches and exemplary texts, has been a knotty one. What single occasion or strategy of self-presentation can possibly embrace the public memoirs of Margaret Sanger or Eleanor Roosevelt, Emma Goldman or Ida B. Wells, Mae West or Isadora Duncan or Abigail McCarthy? Or, to sample an even richer record, the private histories of Mary Antin and Maxine Hong Kingston, Zora Neale Hurston or Maya Angelou, Mary McCarthy or Gwendolyn Brooks? I have therefore opted for a severe selectivity, hoping to suggest some general issues in this literary-cultural complex by focusing attention on two unique women, Margaret Mead and Anaïs Nin. *Blackberry Winter* and volume 1 of *The Diary of Anaïs Nin* have been chosen in part for reasons already suggested. They also exemplify particular themes, theories, and techniques encountered when a woman recreates her experiences in a man's world. Margaret Mead was arguably the most famous American female scientist and public intellectual of this century, while Anaïs Nin was for decades one of our most famous "unknown" authors and devotees of the private life. Their struggles on both battlefields to forge new female identities have proved inspiring to younger generations of women, here and abroad. This cultural leadership also extends to their autobiographies, which offer rich speculations about this special occasion and original act.

In Chapter Seven we turn to an apparently much more limited

autobiographical occasion. It is, however, one with nearly as many cultural and ideological ramifications as the more varied occasions of women's autobiography. That is the creative act of collaboration between a subject and a professional writer or ghostwriter. The model of this occasion is Malcolm X pacing the floor of Alex Haley's apartment, telling the story of his brief, violent, remarkable life. From such temporary partnerships has come a spate of popular and equally temporary paperback autobiographies. Many of these are at best ephemeral best-sellers, but occasionally this characteristic commercial activity produces remarkably permanent results. In a way, the usual Madison Avenue gears were grinding as Alex Haley, a black journalist writing for *Esquire, Playboy,* and *Reader's Digest,* approached Malcolm X in 1959 and initiated the midnight conversations that eventually led to *The Autobiography of Malcolm X.* Since 1965 this remarkable book has won enthusiastic acclaim from, and changed the perspectives of, many white readers and critics, and it occupies a special spot in the literature of liberation and martyrdom treasured by black readers here and abroad. With *Black Elk Speaks* and perhaps *All God's Dangers,* it is a triumph of collaborative autobiographical art as well as a powerful ideological testament and confession. How such works emerge from much the same social circumstances as Dick Gregory's *nigger* or *Ossie: The Autobiography of a Black Woman* is one of several cultural issues raised in Chapter Seven, for in examining collaboration in black autobiography one inevitably questions definitions of authorship which literate classes have assumed for themselves and imposed upon others. Ideological conflicts in this cultural situation will, it is hoped, be clarified by the choice of three representative autobiographies created not by one consciousness but by two.

Between *The Autobiography of Malcolm X* and Du Bois's *Autobiography* (to look back at Chapter Two), there are important similarities and continuities. Many of these flow from their subjects' final sense of themselves as historic figures standing on a world stage and recreating themselves in memoir. Both books stand on one side of a narrative divide within modern black autobiography which Elizabeth Schultz has deftly described.[52] On one side there is outward-looking history, a chronological narrative containing the appropriate authenticating mechanisms for a public self. On the other side are works, equally autobiographical and often just as ideologically explicit, which resemble novels more than they do biographies. These include *Black Boy, Manchild in the Promised Land, I Know Why the Caged Bird Sings,* and (for some readers, at least) even more fictional works like George Cain's *Blueschild Baby.* Like Aiken's *Ushant* and Maxine Hong Kingston's *The Woman Warrior,* these are products of a subject's memory and imagination recreating his or her private life in language which strikes many readers as virtually indistinguishable from that of a novel. This terrain of contemporary autobiography which abuts the continent of fiction is surveyed in the final chapter. Here we seek to justify the use of the traditional term "autobiography" to encompass several experimental narratives of modern experience. Through a particular comparison of Mailer's *The Armies of the Night,* Frank Conroy's *Stoptime,* and Lillian Hellman's second autobiography, *Pentimento,* I try to sort out the controversial aesthetics and historicism of parafictionists, the New Journalists, and other present-day artificers of the self. Preserving the concept of personal identity and using it to bridge history and discourse, and thus to continue to celebrate autobiography as discourse-history, becomes highly problematic for many writers of the 1960s and 1970s. It is a desperate, personal necessity for some. Whether one has a public identity to record and defend like Mailer and Hellman, or a wholly obscure life to recapture like Conroy, the situation of the autobiographer today juxtaposes unprecedented cultural, literary, and psychic problems. Neither Henry Adams nor Gertrude Stein had such chaos to consider. Like the issue of collaboration, the twilight zone of fact and fantasy will doubtless constitute a future battleground for autobiographers in America and for their audiences as well.

Lillian Hellman's *Pentimento,* the last of the sixteen or so texts to be singled out, strikes a significant closing note for several reasons. Through it (and in the parallel pieces by Mailer and Conroy), I examine the ways beginnings and endings are treated in contemporary autobiography. Furthermore, *Pentimento,* as the second of three or four autobiographical narratives Hellman has published, brings to attention other serial attempts to rewrite and re-rewrite the past. Frederick Douglass, Gertrude Stein, Sherwood Anderson, Theodore Dreiser, Anaïs Nin, Maya Angelou—the list of multiple autobiographers in our literature is surprisingly long and various. *Pentimento's* recapitulation and development of themes and tropes from *An Unfinished Woman* is only one variant of this unusual autobiographical occasion. But like other comparisons and individual examinations in this book, the particular case may suggest analogous situations and solutions.

Pentimento makes a convenient (though by no means definitive) stopping-point for yet another reason. As I discovered when I completed this manuscript, Lillian Hellman has provided a rough model for this work. She opens her *Book of Portraits* (as *Pentimento* is subtitled) with Bethe and herself as a girl of sixteen, and closes with memories of Jimsie, Helen, and the death of Dashiell Hammett—all relationships of the aging survivor. Similarly, this book begins with two significant acts of repossession of the nineteenth-century past. We conclude with quite recent experiments in autobiographical form and strategies of self-construction. Yet both her book and this book cut back and forth across time. In "Bethe" many intervening experiences and later relationships are introduced, through whose juxtaposition the presence of the older author is always felt. Moreover, Hellman has selected each of the figures in *Pentimento* to dramatize not only significant moments in a historical past but also to highlight different dimensions of her own identity. In these chapters, too, I have also a dual objective in mind: to establish some continuities in the development of modern American autobiography but also—and more important—to illuminate selected, significant facets of the subject itself. Autobiography in modern America is, then, my Lillian Hellman.

IV

The choice of Hellman, Conroy, and Mailer also reflects the conviction that, despite the strictures of parafictionists and the chaos of public history, autobiography today remains vital as an individuating language act and shared cultural activity. As to the future, however, threats and doubts abound. For instance, Elizabeth Bruss in "Eye for I: Making and Unmaking Autobiography in Film" perceptively compares linguistic and filmic images as vehicles of self-construction within a culture rapidly given over to impersonal technologies.[53] Though she foresees serious threats to traditional narrative as movies and television turn us all into viewers, button-pushers, and screen images, Bruss's eloquent argument celebrates the unique power of words to satisfy the deep desires people have to share and confirm not only ideas but identities. Unless literacy, the individuating impulse, and the institutions which sustain both are driven completely underground, autobiography stands as good a chance of surviving as any other mode of story-telling. This will happen, however, only through the continued creation of fresh forms and idioms for the new experiences and changing values of future men and women everywhere.

Meanwhile the aim here has been to collect, compare, and clarify present understanding of certain exemplary texts and typical occasions which in the present century are invigorating the American tradition in autobiography. The variety and interest characteristic of this literature directly reflects the culture. As Robert Sayre puts it, American autobiography is the Song of Ourselves.[54] Yet the whole oratorio is, I repeat, composed of separate Songs of Myself. Until we learn to read these scores as individual stories and cultural narratives, it will be dangerous or impossible to imagine or hear the whole. Therefore the following comparisons, contrasts, and comments are offered, taking as theoretical and methodological guides those historians, social scientists, literary critics, and philosophers whose names have been already invoked. Their advice may be summarized through the following concluding—and prefatory—statements. The first is by H. Stuart Hughes, who writes of the marriage of history and psychoanalysis, two disciplines essential to autobiography: "the path to the fuller understanding of the individual lies through the group—and vice versa. In both cases, the explanation of motive runs from the single human being to others comparable to him, and then back to the individual once more, as the ramifying thought and action of both are gradually illuminated."[55] This underscores the need to adjust critical focus from *individual text* to *social context* to *appropriate conceptual framework* —and *back to the single text again.* Since each autobiography is, in Clifford Geertz's terminology, a "thick description," each must be assessed differently, though always with an eye to common patterns and similarities.[56] Michael Agar is another anthropologist whose actual work with autobiography has involved collecting the life-stories of drug addicts and urban tramps. From this experience, which superficially differs greatly from reading *The Education of Henry Adams,* he offers a succinct methodology. "Complex forms are approached recognizing the simultaneous relevance of different kinds of explanatory schemata," he writes. "The form is untangled to facilitate analysis, and then retangled to learn what has been gained in understanding the original complex form."[57]

Heeding these instructions for untangling and retangling the complex forms of autobiography, we begin with the two aged historians W. E. B. Du Bois and Henry Adams, who seek to educate their readers about the chances of making sense of twentieth-century change and chaos by placing the time-conscious self at the center of their nineteenth-century worlds.

27

2

History and a Final Self:
W. E. B. Du Bois and Henry Adams

FOR OLD AND YOUNG ALIKE, the desire to reenter one's past, repossess it in words, and thereby connect the self to the greater world is *the* basic historical act. We repeat this pattern in many different ways: writing entries for the high school yearbook or *Who's Who,* filling out applications, consulting a psychoanalyst, composing a loved one's obituary, and imagining one's own obituary. Organizing the world around the self on a larger scale occurs less frequently, but for some it is a vital necessity. The autobiographical impulse can be responded to at any point in a lifetime. For certain individuals—Frederick Douglass, Mary Antin, and Claude Brown come to mind—it arises early, for surely Philippe Lejeune does not have American autobiographers in mind when he observes "rares sont les autobiographies écrites par des jeunes gens."[1] But for others, autobiography is an act deferred, a duty often imposed by fate at the end of a long career and enjoined by family, friends, publishers, and the curious public. Underlying this late reenactment of a life and readers' responses to it is the Diltheyan conviction that human beings stand a better chance of understanding themselves as social beings and historical forces retrospectively. As Henry Adams characteristically phrases it, "the man of sixty can generally see what he needed in life."[2]

Thus many, if not most, American autobiographies, both before and after 1900, are memoirs written by old men and women. Public personages like Franklin, Grant, Carnegie, or Eleanor Roosevelt turn to autobiography when their careers are almost over. For such people, autobiography is a summing-up. Its nature and public acceptance rest on the assumption that the passage of time—long decades in some instances—is required for personal experience and historical consciousness to coalesce. Therefore the necessarily retrospective focus of all autobiographical narrative, which may seem a drawback to more purely imaginative writers, is far from a limitation on the memoirist. Time lends authority to assertions of fact and serves as a strategic perspective to be manipulated for a range of rhetorical effects. The stance of the wise and fatherly elder addressing the reader as son or niece thus becomes early established as a principal model of the autobiographical relationship. For this as for other features of the modern memoir, *The Autobiography of Benjamin Franklin* is the original American act.

From Franklin's time to Adams's and Du Bois's, a number of other assumptions about personal history accumulate, inherited also from several centuries of European practice. Authors and their growing audiences come to agree that historical intentions and assertions about a personal past are signaled and substantiated through a variety of specific autobiographical cues. These include commonsensical considerations like the book's title and subtitle; its preface, introduction, or epilogue; a linear narrative often dotted with quotations from letters, diaries, newspapers, or other verifiable, external records. Even the footnote and the photograph become part of this historicizing paraphernalia. When an old man's memory is buttressed—and presumably corrected—by such testable information and self-authenticating devices, the reader is led to trust the firmly detailed image of the past actor moving within a specific social context. Attention to chronology and to causes, a sense of what Weintraub calls "the external realm of fact" rather than the interior world of self-consciousness, are also hallmarks of the memoir.[3] Still another is the general nature of the metaphors of the self by which the writer brings order to the disparate circumstances of a long life. In traditional memoir, these tropes make patterns (and thus establish identity) out of specific details of remembered events, objects, or places; they stitch together images of a recovered actuality rather than display the freewheeling imagination of the reminiscing writer. Presiding over these narrative devices and uses of language is always the historical consciousness of the present author, brooding on his or her own past and searching for its continuities and changes. Commonly this reflecting consciousness reveals itself quite openly in didactic messages to the reader—in the aphorisms and adages of a Franklin or Adams, in the ideological statements of a Du Bois or Stein.

These are the kinds of assumptions at the back of the minds of many readers as they glance at pictures of the two bearded, balding old men on the paperback covers of *The Education of Henry Adams* and *The Autobiography of W. E. B. Du Bois.* In the Sentry edition, Adams sits at a desk, pen poised. On the back cover are pictures of two houses, the ancestral one in Quincy and the mansion on Lafayette Square across from the White House. These represent his past and present. On the New World paperback, Du Bois also sits, perusing a journal. His round spectacles, swarthy complexion, and clipped goatee suggest some German professor more than an American Negro. To the knowledgeable reader this is not surprising, since after Fisk and Harvard, Du Bois studied history in Berlin. That Adams was actually a whole generation younger than Du Bois—only sixty-five when he began *The Education* in 1903—cannot be surmised from these covers, but one clue is Du Bois's long subtitle, *A Soliloquy on Viewing My Life From the Last Decade of Its First Century.* Few autobiographers can boast of being over ninety when they compose their memoirs. Recollections told from such a vantage point are indeed unusual, and they are likely to be viewed skeptically. Readers will be on the lookout for lapses of memory and factual errors, sentimentality and a meandering narrative, preoccupation with the past but scarcely with the future, and a natural concern over imminent death. How Du Bois copes with such anticipations becomes part of the representative value of his autobiography. Adams, on the other hand, faces different problems with his posterity. The symbolic houses (selected not by the author but by an editor) signal ancestral fame and hint at personal failure, since they suggest the third building which for good reason is not represented: the White House across the square. What Adams makes of his unique family context and perspective on the American past helps to define *The Education* as a more unusual and certainly a more ambiguous memoir than Du Bois's.

If a preliminary inspection of covers provides only limited access to the complexities of these narratives, it does underline the fact that present-day readers always respond to older autobiographies differently from their original audiences. Paperback covers and dust-jacket illustrations played no part in focusing nineteenth-century responses to Franklin's or Grant's memoirs. Today the camera and the book designer send advance messages to audiences and emphasize the presence of others beside the author participating in the autobiographical occasion. Confronting these new techniques and added images, one must sometimes struggle to determine by what means, by whom, and to what ends the self has actually been recreated in its world. A useful guideline to follow comes from Erik Erikson, whose study of Gandhi contains this pregnant remark: "autobiographies are written at certain late stages of life for the purpose of re-creating oneself in the image of one's own method; and they are written to make that image convincing."[4] This insight provides one avenue into these two famous memoirs and suggests a rationale for beginning with Du Bois, whose posthumous *Autobiography* appeared only in 1968, rather than with Adams, officially also a posthumous autobiographer but actually the author who had his *Education* privately printed in 1907. Du Bois's method of self-construction may be no more "convincing" than Adams's, but it is demonstrably simpler, more explicit and conventional. Certain aspects of Adams's oblique and ironic manipulation of the memoir tradition come into sharper focus when seen in contrast to Du Bois's more direct treatment of language, narrative structure, and ideology. Though such comparison may emphasize themes and techniques shared with other twentieth-century autobiographers, my prime motive is to show how these particular aging authors confront and connect nineteenth- and twentieth-century experience and, by placing themselves at the center of their repossessed pasts, bring a measure of order to history.

I

As a final look at an immensely long, historic life, Du Bois's *Soliloquy* opens with the blend of tradition and novelty which marks the whole narrative.[5] Though some may miss its significance, the preface by Herbert Aptheker harks back to the earliest slave narratives, most of which were introduced to their abolitionist readers by white sponsors like William Lloyd Garrison or Wendell Phillips. Aptheker, the white Marxist historian, does not explicitly sponsor Du Bois. Ostensibly his preface simply underlines the crucial fact that *The Autobiography* is a comparative rarity in black American autobiography; it is the third version of Du Bois's life-story. Aptheker also emphasizes the "intense subjectivity" (6) which distinguishes this volume from its predecessors, *Darkwater: Voices Within the Veil* and *Dusk of Dawn: An Autobiography of a Race Concept.* What must also be stressed, however, is Du Bois's characteristic spacing of his several experiments in autobiography. *Darkwater* was written in 1920 and *Dusk of Dawn* in 1940. Since the final *Autobiography,* though published in full in its author's centennial year, was apparently completed in 1960, Du Bois has reexamined the course and meaning of his own experience as modern American and black man every twenty years. Indeed, if, like Houston A. Baker and Stephen Butterfield, one considers *The Souls of Black Folk* to be an experiment in personal history, the pattern of periodic reassessment extends back to the turn of the present century.[6]

An analogous plan to return and reconsider Negro life and culture at periodic intervals also characterized Du Bois's sociological studies at Atlanta University. Here, clearly, is a deeply felt and long-lasting impulse to order time and history around the self, a desire which unites the diverse aspects of Du Bois's multifaceted career as historian, sociologist, NAACP official, and imaginative writer. That this practice is a social scientist's method of assessing change and continuity is also suggested by Margaret Mead's life as field-worker and world traveler. "Going away, knowing I shall return to the same place and the same people—this is the way my life has always been" (14), the anthropologist observes in *Blackberry Winter.*

This principle of periodic return also reflects Du Bois's attempts to link his own life and thought with those of his fellow blacks, as Douglass, Washington, and Malcolm X do in their no less didactic autobiographies. All Du Bois's essays are anchored in the great central theme announced in the "Forethought" to *The Souls of Black Folk:* "the problem of the Twentieth Century is the problem of the color line."[7] *Dusk of Dawn,* with its revealing subtitle, illustrates the younger author's willing subordination of self to the larger social issue. Twenty years later, however, the aged historian acknowledges the more personal focus of his *Soliloquy* and warns the reader about this new subjectivity. "Autobiographies do not form indisputable authorities," he begins.

> They are always incomplete, and often unreliable. Eager as I am to put down the truth, there are difficulties; memory fails especially in small details, so that it becomes finally but a theory of my life, with much forgotten and misconceived, with valuable testimony but often less than absolutely true, despite my intention to be frank and fair. . . .
> This book then is the Soliloquy of an old man on what he dreams his life has been as he sees it slowly drifting away; and what he would like others to believe. (12–13)

Later Du Bois contrasts his earlier autobiographical aims with present priorities by remarking that as a younger writer "the content rather than the form of my writing was to me of prime importance. Words and ideas surged in my mind and spilled out with disregard of exact accuracy in grammar, taste in word or restraint in style. I knew the Negro problem and this was more important to me than literary form" (144). Now, however, the old historian and novelist has more deliberately constructed an appropriate form to express the historical truths he has lived and seen.

The framework Du Bois erects to contain the theory of his life and reflect its changes during seven crucial decades is both traditional and yet perfectly suited to his special experience. Despite great age and the temptation to use time as the skeleton of his story, the autobiographer chooses instead geography and travel as the chief features of his autobiographical design. The *Autobiography* thus locates itself in the mainstream of American personal narratives, which from the time of Thomas Shepard to that of Malcolm X are stories of travelers and pilgrims. Like Franklin in the eighteenth century and Adams in the nineteenth, Du Bois images himself as a transatlantic traveler carried on the currents of a crucial historical epoch toward a new personal identity. But because his is a black identity, the forces whirling him around the world assume a pattern of coherence different from that in earlier lives of the other Massachusetts-born autobiographers.

This familiar shape of experience is introduced in the narrative's opening chapters which record the old man's fresh impressions of his latest journey in 1958–59 across Europe and Asia. It is the fifteenth trip in a very peripatetic career. The present cosmopolitan has been decisively shaped by such European, Asian, and African encounters, as well as by earlier American ones stretching all the way back to Reconstruction days. Because the railroad car and the ocean steamer constitute the content and metaphoric meaning of Du Bois's life, they must appear first in any truthful history. What can then follow is the ideological declaration, contained in the italicized interlude, of his conversion to communism. This late decision colors the whole history which follows. But Du Bois takes pains to show that it is not simply the outcome of a single tour to Russia and China; it results from everything that has preceded it. Only after these two basic factors in his present identity—constant travel and ideological commitment—have been presented in their proper sequence does the old narrator return to beginnings: his birth "by a golden river and in the shadow of two great hills" (61). Great Barrington must be approached by the Great Circle route, via Prague, Moscow, and Peking.

Such dislocation of conventional chronological structure underlines the fact that Du Bois images his life and world as moving in one long spiral as well as in continuous line. The ascending circle is maintained by successive journeys which keep taking the author back across terrain previously covered. These itineraries establish repetition, continuity, and change. For although in important respects his life as a black American has not essentially changed, Du Bois as historian is acutely aware of new cultural forces (one of which is himself) sweeping him and all mankind into radically different paths. His vision of history is thus linear *and* cyclical, and the tensions between these forms of motion and meaning are reflected everywhere in the *Soliloquy*.

Juxtaposing one trip and one traveler against another begins early with the fifteen-year-old youth's first visit to his grandfather in New Bedford. Faring forth alone represents a sharp break with family tradition, for his Dutch-African forebears had "a reluctance to venture into unknown surroundings," a "fear of a land still strange to family mores which pictured travel as disaster" (63). Far from disastrous, traveling represents here and later Du Bois's appropriation of an America which neither his slave nor free ancestors could or would know. On this first outing, he misses a train connection because of the new standard time and sees his first electric streetlight. But more important than either harbinger of progress are two vividly recollected sights. The first is of his grave, courteous mulatto grandfather raising a glass of sherry to greet a black visitor. "I had never before seen such ceremony," he exclaims. "I suddenly sensed in my grandfather's parlor what manners meant and how people of breeding behaved. . . . I never forgot that toast" (98). Unforgotten too is the later sight of thousands of Northern Negroes enjoying an annual picnic at Narragansett Bay. The sight of "the swaggering men, the beautiful girls, the laughter and gaiety, the unhampered self-expression" (99) defines a different dimension of black culture. His personality and the guarded emotion of his autobiography take their imprint from these contrasting memories. For seventy years Du Bois's social self is shaped in imitation of his proud, reserved grandfather and by his equally genuine attraction to the easygoing company of backslapping men and pretty women. Within his own world this tension parallels Adams's sharply contrasting feelings about Quincy and Boston. A few years later, traveling south—not as young Adams does to Washington but further on to Fisk University in Tennessee—also affects Du Bois's Negro identity in ways that are fundamentally different from the way he would doubtless have felt had he gone directly into the white intellectual world of Cambridge from Great Barrington. Thus the austere Yankee with the Bismarck beard is a cosmopolitan self carefully constructed out of experiences and emotions derived from New Bedford and Berlin, Nashville as well as Cambridge.

"To the world in general I was nearly always the isolated outsider looking in and seldom part of that inner life" (283). This characteristic confession applies with equal cogency and pathos to the shy graduate student in Germany who remarks of his twenty-fifth birthday celebration, "I asked in no companions" (170), to the indefatigable sociologist in but not of the Philadelphia ghetto, and later to the brusque NAACP officer. Moving actively in the world but encased in his solitary sphere, separate in important respects from both black and white worlds, Du Bois lives in deliberate acceptance of the doubleness of his special existence. Black and American, scholar and politician, elitist of the Talented Tenth and convinced communist, separatist and integrationist, cynic and hopeful idealist, he came closer, Harold Cruse believes, than either Washington or Garvey to embodying the full range of thought and social action of early twentieth-century blacks in the United States.[8] "I began to feel that dichotomy which all my life has characterized my thought," he remarks of his Berlin days. "How far can love for my oppressed race accord with love of the oppressing country? And when these loyalties diverge, where shall my soul find refuge?" (169). Despite unique advantages of intelligence and education, Du Bois articulates and embraces the basic emotional and ideological dilemmas of black Americans living behind the Veil. Though his acute consciousness of doubleness grows out of the particular movements of his career and character, it represents the situation of countless other lives.

By using travel as the comprehensive metaphor of his remarkably productive career, Du Bois also places himself in an understanding relationship to white Americans. For instance, the ambitious graduate student returns in 1894 in the steerage of an ocean liner to America and his first teaching job, thus repeating an archetypal Americanizing act of millions of immigrants like Mary Antin. Though his light complexion and Caucasian features have only recently led him to be taken for a Jew in Central Europe, here on shipboard he is one of five black Americans among 350 poor immigrants, mostly Jews. This unusual situation and Du Bois's tolerant and good-humored commentary on it suggest the openness and promise of an ideal America in which, taken on their own merits, "the blacks would by no means stand at the bottom of the row" (181). Moreover, this Harvard graduate's mixture of loneliness and sociability, overlaid with a recent communist convert's egalitarianism and pro-Semitism, contrast strikingly with Henry Adams's quite different sentiments under the same circumstance. As he lands in New York in 1868, Adams remembers feeling more out of place in Grant's America than "a Polish Jew fresh from Warsaw or Cracow [or] a furtive Yacoob or Ysaac still reeking of the Ghetto, snarling a weird Yiddish to the officers of the customs . . ." (238). The contrasts in tone here reflect far more than the usual differences between passengers in first class and those in steerage.

Du Bois the traveler merges naturally into Du Bois the participant-observer who looks *in* on many other lives but always looks *outward* from behind the veil of blackness. The freedom of the railroad car for such a cosmopolite is frequently a mixed blessing. During his Atlanta University years he made many forays into the rural South, out of which came his masterpiece *The Souls of Black Folk*. In that and subsequent personal narratives Du Bois faced the problems many other black autobiographers from Douglass to Baldwin have faced: how to turn a unique and often privileged situation as black leader and artist into a representative enactment of black experience generally. Du Bois's prose in *The Autobiography* proves adequate to this task as he vividly recaptures the reality of "jim crow" cars in which he and all blacks were forced to travel at the turn of the century:

> An impertinent white newsboy occupies two seats at the end and importunes you to buy cheap candy, Coca-Cola and - worthless if not vulgar books. He yells and swaggers and a continued stream of white men saunters back and forth from the smoker to buy and listen. . . . Lunch rooms either "don't serve niggers" or serve them at some dirty and ill-attended hole in the wall. Toilet rooms are often filthy. . . . You are apt to have the company of a sheriff and a couple of meek or even sullen black prisoners on part of your way and the dirty colored section hands will pour in towards night and drive you to the smallest corner. "No," said the little lady in the corner (she looked like an ivory cameo and her dress flowed on her like a caress), "we don't travel much." (235)

But Du Bois did travel much. Despite difficulties and affronts, he accomplished much precisely because (unlike many other black leaders) he "knew something of the seething world" (298) of Europe, Asia, Africa, and America. Knowing, in fact, a wider world than most previous American memoirists—including, I would suspect, Franklin, Jefferson, Douglass, or Grant—Du Bois anticipates by a generation or more the Third World consciousness of a Richard Wright and Malcolm X. Thus his double legacy to twentieth-century America—helping to revolutionize American black attitudes toward caste and almost single-handedly creating conditions for a black intelligentsia—is symbolically and literally represented in *The Autobiography* by the ceaseless train trips and steamer crossings which punctuated his life for over seventy years. The aged autobiographer looking back sees his earlier career as "a clearly planned path" (192), though he admits that "the world seized and whirled me" (195). Both characteristic metaphors come together in Du Bois's later affirmation of "lurch and stagger" progress (398), which he is able to discern in world history.

This guarded optimism is voiced at his ninetieth birthday party where, surrounded by admirers of both races, he reiterates his belief in "a world of men going forward" (398). In the audience sits his great-grandson, to whom Du Bois addresses his message of qualified hope. The little boy, he reports, "behaved with exemplary decorum" (397–98). The occasion is rich in autobiographical significance. The crowd of well-wishers gratifies the lonely old man whose crusty manner and biting tongue in the past were all too familiar to his contemporaries. He could doubtless recall Claude McKay's comment in his autobiography *A Long Way from Home* about Du Bois's "cold, acid hauteur of spirit."[9] Yet in his great-grandson he sees the redeeming presence of the future. It is also a consolation and justification to note the child's good manners which recall Du Bois's own grandfather in New Bedford. Six generations of family breeding are thus brought together in Du Bois's truly historical consciousness. Here again the contrast with Adams is instructive. Although the scion of presidents and ambassadors can evoke an American lineage even longer than Du Bois's, the childless widower of Lafayette Square cannot anchor his imaginative movement into the later twentieth century to his own flesh and blood. Adams's impulses toward what Erikson terms "generativity" must therefore be displaced onto the "nieces" and young men who form the audiences of *Mont-Saint-Michel and Chartres* and *The Education*.

Equally characteristic of Du Bois's sense of self and history is his confession on the same occasion of the secret of his long and productive life. It is, he tells the audience, the simple "fact that I have been able to earn a living by doing the work which I wanted to do and work that the world needed done" (398). The value of public service—important, prolonged, satisfying, and self-identifying effort over many decades—connects this autobiographer backward to Franklin, the grandfatherly advice-giver who shares the black scholar's deep pleasure at recalling acts of social service. More to the point, work unites Du Bois with other black leaders like Douglass, Washington, King, and Malcolm X, none of whom ever takes time lightly or ignores history, either in their lives or their autobiographies. Unlike any of these, however, Du Bois accepts no limitations of health, retirement, or even death as putting an end to autobiography. His third or fourth essay in self-construction closes with a reluctant recognition of the factor of time. "I am a little puzzled now about the ordering of my life," he confesses in the "postlude." "Several times in the past I find that I have prepared for death and death has not come. Always on my desk lies a calendar of my own devising with daily and hourly tasks; with plans for the week and the next week, the month and months ahead and the sentinel of my main task for the year" (409–10). This laconic reference to his desk calendar appears to reverse the pattern of the preceding pages by finally emphasizing time over space, sitting still rather than moving. In fact, however, the crowded calendar cannot help evoking those periodic tasks of Du Bois's remarkable past, many of which for their success depended upon the cosmopolitan experience and skill of a world (and worldly) traveler. Moreover, the present-day reader, reminded by Aptheker's preface, also knows that completing his *Autobiography* did not complete Du Bois's traveling. The key event of his "last decade" which is not here recorded is Du Bois's removal to Ghana where he died in his ninety-sixth year. A return to Africa thus completes this unique *and* representative black life.

The final image of the handmade calendar also underscores the *Soliloquy* as a chronological history after all and an outwardly directed memoir. Its author's grappling with twentieth-century racial realities is made coherent and convincing by the oldest, most familiar metaphor of the self in our literature. Of his several attempts at personal history, the *Autobiography*—though it cannot match the imaginative power and range of *The Souls of Black Folk*—presents the fullest account of Du Bois's individual awareness and accomplishment. On his last try Du Bois places himself most fully and originally on record as an American, a black man, and a citizen of the world. He thereby justifies Truman Nelson's apt description of the indomitable author who "nearly ninety . . . has endured every variety of abuse, accusation, and infamy, and all this with a nature sensitive to an extraordinary degree; endured it for his color, his religion, his politics and most of all for the sheer, cussed unchangeability of his *self*."[10]

II

Although Adams denies that his *Education* is in fact autobiography (a position which Ernest Samuels, his most meticulous biographer, accepts),[11] his disclaimer assumes a characteristic ambiguity when examined from the perspective of Du Bois and the conventions of the modern memoir. Striking contrasts in content, tone, ideology, and authorial persona between the two works cannot obscure the root fact that Adams and Du Bois are professional historians who have successfully translated themselves into the image of their different literary methods. Adams's happens to be so ironic and indirect that the careless reader may be taken in, miss some implications in his explicit statements, and misread even more seriously the authorial Ego which, despite disclaimers, powerfully pervades this exemplary parable of modern historical consciousness.

One revealing similarity between *The Education* and *The Autobiography* illustrates the particular complexities facing Adams's reader. That is the fact that while both were pioneer American historians, their contributions to this field—indeed, the very titles in their lengthy bibliographies—are in these narratives downplayed or omitted. Historical thought and achievement have been translated into personal terms, and the acts of research and writing which produced *The Suppression of the African Slave Trade* or *The History of the United States During the Administrations of Jefferson and Madison* are largely ignored. Furthermore, each author's imaginative achievements are also neglected; neither Adams's fiction *(Democracy* and *Esther)* nor Du Bois's *(The Quest of the Golden Fleece* and *The Dark Princess)* is mentioned at all. What such omissions signify in each case must be inferred from the rest of each narrative. But while Du Bois's choice seems more clearly governed by his presiding theme (America's color line in changing world perspective) and his principal metaphor (the solitary traveler), Adams's reasons appear more mysterious. Why his major writings of history and fiction are in retrospect considered *not* educational, while the memory of a boy's rebellious refusal to go to school is recaptured with powerful emotion, is part of the paradox of this ostensibly nonautobiographical narrative. And the enigma is not dispelled when the reader learns that both of Adams's novels were published anonymously or that their author, whom Samuels aptly characterizes as "an addict of paradox and contradiction" (xvii), relished listening to Washington guessing-games about the authorship of his books. In part, *The Education* is also the occasion for a guessing-game. The modern reader might imagine himself sitting at table with the cagy old author, who alternately denies and exposes his motives for writing a work which possesses many of the earmarks of a memoir, a few features of confession, some of the style and drama of an historical novel, and (in its later chapters) reads like a collection of essays on modern history.

Approaching Adams from the perspective of a puzzled present-day reader raises at once the issue of historical context and audience—crucial factors affecting any cultural critique of *The Education.* Unlike Du Bois, whose readers of 1960–68 are treated as a single, undifferentiated body, neither black nor white, Adams writes elliptically or ironically in part because he addresses two distinct readerships. To identify these, and the context within which the book was composed in 1903–6, demands the kind of external evidence which Samuels's or Elizabeth Stevenson's biographies provide. His manifest audience—the one characterized in Adams's preface as "young men, in universities or elsewhere," who are to be fitted "to be men of the world, equipped for any emergency" (xxx)—is not the actual readership Adams had in mind for his privately printed work. An edition of but one hundred copies was sent out in the late winter of 1907 to close friends and public figures mentioned in the narrative who were still alive. To each Adams explained his book and invited comment and censorship. It was, he insisted, only a draft, "in the nature of proof sheets." The typical recipient was told "in case you object to any phrase or expression, will you please draw your pen through it, and, at the end, return me the volume."[12] That only two or three chose to comply attests to Adams's tact, historical accuracy, or perhaps to the intimidating boldness of his ploy. Probably some among his intimate audience squirmed at the cleverly cruel characterizations; others no doubt enjoyed his ironies while observing and appreciating his omissions. However, in later preparing *The Education* for posthumous publication he did not, according to Samuels, extensively revise the text or redefine its readership. "The volume sent to you was meant as a letter," he wrote as late as 1909, "garrulous, intimate, confidential, as is permitted in order to serve a social purpose; but would sound a false note for the public ear. In truth, for the occasion, I am frankly a conspirator; I want to invite private confidence, and the public is my worst enemy."[13]

One might combine Adams's historical and literary audiences of 1907 and 1918 by imagining his ideal reader to be someone like Henry Cabot Lodge. Once a young Harvard student under Adams, then his assistant editor of the *North American Review,* Lodge became later both a writer and a powerful senator from Massachusetts—and husband to one of Adams's favorite younger friends. Furthermore, in chapter 28 he is dissected in one of the book's most deft thumbnail sketches. Finally the old historian appointed Lodge editor of his posthumous volume, coolly leaving a ghostwritten preface signed with Lodge's initials to confuse further his unwary readers.

The game with Lodge and the reader (utterly different from Aptheker's role in Du Bois's posthumous work) gives itself away in the style of the editor's preface, so transparently Adams's own. Decoding other enigmas is more difficult. In general, however, manifest meanings outnumber inside allusions and deliberate omissions, momentous as some of these are. Thus the broad outline and year-by-year momentum of Adams's long life can be retraced as readily as Du Bois's. Chronological order, in fact, reigns uninterruptedly until halfway through the narrative, when the famous twenty-year gap in time between chapter 20, "Failure" (1871), and chapter 21 "Twenty Years After" (1892), occurs. But the book's title and subtitle are indeed more ambiguous opening signals. The subtitle often used is *An Autobiography* and was appended posthumously by a Houghton Mifflin editor, Ferris Greenslet. This raises legitimate questions as to the publisher's manipulation of authorial intent and audience expectation. Such doubts aren't easily dispelled by the title itself, which promises a narrower and more didactic purpose than DuBois's. *Education* suggests the narrator's not entirely metaphoric role as a retired professor lecturing to youths and dispensing useful information, chiefly occupational, about the past. Of course, Henry Adams is himself one of these young men. His own education is being conducted by an older self, the sardonic denizen of Lafayette Square, with their common life as textbook. Many critics, including David Minter in *The Interpreted Design*, have discussed this classic relationship, surely one of the most common in our literature of the self.[14]

These difficulties in immediately pigeonholing *The Education* highlight larger questions about life-history itself. Adams's strategy of self-construction deliberately invites such suspicions. He forces both his intimate friends and us strangers to ponder the nature and limits of autobiographical art and historical truth. Sometimes he supplies his own evidence to expose the deceptions—or, as some would say, his narrative artistry. Thus the death of his Brooks grandfather is first reported as occurring in 1848, though twelve pages later the literal date becomes January 1, 1849. This minor discrepancy silently underlines Adams's desire to "tell the truth" but also to heighten contrasts between his two grandfathers (for John Quincy Adams died in 1848) and thereby between Boston and Quincy. In other places the book is decidedly more duplicitous. Its biographical accuracy has been so often challenged that, more than most autobiographies, it requires continual reality-testing if it is to be used as a source of historical information. Ernest Samuels, in *Young Henry Adams*, emphasizes how untrustworthy *The Education* is as literal record. Major suppressions and distortions occur which continually serve to subordinate the youthful actor to the wise old narrator, who, Samuels insists, constantly drapes the past in "mortuary gauze" and keeps bending history to fit his twin themes of personal failure and cultural chaos.[15]

One flagrant case of revising the past is Adams's account of his undergraduate experience. Harvard is represented as at best a "negative force" on the young man. As intellectual preparation for life, *The*

Education declares, "the entire work of the four years could have been easily put into the work of any four months in after life" (60). Moreover, he complains at not having been exposed to *Das Kapital*, though he does not bother to point out that Marx's work was published nine years after his graduation. An actual undergraduate admiration for Asa Gray (who remains unmentioned in this selective history) is replaced by the formative influence of Louis Agassiz. Whereas Du Bois is fond of quoting from letters or journals in order to illustrate youthful impressions of a scene or problem, Adams does so relatively seldom. Thus we must turn to Samuels his biographer to read the 1858 Harvard class history which contained Adams's first autobiographical sketch, which is unmentioned by its author. In some respects, it turns out, the Harvard senior characterizes himself and prophesies his future career and mature character more accurately than the old Adams of 1905 describes his past and younger self—a curious reversal, indeed, of youth's blindness and the hindsight of age.[16]

   The Education necessarily presents a different image of the past from the undergraduate's class book, for it is an old man's history. Like *The Autobiography of W. E. B. Du Bois,* it is "a theory of my life," "what he would like others to believe." Inasmuch as both accounts reflect a present writer's situation, neither is, or can be, complete. Adams's "ideological problematic" filters information just as decisively as does Du Bois's communism, even though Adams's beliefs carry no convenient party label. Samuels and other biographers are of immense help here, just as a careful critic like Richard Bridgman assists the reader of *The Autobiography of Alice B. Toklas* to detect and understand Gertrude Stein's suppressions and distortions in *her* Harvard years.[17] Adams's most perceptive early critic, Richard P. Blackmur, points the way to the deep autobiographical truth expressed in the often unfactual account of Adams's Harvard education: "surely the dominant emotion of an education, when its inherent possibilities are compared with those it achieved, must strike the honest heart as the emotion of failure." Then Blackmur proceeds to define "failure" as the aged Adams means us to understand it. "It is the failure of the ability to react correctly or even intelligently to more than an abbreviated version of knowledge and feeling: failure in the radical sense that we cannot consciously react to more than a minor fraction of the life we yet deeply know and endure and die. It is the failure the mind comes to ultimately and all along when it is compelled to measure its knowledge in terms of its ignorance."[18] Though "knowledge" represents for Henry Adams the merger of past experience and present insight, his twentieth-century perceptions are clearly much more valuable than

42

the shallower though more verifiably "truthful" memories of the Harvard senior of 1858.

What indeed is historical truth? Can we ever say, with Dilthey, that retrospective historical knowledge affords a trustworthy basis for understanding ourselves and our world? Adams broods over these matters continually throughout *The Education*. Many of his memories, when scrupulously exhumed, reveal the chilling fact that neither the past actor, immersed in a scene like the American ministry in London during the Civil War, nor the present historian, with all sorts of records in hand to correct and complete the picture, understands what really transpired in the past. Hence any account like that of chapter 11, "The Battle of the Rams (1863)," can only conclude with Adams throwing up his hands at the complexities (or the equally mysterious simplicities) of human nature, of national character, and of all historical explanations, including his own. Yet his characteristic decision is to continue energetically itemizing and examining the failures of past and present history-making.

In challenging the impossible past, Adams makes brilliant use of several narrative strategies which, though fitted to his particular case, are meant to serve as exemplary illustrations of possibilities and limitations of historical autobiography generally. The first means of imposing rational order on his world is carefully to distance author from actor by the use of an unusual third-person narrative. Then, after limiting chances of intimate self-revelation, he marches the character "Henry Adams" through the changing landscapes of the past—Boston, Quincy, Cambridge, Washington, Europe. Names, dates, social institutions, books, and prevailing ideas surround the younger adventurer and "circumstance" him in specific times and places. Yet throughout this long narrative of travel, it is the geography of the old man's mind which is lit up more vividly than past scenes and settings. Authorial presence is confirmed both in the adages and aphorisms which dot the text and constitute the old professor's conclusions and in the metaphors which pattern the past and display the writer's associative imagination.

"Education" is at once Adams's comprehensive theme and all-embracing metaphor. The word compresses historical, literary, psychological, and metaphysical dimensions of experience as recovered and imaginatively recreated by a final self. The constituent metaphor for education offered in the preface is the Carlylean image of tailor, manikin, and suit of clothes. By this well-known device Adams seeks to unite the data of his life as historical actor with the recreating writer whose conclusions are derived from retrospective analysis and moral scrutiny. In the act of composing this careful mixture of treatise and personal narrative, Adams as "tailor" discovers the full extent of historical disorder in his remembered world. If the tailor represents himself as an active force, the image of the manikin suggests Adams's opposite sense of passivity and impotence, of being controlled by forces. This outlook is reinforced by the somatic fact that as an adult he measured but five feet three inches tall and always felt himself a diminutive figure among his taller family and friends. But though this tailoring trope is repeated later in the text, one notable feature of *The Education* is the increasing predominance of explicit generalizations over such symbolic imagery. The metaphors which stand for the self in this autobiography—tailoring, travel, architecture, Pteraspis the ganoid fish, and others even more fanciful—are curiously abstract when compared to the characteristic imagery of other historical autobiographers like Franklin, Du Bois, or Malcolm X, whose metaphors of the self evoke much more specific events and relationships. Thus *The Education* contains no memorable scenes in which clothing actually figures to connect and define Adams's life as is the case, for example, with Malcolm X's many and meaningful changes of costume. On the other hand, what American autobiography—Du Bois's, Franklin's, or Malcolm X's included—yields a thicker anthology of memorable and pithy quotations than *The Education of Henry Adams?* A variety of explicit and oblique meanings are communicated in these numerous summaries of personal experience and belief. Aphorisms and adages are Adams's characteristic vehicle of ideological expression, commonly fusing intellectual order and emotional values in statements that are memorably explicit yet often mysteriously poetic.

Three of the most eloquent *sententiae,* which among them express the intellectual style and character of their creator and define in essential ways the persona created to address his several audiences, are the following familiar passages, one early and two later:

> From cradle to grave this problem of running order through chaos, direction through space, discipline through freedom, unity through multiplicity, has always been, and must always be, the task of education, as it is the moral of religion, philosophy, science, art, politics, and economy; but a boy's will is his life, and he dies when it is broken, as the colt dies in harness, taking a new nature in becoming tame. (12)

> But he insisted upon a relation of sequence, and if he could not reach it by one method, he would try as many methods as science knew. Satisfied that the sequence of men led to

nothing and that the sequence of their society could lead no further, while the mere sequence of time was artificial, and the sequence of thought was chaos, he turned at last to the sequence of force; and thus it happened that, after ten years' pursuit, he found himself lying in the Gallery of Machines at the Great Exposition of 1900, his historical neck broken by the sudden irruption of forces totally new. (382)

The pen works for itself, and acts like a hand, modelling the plastic material over and over again to the form that suits it best. The form is never arbitrary, but is a sort of growth like crystallization, as any artist knows too well; for the pencil or pen runs into side-paths and shapelessness, loses its relations, stops or is bogged. Then it has to return on its trail, and recover, if it can, its line of force. The result of a year's work depends more on what is struck out than on what is left in; on the sequence of the main lines of thought, than on their play or variety. (389)

Central as these summations are, they are by no means adequate synecdoches of *The Education*. Yet though they do not speak symbolically to all areas or levels of Adams's experience and consciousness, they do express much that is most characteristic of the man in this work. Running through them is a common theme and dilemma. The personal impulse to find or create order is ultimately grounded in the act of writing. But before this can occur the self has had to suffer confusion and imaginative death at the hands of the forces governing its existence. Adams's syntax and punctuation in the first two passages are significant, his images surprisingly violent. His grand passion for order is linked by semicolons to the brutal fact of a boy's and old man's broken wills and necks; both are parts of a single, long, complex, balanced sentence. Such syntactical structures are typical. Sweeping philosophical declarations and scientific analogies are often expressed in a rhetoric which often strains limits of rational language. A powerful tension is thus generated between reason and instinct, linear movement and waywardness, detachment from and passionate involvement in ideas, the demand for order despite the bleak recognition that such tropism is illusory. All three statements therefore dramatize Adams's historicism, his deep need to assert continuity as he identifies catastrophic change within human experience. Elsewhere in *The Education* one finds similar nuggets of ambiguously hopeful and despairing wisdom. Together they form a puzzling anthology of historical generalizations: "All experience is an arch, to build upon" (87); "One's

45

instinct abhors time" (228); "Any historian who means to keep his alignment with past and future must cover a horizon of two generations at least" (395); "Chaos was the law of nature; Order was the dream of man" (457). Each is a partial reflection of Adams's thought and temperament. As one follows their interplay in the unfolding narrative, the tensions and contradictions they give rise to are seldom resolved. Instead, the categories traditional historians like DuBois cling to—chronological sequence and casuality, the ideology of social progress, and the unitary or stable self—are dissolved into Adams's final category, the sequence of force. Together with "education" and "drift," "force" becomes, as in the second quotation, a presiding metaphor in the autobiographer's private lexicon.

Force refers, however, not only to abstract physical laws or concrete chemical structures. As William Jordy points out, Adams could not even formulate generalizations about the meaning of the dynamo if he did not believe in the categories of "man," "society," "time," and "thought." "None of these series could be separated from the others as Adams jokingly pretended," Jordy observes. "His statement in *The Education* merely indicated the range through which the pendulum of history swung, from personality on one side to impersonal force on the other. As he admired the novelist's ability to make personality purposeful, so he yearned for the scientist's competence to make force equally meaningful."[19]

Autobiography for Henry Adams is, then, a scientific fiction which seeks a delicate balance between human ego and ungovernable forces. No less than Du Bois, his is the consciousness of doubleness. Its presence and modus operandi are the subject of the third quotation. Adams's disembodied pen claims a line of force which makes order and meaning at least possibilities. Two conditions for success must be met, however. First, narrative structure cannot be capricious; it must conform to actual experience as, in his analogy, crystallization occurs around a core. Life's "plastic material" molded by the artist's pencil or writer's pen determines the achieved form fully as much as the creative imagination. Furthermore, a unifying structure of ideas must be discerned and emphasized over merely "playful" operations of memory which cling to people, events, emotions—the minutiae of most memoirs. Both these requirements are exemplified in *The Education*, which is a true crystallization of Henry Adams's present thoughts and feelings around his past.

The crystal, therefore, is still another metaphor of the self in this rich narrative. Its intellectual core connecting self and the experienced world is the theme stressed by Blackmur and identified by the title of chapter 20, at the point where Adams's story breaks in two. Ostensibly, "Failure" summarizes his Harvard years as teacher, historian, and editor. Actually it is a comprehensive judgment on the entire pre-1871 past and a prophecy of the future. Samuels and Blackmur agree that failure applies to both dimensions of Adams's life: preparation for a useful public career in the family tradition and the search for truths. Teaching medieval and American history is, on the one hand, serious business, for "a teacher affects eternity; he can never tell where his influence stops" (300). Yet examining the past finally convinces him that "in essence incoherent and immoral, history had either to be taught as such—or falsified" (301). Neither concrete facts nor historical method could provide grounds for intelligent action or even for proper reaction to the forces controlling man and nature. Whatever it once was for the younger man, history for the educated Adams is simply a heuristic collection of techniques for probing chaos. This is the reason why in 1877, after five years as assistant professor, Adams says he left Cambridge. "With this result Henry Adams's education, at his entry into life, stopped, and his life began" (308). This apparent opposition here between "education" and "life" is another of Adams's serious jokes; it denotes those parts of personal experience the author is willing to talk about openly and those he intends to remain silent on or treat obliquely. Since "education" stops and begins again several times in *The Education*, the terms are by no means exclusive.

People constitute the major thread in the tapestry of words whose design spells failure. One of the most "educational" lives to have touched his own is that of Clarence King, the geologist and one of Adams's closest friends. King's energy, brains, and charisma seem ideal equipment for seizing life and affecting history. This "best and brightest man of his generation," as John Hay called King,[20] had "moulded and directed his life logically, scientifically, as Adams thought American life should be directed. He had given himself education all of a piece, yet broad. Standing in the middle of his career, where their paths at last came together, he could look back and look forward on a straight line, with scientific knowledge for its base. Adams's life, past or future, was a succession of violent breaks or waves, with no base at all" (312). So writes the disillusioned old man only a few years after King's untimely death in 1901. His friend's enormous promise as scientist, businessman, and poised personality had ended in a series of bitter personal and professional failures. King heads the cast of historical personages whose achievements fall far short of potential and whose fates underscore for Adams the deep split

47

in American culture between intellectuals and men of industry, between artists and politicians. Clarence King's disorderly later life and death vividly illustrate Adams's conclusion that "the sequence of men came to nothing." He epitomizes the bleak conclusions about American society, in which, as Adams sees it, public affairs are divorced from private life, reason separated from feeling and moral sensibility, practical knowledge from aesthetic experience. Though Adams's Gerontion vision is partly an assumed role in *The Education,* the case of King reveals its sources in personal memory as well as reading and reflection. Whether such an assessment of culture at the turn of the century is historically accurate is always an important question for Adams. His answer is an autobiographical one: all such conclusions about the past will be the fruits of personal experience and will reflect emotions and moral values within the critic. As a cultural generalization, "failure" is Henry Adams's chief ideological principle which by its very nature is intellectual, moral, and psychological.

In order to use autobiography as a way to test Adams's hypothesis about American life in the Gilded Age, one would need to consult and compare other texts written in or about the same period. Since a split between the public and private, between the worlds of art and thought on the one hand and the world of business and politics on the other, is a principal cultural issue, *The Education of Henry Adams* might profitably be compared with Louis Sullivan's *The Autobiography of an Idea.* Commercial architecture provides an appropriate bridge between these cultural spheres, and Sullivan's autobiography deals in part with Adams's theme. But since the architect's backward-looking consciousness is, as we shall see in Chapter Four, focused much more fixedly upon his childhood and the origins there of his creative genius, a comparison of Adams and Sullivan would of necessity bend the latter to the former's formulations. A nearer, more appropriate contrast exists within the Adams family. Henry's older brother also left a memoir which was published posthumously in 1916, two years before *The Education.* In *Charles Francis Adams, 1835–1915: An Autobiography* and *The Education of Henry Adams* we possess an unusual and promising autobiographical occasion: two brothers' life stories written out of common family memories, many shared adult interests (despite their different careers), and intimate knowledge of each others' autobiographies. Personal failure, too, is Charles Francis's announced theme. Its presence and prominence may in part have resulted from his intensely personal response to reading *The Education.* Upon receiving his copy in 1907 he wrote at once to Henry: "Curious! that old Boston and Quincy and Medford atmosphere of the 40's; and you brought it all back out of the remote past!" Then he added, "But you're not a bit of a Rousseau!"[21] Writing his own memoir five years later, Charles Francis also turned his back upon Rousseauistic confession to record (in a much more pedestrian style than his brother's) his public activities and achievements.

"As the twig is bent, the tree inclines," he begins. "I know this has been so in my case, and my youth and education now seem to me to have been a skillfully arranged series of mistakes, first on the part of others and then on my own part."[22] Given his later accomplishments as Civil War officer, railroad executive and businessman, amateur historian and Harvard Overseer, this opening description of Charles Francis's life as a string of failures sounds as false a note as Henry's parallel but much more comprehensive assertions in the same vein. Both brothers trace their pessimism to early experiences and family heritage. To be sensitive to unsuccess comes easily to Adamses, and Charles Francis assesses as clearly as Henry the drawbacks of their family inheritance of intelligence, moral scruple, and social stiffness. Being a fourth-generation public figure, intensely conscious of oneself in relation to history and institutions, is a situation both brothers accept and explore. Their common location is announced in characteristic language in the autobiographies' opening sentences. Here is Charles Francis Adams's initial presentation of self:

> I came into this world in a house on Hancock Avenue, as the narrow footway on the right-hand side of the statue of Horace Mann, west of the State House grounds in Boston is still designated, between nine and eleven P.M. of the 27th of May, 1835. My father and mother had passed the winter at the house of my grandfather, Peter C. Brooks, on Pearl Street; but on the 11th of May they moved up to Hancock Avenue, their own house, with a view to the approaching event. In my father's diary there is a reference which fixes another and, to the generality, far more interesting date. Quincy granite was then in great vogue. On the 27th of April my father went out to Quincy, and up to the Old Granite Railway in Milton . . . and he there "observed some beautiful specimens which are in process of sculpture for the new Hotel of Mr. Astor in New York." These were the familiar Astor House monoliths, until recently so conspicuous a landmark in the architecture of Broadway. (3–4)

The Education has the briefer, more artfully historical opening of a life in the same setting:

> Under the shadow of Boston State House, turning its back on the house of John Hancock, the little passage called Hancock Avenue runs, or ran, from Beacon Street, skirting the State-House grounds, to Mount Vernon Street, on the summit of Beacon Hill; and there, in the third house below Mount Vernon Place, February 16, 1838, a child was born, and christened later by his uncle, the minister of the First Church after the tenets of Boston Unitarianism, as Henry Brooks Adams. (3)

Though each Adams locates his birth within the rich matrix of place and family, Charles Francis does so quite matter-of-factly, Henry with a tighter, more metaphoric awareness of political and religious tradition imposing themselves on the little infant. The Old Granite Railway, Horace Mann, and the Astor House point toward the busy commercial world in which the older brother is later to move. Henry's single serpentine sentence resonates differently—especially to readers of *Mont-Saint-Michel and Chartres.* Political power is something already turned away from or skirted in the topography of his birthplace, while religious heritage is an unavoidable part of the child's identity imposed by family, theology, and history.

In the same comparatively unimaginative style Charles Francis moves directly into an account of his life, whose manifest achievements are always measured by the monitory Adamsian motto "So much to do, so little done!" In his childhood and youth he notes more openly than Henry the fact of family isolation on Presidents Hill and the unusually long and dependent relationship there of children to parents. He also laments not being taught sports and a love of nature: "I would today give much to feel at home on a boat or bicycle" (13). The retired gentleman's sigh recalls his brother's similar but far more resonant remark: "At past fifty, Adams solemnly and painfully learned to ride the bicycle" (330). Unlike Charles's literal lament, Henry's bicycling becomes part of a metaphoric pattern clustering around the question of balance and precarious adjustment to life's challenges. Where Henry sees his life, especially in contrast to Clarence King's well-planned career, as a series of "violent breaks or waves," Charles Francis assesses his failures within a much more rational pattern. Like Du Bois and Franklin, Charles Francis Adams had a master plan. "I began with a scheme of life; nor was it a bad one. It was to establish myself at fifty; so that after fifty, I would be free to exert myself in such a way as I might then desire. Life also I regarded as a sequence—one thing, accident apart, leading to another" (190–91). The mistakes which sidetracked his ambitions prove, however, quite unspectacular:

turning down an inspector-generalship during the war to remain with his black regiment, remaining longer in the Union Pacific presidency than was politic and hence getting caught in the Panic of 1893. His beloved historical writing and speaking, his devoted services to Quincy and Harvard, were consequently often relegated to weekends and holidays. The picture of a harried, public-spirited businessman caught up in more activities than he would like—this is the rather pallid picture of "failure" which emerges from Adams's modest, unemotional memoir. In an old man's perspective of 1912 he summarizes his life in terms many conscientious, ordinary readers not born on Presidents Hill could understand: opportunities abounded, but too seldom they were matched by capacity or decisiveness.

As a measuring stick, then, *Charles Francis Adams, 1835–1915: An Autobiography* provides the example of one old man's memoir which, despite the Adams ingredient and the unusual theme of failure, might fit many another businessman's autobiography. It therefore offers some revealing contrasts to the far more ambitious and problematical narrative of his famous brother. It is of course dangerous to check one personal history's truths by another's equally subjective account. Indeed, though these men were brothers and remained close friends and collaborators, their autobiographies provide surprisingly divergent accounts of their common childhood. Thus Charles Francis's autobiography does not refer to his brother's revolt against school or the role their grandfather played in breaking a young boy's will. Older brothers, even when equipped with sympathy and hindsight, cannot often be expected to recall events or relationships important to their younger siblings. Even ties to a common father or mother are remembered and valued differently by one child and another. The lesson to be derived from contrasting these memoirs, then, is that even belonging to the same famous family and growing up in a self-consciously historical ambience will not guarantee much overlap in autobiographical subject matter, artistry, or historical consciousness.

The essential difference between Henry and Charles Francis Adams as autobiographers is clearly imaginative. From certain common memories and shared ideological values the younger brother has derived wider cultural conclusions, has infused these with different private associations, and embodies his perceptions in a far more complex and artful narrative. Unlike his brother or W. E. B. Du Bois, Henry Adams cannot accept the conventions of the memoir because he entertains profound doubts about the nature of facts and the chances of deriving reliable beliefs or meanings from memory. As he puts the matter in chapter 27, "all opinion founded on fact must be error, because the facts can never be complete, and their relations must be always infinite" (410). In measuring the bewildering distance between what he once thought and what he knows now, between potential and accomplishment in all realms of experience, Adams transcends the merely personal to create a cultural parable of modern historical existence. He composes what Vern Wagner calls "a treatise on inconclusion."[23] In the process, virtually all the traditional elements of historical autobiography unquestioned by others are dissected and challenged. The result is a powerful imaginative expression of the modern dissociated sensibility from which T. S. Eliot, Ezra Pound, Conrad Aiken, and others drew inspiration for some of their most vivid verse in the 1920s. Yet unlike *The Waste Land,* Adams's modern myth is a crystallization of American history and the actual experiences of a unique self.

Linking *The Education of Henry Adams* to literary history underlines the fact that many sensitive readers like Eliot have responded to this autobiography as if it were almost entirely an experiment in imaginative prose. Adams himself anticipates this, while still insisting upon the historicity and didactic seriousness of his story in characteristic comments to members of his private audience. "An experiment like this volume is hazardous, not as history, but as art," he wrote Whitelaw Reid. "To write a heavy dissertation on modern education, and fill up the background with moving figures that will carry the load is a literary *tour-de-force* that cannot wholly succeed even in the hands of Saint Augustine or Rousseau."[24] Again to William James he described his book as "a literary experiment, hitherto, as far as I know, never tried or never successful."[25] James's response to *The Education* and its author's description of it was sympathetically critical and prescient. "The boyhood part is really superlative," he wrote. "It and the London part should become classic historic documents." But James characterized the second half quite differently: "There is a hodgepodge of world-fact, private fact, philosophy, irony (with the word 'education' stirred in too much for my appreciation!) which gives a unique cachet to the thing, and gives a very pleasant *gesammt-eindruck* of H.A.'s *Self.*"[26] Furthermore, James's criticism of Adams's scientific and historical generalizations was even more trenchant. He took philosophical exception to the positing of a sequence of force extending through history from the Middle Ages, ascending steeply in the twentieth century, and pointing inevitably to catastrophe in the near future. What bothered James more than this quasi-mathematical plotting of historical change was the pessimistic determinism accompanying Adams's schema. "But unless the future contains genuine novelties," he observed, "unless the present is really creative of them, *I don't see the use of time at all.* Space would be a sufficient theatre for these statically determined relations to be arranged in."[27]

As one sympathetic inside reader, James shows a keen awareness of the two striking successes in his friend's literary experiment—the vividly evoked early years and the strong presence of a distinctive self infusing even the densest thickets of speculation. Adams's scientific analogizing, James saw, were less compelling as didactic messages than as dramatic acts of an aged, curious, idiosyncratic mind. Personal identity—"H.A.'s *Self*"—not historical theories or scientific theses, unifies and defines *The Education* for William James. This makes it, despite duplicities and eccentricities, an experiment in autobiography.

What James fails to pursue in his letter are the private facts and factors defining this presiding presence in *The Education,* for he belonged to Adams's intimate audience to whom the silences and suppressions would have been both more obvious and forgivable than for the general reader. Moreover, as a psychologist he doubtless understood that certain concepts appeal to certain temperaments for a variety of unstated and unacknowledged reasons. The psychological dimensions of Adams's history—its focus on a perennially adolescent self with an adolescent's exaggerated contradictions in thought, feeling, and language, the combination of secrecy and the surprising glimpses inward—point to the presence of powerful preconscious pressures shaping a narrative of ideas and worldwide experience. The symbol of these inner forces is Saint-Gauden's bronze statue in Rock Creek Cemetery. Why Adams commissioned it, what the unidentified, draped, and sexless figure signifies, are double mysteries hinted at but never explained in *The Education.* "The interest of the figure was not in its meaning," the author remarks with typical indirection, "but in the response of the observer" (329). The contrast here with Du Bois could hardly be clearer. Du Bois, too, is a secretive self. But in one separate central chapter of the *Soliloquy,* entitled "My Character," he makes an awkward but honest stab at self-portraiture and confession. On the contrary, Adams always treats his own autobiographical persona as a friend or public personage whose motives are interesting but remote, mysterious, probably unknowable. Clues are all we have to go on. Instead of a confessional chapter near the narrative's middle, Adams leaves a large hole there with a brooding figure in bronze as its guardian symbol.

Given the complexity of Henry Adams's psyche, it is a dangerous simplification to suggest that the man and his masks can be "explained" by the traumatic event indicated by that statue—the suicide of Marion Hooper Adams on December 8, 1885. This event—indeed, the very existence of a beloved spouse—are facts never mentioned in the autobiography. Patricia Meyer Specks urges us to pay particular attention to all such "systematic exclusions,"[28] for she believes these omissions illuminate cultural as well as private values. Since glaring suppressions occur in other American autobiographies (we shall later mention particularly Louis Sullivan's and Anaïs Nin's in this connection), it is important here to point out that Adams has, in fact, found several indirect ways of hinting at the impact of the tragic death of a wife upon himself. These include the twenty-year gap in the narrative which calls attention to itself, *The Education*'s theme of unsuccessful action but somewhat more successful reaction, Adams's illogical juxtaposition of determinism and moral responsibility, and the metaphors like the tailor's dummy, the architectural image of the broken arch, and the fossil fish—all symbols of inert, passive, or frozen feeling. Finally there is the actual episode of the death of Louisa Adams Kuhn by lockjaw, which occurs just before the break in the story and is a symbolic reenactment (in Adams's memory, that is) of Clover Adams's death almost fifteen years later.

In the face of his sister's meaningless death, it is "the insanity of force" which bears the special weight of Adams's rage: "the human mind felt itself stripped naked, vibrating in a void of shapeless energies, with resistless mass, colliding, crushing, wasting, and destroying what these same energies had created and labored from eternity to perfect" (288). As we learn from biographers, Clover Adams committed suicide in a fit of depression over the death of her widower-father, to whom she was abnormally close. Hence this brother's and widower's feelings about death and madness are understandable. Characteristically, however, he hides private emotions under general ideas. This explains his reaction to modern psychology, from which he derives this chilling picture of the human mind:

> The mind, like the body, kept its unity unless it happened to lose balance . . . ; [man's] normal condition was idiocy, or want of balance, and . . . his sanity was unstable artifice. . . . He was an acrobat, with a dwarf on his back, crossing a chasm on a slack-rope, and commonly breaking his neck. (434)

Adams's image of the acrobat resonates with several we have already noted: the innocuous one of the middle-aged autobiographer learning painfully to ride a bicycle and the two references to a broken body and will in the quotations cited earlier. It accords with his intellectual interpretations of modern science. "As for himself," he writes of three physicists, "he was henceforth to be a conscious ball of vibrating motions, traversed in every direction by infinite lines of rotation or vibration, rolling at the feet of the Virgin at Chartres or of M. Poincaré in an attic in Paris, a centre of supersensual chaos" (460).

An insanity of force, nightmare, an acrobat with a dwarf on his back, a rolling ball of matter with a center of supersensual chaos—with such violent language Henry Adams epitomizes himself as modern man precariously perched between the worlds of nature and history. Such freighted imagery is, on the one hand, less philosophical or psychological than William James's but, on the other hand, less poetic than T. S. Eliot's. It is the *autobiographical* shape of Adams's ideology, for it carries an urgency derived from the author's present consciousness of persistent past memories. Private as well as public experiences over sixty years and Adams's reading and reflection in the years just before and during the writing all contribute to *The Education*'s imagery. These are components not primarily of the author's didactic messages but of his identity—"H.A.'s *Self.*" In Grele's terminology, their value as public information can be established only by understanding them as private utterance. Reality-testing, again, is essential for grasping the reasons order, balance, and reason possess such desperate significance for this historian who, as we intuit but are never told, was also a husband and survivor of family madness and suicide. Precisely because Adams was a historian and recreates himself in the methods of that discipline, more than through the methods of fiction, psychology, or spiritual confession, his autobiography seldom dramatizes merely private experience. The secretive narrator and the silences in his speech are historical choices. They are made by an author who comprehends with other modern minds that all knowledge is distilled from personal experience and filtered through psyches that are ultimately as mysterious and untrustworthy as the rest of the universe. Thus, for all his doubts Adams accepts the primacy of the realities of nature, time, and history. He employs literary and confessional modes to depict himself in the act of accepting social and historical existence. *The Education* is exemplary, too, in dramatizing the sheer *quantity* as well as the *relativity* and *complexity* of modern thought. Far more than earlier historical autobiographers like Franklin or his own brother, indeed, more than Du Bois and many who come after him, Adams demonstrates how much the modern autobiographical consciousness can and must comprehend—and therefore how many problems of selection and exclusion this creates for the modern memoirist.

Although Adams's account of his historical existence is shot through with mysterious gaps and qualifying silences which only the privileged reader may hope to understand, the final impression of *The Education* is not of a self traumatized and arrested by private crisis or world chaos. Instead of the posthumous existence after 1885 which his brother Brooks Adams says Henry accepted for himself, we see the vital continuity of "H.A.'s *Self.*" The test of this continuous self is the book's comic tone and the fact that personal tragedies like Louisa Kuhn's and Clover Adams's have in particular oblique ways actually been incorporated into a single sustained narrative. Despite Samuels's assertion that the past is draped in "mortuary gauze," other readers detect the presence of a "cheerful nihilist"—to appropriate Richard B. Hauck's title[29]—someone who is able after personal tragedy to "resume his humanity or simianity in face of a fear" (457) and to satirize his own endless theorizing by observing, tongue in cheek, that "the motion of thought had the same value as the motion of a cannonball seen approaching the observer on a direct line through the air. One could watch its curve for five thousand years" (457). Still clearer evidence of the continuous self's triumph over the past is the fact that *The Education,* despite its artistry, remains "in the nature of proof sheets," not a completed repossession of the past. Even after correcting it for posthumous publication, Adams described his book to Charles Francis in 1915 as "an incomplete experiment which I shall never finish."[30] Here speaks not only the cynical poseur but the experienced historian who, like Franklin and Du Bois, recognizes that in striving for the symmetry and finality of art the autobiographer inevitably betrays the historical validity and ideological trajectory of his act. Personal history, as subsequent twentieth-century experience was to show, becomes a juggling act for many whose pasts, presents, and futures are united, if at all, in tenuous and temporary balance.

III

The Education of Henry Adams and *The Autobiography of W. E. B. Du Bois* are for many readers singularly convincing and meaningful histories of the self. Significant segments of American experience during a crucial historical epoch are recorded and, what is clearly more important, interpreted by these two aged historians. Though they have lived and worked more on the fringes of social and political influence than at the centers of power, this location strengthens the force of their assessments of American culture as it undergoes the transformations and challenges of the twentieth century. Standing *outside* as well as *within* gives Adams and Du Bois imaginative leverage and ideological perspective on certain social issues and cultural values. The freedom to criticize American racism in international terms, as Du Bois does, and to examine the cult of success and material progress through science and technology, a central theme in Adams's account, derives in part from their personal sense of relative powerlessness and marginality. Each narrative takes its shape from this social, historical, and imaginative location. Thus Erikson's thesis about self and method is exemplified. Both autobiographies, then, are prophetic for later American writing about the self. Their critiques identify major forces and ideas which also shape American experience for millions of others. The effect of such changes is to turn many Americans, white and black, into dissociated sensibilities like Adams or marginal men like Du Bois.

Both autobiographers are exemplary, too, as instructors in fundamental connections between experience, language, knowledge, and the self. As expert writers in many genres, both are sensitive to their audiences and to the expectations modern readers bring to the autobiographical occasion. Du Bois establishes the clearer relationship with the ordinary reader and serves as a general model for other twentieth-century historical autobiographers who, like him, accept the possibility and sovereignty of verifiable nonfictional statements. Du Bois's commonsensical faith in communication includes recognition of his fallible human memory and the weighty presence of ideological belief. But he never doubts the possibility of making factually accurate statements about, as well as personal interpretations of, his past. A comprehensive acknowledgment of gaps and omissions at the outset is sufficient to underline Du Bois's notions about the way memory works. In *The Autobiography,* the reader finds bias and personal animus, but despite his initial description of the *Soliloquy* as an old man's dream, there are few if any evidences of imaginative flights or plunges into the unconscious. There are no eponymous characters or fictionalized episodes. Such signals of the private imagination molding the plastic material of the past into satisfying aesthetic shape have been removed. His autobiography therefore demonstrates the possibilities of ordering modern experience through commonly accepted techniques of narration: chronological sequence, metaphors of space and travel closely linked to actual experience, an ideological point of view easily identified as plausible beliefs for this self. Past, present, and future are nicely balanced in a narrative which is as devoid of nostalgia as of blind ideological certainty. "Lurch and stagger" progress toward an egalitarian, raceless world community is not very different from the traditional ideals of American democracy. In this respect Du Bois is clearly closer to his predecessors Douglass and Washington than to younger black autobiographers like Angela Davis and George Jackson.

On the other hand, because it is "a literary experiment" deliberately intended to be a "failure" in conventional autobiographical terms, *The Education* is less accessible to the general reader and less imitated by subsequent autobiographers. Adams's "treatise on inconclusion" has become a literary classic, revered by sophisticated readers and frequently assigned as the opening book in courses on twentieth-century American history. But as autobiographer, Adams stands more alone; he is less clearly linked backward to Franklin and forward to Henry James or Stein than Du Bois is to his lineage, Douglass and Malcolm X. If so, this fate may be explained not only by Adams's immense and intimate mental grasp and his inimitable narrative form and imagery, but also by the idiosyncratic ideology he espouses with such comic, snobbish intensity. Too historical for literary successors in flight from history, too artful and duplicitous for ordinary historians, not confessional enough for post-Freudians, Adams makes a party of one, even more than other autobiographers. The great lesson of his life—that a summing-up is impossible for the mature modern consciousness but that a great work of art can be forged out of personal disaster and cultural disorder—has inspired the poetic more than the autobiographical imagination of Conrad Aiken, as we shall see in Chapter Five. Yet virtually all critics and readers find him at the crossroads of their journeys into the American self. With Du Bois, Adams is a chief exemplar of the modern memoirist who, confronting the loss of private values yet drawn to assert a collective identity with his fellows, attempts a personal history of his times which is as little private as possible. In subsequent chapters we shall examine ways Malcolm X, Norman Mailer, Lillian Hellman, and others participate in the "collective and personal, public and private, participatory and spectatorial . . . struggle" which are "the constitutive dialogues of contemporary memoir."[31]

3

The Soul and the Self:
Black Elk and Thomas Merton

SPIRITUAL AUTOBIOGRAPHY IN AMERICA, as in the rest of Christendom, discovers and communicates an individual's "search for God in time and memory." This phrase is the title of a theological study of European autobiography by John S. Dunne and suggests at once a typical structure, standpoint, and purpose for this variety of life-history.[1] The narrative structure most frequently chosen to dramatize the inward search for God is the journey or pilgrimage. The actual or time-bound self may be recreated in symbolic movement on and across the ocean, as occurs, for instance, in the colonial autobiography of Thomas Shepard or in the later narrative of Olaudah Equiano, the Nigerian ex-slave. Travel in and through the American wilderness is another representative pattern which provides apt metaphors for the eighteenth-century Quaker John Woolman and for the nineteenth-century Methodist circuit rider Peter Cartwright. The ideal standpoint from which the life-as-search is often narrated is a facsimile of God's—a timeless and absolute perspective embracing and transcending the limited subjectivity of human events, social identity, historical horizons. By standing imaginatively on the edge of time and the natural order, the soul's historian strives to repossess his or her time-bound self in the act of moving toward timelessness. Thus the purpose of writing personal history becomes twofold: to share with others the discovery of all that is within one's humanity and then, in a sense, to extinguish that self in what Thomas Merton calls in *The Sign of Jonas* "the clean desire for death" (340).

"Man does not live by self alone," Dunne declares, challenging what many critics see as the fundamental value of contemporary American culture.[2] In denying the absoluteness of the self, Dunne raises radical questions about autobiographical intention and expectation, as these come to focus upon historical identity. In the cultures from which most white Americans stem, the tension between self and soul is a familiar and knotty problem. From Saint Augustine on, Western spiritual autobiographers have tried to balance their culture's commitment to the individual with the traditional Eastern belief that autonomous selfhood is the source of sin and suffering. If most secular autobiographers since Franklin and Rousseau celebrate the social self and accord it a sovereign place in history, there is another strain, less prominent perhaps, but no less authentic, which insists upon a more paradoxical proposition. We are both self and more than self; we exist both within and beyond social space and historical time. Men and women become fully human only by reaching the limits of personal or collective identity. Such belief provides common ground for a variety of spiritual narratives written out of different religious traditions but within (and usually against) our now largely secularized culture. This chapter examines the strategies of two of the most famous historians of such transcendental experience in modern America. In the process of locating the autobiographies of Black Elk and Thomas Merton culturally and historically, I hope to suggest ways of discerning the spiritual dimensions of other, more specifically secular life-stories and of evaluating certain salient aspects of American culture from the radical perspective of the pilgrim, the visionary, and the saint.

"I find myself traveling toward my destiny in the belly of a paradox," Merton writes in the epigraph to *The Sign of Jonas.* The image of God's reluctant prophet inside the swimming whale becomes the metaphor of one life and of the whole human condition. Jonas is the biblical type of the traveler and testifier, who represents spirit within the body, death within life and resurrection in the belly of death, God's presence in the natural order, the unbounded soul in the finite social self. As one version of a life-story, *The Sign of Jonas* is the spiritual journal of a Trappist monk (once a young college teacher and aspiring poet) who in December 1941, as America went to war, traveled to Gethsemani, Kentucky to join the Cistercian Order of the Strict Observance. Though to some this act constituted an escape from the world, for Merton the motive was precisely the same as Thoreau's in heading for Walden Pond: "to front only the essential facts of life."[3] His journal appeared in 1953. Like its predecessor of 1948, *The Seven Storey Mountain,* it was written to document and defend this journey into silence.[4] By then, however, thanks to paperback publication, newspaper reviewers, and book clubs, *The Seven Storey Mountain* had already made its author if not the most famous American Catholic of the postwar era, probably the most widely read spiritual autobiographer of his generation. That success confirmed Merton's career as writer and apologist for the contemplative life.

For many American readers, *The Seven Storey Mountain* has been the occasion of their first encounter with the realities and ideals of the monastic life whose daily motions and silences also fill *The Sign of Jonas.* Both books invoke a centuries-old tradition of testimony and confession brought to the New World first by Puritan and Quaker memoirists and journal-keepers. But Trappist monasticism is a strange context for this literary and spiritual tradition. Twentieth-century readers, Catholics included, may well find it easier to share the experiences and viewpoint of a quiet-spoken Quaker like Woolman, traveling through the colonies preaching emancipation of slaves and love of Indians. Similarly, the muscular evangelism of Cartwright at a camp meeting on the banks of the Ohio is more comprehensible than Merton's elected world of silence, contemplation, obedience, and hard labor. Gethsemani, like other utopian communities, exists disturbingly within and yet apart from American culture.

A perspective even more alien and exotic characterizes another modern autobiography which, though written a dozen years or more before *The Seven Storey Mountain,* became widely known only some years later. *Black Elk Speaks: Being the Life Story of a Holy Man of the Oglala Sioux* is the remarkable result of an unlikely partnership between an aged, blind, illiterate Native American who spoke only Lakota and a younger white poet and historian from Nebraska. The book Black Elk and John G. Neihardt together created in 1930 and 1931 was at first known to relatively few (one of whom, however, was Carl Jung). Upon its reissue as a paperback in 1961, in part because of a new interest in visionary and non-Western religions, it suddenly became popular. For historians and religious anthropologists, Black Elk's accounts of Sioux rituals are also accessible in a subsequent book, Joseph E. Brown's *The Sacred Pipe.* But for aficionados of autobiography *Black Elk Speaks* represents far more than a source book of comparative religions; it is at once the self-portrait of a visionary, a history of Sioux culture during several crucial decades, and the first of several masterful collaborations in modern American writing about the self. Even more than *The Autobiography of Malcolm X* or *All God's Dangers, Black Elk Speaks* both fits and evades the conventional categories of confession, apology, and memoir. Black Elk speaks through Neihardt to Wasichu readers from the dual perspective of age-old tribal traditions and his own historical location as survivor of Wounded Knee and present resident on the Pine Hill reservation at Manderson,

South Dakota. Thus two radical definitions of "Western" and "American" values are expressed in this pair of narratives, which are in several senses boundary markers in the geography of the American soul.

The impulse to trace in retrospect one's spiritual trajectory beyond time and human society is not limited to monks, saints, and other professional holy men. It surfaces strangely and suddenly in secular stories as well. Indeed, the distinction between "secular" and "spiritual" virtually collapses as one examines certain contemporary autobiographies like Anaïs Nin's *Diary-I,* Shirley MacLaine's *"Don't Fall Off the Mountain,"* or Annie Dillard's *Pilgrim at Tinker Creek.* These are, among other things, accounts of epiphanies erupting in the lives of a novelist, a movie star, and a naturalist. Illumination here, as also in the very different autobiographies of Frank Conroy and Malcolm X, can occur anywhere: in a hospital or prison cell, on a journey (thus conforming to convention), or in special sacred spots where the "anchorhold" imagination can penetrate, like Thoreau's, deep beneath the surface of nature.[5] Though exotic in other respects, Black Elk and Merton are fully representative in this, for their lives are reconceived, symbolically and literally, as journeys anchored paradoxically in a specific spiritual spot. Furthermore, sickness and confinement are physical and spiritual conditions exploited to their full metaphoric limit. Each of these twentieth-century narratives therefore records the transformations in consciousness—and hence in identity—occurring when "one reaches the limits of experience with the experience of non-experience."[6]

Within modern culture, such interactions of self and soul are commonly reexperienced as tension or contradiction. Though conflicts may find temporary resolution in the act of autobiography, the consciousness of doubleness or dissociation suffuses such stories. However, this sense of living inside and beyond society, alone and yet identified with all nature and the rest of humanity, is by no means identical with the duality expressed by Du Bois or Adams. Theirs, as we have seen, results from a radical awareness of time and change within an ideological universe of historical events, ideas, and cultural institutions. Even for Malcolm X, as will be shown in Chapter Seven, time and history are the presiding categories of his and Haley's imaginations, and these values embrace even the visionary moment in Norfolk Prison Colony. But for others the only adequate response to the intrusion of the Other is to organize one's story around that vital fact. Language (although it belongs to culture), the autobiographical act (though it always exists within a specific historical context), and audience (which necessarily includes those one seeks to touch but from whom one is also alienated) are the problematical conditions and resources which make such responses possible. If words prove ultimately inadequate to represent the spiritual crises and revelations which have decisively shaped the soul, nonetheless, a deep human impulse persists to try to record the inexpressible, to inform one's fellows about mystery, to address one's God. Black Elk and Merton are exemplary autobiographers precisely because their eccentric locations on the borders of secular modern culture become a model of the alienation and dual consciousness afflicting other, more ordinary twentieth-century readers. How the old Indian and the young monk establish bridges from their special worlds to their readers', how they find different but appropriate story forms and metaphors for their experiences of otherness—these are my specific concerns in the following comparison and juxtaposition.

I

If one approaches *Black Elk Speaks* looking for explicit links to earlier American narratives like those of Shepard, Woolman, Equiano, or Cartwright, one's immediate reaction is likely to be disappointment and confusion. Gradually, however, underlying similarities and shared assumptions emerge to span the gap between radically different religious and cultural vocabularies. The awareness of a deeper congruity derives not only from Black Elk's vividly evoked vision and his passionate desire to communicate it properly, but also from the carefully explained collaboration by which the holy man's Sioux world has been repossessed. From the outset, the fact of dual authorship is linked to questions about authority and authenticity which are not simply literary or historical issues. They prove to be existential problems of long standing for Black Elk. How to tell a convincing story becomes, then, inseparable from recreating Black Elk's identity as a holy man in terms both collaborators can understand.

In order to define this original act one must first identify the circumstances of the book's creation. As the title and preface attest, *Black Elk Speaks* is the transcribed and transformed record of an actual oral recitation. Through words and pictures it memorializes the interaction, during the summer of 1930 and the spring and summer of 1931, of the sixty-seven-year-old Sioux and his fifty-year-old visitor who had come to South Dakota seeking spiritual knowledge and firsthand material for his historical epic poem, *A Cycle of the West*. For days the two sat under a pine-bough sunshade outside Black Elk's log cabin. Several others shared the occasion and contributed to its results: Black Elk's son, Neihardt's daughters, Standing Bear (who gives his own version of certain events and drew the fifteen illustrations), Iron Hawk, Fire Thunder, Flying Hawk. A phrase from the 1961 title page helps to focus this complex communal authorship: "As Told Through John G. Neihardt (Flaming Rainbow)."[7] This identifies the white writer's special function as audience, scribe, and sympathetic conduit of hitherto secret spiritual experience. Neihardt never suppresses the contributions of the others. Moreover, "Flaming Rainbow" is no ordinary Indian name conferred upon an honored white visitor. In the account of the vision which came to Black Elk in 1871 there is a flaming rainbow over the door of the Sacred Tepee. The point is clear: Neihardt has become the doorway to another Sacred Tepee reconstructed sixty years later. Although Wasichu readers must enter through the words and the style of the white poet, they recognize at the same time how successfully Neihardt has surrendered himself to his Indian subject. The unique presence and voice of the blind holy man shines throughout. Neihardt's later remark is fully authenticated: *"Black Elk Speaks* is a work of art with two collaborators, the chief one being Black Elk."[8]

Because it is a true collaboration, the narrative gives appropriate expression to the necessarily divergent intentions of the subject and the writer. Just as Neihardt lends his verbal artistry to the old man's wishes, so Black Elk willingly uses Neihardt to speak to white readers in their culture's terms as well as his own. His overriding motive is to preserve and communicate the vision which came to him when he was nine, which he first performed for his people when he was eighteen, and which finally proved unavailing in averting the massacre at Wounded Knee when Black Elk was twenty-seven. As they drove away from their first talk with Black Elk, Flying Hawk remarked to Neihardt, "The old man seems to know you were coming" (ix). This eagerness is prophetic and emphasizes the Sioux's desire to bridge differences in religious and cultural outlook, differences Neihardt is equally anxious to overcome. As Robert Sayre emphasizes, Neihardt is no Chicago sociologist or Harvard anthropologist come out to South Dakota to record primitive beliefs and rituals.[9] His aim as a poet is empathic and inclusive: to enter and articulate Black Elk's spiritual world while at the same time repossessing his historical past. Indeed, one of the book's notable achievements as self-construction is its combination of exalted mystical transport, deep personal anguish, and firm involvement in the everyday world.

Both creators realize that although Black Elk's life overflows with spiritual energy it is not therefore harmonious. "Truth comes into this world with two faces" (192), Black Elk observes, recalling the *heyoka* ceremony. His remark reminds us that its author, like Du Bois in a wholly different context, experiences himself as two distinct persons. He is the holy man with the consuming vision that has changed his life but not the fate of his people. He is also an ordinary Lakota Sioux whose memory, like all men's, is fallible, whose words are inadequate to encompass his visionary imagination. Like other men, he is plagued with fear and doubt. Hence the psychological questions of expressive intent, self-revelation, and manifest and latent meanings which the white reader brings from Western autobiography will prove helpful here as well. Nor are traditionally European-American concerns about personal identity to be completely abandoned simply because Black Elk lives in a tribal community with very different notions of human personality from those which animate and explain Thomas Merton. Sayre is indeed right to warn against an exclusively white vocabulary and frame of reference; "civilization," "savagery," "life," "self," and "writing" are all terms with radically different implications in the Sioux world—or, in some cases, with no meaning at all. Speaking of Indian autobiographies generally, Sayre writes, "There is the danger in all of these books of numerous kinds of misrepresentations, equivalent to P. T. Barnum's exhibiting captive Indians on his New York stage, where they looked very real to the audience, but very strange to themselves."[10] In a sense, all autobiographies, though more or less real to their readers, seem very strange to their authors, for the act of translating a "who" into a "what" through words must always strike the author as inevitably a misrepresentation. Thus Black Elk's willingness to historicize and confess his inmost self and Neihardt's willingness to place Black Elk's vision at the center of his history come together in *Black Elk Speaks*. A wholehearted collaboration locates this unusual story more within the Western frame of autobiographical reference than might at first be expected. Because it exists between, and derives its power from, two distinct worlds of time and social space, this seemingly eccentric work becomes one paradigm of modern spiritual autobiography.

Although Neihardt properly centers attention upon Black Elk's vision, it is essential to note that the speaker does not begin his story there. Instead, the narrative opens with Black Elk's invocation ritual and scriptural parable. Therefore, reading this book becomes a religious ceremony whose purpose is to connect red speaker and white audience and create the double ambience of spiritual and secular time and reality within which the story moves. "My friends, I am going to tell you the story of my life, as you wish," he remarks. He immediately deprecates this personal focus: "what is one man that he should make much of his winters, even when they bend him like a heavy snow?" The aim, therefore, is larger than personal. "It is the story of all life that is holy and is good to tell, and of us two-leggeds sharing it with the four-leggeds and the wings of the air and all green things; for these are children of one mother and their father is one Spirit" (1). Then Black Elk presents his past as a temporal journey now seen "from a lonely hill-top" (2). Next he invites the reader, in the person of Neihardt, to feel, fill, and smoke the sacred pipe. This little ritual consecrates the book as the communal communication it actually is, "because no good thing can be done by man alone" (2). The pipe symbolizes timeless reality, even though the leather on its mouthpiece, as Black Elk points out, "should be bison hide" (3) but is not—a reminder that although the buffalo are gone he has faithfully renewed the hide with some modern substitute. Finally, Black Elk closes the ritual by relating a legend about the bringing of the pipe to his people.

What Black Elk and his collaborator together accomplish with this ceremonial opening is the establishment of the ensuing account of the vision and the life within an Indian framework of a vertical and circular conception of life and self. Then in the second chapter the horizontal or linear perspective of the white man is introduced as Black Elk is quickly located in historical time. "I was born in the Moon of the Popping Trees (December)," Black Elk relates, "on the Little Powder River in the Winter When the Four Crows Were Killed (1863), and I was three years old when my father's right leg was broken in the Battle of the Hundred Slain. From that wound he limped until the day he died, which was about the time when Big Foot's band was butchered on Wounded Knee" (1890). "He is buried here in these hills" (7–8). Neihardt's controlling presence is here telegraphed not only in the parenthetical dates but also by the succinct evocation of a whole historical experience—and its natural locale—which is to be recreated in the narrative. The poet-historian also inserts a footnote to point out that the Battle of the Hundred Slain is known as Fetterman's Fight in white history books. Black Elk's different historical perspective on these events emerges as he explains: "When I was older, I learned what the fighting was about that winter and the next summer. Up on the Madison Fork the Wasichus had found much of the yellow metal that they worship and that makes them crazy, and they wanted to have a road up through our country to the place where the yellow metal was; but my people did not want the road" (9). Several important cultural themes which become personal preoccupations are here introduced: the white man's greed for gold and the road through the wilderness which results, the crazy behavior of the intruders from the

East. A third motif, closely tied to these, is expressed in Black Elk's ensuing remarks:

> But the Wasichus came and they have made little islands for us and other little islands for the four-leggeds, and always these islands are becoming smaller, for around them surges the gnawing flood of the Wasichu; and it is dirty with lies and greed.

Then he repeats the prophetic dream of another, older holy man:

> He dreamed that the four-leggeds were going back into the earth and that a strange race had woven a spider's web all around the Lakotas. And he said, "When this happens, you shall live in square gray houses, in a barren land, and beside those square gray houses you shall starve." . . . You can look about you now and see that he meant these dirt-roofed houses we are living in, and that all the rest was true. Sometimes dreams are wiser than waking. (9–10)

Like the tepee, the coyote's hole, and the bird's nest, the Lakota's island is round like the hoop that represents the Indian nation. Circular forms are natural and holy, while the straight lines and square shapes characteristic of the white man's world—imaged here as a spider's web but elsewhere as the black road—are evil and unnatural. In his vision of the Six Grandfathers or Spirits, the boy is carried into the air like a bird. "Behold the earth!" says the Fourth Grandfather.

> So I looked down and saw it lying yonder like a hoop of peoples, and in the center bloomed the holy stick that was a tree, and where it stood there crossed two roads, a red one and a black. "From where the giant lives (the north) to where you always face (the south) the red road goes, the road of good," the Grandfather said, "and on it shall your nation walk. The black road goes from where the thunder beings live (the west) to where the sun continually shines (the east), a fearful road, a road of troubles and war." (29)

As the rest of the vision unfolds, Black Elk's imagination is revealed in its representative and personal richness of reference. Thus the "skyful of horses dancing around me" signifies ecstatic awareness of his participation in all nature and of loving unity as a source of effective power within the world of men and time. Though Jung links these elements of the vision to a universal psyche, it is also significant that at the vision's climax all forty-eight of the handsome horses are dancing around Black Elk; *he* is the center of the universe for that moment.[11] In this way the vision *is* the self—or becomes so as the narrative unfolds. The special symbol of Black Elk's historical or temporal self is the Sixth Grandfather, through whom the boy sees himself and his future. "Now I knew that the sixth Grandfather was about to speak, he who was the Spirit of the Earth," he relates,

> and I saw that he was very old, but more as men are old. His hair was long and white, his face was all in wrinkles, and his eyes were deep and dim. I stared at him, for it seemed I knew him somehow; and as I stared, he slowly changed, for he was growing backwards into youth, and when he had become a boy, I knew he was myself with all the years that would be mine at last. (30)

This is a truly autobiographical touch. For as the Sixth Grandfather "rose and tottered out through the rainbow door" of the tepee we realize that the Indian narrator of this collective dream has created a palimpsest image of his historical self. The soul's capacity to dream recreates the self; the reel of one lifetime is run backward, as it is in all personal histories. The particular and universal are thereby conjoined, as they also are at the vision's second climax when the boy, astride a bay horse, is taken atop "the highest mountain of them all" to see in another form the sacred circularity of all life. The mountain is both a spiritual symbol of illumination, like the holy mountain in John Woolman's *Journal,* and refers specifically to Harney Peak in the Black Hills, to which Black Elk and Neihardt go at the end of the book. "But anywhere is the center of the world" (43), the holy man asserts, thus reiterating the interchangeability of temporal and spiritual experience in his imagination.

Black Elk's vision, then, alters his life as it gives that life meaning and metaphors through Neihardt's re-creation. The nine-year-old child is defined by the old man as the one who actually experienced such a vision and then lived out its prophetic meanings. Like Louis Sullivan's vacation from school (as we shall see in the next chapter), the event is carefully placed to stand as the source of personal identity and creative power. For Sullivan, his sojourn in nature must be translated into buildings by the adult designer in order for the childhood experience to be fully realized. For Black Elk, his vision must be ceremonially performed for its power to help his people undergo the tragic rigors of history. Many events intervene between the vision and its performance. Some of these simply do not make a story and so are skipped over because they do not fit the recurrent image of Black Elk's and his people's experience as the intersection of a red road and a black road.

But before life can be made to follow inspiration and vatic utterance, the storyteller must come to terms with the fact that he is now split in two. After having the vision, Black Elk remembers, he is filled with the memory of its power. But he is likewise afraid to speak about it "because I knew that nobody would believe me, little as I was, for I was only nine years old" (48–49). Moreover, he is not certain of the correct words. Memory as a source of power splits apart. As for memory of the vision, he remains certain of that, "for nothing I have ever seen with my eyes was so clear and bright as what my vision showed me. . . . I did not have to remember these things; they have remembered themselves all these years" (49). In sharp contrast to spiritual sight (which bears a special poignance when we remember that the speaker is blind) is his ready confession of a faulty memory in other areas. "I think," "so I have heard," "they say" are typical phrases by which he registers his fallible understanding and reassures the reader of his (and Neihardt's) honest wrestle with historical truth.

As a participant now in two worlds, the boy feels cut off from both; even his family "were almost like strangers." One incident nicely dramatizes his new sense of "queerness":

One day during this time I was out with the bow and arrows my Grandfather had made for me, and as I walked along thinking of my vision, suddenly I felt queer, and for a little while it seemed that the bows and arrows were those that the First Grandfather in the Flaming Rainbow Tepee had given me. Then they were only those that Refuse-To-Go had made, and I felt foolish and tried to make myself think it was only a dream anyway. So I thought I would forget about it and shoot something. There was a bush and a little bird sitting in it; but just as I was going to shoot, I felt queer again, and remembered that I was to be like a relative with the birds. So I did not shoot. Then I went on down toward a creek, feeling foolish because I had let the little bird go, and when I saw a green frog sitting there, I just shot him right away. But when I picked him up by the legs, I thought: "now I have killed him," and it made me want to cry. (51)

Though readers may at first miss the distinction between the two grandfathers or the reason for Black Elk's new kinship with birds (their wings are equivalents of man's powers of spiritual ascent), the boy's frustrated self-doubts which lead to the killing of the frog are powerfully evoked and easily understood. A succinct parable of a specific cultural view of man and nature, this little episode also illustrates the psychology of the spiritual calling.

John Woolman once had a closely similar experience and records it in his *Journal*'s opening chapter. Subtle differences in language and outlook do not obscure underlying similarities. "I may here mention a remarkable circumstance that occurred in my childhood," the Quaker writes with characteristic directness.

> On going to a neighbor's house, I saw on the way a robin sitting on her nest, and as I came near she went off; but having young ones, she flew about, and with many cries expressed her concern for them. I stood and threw stones at her, and one striking her she fell down dead. At first I was pleased with the exploit, but after a few minutes was seized with horror, at having, in a sportive way, killed an innocent creature while she was careful for her young. I beheld her lying dead, and thought these young ones, for which she was so careful, must now perish for want of their dam to nourish them. After some painful considerations on the subject, I climbed up the tree, took all the young birds, and killed them, supposing that better than to leave them to pine away and die miserably. In this case I believed that Scripture proverb was fulfilled. "The tender mercies of the wicked are cruel."[12]

Woolman concludes his confession with a characteristic Christian homily: "Thus He whose tender mercies are over all his works hath placed a principle in the human mind, which incites to exercise goodness towards every living creature" (25). The fact that this principle did not operate in the boy's mind until after the killing is not emphasized, though his story does underline the white man's moral distance from the animal world. Black Elk, in contrast, shows an intimate spiritual kinship with all animal life which his vision has only sharpened. Yet even more striking is his ability to reenter and recreate the psychological conflicts of sixty years ago, to become a boy again.

Black Elk is never the completely confident mystic, and this duality permits him to reenter the past fully and feelingly. Right up to the moment when the vision is performed, he continues to consider himself queer or "crazy." In fact, a major motif in Neihardt's narrative is the contrast between these youthful worries about being "crazy" or being thought so by his fellows and his growing realization of different ways others have of acting crazy. Initially his fear is that Whirlwind Chaser, the holy man who cures him of his sickness at the occasion of the vision, will look into his soul "and see my vision there and tell it wrong, and then maybe all the people would think I was crazy" (50). These doubts about the reality and accuracy of visions are connected through Whirlwind Chaser to others' doubts—including, of course, most readers'—about self-proclaimed mystics. In particular, his possible role as a future leader of his people is tied to his cousin Crazy Horse, whose name Black Elk explains at some length. His kinsman's fate and his own futile actions at Wounded Knee are connected by their visions, in which horses figure prominently and to which the ambiguous term "crazy" applies.

Even more strikingly modern and understandable for Wasichu readers is the crisis of self-doubt—or, more properly perhaps, soul-doubt—which overtakes Black Elk during the winter he is seventeen. Few present-day readers can read these pages without thinking of an identity crisis or psychic storm. "A terrible time began for me then," he recalls, "and I could not tell anybody, not even my father and mother."

> Sometimes the crying of coyotes out in the cold made me so afraid that I would run out of one tepee into another, and I would do this until I was worn out and fell asleep. I wondered if maybe I was only crazy; and my father and mother worried a great deal about me. They said: "It is the strange sickness he had that time when we gave the horse to Whirlwind Chaser for curing him; and he is not cured." I could not tell them what was the matter, for then they would only think I was queerer than ever. (163–65)

In a collaboration like this one, it is impossible to determine if Black Elk actually uttered phrases like "only crazy," "only a dream," and "queerer than ever." Whoever originates them, "only" is one of the crucial words for communicating Black Elk's sense of different levels of being and his participation (indeed, his entrapment) in all of them. But confusion and lonely terror are turned to triumph when the following summer Black Elk secures the assistance of two older men and they perform the horse dance for the whole band. When all the horses in the dance and in the surrounding village neigh together, Black Elk experiences another ecstatic revelation. "Then suddenly, as I sat there

71

looking at the cloud, I saw my vision yonder once again—the tepee built of cloud and sewed with lightning, the flaming rainbow door and, underneath, the Six Grandfathers sitting, and all the horses thronging in their quarters; and also there was I myself upon my bay before the tepee" (173). As Black Elk is seated on a bay horse at that moment, it is easy to imagine the process by which the young man's imagination has projected a living situation and communal set of symbols upon the imaginary world. For Black Elk, however, it is just the reverse: "I looked about me and could see that what we then were doing was like a shadow cast upon the earth from yonder vision in the heavens, so bright it was and clear. I knew the real was yonder and the darkened dream of it was here" (173). Soon after, when Black Elk cures a sick boy, the process is completed. The story comes full circle, for the little boy has grown to take the place of Whirlwind Chaser and is now a successful healer.

In the act of performing his vision Black Elk achieves a mature, socially confirmed identity and a temporary end to agonizing division and self-doubt. In Eriksonian terms, his is a successful identity crisis; his vision has provided a convincing ideology by which to live. Nevertheless, the consciousness of existing in the two worlds represented by the red road and the black road never departs. History proves inescapable; he and his people cannot live out their lives "by the power of the circle" (200). Furthermore, contact with the intruding Wasichus teaches Black Elk many new meanings of "crazy." If circular living is the Grandfather's way whereby the red road represents traditional Sioux harmony with nature, then square is the shape of "crazy" existence brought in by the white man over the black road. That east-west road signifies several realities: wagon tracks and the Union Pacific Railroad, conflict and greed, selfishness and abstraction, spiritual sterility and death. After the Sioux fall under white influence he describes them as "traveling the black road, everybody for himself and with little rules of his own" (219). Literally and figuratively, the black road divides the land and destroys the bison herd. One symbol of this "crazy" value system of greedy aggression and self-aggrandizement is the gold watch he pulls from the dead soldier's belt at the Little Big Horn. "It was round and bright and yellow and very beautiful," he recalls, "and I put it on me for a necklace. At first it ticked inside, and then it did not any more" (130).

An even more extended demonstration of the white man's "crazy" culture occurs on Black Elk's longest journey, his trip to the East and Europe as a member of Buffalo Bill's circus troupe. While in London he witnesses Queen Victoria's Diamond Jubilee. Though

the Sioux regard "Grandmother England" as a friendly Wasichu—
since many of them fled to safety over the Canadian border during
fights with the U.S. cavalry—her celebration is described with ironic
candor. "Her dress was all shining and her hat was all shining and her
wagon was all shining and so were the horses. She looked like a fire
coming." Then he adds tactfully, "Afterward I heard that there was
yellow and white metal all over the horses and the wagon" (226).
Though the occasion is recalled as "a happy time" in an otherwise
nightmarish journey into the white world, the connections between
gold, greed, and imperialist splendor, which like the trooper's watch
give Wasichu culture its "crazy" beauty, are heightened by the observer's outside perspective.

Spiritual consciousness, historical experience, and cultural commentary intersect even more vividly and violently in the denouement
of *Black Elk Speaks* in the Ghost Dance craze and the Wounded Knee
massacre which is its tragic consequence. When Black Elk returns
from his European trip he hears of Wovoka, the Paiute in the Far West
whose visionary message promises to "save the Indian peoples and
make the Wasichus disappear and bring back all the bison and the people who were dead" (236). Black Elk is not at first convinced of this
vision of "a new earth." As a realistic mystic, he "thought maybe it
was only the despair that made people believe, just as a man who is
starving may dream of plenty of everything good to eat" (237). Finally,
however, when he attends a Ghost Dance he sees many details from
his own vision reenacted. As he joins in the dance he is transported
on two visionary journeys to the land of the Six Grandfathers. Later,
too, he sees his Flaming Rainbow again. Such recurrences, however,
prove ultimately false. From his present vantage point forty years
later, the storyteller confesses that it was a great mistake to participate
in the Ghost Dance.

While Black Elk graphically describes his travels into the Other
World, Neihardt takes pains to insure that he also recaptures the historical circumstances of his story's climax. With him we look back in
sorrow across the gulf of time from 1931 to the fateful year, 1890. As
he comes to recount the dreadful event, the reader is again reminded
of the geographical setting which has all along contained Black Elk's
narrative and which binds past and present together. "In a little while
we had come to the top of the ridge where, looking to the east, you
can see for the first time the monument and the burying-ground on
the little hill where the church is," he observes, and we realize that
these are both actual and symbolic South Dakota places and buildings
which Neihardt—and the blind old man—are looking at. The descrip-

tion of the massacre, however, is not at all symbolic, but grimly, poetically realistic.

> We followed down along the dry gulch, and what we saw was terrible. Dead and wounded women and children and little babies were scattered all along there where they had been trying to run away. The soldiers had followed along the gulch, as they ran, and murdered them in there. Sometimes they were in heaps because they had huddled together, and some were scattered all along. Sometimes bunches of them had been killed and torn to pieces where the wagon-guns hit them. I saw a little baby trying to suck its mother, but she was bloody and dead. (265)

This scene, surely as gripping as any in Arthur Penn's film version of *Little Big Man* or the fictional account in Thomas Berger's novel—both of which draw upon *Black Elk Speaks*—continues to its dire conclusion with Black Elk and Neihardt working closely together.

> It was a good winter day when all this happened. The sun was shining. But after the soldiers marched away from their dirty work, a heavy snow began to fall. The wind came up in the night. There was a big blizzard, and it grew very cold. The snow drifted deep in the crooked gulch, and it was one long grave of butchered women and children and babies, who had never done any harm and were only trying to run away. (268)

That Black Elk has stamped his consciousness upon this spare and poetic passage may be more readily believed by looking at Neihardt's separate version of the same event which he later used in his 1935 poem, "The Song of the Messiah," the concluding segment of his cycle. In retelling the story of Wounded Knee, Neihardt focuses upon an older Indian, Sitanka, and his starving band, though Black Elk is passingly mentioned as a participant in the Ghost Dance. As the soldiers' rifles reverberate, the poem concludes:

> Beneath the flaming thunders of the hill,
> That fury heaped the dying and the dead.
> And where the women and the children fled
> Along the gully winding to the sky
> The roaring followed, till the long, thin cry
> Above it ceased.
> > The bugles blared retreat.
> Triumphant in the blindness of defeat,

> The iron-footed squadrons marched away.
> And darkness fell upon the face of day.
> The mounting blizzard broke. All night it swept
> The bloody field of victory that kept
> The secret of the Everlasting Word.[13]

Sally McCluskey and others have praised Neihardt for the poetic precision of the prose he put in Black Elk's mouth. But these passages suggest to me that Black Elk has contributed fully as much to the "work of art" as he has to its historical and spiritual authenticity. The result of their collaboration is a far more powerful narrative than Neihardt alone created in the "Song of the Messiah" or "The Song of the Indian Wars."

More important than speculating on whose voice and words predominate is to note the personal and social significance of the massacre story. Black Elk's role in the tragedy is fully described, though it shares our attention with the bloody event itself. Both the potential power and actual failure of his life as holy man are visually enacted in the two attacks on horseback which Black Elk leads. In the first he wears the sacred shirt (all covered with symbols from his vision) and carries the sacred bow, but no arrows or other weapons. He is not hit by the soldiers' bullets. Following the massacre, however, he abandons the bow and takes a rifle. "After what I had seen over there, I wanted revenge; I wanted to kill" (270). Yet he fights and risks death as he has lived—in a sacred manner. Imitating the geese of the north in his vision, he stretches out his arms and charges.

> All this time the bullets were whizzing around me and I was
> not touched. I was not even afraid. It was like being in a dream
> about shooting. But just as I had reached the very top of the
> hill, suddenly it was like waking up, and I was afraid. I dropped
> my arms and quit making the goose cry. Just as I did this, I
> felt something strike my belt as though someone had hit me
> there with the back of an ax. I nearly fell out of my saddle,
> but I managed to hold on, and rode over the hill. (272)

The wounding of the *wanekia,* or savior, of his people reaffirms the sense of doubleness that marks his whole life. Equally powerful and poignant is his sense of failure:

> And I can see that something else died there in the bloody
> mud, and was buried in the blizzard. A people's dream died
> there. It was a beautiful dream. And I, to whom so great a vi-

sion was given in my youth—you see me now a pitiful old man who has done nothing, for the nation's hoop is broken and scattered. There is no center any longer, and the sacred tree is dead. (276)

Though this is a moving conclusion to the story Black Elk chooses to tell, it is not the actual end of *Black Elk Speaks.* Nor are these the literal words of the holy man; like the author's postscript which follows, they have been supplied by Neihardt. The postscript anticipates and contrasts markedly in tone with Haley's epilogue to *The Autobiography of Malcolm X.* Neihardt's aim in having the last word is not to record Black Elk's death (which did not occur until 1950) but to bring readers back into the present, to remind them that this is a collaboration, and to complete Black Elk's spiritual journeys by taking him atop Harney Peak. "What happened there," he observes, "is, of course, related to Wasichu readers as being merely a more or less striking coincidence" (277). The aged holy man, dressed and painted as he was in the vision that brought him in spirit to this very spot sixty years before, sends forth a thin, quavering voice to the Six Grandfathers. It is a plea for forgiveness couched in the language of his vision. Then something like a little miracle occurs. Though the day is clear—South Dakota having experienced a summer drought in 1931—thin clouds begin to gather around the peak. A thin, drizzling rain falls upon Black Elk's weeping face. The Thunder Beings have listened to his confession, apologia, and intercession just as the reader has listened to Neihardt rehearsing his history. Though nothing may have changed in the natural and social worlds, the holy man's prayer echoes in the reader's imagination and memory, fixing itself there in the timeless realm of art and history which it has been Black Elk's aim to reach. There it completes the picture of a man whose efforts to serve his people and to merge with all vegetable and animal life paradoxically endow him with an unmistakable individual voice. In autobiographical terms, Black Elk has recreated himself convincingly in the image of his literary method, for in speaking to and through John G. Neihardt, the old man demonstrates over again the paradoxical fruits of his long experiences: that "no good thing can be done by any man alone," that he and his vision could not alter history, that truth indeed "comes into this world with two faces."

II

Although Black Elk's vision of a sacred, circular, natural world, in which the spiritual traveler returns to the mountaintop he has seen all his life on the South Dakota horizon, is foreign to modern readers, an act of collaboration succeeds in spanning many cultural gaps and keeping a self and a soul in remarkably clear focus. Furthermore, the character of Old Lodge Skins in Berger's novel and Penn's film serves, for those aware of the connections, as a serio-comic stand-in for Black Elk, familiarizing the mysterious and making visual certain aspects of this life. No such alternate versions, so far as I know, exist to domesticate or dramatize Thomas Merton and his world. A Trappist monastery evidently holds little appeal for a novelist and is perhaps even more inaccessible to the filmmaker. Moreover, Merton's childhood and youth lack the obvious color of Black Elk's vision or the romantic appeal of the Battle of the Little Big Horn. Though expatriate experiences in Europe and college days at Columbia might have given Merton's autobiography something of the literary and historical interest of, say, Hemingway's *A Moveable Feast* or Cowley's *Exile's Return,* such is not the case with *The Seven Storey Mountain.* When Black Elk's mind is elsewhere, at least Neihardt is present to jog his memory about battles and Buffalo Bill. Thomas Merton, on the other hand, had no such collaborator available in his Cistercian world of silence to focus dramatic attention upon his secular past, which is reentered not for its own sake but as exemplary illustration of the stages of spiritual movement toward the Mount of Purgatory.

Notwithstanding these obvious differences, the young monk experiences his transformed identity and present location almost as paradoxically as the old Sioux. The fame Merton won with his autobiography becomes the chief reason for this spiritual traveler's continued—indeed, accentuated—self-consciousness. As Frater Louis, he was renamed to a life of prayer, contemplation, and silence. Yet before his untimely death in 1968, he had written and published more than fifty books under his old name, Thomas Merton. "Thou shalt be silent" was the passage the anxious convert found when he opened his New Testament in 1941, looking a bit superstitiously for a sign. But when he entered the monastery, far from giving up writing, he was specifically instructed by his superiors to continue. Thus the *nihil obstat* and *imprimatur* at the head of this volume attest both to censorship and an encouragement without which Merton might never have written this or any autobiography. As it was, he became at Gethsemani a writer with a vengeance. Provided with a private secretary, Merton found himself working at times on three or four manuscripts at once. For a monk whose real calling, as he felt for years, was to the hermit's life, this busy career seemed to contradict and subvert the life of prayerful silence. Contracts, book clubs, deadlines, visits from agents and publishers, correspondence with other writers—these preoccupied him. More than a simple distraction, this situation threatened to separate him from his fellows; "an author in a Trappist monastery is like a duck in a chicken coop," he once wrote. *"And he would give anything in the world to be a chicken instead of a duck."*[14] Moreover, it kept reraising the question of identity, which he thought had been settled once and for all. At the close of *The Seven Storey Mountain* he recalls standing near the cloister cemetery with a fresh copy of *Thirty Poems* in hand. "By this time I should have been delivered of any problems about my true identity," he remarks in the epilogue.

> I had already made my simple profession. And my vows should have divested me of the last shreds of any special identity.
>
> But there was this shadow, this double, this writer who had followed me into the cloister.
>
> He is still on my track. He rides my shoulders, sometimes, like the old man of the sea. I cannot lose him. He still wears the name of Thomas Merton. Is it the name of an enemy?
>
> He is supposed to be dead.
>
> But he stands and meets me in the doorway of all my prayers and follows me into church. He kneels with me behind the pillar, the Judas, and talks to me all the time in my ear. . . . He generates books in the silence that ought to be sweet with the infinitely productive darkness of contemplation. . . .
>
> Maybe in the end he will kill me, he will drink my blood. (400)

This split or struggle between an active creative self and passive contemplative soul also infuses earlier sections of *The Seven Storey Mountain* and continues, in a different spirit, in *The Sign of Jonas*. His is but a particular version of the universal Christian paradox which Merton, like John Woolman, expresses in the image of the man in motion who has already reached his destination. "We cannot arrive at the perfect possession of God in this life," he writes, "and that is why we are travelling and in darkness. But we already possess Him by grace, and therefore in that sense we have arrived and are dwelling in the light" (409). No escape from this seesaw was achieved in Merton's lifetime, though his writing is filled with the calm anticipation of death as the doorway to resolution. Yet even more paradoxically, it was in the act of writing itself that Merton gradually came to experience harmony and union; "my work is my hermitage," he was able to say in *The Sign of Jonas*, "because it is *writing* that helps me most of all to be a solitary and a contemplative here at Gethsemani" (269). Moreover, in solitude he discovers and affirms his truest individual identity; "some of us *have to be alone* to be ourselves," he wrote later.[15]

In *The Seven Storey Mountain,* therefore, autobiography becomes the record of a movement toward and within the solitary activity of writing, a pilgrimage through what Merton calls (in language close to Black Elk's) the "crazy" secular world. But the resting point he reaches is not the actual mountaintop Black Elk climbs in imagination and on foot. Rather, Merton's is a purely symbolic place on the side of the Mount of Purgatory. The standpoint from which he speaks also fits Dunne's anatomy; it is Merton's approximation of a divine perspective on time and society. Through image, event, and explicit meditation and proclamation he juxtaposes the darkness of his secular journey and timebound consciousness against the illumination discovered in the Roman Catholic faith and monastic ideal. However, unlike Malcolm X, another convert, Merton refuses to accord his worldly past and self much dignity or authenticity as stages on the holy way. Indeed, Merton's severe, almost arrogant judgments on the small boy on Long Island, the hellraiser at Cambridge, and the campus leader at Columbia do not present him in an appealing light. A detestation of the secular world which smacks of moral smugness sets his story's tone in many passages and marks a striking difference from Black Elk.

There are several sources for Merton's youthful absolutism. One is a recent convert's ideological enthusiasm. Then, too, he must play a semipublic role even in his private meditations, for he writes as the apologist and propagandist for his Order and for monasticism generally within his Church. The audience to be addressed kept changing in his mind but always included fellow Catholics curious about this well-known convert's story and the realities of the Cistercian life. "I am trying to tone down *The Seven Storey Mountain,*" he observes in 1947 in an entry in *The Sign of Jonas.*

> When I wrote it three years ago, I didn't know what audience I might have been thinking of. I suppose I just put down what was in me, under the eyes of God who knows what is in me. But not everything I remember will please—or help—everyone who may happen to read the book. Now I have suddenly thought of all the different kinds of people who may some day read it: men riding on the Long Island Railroad, nuns in Irish convents, my relatives, secular priests, communists . . . and young girls in boarding schools, whom the censors are afraid to scandalize. (50–51)

With this diverse but still specialized readership in mind, and with his superiors' attitudes to take into account, Merton was led to downplay realistic treatment of his secular life and emotions. The past inhabited by his sinful self is recaptured in a chronological narrative with few intimate confessions but many moral judgments and frequent anticipations of its outcome. It is an absorbing, quietly passionate, somewhat rough-hewn narrative. Though written by a poet most would consider more accomplished than Neihardt, the story possesses few narrative passages as evocative as Black Elk's description of Wounded Knee. Merton, admittedly, has not witnessed any such memorable historical scenes. His is rather the uneventful life of the elder son of a New Zealand painter and an American mother. His was an expatriate childhood passed in France, England, and Long Island in an ambience remote from the political and social realities of the between-war era. The truth is that, like Black Elk, Merton's mind is elsewhere. The family past and his schoolboy emotions and experiences interest him chiefly in relation to changes in consciousness which have since made him a new person. Thus the paradigmatic scene in his boyhood which recaptures the essence of self in relation to others is a memory of his younger brother John Paul, who later provides the story's narrative climax when, as an airman about to go into combat, he visits Merton at Gethsemani and is converted to Catholicism. Shortly after, Merton receives word of his death over the English Channel. This death in the family completes, in a sense, Merton's separation from the world, for his parents and grandfather are already dead. Separation is therefore the theme of this recollected scene of their Long Island childhood:

> When I think now of that part of my childhood, the picture I get of my brother John Paul is this: standing in a field, about a hundred yards away from a clump of sumachs where we had built our hut, is this little perplexed five-year-old kid in short pants and a kind of leather jacket, standing quite still, with his arms down at his sides, and gazing in our direction, afraid to come any nearer on account of the stones, as insulted as he is saddened, and his eyes full of indignation and sorrow. And yet he does not go away. We shout at him to get out of there, to beat it, and go home, and wing a couple of more rocks in that direction, and he does not go away. We tell him to play in some other place. He does not move. (28–29)

Though a genuine pathos is generated by this memory, its true significance for the writer emerges only later. When John Paul in uniform brings his aimless, Cornell college-boy existence to Gethsemani and is suddenly converted by his brother, there is barely enough time for him to receive instruction and be baptized. Merton recalls entering the chapel for that blessed event.

> At the end of the long nave, with its empty choir stalls, high up in the empty Tribune, John Paul was kneeling all alone, in uniform. He seemed to be an immense distance away, and between the secular church where he was, and the choir where I was, was a locked door, and I couldn't call out to him to come down the long way 'round through the Guest House. And he didn't understand my sign.
> At that moment there flashed in my mind all the scores of times in our forgotten childhood when I had chased John Paul away with stones from the place where my friends and I were building a hut. And now, all of a sudden, here it was all over again: a situation that was externally of the same pattern: John Paul standing confused and unhappy, at a distance which he was not able to bridge.
> Sometimes the same image haunts me now that he is dead, as though he were standing helpless in Purgatory, depending more or less on me to get him out of there, waiting for my prayers. But I hope he is out of it by now! (391)

This pair of scenes pointedly contrast mankind's natural and redeemed state; they dramatize the divine standpoint from which, as Dunne states, spiritual autobiography is commonly written. There is a vast distance not only between the two brothers but also between the kinds of isolation suffered by the little boy and by the airman in the chapel. Merton, too, occupies a dual position. In the remote Long Island scene he is selfish secular man callously excluding another from the circle of sociability. At Gethsemani, however, he stands in Christ's place, beckoning to man to come round into the holy place of His presence. In the process of dramatizing actual family relationships, Merton also reveals his own deep attraction for solitude and separation, a situation which in his former life expressed itself as alienation and emptiness but which at Gethsemani has become God's treasured gift.

In scenes and descriptions like these the writer combines a vision of his whole life with a depiction of the embracing experience of *metanoia*, that complete transformation in which the ordinary time-bound self is lost in union with God. Casting his life-story in the form of a continuous journey surveyed from its terminus allows Merton to subordinate specific realities of his once peripatetic past to present spiritual realities of the settled but strenuous life in the cloister. This simple design connects the three parts of the narrative and makes it easier for the layman or secular reader to grasp and sympathize with Merton's ideological assertions.

Part 1 takes for its title "Prisoner's Base." The name of a children's game aptly evokes images of frantic running about and being caught without safe haven. This is how the past looks to the monk who no longer needs to worry about moving at all. Nearly the whole of that past life is therefore recalled as sterile and disordered. "It is almost impossible to make much sense out of the continual rearrangement of our lives and our plans from month to month in my childhood" (24), he observes. Like other members of his respectable, middle-class, nominally religious family, Merton was unknowingly trapped in the "futile search for satisfaction where it could not be found" (165). To his artistic parents living in France, the ideal to be striven for was not fame or wealth or sensual gratification. Life's goal was personal fulfillment, a respectable cultural standard which Merton now sees meant that "all you needed to be happy was to grab everything and see everything and investigate every experience and then talk about it" (10). This trenchant social diagnosis is, however, a general rather than a family critique; it does not do justice to his father's art, which was "religious and clean . . . without decoration or superfluous comment" (9). Nor does it fairly describe his mother's fierce moral sincerity which led her to want her son "to be independent, not to run with the herd. I was to be original, individual. I was to have a definite character and ideals of my own. I was not to be an article thrown together, on the common bourgeois pattern, on everybody else's assembly line" (17). Nonetheless, his beginnings necessarily partook the meaningless mobility of his secular age. "My father and mother came from the ends of the earth, to Prades," he writes of his French birth, "and though they came to stay, they stayed there barely long enough for me to be born and get on my small feet, and then they left again. And they continued and I began a somewhat long journey." Then he concludes, "For all three of us, one way or another, it is now ended" (10). Death—a spiritually empty death in both cases—has ended the parents' travels. But his own coming to rest at Gethsemani has proved a quite different release from meaninglessness, for upon first entering the cloister door he felt immense joy that he finally "was out of this world" (314).

Thus Dennis McInerny is correct but actually understates the pattern of Merton's life and identity when he observes that "perhaps one of the unconscious promptings which eventually led Thomas Merton to take a vow of stability in a monastic order was the intensely peripatetic nature of his early life."[16] Furthermore, the present walled perspective of the Catholic convert Frater Louis gives the geography of his past its special significance. France is indisputably the key. His birthplace and early schooling, the friendship of simple believers like the Privats, the sight of monastery ruins glimpsed from train windows, even the sailing date of one transatlantic voyage begun on the feast day of Saint Louis—such scattered facts and memories unite now to establish France (and to a lesser degree Italy) as Merton's spiritual homeland. However, he takes pains to point out that the boy he once was never recognized the spiritual aura of these locales and movements. In this the contrast with Black Elk is striking.

England, on the contrary, is a different matter and memory. Though Black Elk's Indian eye observes with a certain tolerance the imperial splendors of Victorian London, Merton recalls that same world (a few decades later) as smugly Protestant, middle-class, little more than a genteel wasteland. In fact, even the schoolboy realizes at the time its shortcomings. Though English culture has produced his beloved poet William Blake, that achievement no longer matters as it once did. The Prophetic Books are now safely locked away in the monastery library; "he has done his work for me: and he did it very thoroughly," he observes sententiously. "I hope that I will see him in heaven" (187). Perhaps the most devastating critique of Anglican culture is Merton's memory of a sermon preached at his public school, in which the chaplain, apparently in dead earnest, invites the boys to substitute the word "gentleman" for "charity" when reading the thirteenth chapter of First Corinthians. "It is a class religion," he writes of the church into which he was baptized, "the cult of a special society and group, not even of a whole nation, but of the ruling minority in a nation" (69). His mother's Quakerism, too, proves equally unsatisfying, though it is not so intimately tied to the detested British culture; "when I read the works of William Penn and found them to be about as supernatural as a Montgomery Ward catalogue I lost interest in the Quakers" (119). Thus in nearly every respect the Europe of Merton's prewar past is recreated as a sick world, poised on the brink of chaos, sunk in spiritual nothingness. For the present Cistercian, the only significant differences between one part of hell and another are memories of the Latin Catholic countries which, all unknown to the child and youth, held promise of future redemption and escape.

Past memories as well as current ideological commitments also help to account for Merton's intense Anglophobia. During his difficult adolescent years his father died in London, and Merton began there to assert a rebellious, sensual willfulness. The monk looks back with icy distaste on the green youth drinking raisin wine at school and carousing at Cambridge. Self-centeredness is captured in a characteristic image: "I had begun to bare my teeth and fight back against the humiliation of giving in to other people" (80). In the course of the narrative, this commonplace dental metaphor accumulates other meanings besides egotism, appetite, and pride. Merton's condition as sinful, mortal man is repeatedly evoked through references to toothaches, infected or broken teeth, visits to the dentist, and finally by the army induction examination in 1941 which he fails for lack of enough sound teeth. The mark of flawed humanity is always in Merton's mouth. It is not at all facetious to say that the two major metaphors of the self in this spiritual autobiography merge in the vision of a pilgrim with the toothache, for self and soul are indeed yoked together in this particular image. Even more insistently than his several bouts of sickness, bad teeth are Thomas Merton's stigmata. He has broken his teeth, literally and figuratively, on the cheap candy of Contemporary Civilization— the symbolic title of one of his courses at Columbia—whose attractions are now valued even less than Blake's poems.

America is the goal, in terms of human geography at least, of the unwitting traveler with the decaying teeth. In his mother's country Merton experiences most acutely the alienation from self and society which precipitates his conversion in parts 2 and 3 of the narrative. He starts on the road to Kentucky as an almost archetypal college liberal of the 1930s, mixing fraternity and Young Communists, nightclubs and Mark Van Doren's Shakespeare course, cross-country running and writing verse. In New York's "alien and lunatic street" (325) he feels painfully "the triviality and pathos of normal human experience—the talk of my friends, the aspect of the city, and the fact that every step down Broadway took me further and further into the abyss of anti-climax" (223). As war clouds gather in Europe he falls under the benign influence of Dan Walsh, a Catholic professor who has made a retreat at Gethsemani, and of medieval philosophy. Simultaneous exposure to political chaos and to the Catholic contemplative tradition finally lead him, three days after Pearl Harbor, to flee the horrors of history. He arrives in the dead of night at the spot which, he now knows, "is the center of all the vitality that is in America" (318).

As his secular wanderings are deliberately ended in the Kentucky citadel of silence and solitude, Merton's story attains its most arresting contrasts between the two realms. Urging on the traveler are recent memories of an urban civilization epitomized not only by world war but also by Harlem. North of Columbia he has discovered "the huge, dark, steaming slum" (338) under the tutelage of Baroness de Hueck, a remarkable Catholic social worker. "Harlem is, in a sense, what God thinks of Hollywood," Merton exclaims with mordant humor. "And Hollywood is all Harlem has, in its despair, to grasp at, by way of a surrogate for Heaven" (338). As McInerny reminds us, it is Merton's unsparing vision of a racist society, observed at first hand and then from the moral perspective of the cloister, which later seized the imagination of Eldridge Cleaver in prison and helped to make possible the writing of *Soul on Ice*. [17] To the man who has surrendered his self and now seeks to live in the imagination of God, the special horror of Harlem, Hollywood, and the rest of secular America is "the strange error that our perfection depends on the thoughts and opinions and applause of other men! A weird life it is, indeed, to be living always in somebody else's imagination, as if that were the only place in which one could at last become real!" (323).

Although the landscape of this secular hell is at times brightly lit by Merton's minatory descriptions, the more important achievement of *The Seven Storey Mountain* is recording a new, authentic identity as Christian, Catholic, and monk. The young autobiographer cannot always find for this inward development such striking images as the natural order provides with its toothaches, noisy nightclubs, and Harlem. Spiritual transformation, he finds, is much harder to represent than travels through the wilderness of secular experience. At key moments, therefore, the metaphor of the pilgrimage is replaced by one equally traditional. That image is the conquest of man's darkness by God's light. His soul is imagined as a crystal: "The soul of man, left to its own natural level, is a potentially lucid crystal left in darkness. It is perfect in its own nature, but it lacks something that it can only receive from outside and above itself. But when the light shines in it, it becomes in a manner transformed into light and seems to lose its nature in the splendor of a higher nature, the nature of the light that is in it" (168). The simplicity and clarity of such language is for Merton a testament to its truth, for it calls attention to its own inadequacy. Even when *metanoia* occurs for Merton with dramatic immediacy in his experience of sudden, ecstatic joy in a Havana church, he cannot summon up precise or original images to communicate this moment of blinding awareness, as Black Elk is able to do. "The reason why this light was blinding and neutralizing was that there was and could be simply nothing in it of sense and imagination," he explains.

When I call it a light, that is a metaphor which I am using, long after the fact. But at the moment, another overwhelming thing about all this awareness was that it disarmed images, all metaphors, and cut through the whole skein of species and phantasms with which we naturally do our thinking. . . .

The strange thing about this light was that although it seemed so "ordinary" in the sense I have mentioned, and so accessible, there was no way of recapturing it. In fact, I did not even know how to start trying to reconstruct the experience or bring it back if I wanted to, except to make acts of faith and love. (278–79)

Merton's autobiographical search for a language adequate to express "acts of faith and love" carries over into *The Sign of Jonas*. Since words are of the natural order, they cannot chronicle or define the state of grace. It is as serious a mistake, he discovers, to consider speech and spiritual experience parts of the same reality as it once was for the new convert to expect the Christian life to be "merely the natural life invested with a kind of supernatural mode of grace" (226). God's neutralizing light is utterly other than the figures of speech used to evoke it—quite different, for instance, from the intellectual light and metaphorical fresh air he remembers circulating through that "sooty factory" Columbia University in 1935. God's speech is truly silence. Living in that presence can be suggested to others only by violating silence and by means of the simplest tropes. As another modern Catholic autobiographer has put it, "in religious matters depth, quality, and simplicity count for more than breadth, quantity, or pyrotechnics."[18] At best, religious language for Merton is like Gregorian chant which "says more than Bach without even exhausting the whole range of one octave" (373).

Metanoia indeed transforms personal identity as it undermines faith in language. But it does not, for Merton, obliterate self or quiet the need to communicate. Though he laments the fact that the more words one uses the greater one's spiritual poverty, he admits that words are necessary; "we need them not only to communicate with others, but also to communicate with ourselves," he observes in *The Sign of Jonas*. "We are divided, exiled from ourselves. We have to talk to the self from which we are separated" (271). Autobiography for Merton therefore becomes an inspired and divinely supervised conversation not only with a public self but also with the private self who has traveled a certain distance on the spiritual road towards God and the extinction of self.

While *The Seven Storey Mountain* chronicles the crossings and recrossings of actual and spiritual seas and wastelands, *The Sign of*

Jonas is a meditative logbook of the transformed, grounded life. The inmost self has reached its center. However, Merton's new identity, though bearing marks of God's presence, can neither be described nor defended; the "I" and "the writer" remain split; ultimately "what really happens to what is really me is nobody else's business" (120). Yet in withdrawing from "an artificial and fictional level of being" (269), Merton paradoxically achieves a clearer perspective on ordinary experience. Nature and Kentucky weather, for instance, are seen with a particular, loving clarity reminiscent of Thoreau. (In fact, during these years Merton finally becomes an American citizen out of the desire to be a countryman to those two specialists in creative solitude, Thoreau and Emily Dickinson.) His social criticism, too, broadens and deepens in sympathy. The biting anti-city attack on contemporary American culture which characterizes *The Seven Storey Mountain* gives way to less doctrinaire statements. "Perhaps I am called upon to objectify the truth that America, for all its evil, is innocent and somehow ignorantly holy," he concludes (323).

But the highest expression of Merton's development toward unity as social being, writer, and contemplative soul comes in a remarkable passage near the end of *The Sign of Jonas.* Here the struggle to match words, spiritual reality, and temporal existence comes to a temporary focus in a soliloquy entitled "Different Levels of Depth."

First, there is the slightly troubled surface of the sea, [Merton begins]. Here there is action. I make plans. They toss in the wake of other men's traffic: passing liners. I speak to the scholastics. I make resolutions to speak less wildly, to say fewer of the things that surprise myself and them. Where do they spring from?

Second, there is the darkness that comes when I close my eyes. Here is where the big blue, purple, green, and gray fish swim by. Most beautiful and peaceful darkness: is it the cave of my own inner being? In this watercavern I easily live, whenever I wish. Dull rumors only of the world reach me. Sometimes a drowned barrel floats into the room. . . . If you make a theory about it you end up in quietism. All I say about it is that it is comfortable. It is a rest. I half open my eyes to the sun, praising the Lord of glory. Lo, thus I have returned from the blank abyss, re-entering the shale cities of Genesis. . . .

Words, as I think, do not spring from this second level. They are only meant to drown there.

The question of socialization does not concern these waters. They are nobody's property. Animality. Game preserve.

Paradise. No questions whatever perturb their holy botany. Neutral territory. No man's sea.

I think God intended me to write about this second level, however, rather than the first. . . .

Third level. Here there is positive life swimming in the rich darkness which is no longer thick like water but pure, like air. Starlight, and you do not know where it is coming from. . . . Everything is charged with intelligence, though all is night. There is no speculation here. There is vigilance; life itself has turned to purity in its own refined depths. Everything is spirit. Here God is adored, His coming is recognized, He is received as soon as He is expected and because He is expected He is received, but He has passed by sooner than He arrived. He was gone before He came. He returned forever. . . . In the wind of His passing the angels cry "The Holy One is gone." Therefore I lie dead in the air of their wings. . . .

Here is where love burns with an innocent flame, the clean desire for death: death without sweetness, without sickness, without commentary, without reference and without shame. . . .

Know that there is in each man a deep will, potentially committed to freedom or captivity, ready to consent to life, born consenting to death, turned inside out, swallowed by its own self, prisoner of itself like Jonas in the whale. (338–40)

Meditations like this emerge from a fully mature consciousness, unencumbered by memories of a particular past and largely free also of present realities of the Master of Scholastics' life. The vocabulary and narrative structure of *The Seven Storey Mountain* can be but dimly felt behind the submarine imagery of this triple-layered vision. Autobiography as the experience of depth here *almost* merges into lyrical poetry or pure meditation.[18] Perhaps only the surrounding context of *The Sign of Jonas* maintains the tenuous balance. This movement toward timelessness characterizes other spiritual journals like *Walden* or *Pilgrim at Tinker Creek*. Unlike these naturalists' testaments, however, Merton's imagery of a transhuman world is far more metaphoric than concrete. (Contrast, for example, his fish and Thoreau's geese and robin in the climactic epiphany recorded in "Spring.") In *The Sign of Jonas* natural history easily becomes "holy botany." It is a subjective terrain even more remote, abstract, and pure than Black Elk's vision.

Thomas Merton's autobiographical acts dramatize as fully and consciously as those of any of his contemporaries the continuing struggle to discover and describe a soul living in depth amid the chaotic circumstances of twentieth-century existence. Although they share the timeless viewpoint, narrative form, and conventional vocabulary of earlier spiritual autobiographies, *The Seven Storey Mountain* and its sequel *The Sign of Jonas* engage many of the complexities, changes, and outright contradictions of secular American life. Moreover, Merton himself changes within and between the books it was his fate to write. The smug convert for whom the seven-circled mountain is at times a privileged place from which to condemn the secular city gives way during the 1950s and 1960s to a more sympathetic and engaged citizen-critic. The postulant who in 1941 left the world with relief and writes joyfully in *The Sign of Jonas* about "that first Christmas when you have nothing left in the world but God!" (352) finds himself over the years sustaining much more tolerantly his dual identity. "Actually, I have come to the monastery to find my place in the world," he finally asserts, "and if I fail to find this place in the world I will be wasting my time in the monastery" (322). Merton's later works contain sharp critiques of culture, with race and war (the two prophetic presences in the background of *The Seven Storey Mountain*) as prime targets. Thus he moves toward the conflict-ridden center of cultural values as that center, in the 1960s, explodes in civil protest and new forms of spiritual consciousness. In that decisive decade, readers were able to share other crucial struggles between self and soul in the personal accounts not only of Merton and Black Elk but also of Malcolm X, Martin Luther King, and Norman Mailer. Each of these life-stories illustrates differently the cruel, often tragic tensions between realms of *being* and *doing* which increasingly characterize modern experience.

In these and still other narratives (several of which will be mentioned in subsequent chapters), spiritual autobiography reveals itself less and less as a specialized activity and anachronism in a post-Christian world. It is, in fact, a surprisingly comprehensive model of modern autobiography. Neither *Black Elk Speaks* nor *The Seven Storey Mountain* is as eccentric today as either was upon their original appearance in 1932 or 1948. The life-history as simultaneously the record of an inward journey toward timelessness and an account of social activity and alienation is a pattern which fits many recreated lives of the past two decades. Often, metaphoric language staggers under the burden of expressing the reality of depth experiences, and this challenge is not greatly eased by defining depth in psychological terms simply as the unconscious. Social dissociation and the post-crisis viewpoint of the narrator in autobiographies like those of Conrad Aiken, Frank Conroy, or Anaïs Nin become common conditions of human existence. In the process the dividing line between religion and depth psychology grows hazy or meaningless, as do commonplace distinctions between the artist, the activist, and the recluse. Thus even a supremely social, political, and artistic consciousness like Norman Mailer's in *The Armies of the Night* is gradually transformed under the pressure of events to merge, at least momentarily, with the souls of the naked Quakers in the Washington, D.C., jail. Equally surprising, perhaps, is the transformation in self-awareness recorded in Shirley MacLaine's *"Don't Fall Off the Mountain."* Though their outer lives bear only the faintest resemblance, the Hollywood comedienne, the Sioux holy man, and the Cistercian monk are connected by more than their opposition to American political and military aggression. She, too, is a spiritual traveler, an escapee from the tinsel world of the jet set and the Sinatra clan. No longer traveling by train, as did Black Elk and Merton, she takes airplanes away from the cultural centers of America to Japan, Africa, India, Bhutan. There in the Himalayas she encounters and embraces a non-Western viewpoint and sense of the self which is closer to Black Elk's than to those of fellow American celebrities like Mae West or Dick Gregory. Moreover, this surprisingly unconventional success story of a movie star opens with a poem on the wind written by a Thai poet from Bangkok, the city in which Thomas Merton, drawn out of the cloister in Kentucky to the East, met his accidental death in 1968.[20]

Such an admittedly superficial connection between two vastly separate lives and consciousnesses is but a faint hint of the range and underlying direction of contemporary spiritual experience and expression. Far easier to document is the tie between Annie Dillard and Thomas Merton. When in *Pilgrim at Tinker Creek* she remarks that "it is ironic that the one thing that all religions recognize as separating us from our creator—our very self-consciousness—is also the one thing that divides us from our fellow creatures" (80), we are prepared seven pages later for her first quotation from Merton. Dillard also opens doorways of imaginative recall further backward to Thoreau and Louis Sullivan. "I want to think about trees" (88), she observes, recalling the ecstatic moment of fusion with nature which is the first signal autobiographical moment in her book.

> One day I was walking along Tinker Creek thinking of nothing at all and I saw the tree with lights in it. I saw the backyard cedar where the mourning doves roost charged and transfigured, each cell buzzing with flame. I stood on the grass with the lights in it, grass that was wholly fire, utterly focused and utterly dreamed. It was less like seeing than like being for the

first time seen, knocked breathless by a powerful glance. The flood of fire abated, but I'm spending the power. Gradually the lights went out in the cedar, the colors died, the cells unflamed and disappeared. I was still ringing. I had been my whole life a bell, and never knew it until at that moment I was lifted and struck. (35)

Pilgrim at Tinker Creek not only suggests continuities between contemporary spiritual narratives but also illustrates how simple metaphors of self like trees and fire are repossessed by an imaginative soul-historian like Annie Dillard. Precisely the same self-identifying images are found in the two autobiographers to be examined in the following chapter. But Louis Sullivan's trees and Richard Wright's fire exist in radically different autobiographical contexts; they are bound to secular and artistic rather than to spiritual and naturalist assumptions about the autobiographer's essential self. Moreover, when Dillard remarks candidly, "I have no intention of inflicting all my childhood memories on anyone" (61), we find ourselves in a value system radically different from those evoked in *The Autobiography of An Idea* and *Black Boy*. Dillard, the naturalist, is glad to walk down a creek bed with a child at her side, for "only children keep their eyes open" (92) and can help find an arrowhead or larva case among the pebbles. For their part, the architect and the novelist are largely indifferent to tensions between self and soul which compel the autobiographical imaginations of Thoreau, Black Elk, Merton, and Dillard. When they reenter the world of childhood, it is to rediscover there the sources of their artistic genius.

4

The Childhood of the Artist:
Louis Sullivan and Richard Wright

SPIRITUAL AUTOBIOGRAPHY, as the preceding pages suggest, is not eccentric but central to modern American autobiography. Soul stories
are sharp lenses through which so-called secular lives may be viewed
and different strategies and occasions of self-construction evaluated.
Not only are autobiographical definitions and expectations often clarified and broadened, but the radical transformation in consciousness
depicted in confessions is seen to be analogous to other life situations
and states of mind. Most autobiographers, it may be argued, achieve
self-consciousness through a kind of *metanoia*. They write as if, and
after, some transforming event or inner crisis has occurred. Visions
and conversions are in this sense simply models for several sorts of experiences through which changes and continuities in identity are dramatically realized. Furthermore, many confessional narratives like
Black Elk's or Merton's direct special attention to particular parts of
their pasts, especially those which psychologists define as the earlier
epigenetic stages of the life cycle. Merton, for instance, traces his time-
bound self through childhood, youth, and young adulthood with surprising care, even though the aim of his narrative is to destruct this
developing social self. Even more dramatically, Black Elk and Neihardt illustrate the vital presence in an Indian childhood of a basic
sense of life which makes both *metanoia* and autobiography possible.
As Adams exhibits an ironic sense of life, as we have seen, and Malcolm
X (as I hope to show) a tragic sense, so Merton, for example, mirrors
an essentially religious and solitary stance toward experience. This is
seen not only in the boyhood memories of his brother John Paul but
also even earlier in his mother's diary, which records her little son's
essential character exhibiting itself in "a deep and serious urge to

adore the gas-light in the kitchen" (11). This natural piety, though un-confirmed by a visionary experience like Black Elk's, develops very early what John Dunne or Norman Holland might call Merton's iden-tity theme or personal myth—a relatively persistent and coherent pat-tern of idea and feeling about the world, the self, and the cosmos. That childhood and youth are exemplary stages in the evolution of such self-awareness links spiritual autobiography to other modes of personal his-tory.

Particularly for readers and critics who believe autobiography is not a distinct literary genre (with subdivisions neatly labeled memoir, confession, apology, etc.) but rather a variety of narrative enactments of self-revealing attitudes and states of mind, this attention to early formative stages of personal development can be of prime signifi-cance. Even a cursory glance into Kaplan's or Brignano's bibliogra-phies reveals that life stories concentrating on remembered experiences and emotions of childhood and youth bulk large in our literature. From Lucy Larcom and Mary Antin to Anne Moody and Maxine Hong Kingston, from Frederick Douglass to Claude Brown, from Mark Twain and Henry James to Edward Dahlberg and Frank Conroy, some of the most popular and imaginative historians of the American self have been preoccupied with the beginning stages of their lives and careers. These names, moreover, are merely represen-tative. The list of histories about coming of age in modern America grows every year, as do the appetites of adult readers for all sorts of reminiscences of childhood.

Patricia Meyer Spacks in "Stages of Self: Notes on Autobiography and the Life Cycle" provides a useful historical-literary framework for approaching this cultural phenomenon. Embracing American autobi-ographical practice within a broader European tradition, she invokes Philippe Ariès, who argues that "to every period of history there cor-responded a privileged age and a particular division of human life."[1] For eighteenth-century Europe, full maturity was typically the stage glorified in memoir and confession. In the nineteenth century, the self as child replaces the rational adult in many English and Continental autobiographies, when Romantic values derived from Rousseau and Wordsworth profoundly influenced writers as different as Aksakov, Ruskin, or Edmund Gosse. "And stormy adolescence itself creates the conventional center of interest," she observes, "for a great many twentieth-century reminiscences. What happens in adolescence *mat-ters*, we believe; our forefathers believed this far less fervently" (8). Although Spacks buttresses her historical hypotheses with some con-vincing examples, she is also quick to admit that particular circumstances—especially those reflecting social status and sexual or racial identity—can affect these emphases upon certain periods or stages in remembered lives. Despite individual variation, however, the past two centuries of Western culture do reveal significant patterns and progressions in attitudes toward human experience and personality development, and these are reflected in autobiographies.

Spacks's speculations, broadly international in scope, call attention once again to the problematic interplay of generalization and individual variation in the study of autobiography. They encourage me to take a closer look at American autobiographies of childhood and adolescence. I am struck at once by the number of such narratives written, either in old age or mid-career, by artists, writers, architects, or other highly creative persons. Genius, childhood, and autobiography are not infrequently found together in American letters, as works like *Life on the Mississippi, A Small Boy and Others, The Autobiography of an Idea, Black Boy,* and *Ushant* (to mention but a few from different decades) attest. Whether such works can be made to fit Spacks's typical pattern of nineteenth-century childhoods and twentieth-century adolescences is but one of several challenges these works present. Creative genius is indeed mysterious, whatever its era or cultural context. The uniquely talented man or woman is likely to slip through all but the most tentative of explanatory nets. Weintraub's list of adjectives describing personality surely applies even more aptly to the genius than to the rest of humankind. Nevertheless, when an artist provides freely and fully an account of his own life, and chooses to focus upon the early years with their intimate experiences and crucial relationships, one might reasonably expect light to be thrown upon speculations like Spacks's as upon yet more mysterious areas like the origins of genius. Where biographies and histories often flounder, when even a writer of case-histories as adroit as Freud falls silent, perhaps autobiographies may come closer to "explaining" creative character and temperament. Looking inward to the self reinvented in autobiography, one may hope to see there vital connections between somatic, psychic, and social development out of which personal identity *and* creativity together emerge. Looking outward to the historical moment, as Erikson instructs us always to do, one should be able to recognize some of the cultural concomitants associated with the creative process. For as Phyllis Greenacre believes, one of the social functions of the creative individual is precisely to explore the frontiers of personal identity. In a culture like ours, in which who we are and how we have become that person are widely shared concerns, the study of artistic careers (and not simply of artistic achievement) leads beyond literary or art history. As Greenacre observes, "only young children, philosophers, artists, and certain sick individuals concern themselves constantly with questions of their own identities."[2] If so, artists who recall and philosophize about themselves as young children would seem particularly sensitive seismographs registering important and prophetic personality patterns within a culture.

Preoccupation with such questions impelled Greenacre in 1958 to offer, like Spacks a generation later, some challenging speculations. Her essay "The Childhood of the Artist: Libidinal Phase Development and Giftedness" was followed the next year by an equally wide-ranging essay in *Daedalus,* Edith Cobb's "The Ecology of Imagination in Childhood."[3] Both women are fascinated by the presence of autobiographical consciousness at the center of many successful artists' imaginations and achievements. Greenacre encounters this outlook not only in her reading but also in the contemporary writers, artists, and actors whom she treats in her psychiatric practice in New York. Cobb discovers the same retrospective self-awareness in close association with creative achievement through her study of more than three hundred autobiographies or personal narratives of Western artists since the Renaissance. This literature leads Greenacre to conclude: "In a naive way it might seem that the study of autobiography supplemented by biography would be the method *par excellence* of understanding the individual genius. What could be more firsthand and authentic than what a man writes about himself? It is, as it were, from the horse's mouth" (2:480). Experience, however, chastens her optimistic faith in the literal accuracy of the autobiographical record; "the individual memory is a great remaker of events," she warns, "modeling and remodeling them throughout life with an extraordinary plasticity to make the cloak of remembrance do duty for one occasion after another, to meet both needs and fashions—with all of the skill and less noise than a good tailor" (2:480). Certain features of this complex re-creative process particularly catch her psychoanalyst's eye. Personal history is "always produced for an audience and often for an occasion. The audience always consists of at least two sections: the self and 'the others' . . ." (2:481). Hence it is particularly difficult to distinguish verifiable memories from imaginative reworkings of a genius's past. She concludes:

If all memory, as we ordinarily use the term, would seem to be but a cloak constantly in process of renovation, sometimes with gross additions of new material—in other words, if all memory has a screening function, how else can we understand the man within it? Certainly we must examine the cloak and know that it reveals much of the man within and is genuinely a part of him, but neither mistake it for the man within, nor discard it as of no value because it is not he. (2:482)

Nevertheless, Greenacre does not proceed to inspect any cloaks. Instead of a close psychoanalytic look at the particular ways memory and imagination interweave in a creative artist's autobiography, she proffers only a series of speculations and generalizations. Though she mentions several American geniuses like Helen Keller and Norbert Wiener, she presents no analyses in depth or anything as detailed as a case-history, which she by no means confuses with autobiography. Hence the cultural critic, enjoined by Allport, Erikson, and others to move carefully back and forth between specific text and general rule, is in a quandary. Greenacre's invitation to speculate about the connections between autobiography and the childhood of the artist can be accepted only by going beyond the scope of her own method.

Something of the same problem affects also responses to Edith Cobb. A thoroughly ecological outlook informs her study of autobiography. This viewpoint underlies her central hypothesis about creativity: "creative and constructive processes do not result from an accumulation of information, but from the maintaining of a continued plasticity of response of the whole organism to new information and in general to the outer world" (538). Imaginative flexibility, she believes, originates in childhood and especially in early intense encounters with nature. She therefore proposes that "the 'unmediated vision' of childhood is the primary evidence, perhaps the source, of the predictive, prefigurative imagination of man, and . . . the exercise of this imagination is dependent upon autobiographical recall in some form" (544). Genius, that is, comprises not only extraordinary powers of perception and expression but also an ability to reenter and repossess the past in some vitalizing way—especially, it seems, childhood in which the first and perhaps most intense perceptions of time and space, of the self in relation to others and to the natural world, occurred. Such autobiographical recall, Cobb asserts, is not nostalgia. Rather it embraces "the deep desire to renew the ability to perceive as a child and to participate with the whole bodily self in the forms, colors, and motions, the sights and sounds of the external world of nature and artifact" (546). Ecology, as the science of relationships of organism and environment, provides an appropriate perspective on questions of creativity, childhood, and autobiography. However, Cobb too speculates widely but never focuses upon specific artists' autobiographies.

This is true even of her slender posthumous volume which appeared in 1977. Thus detailed exploration of the ecological influences upon a uniquely creative individual of nature, family, and culture remains to be done.

We need, therefore, to focus more closely and consecutively upon particular life-histories to see if and how these speculations—the historical hypotheses of Spacks, the psychoanalytic insights of Greenacre, and the ecological perspective of Cobb—may contribute to a better understanding of the "patterned character" and "individualized laws of action" which Allport asserts should be the cultural critic's assumption about all idiographic documents. Many modern American autobiographies suggest themselves as suitable test cases or illustrations. In some respects the most obvious text is Gertrude Stein's *The Autobiography of Alice B. Toklas*, for this supremely artful experiment in self-construction openly employs the term "genius" to distinguish its author from all other artists and writers (except Picasso) assembled in Paris. Yet Stein deliberately turns her back upon childhood (an area of the past she prefers to confront fictionally in *Making of Americans*). She pays equally scant attention to nature. Hence Stein does not seem a suitable test case for Cobb's ideas. Two more native and natural choices are Louis Sullivan's *The Autobiography of an Idea* (1924) and Richard Wright's *Black Boy* (1945).[4] Both are classic accounts of coming of age in America. Though Wright's is the better known and has exerted wider influence upon contemporary writers, Sullivan's autobiography appears to lend itself even more readily to psychological and ecological analysis. *Black Boy*, on the other hand, provides clearer proof of the perennial need to relate autobiography to social contexts as well as to psychological and literary ones. While Sullivan's architectural genius is explicitly attributed by its sixty-five-year-old author to early experiences with New England nature, the younger Wright's past is recreated within a differently balanced framework of natural and social relationships. Thus contrasts between the two men's lives are obvious and important. But the very differences and distance between the nineteenth-century childhood of the Irish-American architect and the twentieth-century experiences of the black novelist from Mississippi may serve as useful correctives against too facile generalizing about "the American artist." The fact that the designer of skyscrapers and the author of *Native Son* came into their own as creative artists after moving to the same city of Chicago may prove pertinent but actually much less important than earlier, deeper parallels in their lives. Such similarities—and the metaphoric language chosen by both men to express them narratively—lead back to scenes of childhood and emotions of adolescence. In such affect-laden memories of family and nature and early experiences with social institutions both artists discover and reaffirm their identities as American artists and prophets.

I

"Prophet" is indeed an appropriate term for Louis Sullivan, whose autobiography, as G. Thomas Couser argues, is on its surface a passionately personal testament by one of the founding fathers of modern architecture.[5] The achievement to which *The Autobiography of An Idea* refers is therefore represented by the Wainwright and Guaranty skyscrapers, the Chicago Auditorium, the Transportation Building at the Columbian Exposition of 1893, the Getty Tomb in Graceland Cemetery, and the Carson, Pirie, Scott department store. The fact that Sullivan discusses in detail only one or two of these historic buildings is part of the puzzle the reader of his autobiography initially confronts. What are the ties between these great structures and the self reconstructed in *The Autobiography?* The author seems almost to sidestep this question by asserting that his is a child's story first and only second the memoir of a world-famous architect. As "a cloak of remembrance," therefore, *The Autobiography of an Idea* is tailored to fit its artificer's personal memories and intentions more than its readers' expectations. As it turns out, Sullivan's readers must indeed play several roles at once—historian, literary critic, and psychoanalyst, in fact—in order to appreciate the sartorial style and motives of this unusual account of a genius's life.

The task of mediating between private motive and public expectation begins at once with the title. Sullivan chooses an awkward and impersonal one to emphasize that his life and identity are more representative than unique. The "idea" of which he is simply a manifestation is the traditional Romantic vision of life unfolding as emotion, instinct, intuition, imagination—or, in his own capitalized synonyms, as Personality, Genius, Egocosm. The "autobiography" illustrating these verities records the growth of a single "compacted personality" (168) created in the natural setting and family crucible of a New England childhood. Therefore this "story of a child's dream of power" (272) devotes fully three-fourths of its length to the first eighteen years of Sullivan's experience. Beginnings, he proclaims, are invariably vital. "Thus from the abysm of memory's stillness," he writes, "that child comes into being within Life's dream, within the dream of eternal time and space; and in him we behold what we were and still are. Environment may influence but it cannot alter. . . . Thus in a memory-mirror may we re-discover ourselves" (93).

Though the rediscovered "child life" is Sullivan's own, it is universalized by a third-person narrative, a strategy similar to Adams's. Yet this emblematic self is invoked in very un-Adamsian language. "The *only one* is Ego," he exclaims, "the 'I am'—the unique. . . . Ego signifies identity. . . . It is what we call the spiritual, a term now becoming interchangeable with the physical. It is the sign of man's immense Integrity—the 'I am that I am' " (271–72). Sullivan's language echoes the romantic rhetoric of nineteenth-century thinkers from Coleridge, Froebel, and Whitman to Nietzsche and Spencer and imparts a deliberately vatic tone to *The Autobiography*. As their capitalization suggests, "Ego," "Identity," and "Integrity" are Transcendental rather than Freudian terms. (In fact, Freud's name is never mentioned by Sullivan himself or by his biographer, Willard Connely, or by his most acute critic, Sherman Paul.[6]) Nevertheless, the careful linkage of spiritual and physical existence and Sullivan's penchant for projection as a basic psychic process connecting inner and outer experiences indicate his awareness of the somatic and social as well as spiritual sources of identity. Because Man is never mere disembodied Spirit, *The Autobiography of an Idea*, far more than *Black Boy*, expresses a powerful sense of its author's male body. The voice emanating from that muscular body speaks a sometimes vague, often clumsy, but always symbolic language. This style has often confused and exasperated readers. Connely, for instance, finds its "by-paths of philosophizing or sentimentalism" ambiguous and annoying.[7] John Summerson, though he also calls Sullivan "a colossal sentimentalist" with a style "singularly unpalatable" to the modern ear, more accurately identifies the expressive power and genuine fascination of this grandiloquent utterance, which he sees as gushing "with the innocent self-love of the self-made America of the turn of the century, the rugged, generous, loose-limbed, eternally philosophizing American invented by Whitman and Emerson."[8]

Viewed in these terms as a late memorial to Transcendentalism, Sullivan's story represents a self-conscious effort to turn back the cultural clock and reinfuse twentieth-century life with nineteenth-century values of subjectivism and organic naturalism. Through metaphors of his own experience the aging designer seeks to express the spiritual tenets of Whitman, Horatio Greenough, and Thoreau in a world now dominated by the pragmatic followers of Dewey and imitative architects like Daniel Burnham. His book is "historical" in other respects as well. The account, though child-centered and spiritual at the core, deals at its edges with significant public events and movements. Cultural experience is recorded from the perspective of a generalized democratic American self who in reality is a highly self-conscious son of Irish and Swiss immigrants. An idyllic childhood in South Reading, the Civil War, the westward and cityward movements ending in Chicago, the Columbian Exposition of 1893—these are some of the personal events and public institutions that are memorialized. But several of these are presented merely in passing; the author recalls them less for their intrinsic interest than as aspects and occasions for the further definition of his own youthful identity. That self is not primarily a historic identity. Despite its assertion of the author as a representative American in the era from 1856 to 1895, Sullivan's story, as Connely's biography makes plain, has too many signal suppressions and omissions for his aim to be principally historical. Even as architectural history, the *Autobiography* neglects many matters of prime concern. Not only are major buildings left undiscussed and the history of Adler and Sullivan's famous firm sketchily treated, but important names, like Frank Lloyd Wright's, never appear. In the private realm, too, the gaps are equally striking. There is no mention of Sullivan's brother, wife, sister-in-law, or many other intimates, male and female. Equally obvious is his virtual silence about the last twenty-nine years of his career. One has only to compare this narrative with the life of another highly self-conscious architectural genius, Frank Lloyd Wright's *A Testament,* to grasp the narrow range of Sullivan's historical and biographical revelations.[9]

Such silences and suppressions may in part be explained by the circumstances of *The Autobiography*'s composition and publication. In 1922, when at the instigation of friends Sullivan began writing his autobiography for the *Journal of the American Institute of Architects,* the old man had to look back on a career and personal life in shambles. Separated from wife, brother, and sister-in-law, Sullivan had long since also been separated from Dankmar Adler. Equally sad were the artistic waste and disappointments of his last three decades, during which he executed plans for only about twenty buildings. So impoverished had Sullivan become that in 1918 the designer of the Auditorium Building was forced to give up the offices he had long occupied in its proud tower. Moreover, his attempts through *Kindergarten Chats* to instruct the younger generation of architects had proved largely a failure. Living alone in wretched health in a run-down hotel, Sullivan had ample grounds for ignoring the bleak present and the bitter years since 1895. Small wonder, indeed, that this autobiography leaps over recent decades to reenter the world of childhood and youth. Philosophy and his intended audience, pain and the prospect of lonely death—all conspired in this choice.

Recognizing these limitations on the book's historical aims and achievements, readers must look elsewhere for an appropriate handle to grasp Sullivan's purpose as autobiographer. One promising option is to accept *The Autobiography* not as history or confession but as a self-conscious work of art, the effusion of a lyric poet in prose. Style, language, and narrative structure all direct attention to an essentially aesthetic effect. This is a work modeled more closely on Emerson's *Essays, Walden,* or Whitman's *Democratic Vistas* than on the personal histories of Du Bois or Henry Adams. Dramatizing himself as the Sayer or the Literatus, Sullivan offers his book as an unparaphrasable prose effusion. This intent is implicit in the opening lines. Here, rather than placing himself in social and historical time, Sullivan establishes his initial identity as a tiny figure in a pastoral romance. He begins:

> Once upon a time there was a village in New England called South Reading. Here lived a little boy of five years. That is to say he nested with his grandparents on a miniature farm of twenty-four acres, a mile or so removed from the center of gravity and activity which was called Main Street. It was a main street of the day and generation, and so was the farm proper to its time and place.
> Eagerly the grandparents had for some time urged that the child come to them for a while; and after a light shower of mother tears—the father indifferent—consent was given and the child was taken on his way into the wilderness lying ten miles north of the city of Boston. (9)

Only after this "once upon a time" rural setting has been evoked does the autobiographer specify his origins in terms anticipated by the "exigent and meticulous" reader. "Now lest it appear that this child had come suddenly out of nothing into being at the age of five," he explains, "we must needs authenticate him by sketching his prior tumultuous life. He was born of woman in the usual way at 22 South Bennett Street, Boston, Mass., U.S.A., on the third day of September, 1856" (9–10). As Sherman Paul has emphasized, this opening establishes Sullivan in a mythic natural world of a pre–Civil War Yankee America.[10] The "tumultuous" Boston world is not denied but is clearly subordinated to the rural image. Sullivan's imaginative intent is repeated in the larger patterns of the narrative which follows; not only are beginnings emphasized over subsequent events, but metaphoric rather than matter-of-fact meanings predominate.

Behind this transfiguration of reality stands the immense presence of Walt Whitman. In style, ideology, and subject matter, Sullivan's story reflects its author's thirty-six-year infatuation with *Leaves of Grass,* announced in 1887 with characteristic passion in the letter to the old poet at Camden.[11] "There Was a Child Went Forth" is the particular lyric serving as *leitmotif* to *The Autobiography.* Sullivan explicitly models himself on Whitman's child who "went forth every day, / And the first object he look'd upon, that object he became." A child's intimacy with nature and "all the changes of city and country" is the specific link. But the identification runs deeper than this. The poet-as-child possesses parents who anticipate Andrienne and Patrick Sullivan in significant respects. The poet's "mother with mild words" exuding peace and protection as a "wholesome odor falling off her person" is an older, gentler figure than the young Swiss beauty who sheds the "shower of mother tears" at Louis's departure into the "wilderness." But in both cases the intimate connection between son and mother is emphasized. Their fathers, too, are similar. Whitman's child possesses a "father, strong, self-sufficient, manly, mean, anger'd, unjust / The blow, the quick loud word, the tight bargain, the crafty lure."[12] As for Patrick Sullivan, "no need for discussion—he was Irish" explains his son, who proceeds to characterize the "indifferent" father as physically powerful and graceful but an "unlovely" dancing-master, with "small repulsive eyes—the eyes of a pig" and a personality "self-centered—not even cold" (11, 14, 16). Though later experiences alter and enlarge this rivalrous first impression, the paternal presence remains one emotionally close to Whitman's. The young creative self, whether as Sullivan's Egocosm or Whitman's Kosmos, is a child grounded and growing in nature and a mother's fond love, but also tied in pride and hatred to a powerful father. Other parallels and debts to Whitman appear—in vocabulary, imagery, and a common fondness for imitating in prose the rhythms of opera and oratorio. None, however, is more central to Sullivan's self than the reiterated evocation of "There Was a Child Went Forth."

As literary artifact, however, *The Autobiography of an Idea* cannot duplicate Whitman's lyric, or any other poem, for it is a *prose* narrative with a particular form as unfolding story about a specific past. The narrative shape Sullivan discovers in and imposes upon his experience is the looping line, an intricate pattern of linear and circular movements in action, thought, and emotion. This design is located before his birth in his parents' separate arrival as immigrants in Boston, wherein "the finger of fate was tracing a line in the air that was to lead on and on until it reached a finger tracing a line now and here" (15). Henceforth Sullivan's story—both as journey and creative achievement with pencil and pen—is imaged as a single direct line (representing the "masculine" realms of history, time, will, action) intersecting with and becoming a series of curves or loops (the "feminine" realm of emotion and the imagination). The first (and most prophetic) outward loop is the "vacation" the child takes from school in the countryside near his grandparents' farm. This is followed by an equally decisive trip by railroad to Newburyport and the ocean. Then he moves cityward and with his father surveys Boston and its environs. Later the loop widens as the boy travels with his grandfather to Lyons Falls, New York. Subsequently his discoveries of Philadelphia and Chicago precede and enclose the largest loop of all, which is the eighteen-year-old Sullivan's journey to Paris and the École des Beaux Arts, the Sistine Chapel, and finally back to Chicago and the beginning of a meteoric career. Each circular movement represents a stage in psychic development as well as the imaginative possession of a larger territory of actual experience. Moreover, it is important to note that the young traveler and the old author both recognize this unfolding shape of fate. Thus on the return trip from Lyons Falls the writer relates how the fourteen-year-old boy deliberately "took account of himself; he viewed the long, loop-like journey he had but recently completed, still fresh and free in memory's hold. . . . All these things, these acts, with their inspiring thoughts and emotions and reveries he had drawn into himself and shaped as one single imposing drama, ushering in a new and greater life" (160–61). Unlike more temporally minded autobiographers like Adams or Malcolm X, Sullivan seldom contrasts former innocence or ignorance with present experience or awareness. Ideologically, it is essential that the child perceived *then* what the man writes *now*.

One reason for this unity of vision is that for Sullivan, as Greenacre predicts, memory and imagination are virtually interchangeable human faculties. Both are expressed in this tension of line and loop, of action and recollection, of historic actuality with creative dream. Memory's marriage with the dreamer's imagination is consummated in the incantatory, Wordsworthian opening to chapter 6:

As one in tranquillity gazes into the crystal depths called Memory, there emerges to his view, as through a thinning haze, a broad vision assuming the color and movement of life once lived, of a world once seen and felt to be real, so likewise, the intensive soul moves eagerly forward descending through intervening atmospheric depths toward this oncoming solid reality of time and place, a reality growing clearer, more colorful, more vibrant, more alluring, more convincing—filling the eye, the ear with sound and color and movement, . . . So moving, the two great illusions, the two dreams of the single dreamer, accelerating, rush onward, and vanish both into a single life which is but a dream. (91)

This is a crucial passage in *The Autobiography,* for it defines memory's intersection with imagination as the "double motion" producing the lines and loops of this rendition of an actual life. The reader familiar with Sullivan's masterful buildings with their facades and inner decorated spaces—for instance, the Carson, Pirie, Scott store—will recall the intricately looped, organic ornament set into their soaring or sweeping lines.[13] Sullivan's artistic imagination, whether expressed in a skyscraper, store, bank, or autobiography, exhibits the same characteristic impulse; a common visual pattern links its varied forms. Moreover, this unity of imagination, design, and decoration, seen at least as early as the Wainwright Building of 1890, remained in Sullivan's mind to the last; it is superbly articulated in the plates Sullivan was working on as he wrote *The Autobiography* and published as *A System of Architectural Ornament* (1924).[14] Here is one concrete link between autobiography and a creative career.

If indeed life as experienced and art as created are equally dreams with a common source in the creative memory, then Sullivan's autobiography may be read—in fact *must* be read—not simply as impressionistic history or Whitmanesque pastoral but as a deliberately constructed "dream" whose psychic meanings, as in all dreams, are symbolically manifested in event, image, and metaphor. These metaphors of self which identify the dreamer arise naturally from a remembered past but are conjoined in patterns created by psychic pressures within the sick and aged author. Exploring Sullivan's narrative through its major metaphorical patterns thus reveals the author's historical experience (or at least his historicism) and confirms his literary skill and imagination. Even more clearly, however, metaphors lead inside Sullivan's creative psyche, for the nature and effect of such images point to preconscious drives within a present self and a past self.

The first such pattern of imagery and event in *The Autobiography* shows a small boy identifying himself—that is, seeing himself in and thus making himself one with—natural objects in the Massachusetts landscape as forms of beneficent beauty and power. At the same time, these objects and artifacts (an elm tree, an ash, a meadow with rivulet and a dam, the iron bridge across the Merrimack River) represent relationships with the boy's mother and father to be achieved, maintained, or altered. Memory summons these symbols from a remote but still vivid past. The field, trees, and bridge in the early chapters of *The Autobiography* therefore represent the fusion of fact and fantasy.

The episode of the ash tree opens as a classic Rousseauistic reenactment of childish rebellion against school. Like Adams a generation earlier, Sullivan recalls being led along a New England road kicking and screaming. Unlike Adams, however, the gentle grandmother is also along. It is she who has dressed her darling in white jacket, bow tie, and pantalettes. These effeminate, aristocratic garments and not school itself are the ostensible cause of the child's rage. Again unlike Adams, Sullivan recalls the elders relenting and allowing him to reappear the next day victoriously reborn as "a tousle-headed, freckled, more or less toothless, unclean selfish urchin in jeans" (27). The grandmother is saddened by the young rebel's sartorial transformation, for she perceives that Louis "would continue to grow bigger, stronger, rougher, and gradually grow away from her—ever more masculine, ever more selfish" (27). Thus the episode exhibits a use of clothing metaphors quite different from the one Adams employs. Here is the first of several successful revolts against social discipline and academic convention by a self-styled "compound of fury, curiosity, and tenderness" (27). And the sequel to this childish revolt does not resemble that of Adams at all. Instead of being an ironic demonstration of the inevitability of social conformity, Sullivan's childish act issues in a vision of nature. This occurs the next day as the boy returns hand in hand with the defeated grandmother. He remembers:

> [As they] leisurely mounted a gentle grade, just behind the stone wall to the right of the road—marvel of marvels—stood a gigantic, solitary ash tree; . . . there it stood, grand, overwhelming, with its immense trunk, its broad branches nearly sweeping the grass, its towering dome of dense dark green; . . . The child stood transfixed, appalled. A strange far-away storm, as of distant thundering, was arising within his wonderself. He had seen many trees, yes; but this tree—*this tree!* . . . It became *his* tree—his Great Friend. (28–29)

Later under the "wondrous tree," the child's earliest embodiment of beautiful power, Louis experiences his first mystical union with nature as he watches one morning "the militant splendor of sunrise—the breaking of night's dam—the torrent and foam of far-spreading day" (61). Such water imagery and other trees are both repeated later in Sullivan's story.

The second symbolic tree emerges from Sullivan's memory-imagination as an elm standing in the field where the six-year-old boy spends the month-long vacation from school celebrated in chapter 4. Though this pastoral interlude recalls Tom Sawyer and his gang on Jackson's Island, Sullivan's solitary escape to the field and trees and his building a dam there differ essentially from Twain's fictional idyll. To this self-liberated boy, landscape is not simply a setting for playful adventures or the occasion for learning useful social truths. Nature becomes, instead, a possession, a part of himself, his "promised land." Under the lovingly averted gaze of grandparents and schoolmistress, the boy enacts on nature's stage his scenario of self-discovery. It is, in fact, a classic instance of Cobb's thesis that the creative child early seeks "to make a world in which to find a place to discover a self."[15] Ecology and Transcendentalism meet to explain this psychosocial turning point, one which occurs even earlier in life than Black Elk's vision.

The account opens with Louis slipping away from home with a plentiful supply of doughnuts, rolls, and cookies in his blouse.

> One bright particular spot was his goal. It lay in the narrow bottom of the ravine just where the gurgling water passed hurriedly among field stones under tall arching oaks. Here was the exact spot for a dam. He got immediately to work. He gathered the largest field stones he could handle, and small ones too. He had seen Scotchmen and Irishmen build farm walls and knew what to do. . . . It was a mighty work.
>
> He was lost to all else. The impounded waters were rising fast behind the wall, and leaking through here and there. He must work faster. Besides, the wall must lengthen as it grew higher, and it leaked more at the bottom. He had to plug up holes. At last child power and water power became unequal. Now was at hand the grand climax—the meaning of all this toil. A miniature lake had formed, the moment had arrived. With all his strength he tore out the upper center of the wall, stepped back quickly and screamed with delight, as the torrent started, and, with one great roar, tore through in huge flood, leaving his dam a wreck. What joy! He laughed and screamed. Was he proud? Had he not built this dam? Was he in high spirits? Had he not built this dam *all by himself?* Had he not planned in advance just what happened? Had he not worked as hard as he had seen big men work? . . .
>
> Then he loafed and invited his soul as was written by a big man about the time this proud hydraulic engineer was born. But he did not observe "a spear of summer grass"; he

dreamed. Vague day dreams they were,—an arising sense, an emotion, a conviction; that united him in spirit with his idols— with his big strong men who did wonderful things. (54–56)

With a habitat now aggressively appropriated, the boy ranges the surrounding fields, carefully defining "the full spread of his domain" (63). Exploration uncovers his second tree:

There, solitary in the meadow, stood the most beautiful tree of all. He knew it at once for an elm; but such tall slender grace he had never seen. Its broad slim fronds spreading so high and descending in lovely curves entranced him. . . . Her beauty was incomparable. Then he thought of his great ash tree. How different it was—so grand, so brooding, so watchful on the crest of the hill; and at times, he firmly believed so paternal, so big brotherly. But the lovely elm was his infatuation—he had adopted her at first sight, and still gazed at her with a sweetness of soul he had never known. He became infiltrated, suffused, inspired with the fateful sense of beauty. (64)

Equipped now with two natural objects with which to identify—one masculine and paternal, the other feminine and motherly—the boy completes his solitary domain. "His breast swelled with pride. It was all his. No other boy should ever enter these lovely precincts. No other boy could understand" (68).

It is significant that the idyll of self-objectivation concludes with the boy and future builder turning away from this creative fantasy about himself, his parents, and these trees, to the social world beyond the meadow. "While his heart was fixed in one spot," he writes, "he made many tours of exploration; he called on many farmers and shoemakers. . . . The child was amazed; a new world had opened to him— the world of handicraft, the vestibule of the great world of art that he one day was to enter and explore" (68).

This whole episode marks a crucial childhood moment in an artist's self-discovery. Childish actor and aged author are both identified and united in this imaginative reentering of the New England landscape which is so transparently also the self and the significant others. Behind the scene's lyrical language, pastoral setting, and transcendental message lie significant psychological truths. Seen in terms of Greenacre's paradigm of the creative genius' childhood, certain features stand out in bold relief. First Sullivan shows that he possesses in abundance the basic qualities Greenacre ascribes to all geniuses: acute sensitivity, empathy, awareness of form, rhythm, and relationship, and the sensorimotor equipment for expression (2:485). To be more specific, the child's early capacity for discovering objects to receive and represent his loving desires offers striking proof of Greenacre's assertion that the genius' communion with external forms always reflects powerful inner feelings. Here begins one individual's love affair with the world. Natural forms constitute what Greenacre calls "collective alternates" (2:490)—that is, external objects or relationships by which the gifted child represents and replaces primary objects (his own body, the mother's body, more generally the mother and the father) with whom, however, he remains deeply involved.[16] Mobility of libidinal energy—the capacity to transfer or deflect feeling from primary to secondary objects—is for Greenacre the first hallmark of the artist or creative genius. Here, particular natural objects express Louis Sullivan's earliest, most persistent wish not only to identify with the mother but to rival *and* imitate the father. The ash, elm, sunrise, broken dam, and the marsh symbolize various things to the growing boy—beauty and power, the self and the parents, solitude and socially useful activity. Here too is one explanation why Louis's brother Albert is never to be named in the narrative. Alone and free to act out impulses, Louis explores and defines his natural self, first in visions of masculine power and feminine beauty, then in creative and destructive play. If total freedom is the first prerequisite of "beneficent power" (255), then the breaking of the dam dramatizes the destructive urges implicit in that freedom. Later, as a restless Boston schoolboy, he yearns for "a teacher" with "a spirit utterly human that would break down the dam made within him by sanctioned suppressions and routine" (100). This releaser of creative libidinal force soon appears as Moses Woolson, Sullivan's teacher at the English High School. Shortly after meeting this dynamo of disciplined energy, the fourteen-year-old Sullivan reviews the recent past and again imagines himself as his "child domain" whose water, "held as by a sinister unseen dam" (161), is now to be released.

As the domain and dam suggest, total freedom—including the power to make and destroy—is the prime condition of Sullivan's creativity. The second is discipline. The necessary transition (psychic and physical) from childhood to boyhood takes place at the end of chapter 4, when the boy's father takes him away to Newburyport, ending the era of total permissiveness. In place of the mother who has "vacillated, oscillated, vibrated, ricochetted, made figures of eight and spirals in her temperamental emotionalism and mother love" (77) and has thereby encouraged the indulgent grandparents, the father now enters to impose order, respect, obedience. Through Patrick Sullivan, the child is initiated into the somatic and social ideal he is to imitate consciously throughout life. Line is about to be imposed on loop and curve. The paternal regimen is spartan: early out of bed, a cold drink of water and a run, then to the sea for swimming. Louis, the later athlete of the Lotus Club in Chicago, recreates the scene in vivid detail:

> At the end of two miles they came upon a narrow arm of the sea, which spread into a beautiful sequestered pool, at the point reached, with water deep, and clear green, and banks quite high. Strip! was the order. Strip it was. No sooner done than the high priest dexterously seized the neophyte, and, bracing himself, with a back-forward swing cast the youngster far out, saw him splash and disappear; then he dived, came up beside a wildly splashing sputtering unit, trod water, put the child in order, and with hand spread under his son's breast began to teach him the simple beginnings of scientific swimming. "Must not stay too long in the water," he said. "Would Sonny like a ride astride Papa's shoulders to a landing?" Sonny would and did. He gloried as he felt beneath him the powerful heave and sink and heave of a fine swimmer, as he grasped his father's hair, and saw the bank approach. (78–79)

Under such exhilarating circumstances he recalls first seeing and admiring his father's naked body.

> On land he took note of his father's hairy chest, his satiny white skin and quick flexible muscles over which the sunshine danced with each movement. He had never seen a man completely stripped, and was pleased and vastly proud to have such a father, especially when the father, an object lesson in view, made exhibition dives and swam this way and that way in lithe mastery. And he asked his father to promise him that he would teach him how to do these things, that he too might become a great swimmer. For he had a new ideal now, an ideal upsprung in a morning's hour—a vision of a company of naked mighty men, with power to do splendid things with their bodies. (79)

Here is another distinguishing psychic event—"the experience of awe in childhood" (2:493)—which Greenacre has observed in the early lives of certain creative artists and geniuses. As part of the gifted child's deep emotional involvement with the parents, there sometimes occurs (between the second and fifth years) an actual experience which typically issues in the same idealization of the father (or father-

figure) as Sullivan articulates. This is an occasion of mysterious exhila-
ration and bodily excitement brought about by a child's first sight of
his father's naked body.[17] The oedipal dimensions of this experience
are here made powerfully plain. The boy's previous hatred of Patrick
Sullivan is now suppressed. Identification and a wholehearted acceptance of his father's order and discipline now overlie the child's still
intense identification with the mother. Continuity with that earlier
maternal phase is maintained, however, by the natural setting with
water as symbolic medium and metaphor.

Still another decisive event confirming the importance of the oedipal phase in this boy's development toward a creative career as architect is his account of a Sunday picnic on the banks of the Merrimack
River which climaxes in Louis's first sight of the Amesbury iron bridge.
As with other crises, this one opens with the writer-as-child again
"musing about South Reading, recalling his rivulet, his dam, his
marsh." Then memory suddenly summons up a more threatening
image: "Meanwhile something large, something dark was approaching unperceived; something ominous, something sinister that silently
aroused him to a sense of its presence . . . —an enormous terrifying
mass that overhung the broad river from bank to bank" (81–82). Here
the autobiographer seems deliberately to be exaggerating the child's
terror. "Papa! Papa! Papa! Instanter Papa appeared—ah, the good
fairy had waved her wand in the enchanted wood!" (83). Patrick Sullivan calms his son's fears by explaining what a suspension bridge is.
"On their way to rejoin Mamma, the child turned backward to gaze
in awe and love upon the great suspension bridge. There, again, it
hung in air—beautiful in power. The sweep of the chains so lovely,
the roadway barely touching the banks. And to think it was made
by men! How great must men be, how wonderful; how powerful,
that they could make such a bridge; and again he worshipped the
worker" (85).

To the future designer of skyscrapers whose technical innovations
are to be profoundly influenced by two midwestern bridges (the Eades
bridge at St. Louis and Shaler Smith's cantilever bridge over the Kentucky), this dreamlike memory is a specific prophecy. Equally significant, however, are its anterior sources in the swimming scene, in
which the boy observed the "lithe mastery" of his father's naked body.
That the two moments, apparently so different, are linked is suggested
not only by the watery locale but by the "shameful fear" the boy first
feels toward the bridge—surely an unusual response toward an inanimate object but one suppressed in the swimming scene where it might
have been expected. One of the iron bridge's overdetermined mean-

ings might be to represent or screen a boy's conflicted feelings about paternal phallic power. As the father's reassuring presence and words transform the boy's fear into "awe and love," we witness not simply an instance of oedipal dynamics but also a concrete demonstration of the linkages between identity, infantile sexuality, and one person's later drive to create massive objects like bridges and buildings.

Subsequent stages in the reimagined evolution of this genius are as rich in evidence of libidinal dynamics as these rural and seaside scenes. One of the most dreamlike episodes is the opening to chapter 7, which records Louis's first encounter with city buildings and his conscious decision to become an "archeetec." This crucial moment has, however, a dramatic prelude. Sullivan begins by recalling an old cobbler, an Uncle Sam figure whom he regularly met on Washington Street in Boston. The encounter leads into the longer dream/memory of himself entering the street in which he had been born:

> As Yankee passed on southward the boy turned east into South Bennett Street following the south sidewalk. About midway to Harrison Avenue a paper bag struck the sidewalk in front of him, burst, and hard candies scattered over the pavement. The boy, startled, looked around, and then up. In a second story window, straight across the way, appeared two fat bare arms, an immense bosom, a heavy, broad, red face, topped with straight black hair. A fat finger beckoned to him; a fat mouth said something to him; and at the doorway of the house was the number 22—the house he had been born in; but the silver nameplate marked P. Sullivan in black script was no longer there. (109)

No scene in *The Autobiography* recreates more powerfully the impression of a remembered dream. Louis's oedipal fears and desires about adult sexual experience, involving a mother-figure utterly and safely different in appearance from Andrienne Sullivan, are obliquely but unmistakably expressed. The oedipal meanings of the screen memory are underlined not only by the setting and the father's black name but in Sullivan's explanation for his visit: "He had been led to the spot," he writes, "which he had not seen for years, by a revived memory of a sweet child named Alice Look, who lived next door when the two of them were three together. He had wished to see once more the sacred dwelling wherein she had lived and the walled yard in which she had mothered him and called him Papa in their play" (109–10).

Mixed childhood emotions vividly resurrected by the sixty-five-year-old writer continue to spill out in other images from this past episode. As the boy, "much troubled," continues along Harrison Avenue, "he noticed that the stately trees were bare of leaves and sickly to the sight, while on the twigs and among the branches and even on the trunks were hundreds of caterpillar nests which made the trees look old, poor and forsaken" (110). He "was examining one of these caterpillars undulating upon his coat sleeve, when his quick ear detected the sound of snare-drums." It is a parade of veterans returning from the Civil War, for if Louis is nine the year must be 1865. History thus impinges upon—but does not trigger or control—the autobiographical dream. The sequel is recounted in prose emotionally evocative as Whitman's in *Specimen Days*.

> Onward, into distinctness and solidity, came the mass of faded blue undulating to the pathos of the drums. The drum corps passed—and in the growing silence came on and passed ranks of wearied men in faded blue, arms at right shoulder, faces weather-beaten, a tired slow tread, measured as a time-beat on the pavement, the one-two of many souls. And to these men, as they marched, clung women shabbily clothed, with shawls drawn over their heads, moving on in a way tragically sad and glad, while to the skirts of many of these women clung dirty children. Thus moved in regular mass and in silence a regiment of veterans, their women, their children, passing onward between two tense rows of onlooking men, women and children, triple deep, many of them in tears. So vivid was this spectacle . . . that the boy leaning against a caterpillared tree, overflowed with compassion. (110–11)

Deeply perplexed by his confused feelings, the boy confides in Julia Head, the family's hoydenish, warmhearted Irish maid. "What did it all mean? Why was it so sad; why did he have to cry?" Julia gives the troubled boy three answers, each of which show how historical and psychic meanings are inextricably intertwined in this rich autobiographical episode. The scene first dramatizes a social truth about war: "those men ye saw had just been mustered out of the army," she explains. "They were good fighting men, but all tired out. From the shawls the women wore and the dirty childer, I know the whole crowd was Irish and poor; and as everyone knows, the Irish won the war. Think of it! Holy Virgin!—the Irish fighting for the naygers!" (113). Then Julia drives home another of the scene's implications—Louis's emotional identification with, but distance from, these poor Irish folk. "And yerself, Louis, wid yere big heart and small head couldn't see with yer own eyes and without any books at all, that thim very childer was part of what as ye say lies behind it all? . . . Yere all sintiment, Louis, and no mercy" (114). Then, to palliate this rather harsh judgment of the boy's self-centeredness, Julia tells the story of a Union volunteer from County Kerry who while "out a-walking fer his health, and faring to and fro" on the battlefield,

> came upon a blanket lying on the ground; and at once he picked it up and with great loud laughter he sed, sed he: Sure I've found me blanket with me name upon it: U fer Patrick and S for McCarty; sure edication's a foine thing, as me faather before me wud say.
> "Oh, Julia, I don't believe that's true. That's just another Irish yarn."
> Will, maybe it isn't true and maybe it's just a yarn; but I belave it's true and I want to till ye this; the man from Kerry had a rale edication. Ye may think I'm a-jokin' now, but when ye get older and have more sinse ye'll be noticing that that's the way everywan rades; and the higher educated they are, the more they rade just as Pat McCarty did, and add some fancy flourishes of their own. (115)

Julia's tale is the key linking the apparently disconnected figures and scenes of this enigmatic chapter. It emphasizes, moreover, her role throughout the later childhood chapters as an intermediate figure between Louis's idolized mother, his Irish father, and other women like the fat seductress in the window of 22 South Bennett Street. Julia's folk wisdom shows Louis's emotion at the sight of the soldiers to be wholly characteristic of the boy and of the older man. Here, as in later Whitmanesque invocations to the people, Sullivan projects private feelings (triggered by the bittersweet return to his birthplace) on to the passing parade. This is what Julia means when she accuses him of sentiment but no mercy. Louis Sullivan can enter others' lives only through his own childish memories and desires, just as Patrick McCarty can read only his own name on the Army blanket. Beyond the evident shame and pride at his Irishness—feelings heavily laden with oedipal energy and here introduced in the counterfigure of the Yankee cobbler—the episode says much about Sullivan's adult character. His democratic philosophy with its intense but generalized ardor for mankind, his self-styled role as the people's architect, his complete silence about mature relationships with women—all suggest that Sullivan remained throughout his life a man with capacities for strong universal emotion which masked underlying ambiguities about personal ties.[18] These Boston scenes exhibit some of the pregenital and genital sources of this outlook, about which Greenacre theorizes thus: "The reaction of the artist to the collective object(s) also involves utilization of the most primitive but acute empathic responses to an extent greater than is true in relation to the personal object" (2:501).

Chapter 7 is indeed one of the richest demonstrations in *The Autobiography* of a struggle, largely successful, to make explicit the pregenital experiences and emotions at the core of his creativity. At the close he remarks that "Julia had told the story mockingly. She seemed to leave in it somewhere a sting he could feel but could not understand; . . . She had seen him vibrating at the suggestion of an unseen power and he became rigid in his resolve to penetrate the mystery that seemed to lie back of the tale she told" (116). The psychic resonances of these two phrases, "vibrating at the suggestion of an unseen power" and "rigid in his resolve to penetrate the mystery," are so pervasively characteristic of the boy and the man that they might well be read as Louis Sullivan's "personal myth."[19] They express a self defined by a lifelong involvement with a mother continually invoked in terms of trembling emotion *and* with a father all rigid power and thrusting will. Both the nine-year-old boy and the aged architect are bound and liberated, inhibited and impelled, by this unseen power and rigid resolve. Greenacre could find ample evidence here for perceiving this creative career firmly anchored in "family romance."

Indeed, the transformation of libidinal energy into a life's work is explicitly announced later in chapter 7 when Louis, now twelve, first sees the dignified, well-dressed "archeetec" who has designed Boston's new Masonic Temple. To Sullivan, the Temple incarnates all his romantic childish ideals. "How beautiful were its arches," he recalls, "how dainty its pinnacles! how graceful the tourelle on the corner, rising as if by itself, higher and higher, like a lily stem, to burst at last into a wondrous cluster of flowering pinnacles and a lovely, pointed finial. . . . If Louis chose to liken this new idol of his heart unto a certain graceful elm tree, the pulchritudinous virgin of an earlier day, surely that was his affair, not ours" (118).

However, in order to duplicate such creative combinations of masculine line and feminine curve, of maternal emotion and paternal energy, the boy must actually become the man and the builder. In somatic terms, this means passing through adolescence; socially, it means education and entry into the architectural profession. These experiences engross the autobiographer's attention throughout most of the remaining pages of his history. The crucial event of Sullivan's adolescence occurs when the boy, now nearly fourteen, travels with his grandfather to Lyons Falls. There he comes under the spell of his eighteen-year-old cousin Minnie Whittlesey. The excursion, the longest loop so far of expanding consciousness, also includes a hiking trip into the Adirondack wilderness, which in context is the boy's escape from the social and sexual dangers Minnie represents. On the train the grandfather predicts the sexual awakening which both does and does not occur at Lyons Falls. When they arrive, Louis's aunt greets them "with the dry kiss of superculture" (141), displaying "the reserve of a gentlewoman whom long practice had enabled to speak with delicate precision in a voice scarcely audible, and to inhale her smiles" (140). Minnie, however, is far less forbidding a representative of refined femininity. She reads him Byron and Tennyson, takes him to church and into the woods for lectures on social and literary deportment. As Paul remarks, she "plays Mary Jane to his Huck Finn."[20] Louis's education is not merely erotic but social, for Minnie and the Whittleseys open horizons on social class previously unimagined by the boy. In later years, after Sullivan has become what he wryly calls "a draughtsman of the upper Crust" (194) and learns to dress like a dandy, he may have reexperienced some of these boyish conflicts and desires.

Far safer than the heterosexual and social temptations of Lyons Falls are the Adirondack woods and male companionship. Louis's account of his camping trip to Brown's Tract, which follows immediately, is less initiation than retreat to the masculine realm first entered when his father threw him into the sea pool at Newburyport. New vistas on that world of aggressive, muscular men open when the boy finds himself in Woolson's class at Boston English High School. The ideal of male power recently reawakened is now definitively confirmed by the "mental athlete" whom more than anyone else Sullivan credits with making him into a "compacted personality, ready to act on his own initiative, in an intelligent purposeful way" (168). As the most important father-surrogate in the narrative, Woolson anticipates other tense, orderly, passionate men like Monsieur Clopet of Paris and Bill Curtis and John Edelmann of Chicago.[21] From each Sullivan relearns the lesson of Newburyport: freedom and power through a disciplined body and will. Like the inanimate models or "collective alternates" drawn from nature, these masculine figures point backward to a common oedipal source in childhood. But their historical counterpart and artistic archetype is the Renaissance genius whose work Sullivan worships in the Sistine Chapel, and it is revealing that Michelangelo's *Last Judgment* captures the young student's imagination more than the ceiling. Herein he perceives that the creative force of the "first mighty

Craftsman" is *momentum*—"the work of a man powerful even in old age" (234) because it is still the outpouring of pure Dream or Imagination. The parallels with Sullivan's own career are obvious and ironic. *The Autobiography of an Idea,* too, is a monument to momentum.

Movement from an impulse, however, always interests Louis Sullivan less than recovering the original impulse itself. Hence his overriding concern in chronicling his education and entry into an architectural career is with beginnings, not climaxes or completions. This principle neatly coincides with reality at several points; biography as well as desire records the fact that he spent only two years at high school before entering MIT, where he remained only one year before leaving for an apprenticeship in a firm. By this extraordinary telescoping of time and training Sullivan became a full-fledged designer by twenty-one and Adler's partner at twenty-five. This much is told in *The Autobiography.* What is not directly revealed, in his dramatic account of cramming for the entrance exams to the École, is the fact that he then remained a student in Paris only one short term. He accuses the École of departing from "the profound animus of a primal inspiration" (240), thus repeating his disdain for academic art and traditional training. Other sources for this characteristic attitude, and for the unusual chronology of a truncated youth and early manhood flowing from it, have already been hinted at. Education and tangible success fulfill a father's rigid drive for abstraction and mastery. They also promise escape from the dubious social status of the Irish immigrant's son. At the same time, however, Sullivan's rebellion against education and profession expresses the infantile ideal—first felt as a little boy hiding under his mother's piano—of life as pure emotion, spontaneity, complete and solitary freedom to create beauty. As with his earliest experiences of discipline, Sullivan accepts only enough educational order to release but not restrict creative energy. As autobiographer, therefore, he must compose a narrative which goes against readers' expectations. As soon as he becomes in actuality the big, powerful worker of his childish dreams, he abandons the account of successful achievement. Instead, he turns preacher proclaiming his Whitmanesque doctrine: "The chief business now is to pave the way for the child, that it may grow wholesome, proud and stalwart in its native powers. So doing we shall uncover to our view the amazing world of instinct in the child whence arises genius with its swift grasp of the real" (275). For some readers, as for the architects who first read these pages in their *Journal,* Sullivan's grasp of the "real" world of postwar building in Chicago is much too "swift," his penchant for philosophizing all too unrestrained. Connely, for one, criticizes *The Auto-*

biography as a masterpiece worthy in some respects of comparison with Cellini but "ill-proportioned, lop-sided, truncated" because its final chapters fail to meet traditional expectations.[22] Viewed in the psychological perspective of Greenacre's hypotheses, however, the writer's aims have been amply, even eloquently, accomplished. Memory has recovered through narrative event and metaphor the intimate connections in this creative career between actual experience, philosophical belief, and psychic drive. Sullivan's lifelong urge to penetrate appearance and reach underlying reality by giving shape in stone, cement, and words to still powerful infantile desires and fears can be traced in these pages. Moreover, what lies behind is also right on the surface of his memory. "Louis, long since had begun to sense and to discern what lay behind the veil of appearances," he observes halfway through his narrative.

> Social strata had become visible and clear, as also that hypocrisy of caste and cant and "eminence" against which his mother, time and time again, had spoken so clearly, so vehemently in anger and contempt. . . . These outbursts of his mother sank deep into the being of her son; and in looking back down the years, he has reason justly to appraise in reverence and love a nature so transparent, so pure, so vehement, so sound, so filled with a yearning for the joy of life, so innocent-ecstatic in contemplation of beauty anywhere, as was that of the one who bore him forth, truly in fidelity, to be and to remain life of her life. Thus the curtain of memory ever lifts and falls and lifts again, on one to whom this prayer is addressed. If Louis is not his mother's spirit in the flesh, then words fail, and memory is vain. (183)

Clearly, words have not failed. Memory lifts the curtain on the presiding presence of *The Autobiography of an Idea*. Andrienne Sullivan, though less sharply etched than several powerful men—Patrick Sullivan, Moses Woolson, John Edelmann—diffuses her inspiration into every corner of the narrative her son has composed in loving praise and continued identification.

Author, reader, and psychoanalytic critic can all agree that on one level this autobiography is indeed the love gift to Andrienne Sullivan written by the true son of Patrick Sullivan. It is, of course, more than this. Tracing through language, metaphor, and narrative style the author's recovered memories of powerful preconscious impulses leads

117

necessarily into social and historical experience. These intersections of psychic, literary, and historical forces reveal the variations of the "personal myth" informing and unifying this book. Such confluence defines the only identity of Louis Sullivan available to us as readers of autobiography.

Greenacre's theories from "The Childhood of the Artist" and, more broadly, Cobb's "The Ecology of Imagination in Childhood" serve effectively to open up this text, accounting for some of its emphases, omissions, and ambiguities and supporting claims for its organic coherence—claims to be denied if the work is read simply as memoir, prose poem, or architectural history. Incomplete as the testing has been, it suggests that Sullivan shares with many other modern autobiographers a willingness "to reveal much of their early emotional life and problems" and that the capacity to do so indeed forms an essential part of his creativity. The artistic self celebrated in *The Autobiography* is one firmly rooted in, but flexibly in control of, infantile and childish drives and dreams. Many of these, though expressed more in the idiom of Froebel than of Freud, are brought to the surface of consciousness. Others remain more deeply masked.

Nevertheless, this narrative is not the case-history of a psychoanalysis any more than it is the biography of an entire career. Hence many questions to which either the clinician or art historian might wish answers cannot be found in it. Other approaches would doubtless provide different, more socially meaningful answers. Certainly an approach like Harold G. McCurdy's in "The Childhood Pattern of Genius" differs markedly.[23] This is chiefly true because McCurdy treats autobiography exactly like other sources of biographical information. He places as much weight on asserted facts from Mill's or Goethe's autobiographies, for instance, as on statements in biographies. His three basic hypotheses—that the genius typically enjoyed in childhood a high degree of parental or adult attention; that much time was spent in isolation from other children; and that geniuses had therefore very rich fantasy lives—are perhaps applicable to Louis Sullivan. This autobiography lends *plausibility* to such generalizations. However, McCurdy's misuse of the special truth of autobiography is a serious error which Greenacre and Erikson do not commit. If the study of autobiography as a special genre proves anything to the cultural critic it is to demonstrate the basic differences in form, language, intent, and truth between it and biography.

A simple but significant example of this fundamental distinction has already been cited: Sullivan's omission of his brother's name and presence. Taking the story at face value, the reader might surmise that

118

this childhood, like those of other geniuses, was passed in isolation. What seems closer to biographical truth, as found in Connely's *Louis Sullivan as He Lived,* is that Sullivan spent a more normally social childhood than his own account gives any sense of. The *autobiographical* truth is that he wishes us to believe with him that he enjoyed in solitude the more or less exclusive attention of parents or their surrogates. These two truths are no closer than are the narrative accounts of the same events in the two kinds of life-history. Thus in Connely we read the following account of Louis's vacation from school in which there is so much autobiographical significance:

> When the winter was passed Louis, at least, experimented in freedom. Bored with his school, he went in for roaming. A great place in the vicinity that appealed more to his fancy was a great marsh; there he staked out a domain for himself, and among the reeds, cedars and cattails peopled it with imaginary retainers. For lunch he had his blouse filled with rolls and cakes. He built dams and formed ponds. And whenever he tired of his kingdom he rambled in the other direction to the village, where he spent the remainder of the day watching a moulder or cobbler.
>
> As soon as Patrick Sullivan discovered this truancy he took Louis away from the genial Lists, also away from his more amenable brother Albert.[24]

In certain respects this version of events related in chapter 4 is doubtless more accurate as history than *The Autobiography.* In other ways it seems highly inaccurate. Apart from factual divergences and simplifications, however, Connely's account shows a real diminution in both personal and cultural significance; it reveals less about the little boy *and* the designer of big buildings. What makes it clear that these events mean more and different things than the biographer perceives is precisely the close, sympathetic reading of *The Autobiography* which theories like Greenacre's facilitate. We recall here the careful wording of her proposal: "that the study of autobiography supplemented by biography would be the method *par excellence* of understanding the individual genius." Despite problems and qualifications, her approach properly recognizes the actual complexity of autobiographical statement, its difference from and superiority (for expressive purposes) over biographical statement. Nevertheless, autobiography's special relevance can never be defined in cultural or aesthetic isolation.

Nor can it be fully communicated without comparison and contrast with other autobiographies. This activity helps not simply to achieve a clearer perception of common (or different) psychological and somatic states and processes—vital as these are to the question of creativity—but also to locate these more precisely within the social and cultural environment which is unique to every artist. How radically different this context proves to be when one moves to another historical epoch and region of the country, for a member of another racial and religious group, and into a novelist's retrospective imagination rather than an architect's, is seen when we turn to *Black Boy*, the record of a later remarkable American childhood and youth.

II

Greenacre bids us begin the autobiography of a greatly gifted individual by asking the same preliminary questions about *occasion, audience,* and *intention* which all life-stories demand. For Wright, this process leads at once in more public and political directions than was the case with the aged architect in his solitary Chicago hotel room. *Black Boy*'s inception is, therefore, simpler to specify, its "ideological problematic" easier to identify.

On April 9, 1943, Richard Wright gave a talk in Commemorative Chapel to the Fisk University students and faculty not off at the ends of the globe in World War II. The visit to Nashville, long urged, had been long delayed, for the already famous novelist was reluctant to face black middle-class intellectuals. "I gave a clumsy, conversational kind of speech to the folks, white and black," he later recalled, "reciting what I felt and thought about the world; what I remembered about my life, about being a Negro." The address must have been less clumsy and more shocking than he thought. "After the speech I stood sweating, wanting to get away. A Negro educator came rushing down the aisle, his face tight with emotion: 'Goddam,' he panted in a whisper, 'you're the first man to tell the truth in this town!' " Wright's own response to his Southern audience was also immediate. "There were more of these reactions from both white and black, so many more of them that I resolved that night I would stop writing my novel and string my autobiographical notes, thoughts and memories together into a running narrative."[25] Two years later, Harper and Brothers published *Black Boy: A Record of Childhood and Youth.* It was the spring of 1945. World War II was ending in Europe, and the desegregation of the American armed forces was slowly becoming a reality. For many, a new era in American social history seemed about to begin. Into this hopeful atmosphere the thirty-seven-year-old author of *Na-*

tive Son projected his bitter remembrances of one American childhood. Stepping from behind the screen of fiction, Wright spoke in the harsh accents of "the first man to tell the truth in this town." In doing so, he again arrested the attention, affronted the feelings, and balked the liberal expectations of whites and blacks who found his story a hard pill to swallow. Thirty-five years after, *Black Boy* is still strong medicine for many American readers.

Hindsight suggests that Wright's talk at Fisk may have had repercussions for the history of American autobiography as important as Frederick Douglass's speech in 1841 to the abolitionists at Nantucket. Both precipitated compellingly candid books which appeared at propitious moments, exactly a century apart. Both, too, enjoyed a wide success. Through the Book-of-the-Month Club, *Black Boy* reached probably the largest American audience up to that time to read the story of an actual black life. This national and international readership reacted much like Wright's Nashville listeners—often with sympathy and admiration, but also with outrage. In later years, too, *Black Boy*'s impact on a generation of younger black novelists and autobiographers has been similar. Ralph Ellison, James Baldwin, Eldridge Cleaver, and Maya Angelou are among present-day artificers of the self who have been fired by Wright's example to imitation, emulation, and opposition. The same thrusting urge for truth and honesty in writing about the experience of being black in America and dramatizing a bitter, conditionally successful struggle for manhood also unites *Black Boy* to its successor *The Autobiography of Malcolm X* as to its predecessor, Douglass's *Narrative*. Speaking out boldly to an American audience which both desires and dislikes the message has provided the occasion through which three black American selves have been recreated in 1845, 1945, and 1965. Of the three, however, Wright is the only creative artist, and this fact is of crucial significance.

As reference to "autobiographical notes" indicates, *Black Boy* was not Wright's first venture into personal history. Like many of his predecessors, the autobiographical impulse came early and lasted long in this black writer's career. From his first three works—*Uncle Tom's Children, Native Son,* and *Twelve Million Black Voices*—through *Black Boy* on to *The Outsider* and *The Long Dream,* Wright repeatedly made literary capital out of personal anguish and alienation. Ralph Ellison therefore properly emphasizes the complex intermixture of public message and personal motive, expressive intention and literary strategy orchestrated in this novelist's autobiography.[26] The "truth" has at least as many facets and depths in *Black Boy* as it does in *The Autobiography of an Idea.* If a mixture of approaches helps to open up the white architect's recreated childhood, the same may prove equally necessary for the black novelist's story.

As happened with Sullivan, Wright's intentions and actual achievement have sometimes been misunderstood or too narrowly construed. Often read as a crypto-novel by some, as a Marxist parable by others, and as the case history of an alienated existentialist by still others, Wright's autobiography escapes each of these simple categories to remain completely and completely autobiographical. For one thing, its historicity, like that of *The Autobiography of an Idea*, is a subordinate but nevertheless essential element. In some obvious respects more "literary" than either Douglass's or Malcolm X's autobiographies, Wright's story nonetheless recaptures an actual Negro childhood in Mississippi during the years 1911–27. Moreover, like other autobiographers, he pictures his past from a specific vantage-point—that of an artist who is an ex-communist in his mid-thirties responding to the cultural pressures and possibilities of the Depression and the World War II era. The four-stage trajectory of Wright's brilliant, brief, and symbolic career—from its Mississippi beginnings to a flowering in Chicago and New York, then to expatriation in Paris and finally into a Third World and African phase—is not fully adumbrated in *Black Boy*, which closes with the nineteen-year-old adolescent leaving Memphis for Chicago. Nevertheless, many of the basic concerns, private and public, of the mature author inform and control this narrative. Michel Fabre's masterful biography *The Unfinished Quest of Richard Wright* provides an indispensable source of information and insight into this historical context and continuity. Even more helpfully than with Connely's biography of Sullivan, Fabre's life supplements and supports the autobiography of this novelist by relating literary matters to personal experience, thereby supplying materials for a fuller understanding of *Black Boy*.

A multilayered approach, and not purely a literary one, is encouraged as well by the author's asserted aim: "I wanted to give, lend my tongue to the voiceless Negro boys. I feel that way about the deprived Negro children of the South. . . . Not until the sun ceases to shine on you will I disown you! That was one of my motives."[27] This emotional declaration of racial unity, with its significant quotation from Whitman, is also a historical statement. Wright's title and subtitle, too, though apparently literary and eponymous, denote a particular life, not just generic experience. Moreover, the "introductory note" by Dorothy Canfield Fisher adds another historical dimension, one edged with an irony Wright doubtless recognized. Resembling the prefaces to Douglass's *Narrative* by Garrison and Phillips, the laudatory sentences by the white Vermont novelist suggest other, more significant parallels to slave narratives. As Sidonie Smith has pointed out, *Black Boy* reenacts the same rebellious *agon,* culminating in flight, which is dramatized in the antebellum accounts of ex-slaves.[28] Like a latter-day Douglass or J. W. C. Pennington, Wright excoriates the moral hypocrisy of racial oppression that cloaks itself in Christian language. Yet like them he often assures the reader of his own allegiance to the highest moral standards of the dominant culture.

The heart of the comparison is the one Smith emphasizes—flight as the immediate, personal answer to social evil. The moral, social, and psychological complexities of escape in Wright's autobiography link it not simply to slave narratives but to countless later stories, white as well as black, secular and spiritual, fictional as well as historical. Robert Bone is but one of several critics to note in Wright's plot of a youth in desperate motion resemblances to a picaresque novel or, since the running boy is the future novelist, to a *bildungsroman.*[29] Several features encourage one to read *Black Boy* as pseudofiction: Wright's liberal use of dialogue, which is much freer than in earlier black autobiographies; the dramatic shape of the tightly constructed narrative; the nature and richness of the imagery; and the symbolic descriptions. However, unlike *Native Son* or *The Outsider, Black Boy* is not intended as fantasy, though it employs imaginative elements which partake of the fantastic, eponymous, and mythic.

Nevertheless, as both W. E. B. Du Bois and George Kent have emphasized, if Wright's is examined as the history of a representative black Southern childhood and adolescence, there are indeed signal—indeed, startling—emphases and omissions.[30] Even though he was closer to the black folk, Kent believes, than any other major black author, Wright by no means presents here the whole range of racial and regional experience sustained by his people in the early twentieth-century South. Instead, in dramatizing one future writer's encounter with naked oppression, he warps social reality in order, like Louis Sullivan, to stress his solitary and imaginative beginnings. In the process he necessarily misrepresents the diversity and warmth of the actual folk culture historically available to himself and to other Mississippi children as emotional supports—including particularly the extended family, church, farm, and street-corner communities. Moreover, Wright's familiarity with black writing, including autobiography, was sketchy or developed late in his career. Thus he apparently read *Up from Slavery* only during the 1940s. As the final pages of *Black Boy* assert, naturalistic fiction by white writers influenced him more compellingly than autobiographical works by black authors. Hence this work fits literary and social tradition even more uneasily than Sullivan's.

Warnings about what is *not* present in *Black Boy* are less necessary when responding to the psychological resonances and revelations in this remarkably expressive story. Even more clearly than with Sullivan, a proud and secret self presides over the text, covertly revealing itself through event, style, and metaphor. The challenge of listening to the undertones of *Black Boy* and, in Erikson's terms, "helping" the author to articulate his inner reality, has attracted a variety of readers and critics. One of the first of these was the social psychologist, R. K. White, who in 1947 published his pioneering eassay *"Black Boy:* A Value-Analysis." Both as man and scientist, White found himself fascinated by a disturbingly powerful story. Three questions particularly plagued him: How can one explain the pervasive and unrelieved bitterness of this book? Why did Richard Wright not become a delinquent or criminal instead of a novelist, given the social circumstances of his childhood? What family situation, in particular, helps to explain this "splendidly stiffnecked rebel" who is at once "such a tragically unhappy human being?" But White is less concerned with the nature of Wright's artistic genesis; moreover, the method he employs to deal "scientifically" with this complex text offers a questionable combination of impressionistic and statistical analysis.[31] It is far more difficult to do a value analysis by coding the various overdetermined meanings or associations in the language of *Black Boy* than White recognizes. Moreover, comparing Wright's Mississippi childhood attitudes to those expressed by eight white California undergraduates is not only dangerous but ignores the central motive—telling the story of a *black* artist's genesis—which makes Wright distinct. To be sure, Sullivan may also prove in certain respects as different from Wright as are the Stanford students. But since we are not using Sullivan as a control but instead seeking similarities and differences in the life-stories of two gifted persons and hoping to illuminate autobiography itself more than creativity, we are encouraged to proceed along a somewhat different tack in dealing with some of the questions White raises about Wright's autobiography.

As readers instinctively know and White explicitly notes, the opening scene of *Black Boy* offers a key to the whole narrative. In fact, this scene and the rest of the brief chapter which follows form as neat a synecdoche as can probably be found in the history of modern American autobiography. Wright has compressed into a single dramatic incident and the crucial events and emotions flowing from it the essential shape of his childhood experience; he offers a primary image of his autobiographical self. Examining the manifest content and underlying emotional pattern of the book's beginning, then, forms the necessary prelude to any adequate understanding of Wright's artistic identity.

The episode unfolds with dramatic suddenness; its violent action is completed within five pages. The autobiographer then signals its symbolic significance (and that of succeeding episodes) with these closing words: "Each event spoke with a cryptic tongue. And the moments of living slowly revealed their coded meanings" (14). Most of the scene's meanings, however, need no decoding, for the writer has made it painfully clear that four-year-old Richard lives in a world of fear, aggression, hunger, nightmare, and frustrated love. Wright introduces the reader to this world by showing first a small boy standing before an open fire warming his hands and keeping quiet. He is in the house of his grandmother who lies ill in the next room. Though Richard's manifest mood is one of anger, fretfulness, and boredom, his underlying one is of fear and longing. "I was dreaming of running and playing and shouting, but the vivid image of Granny's old, white, wrinkled grim face, framed by a halo of tumbling black hair, lying upon a huge feather pillow, made me afraid" (9). Unlike his placidly playing brother, Richard cannot keep still. When "a bird wheeled past the window . . . I greeted it with a glad shout." In retrospect, we realize this cry is virtually the last sound of joy to issue from the boy's lips in the whole story. To be free and fly away from the house of silence and suffering is the stifled wish which becomes actuality in the course of the narrative. His mother enters, rebukes him sternly, and returns to the bedroom. Desperate with boredom and pent-up resentment, he returns to the fire. "Why not throw something into the fire and watch it burn?" Then Richard, ignoring his brother's warning, brings a blazing straw close to "the long fluffy white curtains" framing the windows. "He spoke too late. Red circles were eating into the white cloth; then a flare of flames shot out. Startled, I backed away. The fire soared to the ceiling and I trembled with fright. Soon a sheet of yellow lit the room. I was terrified. I wanted to scream but was afraid." Instead of sounding the alarm, Richard runs outside; "I crawled under the house and crept into a dark hollow of a brick chimney and balled myself into a tight knot. My mother must not find me and whip me for what I had done" (11). As the terrified child listens to the commotion above, he experiences the mood which recurs continually throughout his story: "I felt lonely, cast forever out of life" (12). When discovered

125

he refuses to come out; his father must crawl under the burning house and pull him out; "more than half of the house had been destroyed" but the grandmother had been carried to safety on a mattress.

The sequel to this dramatic opening is even more symbolically fraught with implications for the autobiographical self.

> "You almost scared us to death," my mother muttered as she stripped the leaves from a tree limb to prepare it for my back.
> I was lashed so hard and long that I lost consciousness. I was beaten out of my senses and later I found myself in bed, screaming, determined to run away, tussling with my mother and father who were trying to keep me still. I was lost in a fog of fear. A doctor was called—I was afterward told—and he ordered that I be kept abed, that I be kept quiet, that my very life depended upon it. My body seemed on fire and I could not sleep. . . . Whenever I tried to sleep I would see huge wobbly white bags, like the full udders of cows, suspended from the ceiling above me. Later, as I grew worse, I could see the bags in the daytime with my eyes open and I was gripped by the fear that they were going to fall and drench me with some horrible liquid. Day and night I begged my mother and father to take the bags away, . . . Time finally bore me away from the dangerous bags and I got well. But for a long time I was chastened whenever I remembered that my mother had come close to killing me. (13)

Surely no more striking reversal exists among American autobiographies than Wright's final line. Where the reader expects a confession that the boy had tried (although inadvertently or unconsciously) to attack his own family one finds its opposite. Such heavy rationalization clearly demands examination.

The richness of dramatic detail and complexity of emotion here suggest that the episode must be in large part imagined. Yet neither of Wright's biographers treats it as fantasy. Constance Webb reprints most of the scene as the record of an actual and decisive childhood experience. Fabre, too, seems to accept it as an authentic memory.[32] He connects it with Wright's earliest recorded remembrance, from his first three years passed on the farm of his paternal grandparents. It is significant that these years, like nearly all experience of his father's family, are omitted from *Black Boy*. The contrast here with Sullivan is plain: Wright wishes first to dramatize encounters with the maternal "white" grandmother's town world and not with his father's rural setting. Richard's first memory is "of two women, probably his mother and grandmother, chatting and arguing in the courtyard covered with red clay dust; the heady smell of laundry boiling over a wood fire in the two black pots; the child not being allowed to get near the flame; a pang of hunger; and words that he spoke without understanding what they meant."[33] Common to both memories is the child's deep, frustrated hunger for maternal attention and love, associated already with fire. A similar hunger is clearly represented by the house-burning. Fabre interprets the boy's psychological dynamics thus:

> Whether he really did have the nightmares, described in *Black Boy*, about white, udderlike sacks looming over his bed about to drench him with a horrible liquid, an image that he used to illustrate the transformation of the maternal breast into a threat, he certainly did regard the punishment as a betrayal. . . . How could the source and object of all love turn into a fury, capable of punishing him so painfully and rejecting him so totally? This episode brutally shattered the emotional security he had derived from the exclusive affection of his mother; the same treatment from his father would certainly not have been as upsetting.[34]

Though sound biographically and psychologically, Fabre's explanation concludes disappointingly. "If it is true," he writes, "as Wilhelm Steckel maintains, that neurosis is an attempt at self-expression, of which the man of genius is the embodiment, then it may well be that Wright's original estrangement and deep insecurity are rooted in this incomprehensible punishment for a transgression he did not accept as such, an experience which long predated his first encounter with racism."[35] Assuredly, this event does dramatize Richard Wright's life-long alienation and insecurity. But why, one asks, is the maternal punishment "incomprehensible" to the adult author when it was so clear to the terrified child? It seems that Fabre fails to consider the double perspective of autobiographical narrative. The sense of having done something wrong is, in fact, recognized by the child, but it is the mature man who suppresses the shame, guilt, remorse, or criminality. In Greenacre's terminology, this scene is a cloak of remembrance, tailored to fit adult and child.

Furthermore, Fabre misses a second significance of the fire: far from predating it, this event *is* Richard Wright's "first encounter with racism." For the bitter irony and psychic burden of Wright's recreated childhood is the fact that his own family, a child's first landscape of love, is also the prime locale and instrument of white racial oppression.

127

Whiteness is present here in several significantly related ways: in the white grandmother lying on the feather pillow and demanding by her illness the silence and passivity Richard refuses to give; in the fluffy white curtains of a respectable and confining middle-class household; in the fog of fear engulfing him; and in the "huge wobbly bags" containing the "horrible liquid" of his nightmare. What these repeated images of whiteness underline is Wright's own biological and social identity, against which he instinctively strikes out. The source of this black child's existence is a mother who herself stems from a "white" woman turned "black" by virtue of marriage to a "black" man. The social mystery is for a while hidden from the child by his own family. Even its earliest hints are fraught with power and violence. To be sure, the grandmother's power and violence are connected both to whiteness and, by the word "halo," to her Seventh-Day Adventist religion. Here, however, her power to dominate others operates indirectly through her daughter's demand for silence. After Richard's beating, the doctor, another voice of the dominant culture, reinforces the prohibition: "that I be kept quiet, that my very life depended upon it." Medical and social prescriptions are plainly the same: a black child in Mississippi must be taught to keep quiet, not to pry or protest. In oedipal terms, too, the beating by this child's own mother dramatizes the very depth and hopelessness of his involvement with a loved one who must betray him—who has, in fact, already done so by bringing him into a world and family so mixed and divided against itself.

Ellison suggests still another social-psychological dimension of this scene when he points out "the historical fact that the lower-class Negro family is matriarchal; the child turns not to the father to compensate if he feels mother-rejection, but to the grandmother, or to an aunt—and Wright rejected both of these." Then he adds: "Such rejection leaves the child open to psychological insecurity, distrust and all of those hostile environmental forces from which the family functions to protect it."[36] The crucial term here is indeed "distrust," for the opening scene and the rest of the first chapter of *Black Boy* dramatize Wright's comprehensive lack of trust in his family, in his world, and in himself. This primary task of Wright's ego is presented, unmistakably and unforgettably, as taking place against almost insuperable obstacles. In one situation after another in chapters which follow, Wright acts out of basic mistrust. In each event and relationship, it is the mother who presides over the son's conflicts and misunderstandings. The psychoanalyst's cliché—the mother is the world—describes the inner dynamics of *Black Boy* as it does *The Autobiography of an Idea*. A major function of the opening scene is therefore to direct attention

128

to this maternal presence and relationship as the central motif in Wright's growth. The fact that a beloved mother must mediate between her son and the world through her own illness, poverty, husbandlessness, and racial stigma becomes at once the ideological and psychic burden of Wright's story.

Wright's childhood is, however, no ordinary black life. The fact that he is both the child who tries to burn down his grandmother's house and the novelist who later writes *Native Son* (and dedicates it to his mother) is, although a paradox, implicit in the opening episode. The future creative career is presented not literally but symbolically in the very instrument and form of the child's violent rebellion: fire. More than any other emotion, experience, or image in *Black Boy*— more than hunger, flight, speaking out, or escape—fire is the comprehensive metaphor of self which unites and explains Wright's identity. One can identify at once several aspects of fire's overdetermined meaning in the episode. Its simplest significance is not as a form of violent aggression, for before Richard touches the burning straw to the curtains he has warmed his hands at the fireside. In light of what follows, this gesture expressed the child's strong need for maternal love and family protection. When, however, this natural source and symbol of nurture proves unsatisfying to the yearning boy, he uses fire as a mode of rebellious rage. Setting fire to the house represents his response not simply to the illness, silence, "whiteness," and confinement of his existence, but also to its lovelessness. Fire thus becomes a primary mode of self-expression. Wright's almost unconscious arson prophesies later modes of speaking out in defiance of his black-white family's injunction to keep quiet. Because it is emblematic both of frustrated love for his mother and artistic accomplishments like *Native Son*, Wright *cannot* call it criminal, though it clearly is so defined by both Southern whites and blacks. Furthermore, his rebellion reveals an energy and violent willfulness which matches the very same qualities in other members of his mother's family—including particularly the grandmother and Aunt Addie. Their rigid fanaticism and domineering love are constant forces pressing him into the role of acquiescent black Southerner who knows his "place." For his own part, Richard wishes to shout and play, to fly like a bird, to run away—in short, to express his own nature as freely and spontaneously as Louis Sullivan has been encouraged to do. One of the striking features of *Black Boy,* as contrasted to *The Autobiography of an Idea,* is how little of this spontaneous childish play Wright records, how much creative and libidinal energy is diverted into bitter opposition. In this intrafamily battle Richard's mother, partly through her subsequent illness, partly through her temperament and love, plays a surprisingly passive role. Secretly she is more on the side of the rebel than of her family and society. This is evidenced in the kiss she gives Richard at a crucial moment in his revolt against the grandmother's tyranny.

Thus a psychosocial cluster of symbolic event, emotion, and motive attached to fire creates the core of meaning-as-identity in the opening incident of *Black Boy*. The pattern of its trajectory through the rest of the narrative is as well marked by Wright as Sullivan's tracing of his identification with natural objects and places. Yet *Black Boy* exhibits a number of striking differences from *The Autobiography of an Idea*. One of these is the fact that fire is scarcely ever treated as simple, natural process. In fact, nature plays but a peripheral role in Wright's recollections. Essentially an urban and social person, Wright includes only a few brief lyrical catalogs of natural description. Carefully interpolated between scenes of solitary action and social conflict, these infrequent moments are rendered in a self-consciously poetic prose which marks them off as the conscious memories of the mature writer rather than simulations of a child's awakening sensibility. Nonetheless, these natural descriptions carry "coded meanings" which are always more important than the images themselves. Here, for instance, are several early remembered Mississippi sights:

> There was the liquid alarm I saw in the blood-red glare of the sun's afterglow mirrored in the squared panes of whitewashed frame houses. . . .
> There was the experience of feeling death without dying that came from watching a chicken leap about blindly after its neck had been snapped by a quick twist of my father's wrist. . . .
> There was the hot panic that welled up in my throat and swept through my blood when I first saw the lazy, limp coils of a blue-skinned snake sleeping in the sun. . . .
> And there was the quiet terror that suffused my senses when vast hazes of gold washed earthward from star-heavy skies on silent nights. (14–15)

Recalling Sullivan's trees, meadow, dam, bridge, and river, one recognizes that while the future architect has found in New England nature beautifully powerful objects to receive and represent his creative energy, Wright's imagination is more intimately bound to people whose words, emotions, and gestures threaten rather than sustain his developing self. Here several of his images summon up again the fiery family violence of the preceding scene. Likewise the image of the chicken dead from a twist of his father's wrists anticipates the subsequent scene in Memphis when Richard, using his father's own impatient words, "Kill that damn thing! . . . Do anything, but get it away from here!" (17), hangs a stray kitten. The memory of the kitten's stiff, cold body becomes doubly associated with the memory of the leaping chicken. First, "I had had my first triumph over my father. I had made him believe that I had taken his words literally. He could not punish me now without risking his authority" (18–19). But the event recalls more than a sensitive son's first put-down of the father, for it culminates in still another confrontation between Richard and his mother. As in the fire episode, his mother, not his father, is remembered as the source of pain and punishment. It is she who forces the terrified child out into the black night to bury the dead kitten and repeat a prayer of contrition over its grave. Little wonder, then, that the writer's lyrical memories of a Southern night are suffused with "quiet terror."

Even in passages of natural description, then, Wright recreates a child's earliest social self orbiting around the mother, father, and his black-white family in violently suggestive images of love and hate, need and desire, death and fire. If the mother's figure remains under the spell of still powerful oedipal emotions, the father, though also the object of deep resentment and frustrated love, is seen more from the mature writer's perspective. Both parents are defined and linked by images of the very forces sundering them in the past—hunger, disloyalty, and sexual passion. The simple lack of food becomes a gripping reality to the little boy who associates it ever afterward with the absent and indifferent father.

The final picture representing most poignantly and symbolically Richard's splintered family and ungratified longings is the remembered visit to the father to ask for money. This scene is recaptured in imagery that recalls the house-burning, for when the boy, urged on by a desperate mother to ask for financial support from the father who has left and is now living with another woman, enters his father's house he confronts another fire. Again, it is not one he can warm his hands at. "My father and a strange woman were sitting before a bright fire that blazed in a grate," he recalls (40). The colloquy which follows is again dramatized with a novelist's economical artistry. Mother, father, the other woman, and child face one another, arguing over a nickel that is the only help proffered. The fire in the grate represents the sexual passion which separates and unites father, mother, and mistress and which likewise includes the child who, looking into the coals, sees himself an unconscious participant in the sexual drama.

How such childish emotion is transformed into conscious "meaning" by the mature autobiographer is brilliantly exemplified by the chapter's final paragraphs. "A quarter of a century was to elapse between the time when I saw my father sitting with the strange woman and the time I was to see him again," he recalls,

> That day a quarter of a century later, when I visited him on the plantation—he was standing against the sky, smiling toothlessly, his hair whitened, his body bent, his eyes glazed with dim recollection, his fearsome aspect of twenty-five years ago gone forever from him—I was overwhelmed to realize that he could never understand me or the scalding experiences that had swept me beyond his life and into an area of living that he could never know. I stood before him, poised, my mind aching as it embraced the simple nakedness of his life, . . . From far beyond the horizons that bound this bleak plantation there had come to me through my living the knowledge that my father was a black peasant who had gone to the city seeking life, but who had failed in the city; . . . that same city which had lifted me in its burning arms and borne me toward alien and undreamed-of shores of knowing. (42–43)

Here the "scalding experiences" of childhood have been translated into ideological terms which are the manageable residue of fiery memories of the past. The perfidious parent has been punished by time even more thoroughly than he was by the son's childish murder of the stray kitten. His fate—in a sense also a celebration and almost a reconciliation—is to be turned into a stereotype of the ignorant sharecropper. Yet Wright's Marxist language carries the freight of the preideological past; words and phrases like "scalding," "the simple nakedness of his life," and "in its burning arms" echo not only a child's memories of his father's threatening sexuality as he watched a strange woman throw her arms about the father's neck before a brightly burning fire, but also other memories and later actions of his own in response.

Although fire is plainly the central experience and metaphor informing *Black Boy*'s beginning, it does not comprise the whole range of emotion and event of this remarkably rich chapter. Indeed, fire is not explicitly connected in Wright's imagination with the crucial moment in the first chapter when the growing boy first becomes aware of himself as a separate individual. This takes place in the apartment of Miss Simon, the directress of the orphanage to which Richard is sent when his mother can no longer feed him. Miss Simon seeks to break down the stubborn silence and hungry fear that now characterize the boy's response to the world. She may also, like Sullivan's woman at the window, be trying to seduce him as well. The scene's veiled eroticism is hinted at when she makes Richard stand close beside her writing-desk and blot the letters she is addressing. He is frozen into silent immobility by her terrifying proximity. Suddenly a sense of himself as a single separate person crystallizes. "Dread and distrust had already become a daily part of my being," he observes, "and my memory grew sharp, my senses more impressionable; I began to be aware of myself as a distinct personality striving against others. I held myself in, afraid to act or speak until I was sure of my surroundings, feeling most of the time that I was suspended over a void. My imagination soared; I dreamed of running away" (38).

Though this moment is unaccompanied by actual or metaphorical fire, its other associations—hunger, fear of sexuality, threats of violence, all linked to motherly love—contribute to his self-recognition. The occasion contrasts sharply with Sullivan's discovery of self which, as we have seen, occurs under entirely different auspices and within a natural amphitheatre. Wright has moved along two roads toward discovery of a self defined in opposition and flight. The first is the road of words. Learning to read, write, and count have already become skills picked up in bars and schoolyards (but hardly in schoolrooms, where he is speechless with fear) and from a friendly coal man. Most of the words are four-letter replicas of reality; "whip" and "beat" are two of the politest and commonest. They are not the coarsest, however, and when Richard innocently acquires the vocabulary of obscenity and transfers it in soap to the neighbor's windows his irate mother whips him along the street to wash them off. "Never again did I write words like that, I kept them to myself" (33). From such experience of privies, whorehouses, and bars he derives a vision of sex as violent, unclean, unmentionable. Any hint of its oppressive presence—as in the scene at Miss Simon's writing-desk—is likely to terrify the boy into silence and flight. Thus only certain words afford escape from the traumatic memories of childhood; others are sternly repressed as too threatening to recall.

The second route to a sense of self is physical hunger with its psychic counterpart. Richard's initiation into the realities of adult black Southern life—an initiation early and more intense than Sullivan's—is a process of learning to suffer deprivation. Its commonest form is lack of food, which is never separable in his experience from lack of love. Thus the disappearance of his father, the sudden responsibility thrust upon him to play the father's role in an often foodless household, and his own mother's act of pushing him out the door to fight his way to the grocery store—all are threatening events engendering in Richard a deep bitterness based upon feeling perpetually deprived of sustenance. "The most abiding feeling I had each day was hunger and fear," he recalls.

> Each morning after we had eaten a breakfast that seemed like no breakfast at all, an older child would lead a herd of us to the vast lawn and we would get to our knees and wrench the grass loose from the dirt with our fingers. At intervals Miss Simon would make a tour of inspection, examining the pile of pulled grass beside each child, scolding or praising according to the size of the pile. Many mornings I was too weak from hunger to pull the grass; I would grow dizzy and my mind would become blank and I would find myself, after an interval of unconsciousness, upon my hands and knees, my head whirling, my eyes staring in bleak astonishment at the green grass, wondering where I was, feeling that I was emerging from a dream. (36–37)

This Dickensian episode shows the writer's retrospective imagination dealing with simple natural objects very differently from the way Louis Sullivan did. For Wright, grass has a social and psychological meaning bound more closely to a specific time, place, and affect than are the trees and fields of Sullivan's South Reading. Wright's imagination is less free than Sullivan's to spin out from nature universal and prophetic extensions of meaning. Sullivan's solitary enjoyment of nature as beneficent beauty and power is made possible by the indulgent support of grandparents standing in for the absent parents and is sustained, we recall, by a blouseful of rolls, doughnuts, and cookies. Wright's encounter with the grass is closer to nightmare than to idyll. Miss Simon is as unlike Sullivan's teacher as their two religious grandmothers differ. The binding presence of physical deprivation or pain, of social proximity but spiritual separation, make it impossible for natural objects to serve as the same kind of collective alternates for Richard Wright as they do for Louis Sullivan.

Similarly, Wright's memories are so intensely physical reminders of pain that this accounts for the almost complete absence of humorous scenes or moments in *Black Boy*. To a sensitive future novelist, all memories, even potentially funny ones like that of the black preacher eating up all the chicken while little Richard gags over his soup, are too insistently infused with the original emotions of fear, hunger, and loneliness to permit comic re-creation. The comprehensive metaphor for this bleak battery of memories is fire burning within and around Richard Wright's childish consciousness.

The reader who wonders if a literary artist's imagination has here manipulated historical memory to create metaphoric patterns like that of fire, hunger, and flight has two ways to reality-test *Black Boy*. First, one may note Wright's explicit comments on the interactions of his imagination and memory. An apt instance occurs near the close of chapter 2, where he reports the anecdote of a Negro woman whose husband has been seized and lynched by a mob. This event is not recorded as part of Wright's own experience, though it is the germ for one of the most gripping tales in *Uncle Tom's Children*, "Bright and Morning Star." "I did not know if the story was factually true or not," Wright observes, "but it was emotionally true because I had already grown to feel that there existed men against whom I was powerless, men who could violate my life at will" (83). Then he adds this significant explanation of his use of others' experience in his own story:

> The story of the woman's deception gave form and meaning to confused defensive feelings that had long been sleeping in me. . . .
> My fantasies were a moral bulwark that enabled me to feel I was keeping my emotional integrity whole, a support that enabled my personality to limp through days lived under the threat of violence.
> These fantasies were no longer a reflection of my reaction to the white people, they were a part of my living, of my emotional life; they were a culture, a creed, a religion. (84)

Another way to reality-test *Black Boy* is to see how and in what new variations of social situation and private emotion fire appears as an explicit structuring device in later episodes. This involves noting the numerous minor but revealing incidents or verbal usages which dramatize fire or heat as accompaniments to social conflict. One is the "aching streak of fire" left on his legs by his outraged grandmother's stick after he has innocently told her "to kiss back there" (49) while she was bathing him. This again connects fire to sex and to the boy's growing realization that he can strike back at a domineering family and society with shocking words that burn and sear. Richard becomes fully aware of words' fiery power as he listens to the story of Bluebeard and his seven wives whispered to him by a boarder on his grandmoth-

135

er's porch. "My imagination blazed," he recalls. "I hungered for the sharp, frightening, breathtaking, almost painful excitement that the story had given me" (47–48). Such a response goes precisely counter to his grandmother's rigid religious outlook, which asserts that all stories (except those in the Bible) are to be banned as lies. Hence it is both attraction and reaction that lead him to remark of his disapproving family: "They could not have known that Ella's whispered story of deception and murder had been the first experience in my life that had elicited a total emotional response."

Such moments, minor only in apparent importance, are interwoven with repeated references to fire in larger, more violent events. Two of the most arresting of these dramatize relations with older men who serve as temporary (but, as it turns out, unsatisfying) father-figures. The first is Uncle Silas Hoskins of Elaine, Arkansas. He possesses several qualities that seem to qualify as a male ideal: the food on his table is so ample that the hungry boy can carry away biscuits in his pockets; he is also a successful saloon-keeper who carries a pistol and is feared by white men. But Uncle Hoskins betrays Richard's nascent trust one day when in a jocular mood he drives the horse and buggy down into the Mississippi River. The boy beside him is terrified. Even though he cannot swim, Richard starts to leap over the side into the swirling water. " 'Listen, son, don't you trust me?' he asked. 'I was born on that old river. I know that river. There's stone and brick way down under that water. You could wade out for half a mile and it would not come over your head.' His words meant nothing and I would not re-enter the buggy." (62). This vivid picture of a boy too suspicious to accept well-meant, fatherly teasing has water but not fire in its unfolding. This fact accrues double significance when we learn from Constance Webb's biography that such an episode probably did not happen to Richard Wright this way at all, that it was an incident related later by Ralph Ellison.[37] What actually did occur to Wright's family is the subsequent murder of Uncle Hoskins by jealous, greedy whites. This first and closest intrusion of white violence into the family circle is recaptured in characteristic Wrightian language. "Uncle Hoskins had simply been plucked from our midst," he writes, "and we, figuratively, had fallen on our faces to avoid looking into that white-hot face of terror that we knew loomed somewhere above us" (64). Fire returns to Wright's vocabulary as soon as his own actual experience replaces Ellison's.

Even more arresting is Richard's second encounter with a father-figure who shows him how to strike back at the white world through fiery means. This is Professor Matthews, the silent, well-educated "uncle" whose sexual relation to his Aunt Maggie is complicated also by a mysterious relation to a white woman. One night, the family is again thrown into panic and flight as Matthews enters suddenly. Something terrible has happened between the black man and white woman.

> "The house is on fire," "uncle" said. "And when they see it, they'll know who did it."
> "Did you set the house afire?" my mother asked.
> "There was nothing else to do," "uncle" said impatiently. "I took the money. I had hit her. She was unconscious. If they found her, she'd tell. I'd be lost. So I set the fire."
> "But she'll burn up," Aunt Maggie said, crying into her hands. . . .
> Fear filled me. What was happening? Were white people coming after all of us? Was my mother going to leave me?
> "Mama!" I wailed, running into the room.
> "Uncle" leaped to his feet; a gun was in his hand and he was pointing it at me. I stared at the gun, feeling that I was going to die at any moment. (76–77)

Several strands of fear and desire are here knit into an autobiographical pattern by the quiet black man's incendiary act, the sexual implications of which are so carefully masked that Wright himself can say at the end: "For weeks I wondered what it was 'uncle' had done, but I was destined never to know, not even in all the years that followed" (78). This scene forms a bridge between Richard's own act of childish arson, his visit to his father's house, and later events in which fire even more explicitly symbolizes sexual experience, racism, and aggression.

These subsequent events occur to the adolescent Richard in Memphis, after he has fled Mississippi and Arkansas and the tightening coils of a white oppression that is often evoked as a dangerous fire. Yet before Richard can leave the city which is a way station on the road to Chicago, he must negotiate an emotional rapprochement with his mother, for as is suggested by her physical presence at all the fires, actual and metaphorical, in the early chapters of *Black Boy*, Richard's mother remains for a long time the unquenched and bound libidinal fire in the boy's heart. If Richard is to grow beyond the terrified child trapped in fear and longing, the oedipal tie must be translated into a maturer affection. Only then can he really love her and stop trying to kill or repudiate her. This takes place at the end of chapter 3. A long nighttime meditation takes place as the boy sits beside his sick mother, stricken now with a crippling illness and recently turned away from the white hospital in Clarksdale, Mississippi. Though these thoughts and emotions sound more like those of the mature artist than of the sitting boy, they nevertheless mark a crucial act of autobiographical self-awareness and definition.

> Once, in the night, my mother called me to her bed and told me that she could not endure the pain, that she wanted to die. I held her hand and begged her to be quiet. That night I ceased to react to my mother; my feelings were frozen. I merely waited upon her, knowing that she was suffering.
> . . .
> My mother's suffering grew into a symbol in my mind, gathering to itself all the poverty, the ignorance, the helplessness; the painful, baffling, hunger-ridden days and hours; the restless moving, the futile seeking, the uncertainty, the fear, the dread; the meaningless pain and the endless suffering. Her life set the emotional tone of my life, colored the men and women I was to meet in the future, conditioned my relation to events that had not yet happened, determined my attitude to situations and circumstances I had yet to face. A somberness of spirit that I was never to lose settled over me during the slow years of my mother's unrelieved suffering, a somberness that was to make me stand apart and look upon excessive joy with suspicion, that was to make me self-conscious, that was to make me keep forever on the move, as though to escape a nameless fate seeking to overtake me. (111–12)

This freezing of Richard Wright's love for his mother represents the antithetical and necessary sequel to the "fire" previously felt for her. Although Wright's memory/imagination can recreate a whole series of fiery events and emotions which bring alive the inner landscape and outer circumstances of his childhood, when it comes to demonstrating the transformation, during adolescence, of this oedipal emotion he resorts to explicit statement in which "cold" replaces "hot" as a metaphorical medium. He concludes his self-analysis thus:

> It made me want to drive coldly to the heart of every question and lay it open to the core of suffering I knew I would find there. It made me love burrowing into psychology, into realistic and naturalistic fiction and art, into those whirlpools of politics that had the power to claim the whole of men's souls. It directed my loyalties to the side of men in rebellion; it made me love talk that sought answers to questions that could help

nobody, that could only keep alive in me that enthralling sense
of wonder and awe in the face of the drama of human feeling
which is hidden by the external drama of life. (112)

Just as clearly as Sullivan's self-disclosure in the colloquy with Julia,
this passage describes the mixture of incandescent inner emotion and
outer cold determinism which characterizes much of Richard
Wright's thought and art. One of its sources is the long-suffering love
of Ella Wilson Wright recreated in her son's autobiography and revealed in the epigraph of *Native Son:* "To My Mother, who when I
was a child at her knee, taught me to revere the fanciful and the imaginative." A fanciful and imaginative use of language has indeed liberated Richard Wright from a bondage as binding as racial oppression.

This epigraph suggests why the resolution of oedipal conflict takes
place concurrently in *Black Boy* with the author's discovery of his artistic calling. From a boy who faces the threatening world of school
in speechless terror, Richard grows into an adolescent defined as
"bad" by his pious family because he refuses to be a quiet Christian.
In the eighth grade he becomes an additional danger to the whole
black community when he writes and has published in a newspaper
his first story, "The Voodoo of Hell's Half-Acre." "The mood out of
which a story was written," he observes, "was the most alien thing conceivable to them. They looked at me with new eyes, and a distance,
a suspiciousness came between us" (184). Even more abysmal is the
gap in sympathy and understanding between the fledgling writer and
his first white employer. Wright's Southern world of whites and blacks
defines as positively criminal the very activity which has since become
his moral bulwark and source of personal integrity. Words and stories
are to be his means of attacking or repulsing attacks, of confronting
and resolving the emotional conflicts of his childhood and youth, and
of discovering and defending his manhood. But learning to wield
words is a dangerous apprenticeship. In his varied encounters as an
adolescent with Southern racism, in hotel, optical company, or movie
theatre, Richard seeks desperately "to avoid trouble, for I feared that
if I clashed with whites I would lose control of my emotions and spill
out words that would be my sentence of death" (220). Eventually the
effort of bottling up the pressures is too great; like his ancestors the
fugitive slaves, he must escape northward toward freedom.

The emotional legacy carried along is a frozen fire. "I had developed, slowly and painfully, a capacity to contain it within myself," he
writes. "But my inner resistance had been blasted. I felt that I had
been emotionally cast out of the world." (223). Small wonder, then,

his inhibited response to Mrs. Moss and Bess in the Beale Street boardinghouse. Their instinctive goodwill and simple acceptance, which one might expect to be greeted with open arms, is perceived instead as another threat, for the eighteen-year-old boy cannot bring himself to embrace either Mrs. Moss's outlook or her daughter's willing body; ". . . such simple unaffected trust flabbergasted me. It was impossible" (235).

The author rationalizes his response thus: "I had come from a home where feelings were never expressed, except in rage or religious dread, where each member of the household lived locked in his own dark world, and the light that shone out of this child's heart—for she was a child—blinded me" (238). He has, we recall, already encountered the blinding fire of sexual passion in the person of his father and the strange woman. He is also repelled (though less powerfully) by Bess's intellectual simplicity; "she just did not attach to words the same meanings I did," he remarks (239). Here speaks the symbol-making autobiographer and novelist who has learned to control and express through words like "fire" and "light" the tempestuous emotions of his childhood and youth. The sign of this mastery is the epigraph to *Black Boy:* "For Ellen and Julia, who live always in my heart." Wright's loving dedication to his wife and daughter testifies to his eventual victory over the frozen emotions and repressed sexual fears that still operate powerfully at the close of his autobiography.

If Bess and her mother exemplify acceptance of life on terms too sensually and trustingly simple to satisfy Wright, the black men he meets at his Memphis job at the optical company are equally unsatisfactory models for a sensitive youth. The alternative to Shorty's shuffling subservience comes not from any black man or woman he meets on Beale Street, but from white minds and wills encountered in the books he borrows, with a white man's help, from the public library. Like Mary Antin, then, Richard Wright's first escape from American oppression comes through the American public library. H. L. Mencken is the first author to reveal a new landscape of self-expression, a mode of "fighting with words" against ignorance and prejudice. The gap between the eighteen-year-old's ignorance and Mencken's experience is nicely suggested when Wright recalls, upon first opening *A Book of Prefaces,* that "I was nearing my nineteenth birthday and I did not know how to pronounce the word 'preface.' " Then he adds, "I was jarred and shocked by the style, the clear, clean sweeping sentences. Why did he write like that? And how did one write like that? I pictured the man as a raging demon, slashing with his pen, consumed with hate, denouncing everything American, extolling everything European or German, laughing at the weaknesses of people, mocking God, authority" (271–72).

It is not psychologically reductive to see in Wright's image of Mencken's slashing pen a satisfactory phallic substitute for the black weapons of aggression and criminality already encountered: Uncle Hoskins's and Professor Matthews's guns, Harrison's long gleaming knife. Sublimation is necessary, in part, because of the oedipal guilt and involvement still operating powerfully in Wright's psyche. Later, as he becomes acquainted with the fiction of Sinclair Lewis and Dreiser, these connections to his own life become even clearer. "I read Dreiser's *Jennie Gerhardt* and *Sister Carrie* and they revived in me a vivid sense of my mother's suffering; I was overwhelmed. I grew silent, wondering about the life around me. It would have been impossible for me to have told anyone what I derived from these novels, for it was nothing less than a sense of life itself. All my life had shaped me for the realism of the modern novel, and I could not read enough of them" (274). Here the author makes explicit what many readers feel: *Black Boy* itself owes explicit allegiance to the naturalistic novel, for like certain of Dreiser's works it masks beneath the realistic style deep family memories and oedipal emotions.

Wright's account of his subsequent response to these white writers demonstrates the final synthesis of experience and metaphor in his recreated life. First, he is deeply depressed by the gap that yawns between those vivid pieces of prose and his own lame efforts at writing. "I had a new hunger," he confesses, which "in buoying me up, reading also cast me down, made me see what was possible, what I had missed. My tension returned, new, terrible, bitter, surging, almost too great to be contained. I no longer *felt* that the world about me was hostile, killing; I *knew* it. . . . I seemed forever condemned, ringed by walls" (274). Slowly, however, this biting depression and frustration is replaced by more manageable emotions, "a vague hunger" and a "feeling that I carried a secret, criminal burden about with me each day" (276). It is significant that this transition to the guilty feelings of a conscious criminal coincides with the arrival of his mother and family from Mississippi. "I began to eat warm food," he observes. This simple comment shows how the youth contained for a while the draining emotions of rage and anxiety. Through the language of food he expresses also the language of the libido, which here is recording a diminution of oedipal affect. The "blinding light" of Bess Moss's sensual escape from racial realities is a response he can accept neither emotionally nor intellectually, for it reminds him too insistently of his father, that other "black peasant" in his past. "I could, of course, forget what I had read," he remarks, "thrust the whites out of my mind, forget them; and find release from anxiety and longing in sex and alcohol. But the memory of how my father had conducted himself made that course repugnant. If I did not want others to violate my life, how could I voluntarily violate it myself?" (277). But the more temperate warmth emanating now from his mother, family, and, significantly, his reading provides a cultural climate which can temporarily sustain him. It is important to note here, as some critics have not, that Wright is well aware of the limitations of white literary forms as emotional sustenance during these months in Memphis. "It had been only through books—at best, no more than vicarious cultural transfusions—," he writes in the final pages of *Black Boy*, "that I had managed to keep myself alive in a negatively vital way" (282). Then he adds this revealing comment: "And it was out of these novels and stories and articles, out of the emotional impact of imaginative constructions of heroic or tragic deeds, that I felt touching my face a tinge of warmth from an unseen light; and in my leaving I was groping toward that invisible light, always trying to keep my face so set and turned that I would not lose the hope of its faint promise, using it as my justification for action" (283). These words complete the transformation of the deep fantasy at the core of Richard Wright's life and identity into the manifest "meanings" of his life and career. From the little boy who set fire to the white curtains of his family's house he has slowly and painfully developed into the nineteen-year-old near-man poised for flight into the "burning arms" of Chicago. His adult experiences there, later published as *American Hunger,* are in a deep sense separable and a separate story. The fire that once failed to warm his hands and heart as a four-year-old, and which burned and seared him and his family in a succession of violent acts of arson and aggression, has been slowly translated into a less torrid flame. Oedipal conflicts of childhood are still present—in the energetic stance of defensive aggression, through the words adopted from Mencken and Dreiser, in the power of his recoil from the arms of Bess Moss, but above all, in the pervasive imagery of fire, the language he has learned from his own bittersweet experience to use in forging a version of that appropriately modulated experience in *Black Boy.* Even more his private vocabulary than flight and fight and hunger, fire is the idiom of the authentic self recreated in this remarkable autobiography. No autobiography by an American black employs so consciously or variously this particular metaphor of self. None, therefore, illustrates as powerfully as *Black Boy* Gaston Bachelard's profound observation: "At all times and in all fields the explanation by fire is a *rich* explanation."[38]

III

As reinventors of their own beginnings, Richard Wright and Louis Sullivan provide several significant clues to the ways memory and imagination interact in a highly gifted individual's autobiography. Comparison and contrast help define the characteristic structure, tone, and metaphoric patterns of each artist's narrative of childhood. Whether any sweeping conclusions about the sources of creativity itself can be drawn from two such powerfully idiosyncratic accounts as *Black Boy* and *The Autobiography of an Idea* remains, however, problematic. Perhaps the wisest course is to point out some of the ways examination of particular texts clarifies (and at time challenges) larger speculations, like those of Greenacre, Cobb, and Spacks, as well as narrower approaches to autobiography, like that of R. K. White. This may at least identify pertinent questions—historical and aesthetic but also social and psychological—to be considered in further investigations of this complex cultural phenomenon.

The essential fact is clear, though its sources may not be: these twentieth-century autobiographers, though of different generations and social milieux, deliberately downplay or omit adult experiences and achievement in their concern to recreate as vividly as possible the emotional landscape of childhood and youth. These are explicitly identified as crucial periods in the evolution of their genius. In accentuating beginnings, moreover, both Sullivan and Wright emphasize the earlier events of childhood over subsequent experiences of adolescence. Though both stages are remembered vividly, the first ten or twelve years seem most important to them. If so, this raises questions about Spacks's historical-literary paradigm. For these American autobiographers at least, both childhood and adolescence are significant stages of self; the nineteenth-century penchant for the earlier period seems to have persisted into the so-called era of adolescence. Spacks acknowledges such persistences, though without linking them specifically to creative careers; "all writers have more or less available to them the resources of the past," she observes, "slipping into old languages or modes of perception often with an astonishing air of comfort" (7). Such an easy embrace of former Transcendental modes of perception is especially evident in *The Autobiography of an Idea.* But Spacks mentions several twentieth-century American autobiographers who similarly slant their life stories. As compared, say, to Franklin, Woolman, Thoreau, or Grant, very few modern writers of personal narratives slide over their early years. Hence, in later chapters, when discussing several of the writers Spacks cites, we will note other aspects of personal identity besides the acquisition of a powerful creative drive which are explicitly grounded in childhood and adolescence. The occasions we shall be using to explore the autobiographies of Frank Conroy and Lillian Hellman, as of Conrad Aiken and Alexander Berkman, are each different from the rubric use here. Nevertheless, common to each of these writers—as to others like Mary McCarthy, Alfred Kazin, Claude Brown, Maya Angelou, and Edward Dahlberg—is the extraordinary weight given certain early formative experiences. It will be seen that for many aspects of a mature identity and ideology, childhood and adolescence form a seamless temporal unit rather than falling into the discrete stages which Spacks and Erikson tend to emphasize.

Sullivan and Wright clearly succeed in creating this seamless web of significant experience, each author binding together in one metaphor-laden narrative the first eighteen or nineteen years of his life. This tight unity is the reason for my extended treatment of these texts. What questions, therefore, do they raise which connect them to other autobiographical occasions and acts? To begin with, one needs to inquire how widespread in other twentieth-century accounts is the emotion-freighted image of the author as sensitive, solitary, almost narcissistic child isolated more completely from others in the autobiographer's imagination than he (or she) probably was in actuality. This impression of the future artist is further complicated by the apparently opposite image of a child deeply involved with a few intimate others, chiefly, of course, the mother and father. Greenacre's "family romance" has in fact quite specific features for the genius as personal historian. One notable aspect is the virtual or absolute absence of siblings. Closely allied to this is the neglect of the adolescent love affairs, peer friendships, and first steps toward full genitality and marriage which the lives of "ordinary" people usually exhibit during youth. Are there, for instance, figures in other autobiographies like Bess Moss and Minnie Whittlesey from whom the recreated self carefully keeps an emotional distance? Andrienne Sullivan and Ella Wright are the undisputed muses for these artist-autobiographers; are there analogues or stand-ins in other accounts of American childhoods?

The presence in Sullivan and Wright of intense libidinal energies still mobile in mid-life or old age is central to both autobiographical recreations. These texts instruct us to examine other accounts of childhood to see if they too exhibit the same conflicts between creativity and destructiveness, the same psychic freedom and flexibility which accompanies still-powerful infantile attachments. A fierce energy of will and imaginative self-control unite the childish self to the mature writer of these reminiscences and demonstrate that no crippling dependence upon the mother or obsessive rivalry with the father persist. Moreover, the trajectory of these lives and careers, though not fully traced out, leads away from the affective ardors of family and home as well as circles fondly (and bitterly, in Wright's case) around them. This dual engagement with the past is to be seen in the other manifestations of these men's genius. *Native Son,* for instance, employs for a variety of fictional and ideological effects the same emotions of fear, violence, fire, and flight which are anchored by *Black Boy* in the author's early childhood. Similarly, Sullivan's architectural career, all the way from the early Wainwright Building and the later Bayard Building to the plates in *A System of Architectural Ornament* at the end of his life, shows a characteristic continuity in structural and decorative style which is also expressed verbally in the line-and-loop narrative organization of *The Autobiography of an Idea.*

In canvassing other texts for similar consistencies and connections, we may find Greenacre's psychoanalytic concept of "collective alternates" to be of special value. The future artist's ability to keep alive the libidinal ties to parents and their surrogates and at the same time to deflect these onto natural or cultural objects may well be more widely shared than my focus upon creativity suggests. Furthermore, what Cobb calls "the passionate world-making behavior of the child"[39] may persist as childhood memories even for those who are not able, like Sullivan, to translate emotional identifications with nature, his father's body, or an iron bridge into skyscrapers and banks. Richard Wright's collective alternates, we have seen, are generally remoter from nature than Sullivan's. Their emotional coloration, too, suggests a more deterministic connection between self and social circumstance. Though his story culminates in the dual escape to literature and Chicago, Wright's fire imagery continues to hold him to his Mississippi past. This emotional tie may account for the virtual absence of humor and joy in *Black Boy.* It also tells much about Wright's historical and social warping of what others see as representative Southern and black "reality." If *The Autobiography of an Idea* is, in Spacks's terms, a throwback to nineteenth-century celebrations of childish freedom and innocence, *Black Boy* can stand for a number of later twentieth-century texts in which the immature self is consciously bound and bruised by social forces. I doubt, therefore, if Richard Wright lends support to the Eriksonian proposition of adolescence or youth as a moratorium or temporary escape from adult realities. To be sure, Wright as the recreator of his artistic self is not interested in an accurate or complete representation of social experience. Unlike Sullivan, whose imagination has selected memories enhancing the illusion of childish awareness and choice, Wright just as deliberately stresses or suppresses biographical details palliating the bleakness and alienation of the writer as young black American. Nature helps Sullivan deflect certain bitter memories and actual conflicts; inanimate objects become the displaced representations of the same kind of psychic struggles which Wright confronts more directly. The ideology of each creative individual contributes to such choices, as do the particular artifacts (a building, a novel) each is later to create. Spacks is a useful guide to all such recoveries of the past which will doubtless contain other "systematic exclusions" (7) to be identified and explained.

This parallel analysis of two autobiographies of American artists thus suggests the need, in considering all narratives of childhood and youth, to proceed beyond manifest content, ideological statement, and literary form—important and essential as these aspects are—to deeper levels of fantasy, dream, fear, and desire. The persistence of infantile emotions may be detected in repeated images and events which together give emotional coherence and continuity to the re-imagined self. In identifying and connecting basic elements of an identity, Greenacre's concept of "collective alternates" helps bridge gaps between event and emotion, childhood experience and later career, action, ideology, and moral stance, which are not explicitly bound together by the reminiscing writer. Cobb, too, helps to identify nature not simply as the locale but also as the catalyst of many such crucial childhood events later recaptured as memories by an autobiographical consciousness. Moreover, their common stress upon the pre-oedipal, oedipal, and especially upon the latency stages of epigenetic development correspond nicely to the narrative emphasis of these (and other) narratives. Though autobiographers do not always (perhaps seldom) divide their lives into the same stages used by a Freud, Erikson, or Keniston, there appears to be widespread agreement among modern autobiographers and psychologists that one's life before maturity, marriage, and a career makes a natural narrative unit.

Whether Greenacre provides universally applicable hypotheses about the childhood of the artist remains, however, unclear as a result of this extended comparison of Sullivan and Wright. Her perception of the psychic significance in a creative career of the "moment of mystery or awe" is brilliantly and quite specifically illustrated in *The Autobiography of an Idea*. Yet it rests upon assumptions about the patriarchal family as the normal environment for the growing artist which Richard Wright's experience (or, for that matter, Edward Dahlberg's)

belies. Whether through accidents of death or divorce or more permanent social factors like race, class, different social mores and assumptions about privacy, different autobiographers will have available
childhood experiences which depart from the pattern Phyllis
Greenacre assumes. Certainly my impression is that *Black Boy*'s full
range of personal and social meanings are not elucidated as clearly
through Greenacre's premises as is the case with *The Autobiography
of an Idea.*

Nevertheless, Greenacre, along with White and Bachelard, opens
up psychological depths in *Black Boy* in ways which match, comple-
ment, and possibly correct my more doctrinaire psychoanalytic interpretation of Sullivan's personal history. Yet central to both works—and
hence perhaps to other similar recreations of childhood—is the mother-
son relationship in its dynamic unfolding through time, social space,
and autobiographical imagination. Readers have long noted and responded to this emotional aspect of the architect's and the novelist's
identities. What Greenacre, even more than Cobb or White, helps us
see is overdetermined language and structure as the *present* expression of *past* affects invested in significant others. Neither Sullivan nor
Wright hide the fact that their autobiographies, though written for
several audiences and ideological causes, are at their core love-gifts
to Andrienne List Sullivan and Ella Wilson Wright. This is not to reduce or simplify either autobiography. Sullivan and Wright are creative artists. They each possess memories and imaginations too deep
for facile formulas. Perhaps all that stressing autobiographies as complex psychic structures can achieve is to throw a small beam of light
into the darkness out of which all creative careers come. As Ralph Ellison writes (quoting Hemingway), a life and an imagination like Richard Wright's are "forged in injustice as a sword is forged."[40] What one
learns about American injustice from *Black Boy* is, in an ideological
sense, much more than what one learns from *The Autobiography of
an Idea.* We learn from both that, from the artist's viewpoint, the primal injustice is to be deprived of the mother's exclusive love. What
a creative artist *does* with the universal emotional deprivations and
separations of childhood will vary infinitely according to temperament, accident, and opportunity. What leads deeply into these two
artists' autobiographies—and perhaps beyond them to other American narratives of immaturity and initiation—is Greenacre's perception that "the artistic product has rather universally the character of
a love gift, to be brought as near perfection as possible and to be presented with pride and misgiving" (2:490). Possibly this insight about
the childhood of the artist will illuminate autobiographies like Alexan-

147

der Berkman's and Conrad Aiken's, to which we turn in the next chapter. These lives, too, are anchored in childhood traumas even more violent than Wright's and also in treasured memories of mothers like Louis Sullivan's.

5

Cato's Mirror: The Face of Violence in the Autobiographies of Alexander Berkman and Conrad Aiken

TERENCE MALICK'S REMARKABLE FILM of 1974, *Badlands,* contains a sequence which vividly epitomizes the experience of American violence and deftly connects it to the impulse deep within even the most inarticulate of victims and violators to turn pain into art. Like its predecessor *Bonnie and Clyde, Badlands* is based upon actual history—the Charles Starkweather case of 1958 in which a pair of Nebraska teenagers went on a murderous rampage, killing eleven persons, including the girl's parents and baby sister. In the film, Kit and Holly flee to the prairie shack of Cato, Kit's fellow worker on the town garbage truck. Cato tries to sneak away and sound the alarm. Kit shoots his friend in the back. Cato staggers indoors, bleeding but silent, and collapses on the bed. As Kit and Holly circle aimlessly around the room, the dying man does something oddly significant—he picks up a mirror and carefully examines his face in its surface. Kit says nothing, and Holly offers neither apology nor help. Instead she innocently inquires about Cato's pet spider. What does it eat? Does it ever bite? "It never bit *me,*" he gasps laconically. After he dies, Kit drags the body into the shed, then stalks up and down outside gesturing vehemently to the corpse. Like other victims in this brilliant, disturbing film, Cato has been caught in the spiraling coils of Kit's almost voiceless and casual violence.

But the moviegoer's imagination has been arrested by Cato's looking at his face reflected in the mirror. The momentary act carries several implications. Most obviously, it dramatizes this innocent victim's exquisite sense of loss and thus qualifies the film's lyrical depiction of a brutal chain of events. More broadly, it represents a person's wish to view himself in the grip of experience, to seize his identity as it is

149

being torn away. The image in the mirror recalls the psychological assertion that it is in the face and genitals that humans characteristically epitomize themselves. Cato's looking in the mirror is the filmic equivalent of an autobiographical gesture. Violent, meaningless death only moments away is but the extreme instance of experience to be measured and turned by memory into some sort of acceptable significance. In this desperate circumstance the mirror replaces pen or typewriter with which literate people—those with a longer lease and perspective on life than Cato—traditionally record events, bend them into patterns, and by imaginative remembering recreate themselves. Moreover, the second arresting aspect of this scene, Holly's chillingly innocuous inquiries about the spider, suggests another impulse toward autobiographical art. Throughout *Badlands* the violence is filtered through Holly's voice-over narration. Her appalling schoolgirl rhetoric—a fourteen-year-old's imitation of *True Romance*—resembles her exchange with the dying man and attests to the moral void in both her life and Kit's. But it also serves as a defensive distancing of the horror to which she only vaguely assents. Listening to Holly's flat, expressionless voice repeating phrases about her western outlaw lover, we are reminded that *True Romance* is part of the autobiographical subliterature of our culture. Later, Kit too reaches for words to express himself and his story when he speaks into the dictaphone at the rich man's house. Both voices, like Cato and his mirror, dramatize inarticulateness made articulate and offer proof of Rollo May's insight that in a violent society like ours "the first thing to disintegrate is the language."[1] Perhaps because ordinary communication is impossible, Kit's rifle has spoken and will speak again. Like Billy Budd's fist in another moral universe, violence finds its own medium of expression.

Other American victims, violators, and bystanders have been luckier than Cato, Kit, or Holly in finding a voice for their turbulent, bloody lives. Living before or beyond Hollywood and endowed with the will to write, many American autobiographers have put into words the sudden blinding loss or drawn-out pain from which they have subsequently escaped with a new sense of self. Cato's mirror has a host of literary antecedents and real-life parallels. This is true not simply because American violence, as the Koerner Report and numerous historians remind us, has always been unavoidable, but also because autobiography offers one of the readiest, most flexible instruments for coping imaginatively with damage or death. On the public stage of history, the stimuli for such literary responses are all too obvious: civil and foreign wars, Indian massacres, slavery and racial oppression, labor strife, prison life, the brutalities of an extreme capitalism, all the explosions of urban living for the immigrant and the native-born. Moreover, as we approach the present age of the psychoanalyst and the paperback, an understandable increase in autobiographies dealing with private violence can also be noted.

Whether the writer's retrospective viewpoint is the long one of a Grant or a Whitman or the more immediate perspective of a Malcolm X or Maya Angelou, many experiences of suffering to the self or to another press powerfully upon the memory and imagination. Their force necessarily affects both the decision to write and the techniques chosen to represent them. At the time it occurs, violence usually can be merely endured or witnessed. The mind often goes numb in the sudden apprehension of acute pain. Man's impulse, however, is not to remain in this state but to impose by some means order and significance upon experience and thus reaffirm personal identity. Language is our first and last resort in this battle and has been embraced with particular urgency by many of those who have personally suffered violence. It is scarcely surprising that autobiography should be a favorite medium for these re-creations, since, as the vocabulary of violence suggests, such experience is always violation of some self, its body, space, rights—ultimately of its very identity. Conversely, violence may be in part contained if communication can reaffirm the integrity of the encountering individuals. Autobiography is an appropriate medium for such affirmations since, as Russell Hart points out, it is precisely the function of the autobiographical act to convert historical event and psychological experience into personal identity.

Because autobiography is not pure fiction but an imaginative version of history, it cannot completely rewrite the past, no matter how insistently the traumatized memory calls upon the imagination to do so. Indeed, personal history always seeks to substitute understanding for repression, so that by offering author and audience a plausible explanation of the past its damage may be diminished. Even so-called random events undergo this transformation, which can bring into consciousness hidden motives in the self and others. In his play *The Face of Violence*, Jacob Bronowski explores this dimension of our response to random violence. His character Pollux meditates on the fact that all violence is "the junction of impulse and history":

> The unpremeditated crime
> Conceals indeed no *conscious* long design:
> And yet—and yet
> Years of mutinous repression,
> An ancient misery of mind

151

And festering oppression—
These make the slow fuse that explodes
The strangler's instant act of passion.
The culprit and his age
Conspire in a rage,
And their frenzy makes a fire
That nothing can assuage.[2]

Autobiographers, too, affirm the "conscious long design" behind observed and experienced violence. Because their stories are imaginative versions of real events, the search for some assuaging order always entails explanatory connections between "the culprit and his age." But because autobiographies are also manifestations of "frenzy" and "fire," the culprit's inner desires must also find direct or symbolic voice. Passion and conscience are thus insistently present in any re-creation of violence, just as they were at the original explosive event. But it is one of the special aspects of the autobiographical act that it can balance anarchic impulse and the energies of superego with rational analysis. Memory, as Phyllis Greenacre asserts, is as protean a faculty as fantasy or desire. When its burden is a violent chain of events or emotional relationships, the repressions or displacements are likely to be massive, as we have just observed in the case of Richard Wright. Erikson reminds us again that "at best, memories connect meaningfully what happened once and what is happening now. If they are painful, they at least recover from the defeats of the past the stragglers of unlived potentials."[3] In *Gandhi's Truth* he illustrates this hypothesis by a sensitive examination of the private and largely unacknowledged violence toward wife, sons, and the sexual impulse embedded within Gandhi's empire-shaking doctrine of nonviolence.

These reminders can prove as illuminating for personal histories with violent experience as their source and focus as they were for autobiographies of the creative artist. Violence and creativity, after all, are in important respects polar experiences. That they are intimately related is suggested by the still-powerful associations between making and destroying revealed in *The Autobiography of an Idea* and *Black Boy*. Both impulses are crucial to humans and culture; neither has been exhaustively studied or fully understood. Yet public, legitimated violence is bound to be different, and perhaps easier to contain, than more purely private or domestic suffering. Either experience, to be sure, may prove autobiographically decisive or relatively unimportant. Even war—probably over the years our most socially accepted mode of violence—is memorialized quite differently in classic American autobiographies of the past. Franklin's strategy, for example, in line with his characteristic response to disorder and turbulence, is to ignore or treat very obliquely the revolutionary bloodshed and suffering which Crèvecoeur, in *Sketches of XVIII-Century America,* dramatizes with such chilling irony and autobiographical pathos.[4] *Personal Memoirs of U. S. Grant* and *Specimen Days* offer even more direct and protracted looks into Cato's mirror.[5] Yet both Civil War authors adopt characteristic devices for distancing as well as defining the self vis-à-vis the bloody realities of the past. These are represented for Grant by the corpse-strewn battlefield at Shiloh, for Whitman, by the cartload of amputated limbs outside the field hospital on the Rappahannock. Whereas Grant merges himself with his country's *agon* under the modest democratic metaphor of the unshaven Union commander dressed in "the uniform of a private with the straps of a lieutenant-general,"[6] Whitman reinvents a more mythic persona, the Wound Dresser, whose alter ego, America from 1861 to 1865, is one vast military hospital.

These pre-twentieth-century narratives of meaningful military violence have, however, stimulated surprisingly few modern emulations. War has not proved an American occasion through which many significant selves have been imaginatively recreated. Far more common and decisive as stimuli to contemporary historians of the self are smaller events, public and private, in which individuals recapture themselves in the grip of violent experience. Moreover, when the public dramas of the battlefield or hospital give place to other kinds of violence, the usual certainties of social legitimacy for such violence often disappear or are cast in doubt. The "ideological problematic," which Grele posits as an essential link between individual and cultural narratives, becomes critical but less clear. When the prison autobiography succeeds the slave narrative—and, perhaps, even the war memoir—as a characteristically modern story of public violence, the autobiographical strategies of Alexander Berkman or Malcolm X will necessarily differ from those of Douglass or Whitman. Even in completely private lives, where violence presents itself as psychic storms arising from family strife and mental sickness, the moral atmosphere is often murky.

Since so many modern autobiographers do emphasize violent events and emotions as elements of their later identities, it is impossible to make anything like a representative selection of texts for detailed comparison and contrast. As was the case with creativity, the social and historical, aesthetic and psychological dimensions of this autobiographical occasion are almost endless. In deciding to concentrate

upon Berkman's *Prison Memoirs of an Anarchist* and Aiken's *Ushant,*
we have been guided by several central considerations associated with
this common but complex cultural occasion. Berkman's narrative of
1912, as we will demonstrate, illustrates early and with astonishing
subtlety and power one modern experience of political violence in
which the manifest ideological component—in this case anarchism—
runs counter to popular American political belief. Yet because Berkman accepts the full burdens of his autobiographical act, he searches
his violent past as political assassin and penitentiary prisoner for evidences of both change and continuity in belief and historical identity.
Thus the tensions between the political convictions behind his attempted murder of Henry C. Frick in 1892 and the older, altered self
who emerged fourteen years later from Western Penitentiary are examined in light of lifelong psychic struggles and against the backdrop
of changing historical realities. The result is a candid and convincing
portrait of a tormented, once-violent self recreated by literary methods which at times are almost as "fictional" as those used by Wright
or Aiken.

The increasingly interior focus of *Prison Memoirs* not only exemplifies Bronowski's contention that violence is the "junction of impulse
and history," but also provides several grounds for comparison with
Aiken's *Ushant.* The poet's personal narrative of 1952, as thoroughly
private as Berkman's is political and public, has a crucial childhood
event at its core. In that family trauma—even more decisively, we
shall argue, than with Richard Wright's arson—a uniquely tempestuous artistic career was engendered. One climax of Aiken's career is
Ushant, which like *Black Boy* comes after many of the poems and novels which are also decisively marked by the poet's violent past. *Ushant*
is an intricate, dreamlike narrative which circles around the brutal
transforming event only to reconstruct it near the close of the story.
The energy and imagination with which violent experience and artistic achievement are connected are of course uniquely Aiken's. Yet
Ushant may offer clues to other autobiographical strategies, just as
Berkman's prison memoir provides a perspective on later ideological
testaments and records of American violence. The perennial balance
between the inescapably singular and the possibly representative dimensions of autobiography can be maintained in this case only if we
keep certain central questions in mind as each work is examined and
compared. Most generally, of course, we should look for those particular relationships between self and society which are stressed when
public or private violence is asserted as the center of a social self and
historic identity. One should also note the specific literary methods

154

selected to reenact such powerful memories of pain and loss. Finally, we must be sensitive to all verbal clues to unacknowledged as well as openly perceived psychic forces which, as Bronowski believes, once interacted with outer circumstance and which still energize the memories and pens of survivors of violence.

I

To begin with a glance back at nineteenth-century narratives of American pain and suffering, one notes that *Prison Memoirs of an Anarchist* brings the face of violence even closer to the reader's gaze than Whitman does in *Specimen Days* and holds it there over a longer span of time than is the case with *Personal Memoirs of U. S. Grant.* Berkman thus advances the art of personal history as he furthers his ideological cause by making an initially skeptical audience see, feel, and ultimately sympathize with the violence of an unhallowed public event and a pariah's life. He thus imparts to his past an emotional, intellectual, and moral complexity unexcelled in most previous American accounts of violence, including even most nineteenth-century slave narratives. Furthermore, *Prison Memoirs* stands at the head of an important modern subgenre of life-histories, one likely to prove significant as long as the jail and penitentiary continue to function as punishment centers and training schools for rebellious and violent members of American society. Though their authors may not have heard of Berkman's book (not a common title in prison libraries), Caryl Chessman's *Cell 2455, Death Row, The Autobiography of Malcolm X,* Cleaver's *Soul on Ice,* Jackson's *Soledad Brother,* and James Blake's *The Joint* may all be read against the background of this pioneer prison autobiography.

From first page to last, *Prison Memoirs* exudes emotional and moral power. This is so because it is, in nearly equal degrees, an important historical document, a passionate polemic, a dramatic narrative which often reads like a novel, and a candid self-portrait of a psyche in the agonies of death and rebirth. Hutchins Hapgood was the first to note this particular feature. "This is the only book that I know," he wrote in his introduction to the 1912 edition, "which goes deeply into the corrupting, demoralizing psychology of prison life."[7] A contemporary reviewer in the *New York Globe* echoes this insight by asserting "nothing could exceed the uncanny spell exercised by this story. Berkman has succeeded in making you live his prison experiences with him, and his book is as complete a self-revelation as is humanly possible."[8] Neither admirer, however, grasped the full extent of Berkman's confession, which goes well beyond the mere recording of the emotional realities of the cell block. The psychodynamics of childhood and family relations in czarist Russia, his life in the Pioneers of Liberty (the Jewish anarchist group in New York), and the inner history, brief and bitter, of the released prisoner who moves like a wraith through the last pages—these revelations are as poignant as the "psychology of prison life" and just as essential to Berkman's purpose. Precisely because it brings so much of the past to bear upon fourteen years' experiences, *Prison Memoirs* is a true autobiography. In its 512 pages the lineaments of a full identity emerge.

The title is the first and proper clue to a many-layered record. The story opens firmly within the tradition of the memoir with its assumption of a social and historic self. Though memories and impulses from a private past soon appear, particularly in his symbolic dreams and reveries, Berkman accepts the public identity conferred by the question put by his captors in Frick's office after Berkman's pistol and knife have failed to do their work. "Mr. Frick, do you identify this man as your assailant?" (35) becomes, therefore, both the literal and the larger issue which Berkman contrasts with two other historic deeds of violence. These are the assassinations of Garfield and McKinley which bracket this turbulent era of American history. In particular, differences and similarities between his attack on Frick and Leon Czolgosz's on McKinley are a major ideological concern. These are articulated in letters (many of them smuggled out of Western Penitentiary) to Emma Goldman, his faithful fellow anarchist and "The Girl" of this narrative. This correspondence is an important autobiographical device. The author reproduces a facsimile of one letter and quotes others in order to authenticate his experience and provide a beyond-the-walls perspective on the events and changes in his life.

Berkman's historical self and public acts come first because he seeks to persuade the reader of two truths about political violence. First, his attack on the steel magnate was fully justified as an idealistic yet realistic gesture on behalf of the People. But, second, his subsequent imprisonment demonstrates just as realistically that life in this penal institution is not essentially different from the reader's own world; prison, in fact, is a replica of the parent society. This latter claim, mere metaphor to many readers, becomes a commonplace for later prison autobiographers like Cleaver and Jackson. When Berkman asserts, "Daily I behold the machinery at work, grinding and pulverizing, brutalizing the officers, dehumanizing the inmates. Far removed from the strife and struggle of the larger world, I yet witness its miniature replica, more agonizing and merciless within the walls" (272), he makes a point echoed from Soledad in 1970 by George Jackson: "Inside the joint it is the same only much more intense."[9] Neither man writes metaphorically. Both simply report perceptions and convictions about the raw and subtle modes of exploitation, cruelty, hypocrisy, and injustice in the prisoner's world, as well as the love and solidarity also found in cell block and prison yard.

For Berkman, as for Cleaver, the chief instruments of oppression are capitalism and its willing servant, Christianity. Frick's ruthless suppression of the Homestead strikers makes him, therefore, a more powerful evil than the warden, though the two are merely larger and smaller tyrants. Both have conspired to destroy the dream that brought him to America: his belief in "the land of noble achievement, a glorious free country, where men walked erect in the full stature of manhood" (20). Unlike other disillusioned immigrants, however, Berkman was prepared to act—hence his *attentat*. "I had always taken the extreme view," he declares. "Society is a patient; sick constitutionally and functionally. Surgical treatment is often imperative. The removal of a tyrant is not merely justifiable; it is the highest duty of every true revolutionist" (7). Thus Frick is shot not as a person but as a symbol. The act, moreover, is accomplished by an impersonal instrument: "I am simply a revolutionist, a terrorist by conviction, an instrument for furthering the cause of humanity; in short, a Rakhmetov" (9–10) By naming himself after the hero of Nikolai Chernyshevsky's novel *What Is to Be Done?* Berkman at once fictionalizes, historicizes, and depersonalizes himself. Indeed, he is quite willing to sacrifice this self to the cause. "To remove a tyrant is an act of liberation, the giving of life and opportunity to an oppressed people. True, the Cause often calls upon the revolutionist to commit an unpleasant act; but it is the test of a true revolutionist—nay, more, his pride—to sacrifice all merely human feeling at the call of the People's Cause. If the latter demand his life, so much the better" (7).

Prison Memoirs narrates at length the actual consequences of acting out these violently altruistic beliefs. During fourteen penitentiary years this rigid, arrogant young idealist changes into a middle-aged man who learns to love particular men, not just the People. At first affronted that his fellow prisoners neither understand nor approve his *attentat* ("Too bad you didn't kill him," one whispers. "Some business misunderstanding, eh?" [54]) Berkman gradually drops his disdain and discovers "the man beneath the criminal" and the necessary human element in all ideological equations. Prison experience affirms a wider identity than that of the anarchist assassin. In recreating himself in this altered image, Berkman celebrates a possible function of autobiography for a violent life: the realization in the face of suffering of a unique and changing self. Yet Aleck, the new American self, is not fundamentally different from Sasha, the Russian schoolboy who reacted violently against his bourgeois background by declaring his allegiance to nihilism. Continuity *and* change characterize Berkman's recreated identity, as with all other successful autobiographers.

The historical event confirming this redefinition of a violent political self is McKinley's assassination in 1901. Emma Goldman's public offer to nurse the dying president as her recognition of his humanity forces Berkman, inside his cell, to reexamine his own deed of 1892 from a different perspective. Terrorism in America, he now sees, must be considered from several viewpoints: the private imperatives of the assassin, the political and economic realities, and the ideological understanding of the American workers who are the intended beneficiaries. "To prove of value," he writes The Girl on December 20, 1901, "they must be motivated by social rather than individual necessity, and be directed against a real and immediate enemy of the people." Hence, though he sympathizes with Czolgosz he cannot approve of his deed: "as an expression of personal revolt it was inevitable, and in itself an indictment of existing conditions. But the background of social necessity was lacking." For he now knows by experience how different the United States is from Russia.

> In Russia, where political oppression is popularly felt, such a deed would be of great value. But the scheme of political subjection is more subtle in America. . . . The real despotism of republican institutions is far deeper, more insidious, because it rests on the popular delusion of self-government and independence. That is the subtle source of democratic tyranny, and, as such, it cannot be reached with a bullet.
>
> In modern capitalism, exploitation rather than oppression is the real enemy of the people. Oppression is but its handmaid. Hence the battle is to be waged in the economic rather than the political field. It is therefore that I regard my own act as far more significant and educational than Leon's. It was directed against a tangible, real oppressor, visualized as such by the people. (416–17)

Berkman writes as a wiser ideologue but one who has by no means repudiated his own past or its illusions. He already knows that his fellow prisoners, at least, did not see Frick as the oppressor. Nevertheless, both his original fervor and this sobering later knowledge have been subsumed into a larger truth. "Yet I feel that the individual, in certain cases, is of more direct and immediate consequence than humanity" (399). Abstractions about justice and terrorism remain. But the concrete realities of living—and dying—persons have now an equal or higher priority. John William Ward has succinctly connected the two aspects of Berkman's experience: "Along with his awareness that the revolutionist's dream may only sacrifice people to the myth of the 'People,' the collectivity which has no room for actual, concrete, living individuals," Ward writes, "Berkman came to realize that violence, the decision to kill, finds no sanction in some transcendent ideal, but is finally to be justified only in relation to historical necessity which, in turn, demands political calculation and a pragmatic estimate of the consequences."[10] This ideological redefinition is an autobiographical act.

Prison Memoirs is ultimately personal history, not a political testament or polemic. Facts and beliefs have been retranslated into experience by the author's retrospective realization that political violence, however idealistic in motivation, can never be divorced from the human beings—himself, The Girl, his fellow prisoners, Leon Czolgosz, William McKinley—who must finally affirm or deny its validity. The literary feat of enlisting sympathy for an arrogant ideologue, by tracing his evolution into a lover of individual men, cost Berkman much, but it made him an imaginative artist. "I was filled with wonder," Emma Goldman writes in her own autobiography, *Living My Life*, "to see Sasha emerge from his Calvary an artist with a rare gift of music in his words."[11] Her praise, admittedly that of a fellow anarchist and onetime lover, is a justified response to Berkman's style, careful narrative structure, and deft use of fitting imagery. These and other characteristics of literary artistry are all the more remarkable when one realizes that English was the author's third language.

Because message, style, and self-revelation are truly inseparable in *Prison Memoirs,* exploration of this intimate experience of violence must begin with Berkman's careful selection of narrative techniques. Berkman's reliance upon first-person, present-tense storytelling imparts an almost fictional immediacy to the vivid events and emotions which open the action, while later reproducing effectively the slow movement of prison time and the circular torment of prison thoughts. He seems to have been thus impelled forcibly into his past by the almost overwhelming passions which flooded his memory and imagination as he began writing. This occurred in May 1910, four years after his release and on the anniversary of his decision to go to Pittsburgh and kill Frick. "Day after day he would sit at his desk staring into vacancy," Emma Goldman recalls, "or he would write as if driven by furies. . . . Then would come days when Sasha would vanish into the woods to escape human contact, to escape me, and above all to escape himself and the ghosts that had come to life since he had begun to write."[12] In such a frame of mind, he found it impossible to maintain distance from his history. Several fictional devices suggested themselves as the right ways to reenter and contain the past. Liberal use of dialogue and flashbacks, a tone often highly dramatic and emotional, a network of simple metaphors connecting disparate episodes and feelings, as well as the author's initial sense of himself as a fictional character like Rakhmetov—all these suggest that Berkman has in mind the *bildungsroman* as well as the autobiography. In certain respects, then, his book resembles James Weldon Johnson's pseudoautobiography also published in 1912, *The Autobiography of an Ex-Colored Man.* Nevertheless, these fictional techniques are firmly controlled by the author's historical sense. Hence when one of several New York publishers who refused *Prison Memoirs* suggested he rewrite it under a pseudonym, Berkman stoutly refused. Emma Goldman, whose Mother Earth Publishing Association did issue it, agreed vehemently. "I resented the suggestion and pointed out that *Prison Memoirs* was a personal story, the product of years of suffering and pain. Could the writer be expected to hide his identity concerning something that was flesh of his flesh and blood of his blood?"[13]

In the act of preserving and dramatizing his own flesh and blood, Berkman also memorializes the anonymous lives of many fellow prisoners. These, however, are not named or identified as specifically as Whitman, for example, does his hospital friends in *Specimen Days.* One whose private suffering becomes a symbol of universal social oppression is Harry, a sickly, illiterate lad who at the age of nineteen has not seen a single day of liberty since early childhood. "Tell me, Aleck," he asks, "how does it feel to walk on de street, to know that you're free t' go where you damn please, wid no screw to foller you?"

> Alone in the cell, I ponder over his words. "Everybody was always against me," I hear the boy say. I wake at night, with the quivering cry in the darkness, "Everybody against me!" Motherless in childhood, reared in the fumes of brutal inebriation, cast into the slums to be crushed under the wheels of the law's Juggernaut, was the fate of this social orphan. . . . The blanched face of Misery is silhouetted against the night. The silence sobs with the piteous cry of the crushed boy. And I hear the cry, and it fills my whole being with the sense of terrible

wrong and injustice, with the shame of my kind, that sheds crocodile tears while it swallows its helpless prey. The submerged moan in the dark. I will echo their agony to the ears of the world. I have suffered with them, I have looked into the heart of Pain, and with its voice and anguish I will speak to humanity, to wake it from sloth and apathy, and lend hope to despair. (450–51)

The experienced reader of American autobiography will hear several echoes in this passionate outburst. The clearest, perhaps, is Frederick Douglass's arraignment in his *Narrative* of the slaveholding Christian civilization which also sheds crocodile tears over its victims.[14] Another prototype for Berkman's rhetoric and emotion is Walt Whitman. Though he makes no reference to having read *Leaves of Grass* in the penitentiary, his line "I have suffered with them" echoes the memorable line from section 33 of "Song of Myself"—"I am the man, I suffered, I was there." Furthermore, in moments of anguished fellow feeling like this, Berkman reveals how deeply he has been drawn into a life of pain by the same kind of fascination with death and homosexual love as Whitman felt. These emotions, diametrically opposed to the anarchist's original austere attitudes, are also expressed in metaphors drawn from nature and childhood, as well as from the crude argot of the cell block. All gradually cohere to compose a new identity. Trees, birds, flowers, bread, and the moon are used to symbolize his feelings about and experiences of freedom, escape, self-expression, and homosexual love. This shift in literary affinity from Chernyshevsky to someone like Whitman marks the extent of Berkman's actual and imaginative Americanization. The narrative which opens like a political novel modulates later into meditation and prose poetry. By borrowing features from several genres and traditions, Berkman adapts form to message, translates ideology into dramatic scene and description, and thereby connects Sasha and Aleck. The result is a recognizably American work of vernacular prose.

Berkman's achievement contrasts strongly with more fragmented and one-dimensional versions of later prison experience, such as *Soul on Ice.* Cleaver's book possesses undeniable power and urgency. But it does not stand rereading as well as *Prison Memoirs.* In Erikson's phrase, Berkman has better served "tradition and individual style."[15] Despite the eccentricity of the author's anarchism and the *apparent* crudity of his immigrant's English, his pioneering work establishes with surprising completeness the pattern of experiences and attitudes for subsequent American prison autobiographies, black as well as white. This model might be summarized thus: life in prison is a microcosm of the larger society; courtroom justice is seen as a travesty, as is also the parole system which often traps the convict and convinces him he is a political prisoner; daily routine is at once monotonous and a continuous ordeal of physical and spiritual danger; prison is also, however, a place for reading and reflection, for the discovery of an articulate, outraged self who can some day write *Soledad Brother* or *Soul on Ice;* the natural world is passionately felt as absent pleasure; escape is the eternal dream and occasional reality; homosexual love, often violent but sometimes tender, is an ever-present emotional option; masculinity therefore becomes an insistent identity issue; prison memories persist in the autobiographer's guilt over friends and lovers left behind when the gates open on one's own freedom. Finally Berkman anticipates others by dramatizing a central paradox: his personal victory over violence and his achieved compassion derive in considerable measure from the very ideology of abstract humanity which is slowly replaced by love for special individuals. "You lived in your theories and ideals" (436), his friend George remarks just before his release. That event is marked by a petition signed by two hundred inmates asking that they be allowed to bid Aleck good-bye. Such lived contradictions and reversals recur under quite different circumstances in Cleaver's ideology of rape and his discovered love for Beverly Axelrod, and in Malcolm X's double conversion, first to a racist and then to a raceless Muslim faith.

If contradiction and paradox mark the changing stages of Berkman's historical experiences, the inner imperatives for such complexities are articulated with a candor equally convincing. His anarchism harbors so many conflicting allegiances that it is scarcely surprising that prison uncovers many buried motives, fears, and desires. Psychic forces manifest themselves at several key points: in the *attentat,* which is both a rational political deed and a patently oedipal gesture; in Aleck's tender ties with young prisoners; in his dreams, especially the most desperate dream of all—suicide. In each of these overdetermined acts and attitudes we can detect the child, the assassin, and the convict proclaiming simultaneously their presences. As private impulse merges into public history the power of the past is proclaimed in Berkman's declaration: "Only aspirations that spontaneously leap from the depths of our soul persist in the face of antagonistic forces. The revolutionist is born" (414).

Russian past and Pittsburgh present are first linked in the flashbacks of this richly interwoven narrative. On the railroad trip to his rendezvous with Frick, Berkman's daydreams take him back to childhood scenes. His was a bitterly divided household, where a despotic father and hated uncle foreshadow Frick. Even more important to the young assassin—and to the older author—is his mother. She is recreated as a typical bourgeoise, despite her sympathy for the family's radical members. A crucial memory is of one dinner-table argument when Sasha objects to his mother slapping a servant.

"You forget yourself. My treatment of the menial is no concern of yours."

I cannot suppress the sharp reply that springs to my lips: "The low servant girl is as good as you."

I see mother's long slender fingers grasp the heavy ladle, and the next instant a sharp pain pierces my left hand. Our eyes meet. Her arm remains motionless, her gaze directed to the spreading blood stain on the white table-cloth. The ladle falls from her hand. She closes her eyes, and her body sinks limply to the chair.

Anger and humiliation extinguish my momentary impulse to rush to her assistance. Without uttering a word, I pick up the heavy salt-cellar, and fling it violently against the French mirror. At the crash of the glass, my mother opens her eyes in amazement. I rise and leave the house.

Immediately after this quarrel Berkman recounts his mother's death, which occurs before the two can be reconciled. The scene is as tender as its predecessor was tempestuous.

My heart beats fast as I enter mother's sick-room. I fear she may resent my intrusion: the shadow of the past stands between us. But she is lying quietly on the bed, and has apparently not noticed my entrance. I sit down at the bedside. A long time passes in silence. Mother seems to be asleep. It is growing dark in the room, and I settle down to pass the night in the chair. Suddenly I hear "Sasha!" called in a weak faint voice. I bend over her. "Drink of water." . . . I start to leave the room. "Sasha!" I hear behind me, and, quickly tiptoeing to the bed, I bring my face closely, very closely, to hers, to catch the faint words: "Help me turn to the wall." Tenderly I wrap my arms around the weak, emaciated body, and an ·overpowering longing seizes me to touch her hand with my lips and on my knees beg her forgiveness. I feel so near to her, my heart is so overflowing with compassion and love. But I dare not kiss her—we have become estranged. Affectionately I hold her in my arms for just the shadow of a second, dreading

163

lest she suspect the storm of emotion raging within me. Caressingly I turn her to the wall, and, as I slowly withdraw, I feel as if some mysterious, yet definite, something has at the very instant left her body. (18–19)

This searing moment establishes itself at the core of Berkman's life and self as clearly as Conrad Aiken's life is shaped by the deaths of his mother and father—and even more inexorably than Wright's self is fixed by his bedside vigil. The mother's death in the arms of her proud, estranged son decisively shapes the autobiographical identity here dramatically revealed in Berkman's vivid language. Thereafter, an iron and inexpressible tie—at once infantile, adolescent, and adult in its love and guilt—links him to his past and infuses all his actions and beliefs. When he daydreams in the Pittsburgh train and the swarthy worker behind him says, "Wake up, young feller! Whatcher sighin' for?" (19), the answer is as clear as the meaning of later prison scenes like the poignant one with his beloved Russell, who also needs help turning to the wall in the prison hospital. This cluster of feelings and ideas developing out of the author's early experiences is at once personal and social. Love for the dead mother and abiding hatred of overbearing fathers like Uncle Nathan and Frick lead him to regard Russian and American justice as terrible evils and paternalistic punishments aimed at his own hidden oedipal impulses. Hanging or suicide are therefore bold defiant gestures and appropriate consequences of a son's substitute ties, both heterosexual and "boy love." However, these secret determinants of behavior and character never reduce to a set of psychological categories. At no point is Berkman's reader encouraged to dismiss anarchism, the *attentat,* or the author's arraignment of American justice by a simple recourse to Freudian formulas.

And yet psychoanalysis *does* help to connect Berkman's inner and outer realities. Only a short while before Berkman began to write, Sigmund Freud delivered his epoch-making lectures in Worcester on "The Origin and Development of Psychoanalysis." Emma Goldman, in fact, attended one of these Clark University lectures. In the fifth of the series, Freud enunciated one of his central insights about man's fantasy life:

We men, with the high claims of our civilization and under the pressure of our repressions, find reality generally quite unsatisfactory and so keep up a life of fancy in which we love to compensate for what is lacking in the sphere of reality by the production of wish-fulfillments. In these phantasies is often

164

contained very much of the particular constitutional essence of personality and of its tendencies, repressed in real life. The energetic and successful man is he who succeeds by dint of labor in transforming his wish fancies into reality.[16]

The relevance of this generalization to Berkman's life-history can be seen at many points, though never more clearly than in the reverie in jail of the young assassin. Looking through the bars, he imagines a carpenter building his gallows. It is the actual carpenter who was in Frick's office and frustrated the attack with his hammer. A childhood memory suddenly intervenes: reading an illustrated book, *The Execution of Stenka Razin,* which precipitates a family quarrel about the seventeenth-century Russian revolutionary. When his father calls Razin "a murderer, a common rioter," little Sasha is perplexed. "Anybody could tell the difference between a murderer and a worthy man," he thinks, and draws comfort from his mother's stealthy tears. Then the reverie returns to the present. Berkman wonders if the gallows will support his weight, if some little American boy will some day call *him* a murderer. "No, they shall not hang me!" he cries.

> My hand steals to the lapel of my coat, and a deep sense of gratification comes over me, as I feel the nitroglycerine cartridge secure in the lining. I smile at the imaginary carpenter. Useless preparations! . . . No, they won't hang me. My hand caresses the long, narrow tube. Go ahead! Make your gallows. Why, the man is putting on his coat. Is he done already? Now he is turning around. He is looking straight at me. Why, it's Frick! Alive?
>
> My brain is on fire. I press my hand against the bars, and groan heavily. Alive? Have I failed? Failed? (38–39)

The implications of this daydream are heightened when Berkman actually tries to kill himself. As the chief of police and his men pry his jaws apart, they demand to know what the cartridge contains. "Candy," is the defiant reply. This underlines the fact that one meaning of the *attentat* is as childish defiance to be rewarded with a piece of lethal candy, perhaps in fantasy bestowed by the dead mother. Furthermore, the irony of the carpenter turning into Frick himself, like the obvious link between Frick and his own father, accents the ancient family emotions infusing Berkman's despair. Though he may not exactly fit Freud's pattern of the "energetic and successful man"; manifestly Berkman's violent politics and his autobiography both express wish-fulfillments. Each idiosyncratic response reflects "the pressures of repression"; each defines "the particular constitutional essence of personality" of this violent dreamer.

Indeed, Eros and Thanatos vie ceaselessly in Berkman's prison thoughts and desires. Perhaps the most poignant illustration of this conflict is his relation with Russell. Recounting his young lover's death from meningitis, he confesses to The Girl the depth of his participation in another's suffering.

> In some manner his agony seemed to affect me, and I began to experience the pains and symptoms that Russell described in his notes. I knew it was my sick fancy; I strove against it, but presently my legs showed signs of paralysis, and I suffered excruciating pain in the spinal column, just like Russell. I was afraid that I would be done to death like my poor friend. I grew suspicious of every guard, and would barely touch the food, for fear of its being poisoned. My "head was workin,'" they said. . . .
>
> I was on the verge of suicide. . . . I was put in the strait-jacket. They bound my body in canvas, strapped my arms to the bed, and chained my feet to the posts. I was kept that way eight days, unable to move, rotting in my own excrement. . . .
>
> I am in pretty bad shape, but they put me in the general ward now, and I am glad of the chance to send you this note. (409–10)

For the arrogantly innocent prisoner who first learned about homosexuality in prison and was appalled, such psychosomatic suffering represents an astonishing change. In another sense, however, it fits comprehensibly into the context of childhood and his mother's remembered death. No wonder, then, that images of prison as a dark cavern proliferate while Berkman's narrative draws to its climax. The autobiographer's deepest desires are for death more than for rebirth in love, and these feelings are expressed with a frank urgency quite different from Whitman's hospital memories.

"Resurrection," the brief final section of the story, is thus understandably laced with graveyard images and hints of impending death. Berkman's release and return to Emma Goldman and the Pioneers of Liberty are marked by bitter feelings of isolation. Though he could pour out his soul to her in letters from prison, when he is actually reunited with The Girl he is mute; he can only gnaw at the petals of the bouquet she presses into his hand. Although his "stay in the penitentiary was a continuous struggle that was the breath of life" (498), freedom brings bitter thoughts and rehearsals of oblivion.

That the ex-prisoner's mind still circles back to boyhood is reflected in the most touching of the closing episodes—Berkman's attempt to find love with a Cleveland prostitute. The scene opens prophetically with the purchase of a revolver and closes in Buffalo with the girl abandoning him for a more responsive lover. Like the woman's odd nickname, Frenchy, these details make a coherent pattern. The gun points beyond the last page of *Prison Memoirs* to the event repeatedly predicted which cannot occur in the narrative: Berkman's suicide in Nice in 1934. Together with the Buffalo locale, the revolver also recalls McKinley's assassination in that city and the ideological crisis Czolgosz precipitated. Moreover, the whore's name, her sordid surroundings, her older friend with the brutish, domineering husband, and her pathetic attempts to interest him in love all provide meaningful clues to the autobiographer's emotional state, his psychic "turn to the wall." On the lake steamer, Frenchy seeks to awaken romance by reciting the banal poem which begins "Mother dear, the days were young / When posies in our garden hung." But he remains unresponsive—impotent, in fact—and watches with resigned relief when she goes off with another man. The writer's memory recreates here not merely a particularly painful moment of his postprison ordeal but one which shows unabated oedipal energies still churning. His own mother and father, an assassin's gun and an anarchist's deed, even that long-ago dinner-table quarrel about the chambermaid—all are alive, exerting dominion over the writer's emotions and behavior. Even Frenchy's name has meaning for the reader who recalls the boyish gesture of defiance and frustrated love: flinging the saltcellar against the French mirror. In a literal sense the past is a prison which Alexander Berkman still inhabits. As one realizes the weight of this truth, his title echoes with enhanced aptness and irony.

Prison Memoirs closes with a return to beginnings and the autobiographer's original insight: "The revolutionist is born." In many of the narrative's crucial moments and gestures can be seen a man and a child. The child within the man is an imperious psyche beating its fists against the father's world. But the mature writer who looks back on his prison self and boyish rebellions is also the ideologue who rationally analyzes American exploitation and oppression and carefully distinguishes Russian from American social reality. Western Penitentiary is an actual place recaptured with a proto-novelist's discerning eye and ear. It is as real as any of the hospitals along the Potomac were for Whitman, as real as Shiloh's log house for Grant. If the book turns increasingly confessional and suicidal, its tenuous balance between violence and love nearly lost at the end, these changes reflect an actual prisoner's reentry to the world of 1906. Furthermore, history records

Thanatos's triumph in Berkman's case nearly as inevitably as in the case of Malcolm X. We sense from internal evidence in his autobiography that the suicide will occur, just as we have ample grounds for anticipating the fated moment in the Audubon Ballroom.

By the same process of multilayered communication, *Prison Memoirs* suggests, perhaps more clearly than some other forms of history, why anarchism as an American radical movement aroused the almost hysterical opposition which Berkman, Goldman, and Johan Most suffered during these turbulent decades. Given the actual number of anarchists, the even smaller number of violent deeds committed by these passionate ideologues, their virulent persecution and suppression seems a fit subject for the psychohistorian. Although the matter is doubtless complex, one aspect of this situation is vividly dramatized in Berkman's book. At the manifest level, it records an actual assassination attempt upon a businessman-hero nearly as admired by the American public as Andrew Carnegie. Here anarchism really meant bloodshed. Even more disturbing, however, is the underlying psychological message incarnated in Berkman's career and character. One of Freud's discontents, this anarchist honestly and openly detests civilization. He really wishes to kill fathers and to possess, if only in death, his own mother. Out of an actual family past Berkman generates impulses which are expressed publicly and violently at Pittsburgh in July 1892. Finally, after surviving the horrors of fourteen penitentiary years, he has found the language with which to express inner and outer violent reality. The book's power to move and shock persists. As the first great American prison narrative, *Prison Memoirs of an Anarchist* exemplifies the force of Jean Genet's moral insight about prison autobiographies, which "do not meet in what is still called ignominy: starting in search of themselves from that ignominy demanded by social repression, they discover common ground in the audacity of their undertaking, in the rigor and accuracy of their ideas and visions. In prison more than elsewhere one cannot afford to be casual."[17]

II

As its title foreshadows, *Ushant* stands in sharp contrast to Berkman's ideological narrative of political terrorism, pain, and death. Aiken largely ignores war, politics, and the organized violence of social institutions and ideologies. Instead he recreates himself as an archetypal private person turning his back upon history, chiefly the years between the two world wars, "those giant parentheses between which his life had had to run the gantlet (like all mankind) from beginning to end."[18] He prefers instead to record a passionate lifelong struggle to turn turbulent private experience into enduring art. His title directs attention to this inner landscape of the imagination which, we soon discover, is fully as violent as any of his more public-minded predecessors or contemporaries. The mysterious word "Ushant" is simultaneously a place, a pun, and a symbol of the self. First of all, Ushant is a geographical spot, the tiny island in the English Channel which marks a dangerous but welcome landfall for the traveler from the New World. Hence Aiken reimagines his life initially as a voyage with himself as a secular pilgrim recrossing the Atlantic of previous experience in a Joycean dream which gradually returns to waking reality. As a pun (and Conrad Aiken is one of the master punsters in American literature) Ushant suggests the contradictory prohibitions voiced by an English or a Yankee conscience which is at once his own, his family's, and his culture's. If Aiken's reconstructed life is truly a "comic pilgrimage to death—and love" (149), then Ushant is the comprehensive and ironic admonition—"you shan't"—directed at each one of his obsessive preoccupations: death and profane love, words and wit, social rootlessness and the unremitting exploration of consciousness. He both accepts and rejects these admonitions. In doing so, he defines and celebrates his life as both journey and dance:

> The most intricate and surprising and involved and contrapuntal of dances, and this dance, in which light and darkness were the partners (or all and nothing) was one's life. . . . That shape, which was to be the shape of oneself, and the shape of one's "view" from the little headland of oneself, was immanent, was already there: that map had already been drawn: inward, or outward; one would follow those contours and travel those roads, those seas, make landfall of those shores: they were there, waiting, below the horizon, those houses, those countries, to be lived in and loved: even to the perhaps unattainable—or approachable only at peril of shipwreck—Ushant. (243)

As his language intimates, the author of this autobiographical dance or voyage is a symbolist poet and novelist. *Ushant* is an experimental narrative presided over by the artistic presences of Melville, James, and Joyce rather than the social concerns of Chernyshevsky and Whitman. In approaching the frontiers of fantasy, it opens *in medias res*—"beginning without beginning, water without a seam, or sleep without a dream." It closes in the same way: "like notes of music arranging themselves in a divine harmony, a divine unison, which, as it had no beginning, can have no end—." In between, the reader is continually bathed in a subjective consciousness dramatized—and distanced—as the narrator D. This Kafkalike *persona* suggests even more facets to the authorial identity than Berkman's Rakhmetov. D. recalls, first, William Demarest, the protagonist of Aiken's 1927 novel, *Blue Voyage,* and the kindly amateur psychologist of the later (and finer) novel *Great Circle.* D. also represents the *Doppelgänger,* the dreamer, the musical note, or a detached dimension of the authorial imagination. Aiken launches all these possible implications in the opening dream sequence, which is also an autobiographical dialogue. "The relationship, then—(said D. to himself)—was that of the finder of the camera to the landscape which it 'finds,' and in which it is found: the two are in fact participants of one scene. And is the finder the 'I' as well as the *eye?* the one who sees, the one who knows, the one who is consciousness?" (7). Later he extends this camera metaphor by calling D. the artificer who deploys himself as the shape of his own artifact, thus separating the "narrating" self from the "subject" self (305–6). D. also figures in a recurrent dream as one of four translators of a novella which turns out to be *Ushant.* On still another level—for Aiken's autobiography resembles in several respects a piece of Turkish pastry—D. is the decipherer or dissector of the narrative imagined as a palimpsest, onion, or crystal.

Such a rich profusion of metaphors, analogies, and devices is called for by the challenge Aiken sets himself: "to be as conscious as possible . . ."; to understand "the workings of his psyche, and of the springs and deficiencies and necessities and compulsions, the whole subliminal drive which had made him a writer to begin with. . . . He had discussed, with the farouche John, and with the Tsetse too, the notion, for example, of presenting a poem, or a piece of fiction, complete with the formulative matrix, the psychological scaffolding, out of which it was in the act, the very act, of crystallizing" (246). More fully than *Preludes for Memnon, The Divine Pilgrim,* or *Great Circle, Ushant* represents the realization of this ambition, the dream of self as an imaginative act complete within its "formulative matrix." Nearly every critic of Aiken from Malcolm Cowley to Jay Martin and Arthur Waterman has pointed out how his writings—the poems, stories, novels, plays, and essays which eventually filled more than forty volumes—are all essentially explorations of self, investigations of individual identity. Even more clearly than Stephen Spender, whose autobiography *World Within World* is at once his most characteristic and richest accomplishment, Aiken has made himself *the* representative autobiographical poet of his generation. In this regard his aim and art differ sharply from that of his Harvard friend and rival, T. S. Eliot, the "Tsetse" of the above passage and—by contrast, at least—the arch-bishop of impersonal poetry. Aiken is wholly "concerned with the inner side of personalities, or rather *a* personality," as Henry A. Murray has observed. "He has never even *tried* to get outside himself. At the very outset, it seems, he knew his special fate: to follow the grain of his nature and thereby to discover, in his own singular and undupli-cated mind, the features of other inward turning minds."[19] Neverthe-less, as Murray himself recognizes, Aiken's autobiography creates no imaginary realm. As the explication of a singular self, *Ushant* records a half-century's strenuous and bitter engagement with external reality which, though it contains no *attentats* or prisons, is nonetheless cha-otic and violent enough to call forth all the poet's powers of inner op-position and artful containment.

The central and traumatic event in "that crazy voyage" which was Aiken's life and of which *Ushant* is "its true bill of lading" (249) is so sensational that it would probably be known in advance to many readers had Aiken not pursued so private a career. But Aiken shunned the spotlight of history so successfully (and was ignored by history) that his autobiography never resembles *The Education of Henry Adams* which he so admired. *Ushant* is a mysterious and enigmatic story but was never privately printed for an intimate circle of friends. It is a pub-lic record of very private violence and death. And its three hundred pages, which postpone the brutal fact of his parents' deaths, are not at all like Adams's elaborate narrative with its silent center. Far from it; *Ushant*'s pages are filled with emotional anticipations and imagina-tive translations of the event which, when it comes, is related with al-most laconic drama:

> One was, at one and the same time, retaining the house at Sa-vannah, and the gay card-parties, and the timeless walk to the telegraph office, and the extraordinary quarrels—as in that mysterious episode which he had introduced into an early story, when he had looked down over the banisters to see his father sitting on his mother's knee, with his arm around her, and had heard him say, as he softly retreated, "Yes, if you don't stop this insensate round of party-going, with the inevitable neglect of your children, then there's just one way to put an end to it: I'll have another child!—"—He was retaining all this, and re-enacting it, even to the final scene of all: when, after the desultory early-morning quarrel, came the half-stifled scream, and then the sound of his father's voice counting three, and the two loud pistol shots; and he had tiptoed into

the dark room, where the two bodies lay motionless, and apart, and, finding them dead, found himself possessed of them forever.

Then follows immediately Aiken's extraordinary insight into the personal significance of his violent orphaning: "But, also, even as he looked back at these, and their immobility, as of artifact, he knew that he was irrevocably dedicated to a lifelong—if need be—search for an equivalent to it all, in terms of his own life, or work; and an equivalent that those two angelic people would have thought acceptable" (302–3).

The brute fact of sudden death is, then, one of the central meanings of Ushant. As "that name [which] had dominated the germinal dream, and therefore the theme of the imagined book" (326), Ushant stands for a cataclysmic event pervading and defining all subsequent existence. Dream and reality unite at the symbolic spot around which the narrative, like the life it replicates, is organized. Little wonder, then, the complexity and density of this autobiographical essay. Not only is Aiken attempting the impossible task of total self-explication, but he does so out of a consciousness laden with the legacy of excruciating, crippling loss.

One scarcely needs the testimony of an expert psychologist of suicide like Albert C. Cain to recognize here an instance of "the almost uniquely inexpressible tragedy that a parent's suicide presents to a child, a tragedy reaching even beyond other childhood bereavements."[20] As much as perhaps any account can, Ushant expresses "the almost uniquely inexpressible." Although Aiken does not trace in detail his historic and social identity, the challenge of properly responding to Ushant as psychological confession and act of catharsis remains. Around such a core, Ushant makes a coherent design out of the conscious and preconscious history of its author as small child, eleven-year-old orphan, youthful poet, and older man. To compound complexity, two of these selves are intimately familiar with psychological theory. "Aiken's abettor," writes Murray, "the psychopompos who illumined his pilgrim-rake's progress through the seven circles of the mind, inward, downward, and backward, was quite obviously Sigmund Freud." Murray elaborates the crucial connection thus: "Almost alone in his generation Aiken proved equal to the peril. He allowed the Freudian dragon to swallow him, and then, after a sufficient sojourn in its maw, cut his way out to a new freedom. When he emerged he was stocked with the lore of psychoanalysis but neither subjugated nor impeded by it. . . ."[21] Surely one of the best evidences of such mastery is Ushant, in which Aiken's first reading of *The Interpretation of*

Dreams makes a major moment: "the magical bucket had at last been lowered into the only, the infinite, magical well" (174). This helps to explain his choice of dreaming soliloquy as the form and substance of his story.[22]

The way into Aiken's labyrinth of consciousness and the unconscious is indicated by a hundred hints dropped before the decisive moment and by lengthy explications left in its wake. Nevertheless, one should guard against reducing the story to this single explanatory equation. D. defines his own tale as "that receding *passacaglia* of symbols . . . which, no matter how often one removed the successive surfaces, to reveal a new hieroglyph, forever came up with the same mystic equation: YOU" (19). That YOU is the sum of many experiences, not just one. But it, or he, has been split in two by the violent climax of Aiken's boyhood. Death has annihilated time and decisively and permanently separated a part of him from his world. Thus spatial movement—the countless voyages back and forth from America to Ariel's Island (his name for England), from Savannah north to New Bedford and Cambridge—assumes a curious double meaning. From D.'s "narrating" viewpoint, there is actually a self in the story who lives, moves, writes, and loves. But in another, equally valid sense the "subject" D.'s life demonstrably stopped in Savannah some time before those two pistol shots reverberated through the house on Oglethorpe Avenue. In a fundamental way his psyche has been fixed even more inexorably at and by this moment than Berkman's is by the death of his mother. Artistically, of course, Aiken's psychic arrest produces something quite different from *Prison Memoirs of an Anarchist*. The shape of his poetic narrative resembles the "stillness of motion round an invisible center" (329). As a self translated into words, his life exhibits henceforth no "progress." All narrative motion becomes not linear but "annular" or "spiral," without beginning or end; everything is presented "as on one time level." Aiken's life as "actual" experience within time, geography, and society is therefore firmly held within a time-free dreamer's imagination. That gripping (and gripped) consciousness converts historical actor into autobiographical character:

No, the conversion was clearly, as one could realize after the event, a resolution of feelings and attitudes of long standing, perhaps lifelong: perhaps it was now possible to say that it was only by obeying the ghostly summons of the poet of White Horse Vale, and going to Ariel's Island, and accepting it and being accepted by it, that he had been able to accomplish what essentially and profoundly all this time he had most wanted

173

and needed to accomplish, the retention of that nursery floor, that room, that house in Savannah, that house and the vivid life in it—father and mother, and the tremendous parties downstairs, which D. could watch through the banisters of the curved staircase, and the deeply satisfying sense of belonging to it all, whether there, or at New Bedford, or Cambridge. (300)

Once again the "objective correlative" (250) of converted and arrested existence—of a self transformed by violence and by the energetic and obsessive need to *get back behind* that violence—is the tiny Channel rock. "And hadn't his entire life been simply a *locus* bending itself again and again, after no matter how many interruptions and diversions, as of wars, or storms at sea, to this limit, this perhaps unattainable limit, this imperative and imperishable Ushant?" (300).

But Ushant can never represent simply a resting place, no matter how urgently a part of Aiken's autobiographical consciousness yearns for stasis. Standing in the Channel, the rock and lighthouse point westward to the New World from which Aiken comes and to which he invariably returns. But they also point eastward to England. Ariel's Island is the symbol and substance of civilization and poetic tradition to which Aiken attaches himself when he settles at Saltinge (his name for Rye). Life then is continuous movement—physical, emotional, imaginative—of which the ocean swirling around the rock is the comprehensive symbol. Each time Aiken repasses Ushant he is a different person. Yet he truly remains the same child he was on the upstairs nursery floor in Savannah reading *Tom Brown's School Days*. In one sense, then, he lives "in a world of awareness in which all was in motion, the values and meanings changing their names and faces at will, and the personality itself—if it could be called such—constantly dissolving into the discontinuous and inapprehensible discreteness of causal or temporal series" (304). But for the other self, space and history are truly frozen by the images and intricate rhetoric of *Ushant*. Thus, through his double persona D., Aiken dramatizes the classic paradox of autobiographical identity: continuity and change.

The polarities of this double self are explored in two complementary, interwoven ways. The first is narrative recapitulation of historical experience imagined as geography and map. On this biographical chart everything is depicted in pairs. America precedes, leads to, and succeeds England. Savannah stands over against New England. America is his native land and the prime locus of his imaginative identification with his dead father. England, conventionally *and* psychologically, is the motherland, the locale for sexual initiation, poetic inspiration, and his own attempted suicide. If Savannah represents raw, red memories (not simply of the family tragedy but also of the city's "stinking feculent alleys" with their "rich and rancid" Negro life), then New Bedford and Cambridge stand for the "formed" and colder frame of conscious family tradition which receives the orphan and makes him a cultivated man and a poet. Henry James, the American Master of Lamb House, presides spiritually over his English initiation, while William Blackstone, the gentle English Puritan poet who settled at Shawmut in Massachusetts Bay, serves as mentor to Aiken's loving appreciation of the wilder American landscape. Thus *Ushant* matches *The Education of Henry Adams* in its contrapuntal and symbolic geography.

The second device for containing and expressing the fierce dualities of his life is metaphor, the poet's painfully acquired and characteristic idiom. Aiken's "equivalents of the still shadowy self" (92) are as conventional and intricate as the map of his outward life, to which they are closely connected. The sea, ships and voyages, houses and trees, and lines of verse are major symbolic notes in the rich *passacaglia*. Less frequent but still significant images of the self are certain concrete objects: his father's secret portfolio of poems discovered after the disaster, the revolver purchased on Aiken's first European trip, his own face in the mirror. Each finds its place in the narrative flow as "equivalents of being," evidence of simultaneous existence on social, literary, and psychic levels. Each contributes a note or chord to the rich composition, one imaginatively more intricate even than *Prison Memoirs*. This is scarcely surprising: prison life affords Berkman a narrower (though equally intense) range of experience and metaphor than Aiken's poetry, travels, and loves.

Though *comedy* (in the form of wit, puns, and irony directed at the self as well as at others) also distinguishes Aiken from Berkman, another distinctive motif in *Ushant* is heterosexual love. As sexual passion preeminently, but also in friendships of all sorts, love defines to a surprising degree the tone and tenor of this history. Nevertheless, important as these elements are, they derive ultimate significance in relation to the deepest concern of the inward voyager, one which finally links his life and art to that of Berkman. "Creative *moritura*"—as his friend Hambo (Malcolm Lowry) discusses with lugubrious delight—fills D.'s waking and dreaming thoughts, spilling forth in most of what he writes. "The obsession with death, with abnormal sensibility and death, informed them everywhere: the reek of decay and dissolution and corruption arose from them every morning of his

175

life" (241). These "dark spoutings from the foul unconscious" are as inescapably real as the deaths of his parents or the later deaths (several by suicide) of adult friends and fellow poets (242). Eventually, however, Aiken triumphs over his obsession as Berkman does not. Moreover, he achieves this victory *autobiographically* by confronting and explaining personal morbidity, not by translating it always into poetic symbol, persona, or fictional plot. Unlike his admired predecessor Adams—who can only displace the bitter specter of suicide from his wife to his sister Louisa's accidental death, where it can be voiced and borne—Aiken faces down his violent past, openly acknowledging its compelling power over his adult self. He thereby deals with it *both analytically and imaginatively.* Few American autobiographies manage to depict actual loss and imagined pain on as many levels as this narrative of a reflective poet's life.

In widest perspective, death is embraced as inextricably part of all living, growing, loving, and creating. Violent separation at a crucial age from his father and mother can be seen, then, only as an extreme instance of the necessary separation of self from family and society which initiates "the long and vivid process of dying which we call life. To be able to *separate* oneself from one's background, one's environment—" D. muses, "wasn't this the most thrilling discovery of which consciousness was capable? and no doubt for the very reason that as it is a discovery of one's limits, it is therefore by implication the first and sharpest taste of death" (32). This vital discovery is born in a child's earliest memories of nighttime separations from the beloved mother when the gas flame in the bedroom goes out. Such tiny "deaths" are first steps toward the ultimate end as well as reminders of intermediate crises like D.'s own attempted suicide at Saltinge, when he turns the gas on.

Indeed, Aiken finds death to be the recurrent theme of all family ties. After the searing loss in Savannah commits the orphan boy to the lonely task of attaching himself to his Massachusetts relatives, his joining *them* and their accepting *him* are both confirmed by deaths. One of these is the grandmother's protracted dying in a nursing home. Another, more significant moment is Aunt Jean's funeral, at which he first feels "the simultaneity of belonging and of being, of group anonymity and individual identity: tradition and the individual talent . . . as the Tsetse was to say!" (96). Aiken's initial sense of self, then, is anchored in separation and loss. "Was this perhaps true of everything, and everywhere—and was it perhaps only in the profoundest experience of annihilation, and of the dissolution of all hope and pride and identity, in the great glare of cosmic consciousness, that one could regain one's power to *value?*" (223). Thus the experience of violence—for violence is here an apt synonym for separation—constitutes an education in values, which D. describes characteristically as first "being lost at sea" and then as reading further in that lexicon "of which he had learned the first vast and shocking syllables at Savannah" (223).

But the comforting and creative matrix of family, cultural tradition, and death which replaces Savannah's "more singular violences with a swifter, deeper notation" (91), cannot emerge until D.'s adolescent psyche begins to deal consciously with the parents' suicide. For suicide is no normal death. It cannot be explained by the usual rationalizations. Only an extraordinary act of emotional confrontation can make headway against the devastating feelings of pain, loss, guilt, shame, and rage which this highly sensitive boy must have experienced. We know what this might have been like only from the viewpoint of the "narrating" D., who represents the sixty-three-year-old autobiographer. Any psychological reconstruction or reentry into the repressed or expressed feelings of 1901 can therefore take place only in terms of the literary narrative the older self has created. This fact is underlined by the strategy Aiken adopts of turning himself into a supremely self-conscious poet and "devotee of the word." A whole series of imaginative acts recorded in *Ushant* convert him into successive images of the little boy who first looked into a book and read the magical line: "I'm the Poet of White Horse Vale, Sir, with Liberal notions under my cap." This small ancestral figure who is the core self lies secure within the family past before the cataclysm—doubly secure in his embryonic possession of the means of coping with catastrophe. Before the deaths occurred, that is, the boy has caught the contagion of Hughes's epigraph and decided to make himself a poet. Thus is initiated a course of action of which the departed father and mother would have been proud "and which therefore saw to it that he *thus kept them*" (302). A life of art is the chosen means of appeasing *and* repossessing "those two angelic people" who have in fact committed the monstrous egotism of murdering themselves. Intensely painful facts of private life and consciousness can be translated into poems, stories, essays, novels, and autobiography because they must. Violence makes art vitally necessary for Conrad Aiken. As D. puts it, "the prospect and immediacy of death had made him a poet" (152).

The psychological mechanism for transmitting and transmuting reality is first identification with the father. This massive, early, and conscious identification—which contrasts with a more oblique expression of feelings for his dead mother—is the most notable feature of *Ushant* distinguishing it sharply from *Prison Memoirs of an Anarchist.*

One notices at once the fierce energy and literary focus of Aiken's psychic tie. The deep feelings of anger and guilt, which psychologists insist inevitably characterize the response of actual survivors of family suicide, have been repressed or displaced. So, too, have the complex oedipal emotions of an eleven-year-old boy who, we have reason to believe, was just entering puberty when the tragedy occurred. Related responses to the situation—a boy's overwhelming sense of personal worthlessness, shattered self-esteem, and the need to prove his parents wrong in their low opinions of him—are likewise shadowy or suppressed. Instead, what Aiken finds more manageably expressive is an actual event which points forward to the resolution of the boy's emotional turmoil. That is his discovery of his father's private portfolio in which a whole sheaf of significant papers is contained. This "symposium of the family" reveals a complex three-generation legacy—a penchant for poetry, liberal religious thought, and uninhibited sexual gusto—available from his New England ancestors. Particularly crucial are the secret poems of his physician-father, some of them "startlingly carnal love poems." Among them, too, is the father's suicide poem, neatly folded by the grandparents next to newspaper accounts of the tragedy. D. also discovers himself in the emblematic volume. He is, first, the small child depicted in a comic sketch by his father. This baby looks out at him as the very image of "life's blatant effrontery, its sheer impudence" (33). More important, he is there in the form of his very first poem, which his father has carefully preserved—and actually rewritten as one of his own verses! Writing, therefore, is the "family habit, or cloak, which he must himself, naturally, try on" (108). Furthermore, the actual thinness of this ancestral art—for neither his father's verses nor his grandmother's are very good—offers him the opportunity not simply to join but also to excel. Two of his Massachusetts relatives in particular encourage identification and rivalry with the dead, disgraced parent, whom they conspire with D. to mythologize as "the brilliant but lost one" (106). Through them D. begins to find himself in the effort to overcome the shame and guilt of his family past. "The *persona*, yes, of the father had thus been adopted," he writes, "and with this, had proceeded a parallel adaptation, the taking over of the father's role as a writer. 'The Poet of White Horse Vale, Sir, with Liberal notions under my cap—'; no doubt, this had been the first occurrence of the magic, the all-precipitating word or at any rate the occasion for the first explanation of it: poets, there were such things as poets: they wrote poems! . . . But there was also the further fact that *father* wrote poems; and then typed them on his Blickensderfer typewriter, as, a decade later, the Tsetse was to do" (107).

Two of several ironies in this account of self-definition and catharsis are worth noting. First, the odd fact that the father's poems are typed on prescription pads once used by the brilliant, perverse physician. Poems are prescriptions for all sorts of sickness. The other detail is the Blickensderfer typewriter, which makes the connecting link to T. S. Eliot and his machine. This detail explains both the absence of overt anger and enmity toward the dead father (whom, it is significant, he never accuses of murdering his mother) and Aiken's mixed admiration and dislike of Eliot, feelings clearly telegraphed to the reader in his unsubtle pseudonym. If the son cannot bring himself to express openly all the ambiguous feelings still harbored toward his dead parent, he can—and does—transfer some of these emotions onto others. Eliot makes a good substitute for several reasons: not simply because his pseudonym suggests a deadly disease and because he looks eternally middle-aged and prim, but also because his embrace of religious orthodoxy seems to Aiken an escape (not unlike suicide) from the turbulent realities of modern secular life. Later, D.'s mixture of hostility and love finds another displaced object in Hambo, for Malcolm Lowry plays the son's role in a highly oedipalized master-disciple relationship which dominates the final pages of *Ushant.* Even more clearly than with Eliot, this literary friendship exemplifies the fiercely aggressive and deeply affectionate feelings so curiously blended in D.'s career and identity.

Although Aiken explores and defines his obsession with death with even more energy and fascination than Berkman or Whitman, *Ushant* is finally very different in its thanatoid dimension from either *Specimen Days* or *Prison Memoirs.* The crucial difference, as we have suggested, is the comic candor of D.'s recreated love life. The "importance of the sexual behavior" (306) is the other side of the coin from his death wish. This counterpointed motif is treated more extensively and ironically than Whitman's attraction to young soldiers or Berkman's tragic "boy love" in the penitentiary. Sexual love for Aiken is both autobiographical theme and coefficient of his art. As he records the succession of wives and mistresses D. has known and made love to, the other D. turns these "Loreleis" into artifacts. The women emerge as characters in countless stories and poems, symbols of the ideal and the actual. His canting names suggest the range of feminine character thus transmogrified—Cynthia, Faubion, Maid Marion, Agnes Fatuous, Anabel the Kensington Bluestocking, Irene the London streetwalker with whom he loses his cursed virginity, and his successive wives Loreleis One, Two, and Three. None of these is listed in the "key" which stands at the beginning of the autobiography to

179

identify actual people behind the pseudonyms. Eliot is named there; Pound is "Rabbi Ben Ezra," and many members of his family are found in this list of *personae*. But Aiken's women remain clothed in an anonymity which merges autobiographical discretion and fictional type-casting.

There is another impulse behind D.'s discreet indiscretions. Sexual love in *Ushant* is not simply personal history and picaresque adventure. Though celebrated as the vital counterweight to a morbid preoccupation with death, it has also a darker, dangerous side. In virtually every one of his amorous adventures, some force closely allied to the erotic impulse operates to corrupt and eventually kill the tie D. so incessantly seeks. If, as he asserts, his whole life is a "furious dialogue" between love and death, then D.'s affairs, marriages, and divorces are phases in an equally furious dialogue between man and woman—and within the "nympholept" consciousness of the author as well. Small wonder, then, that he hides the actual identity of all but one or two of the women he has loved and left. Aiken's honesty in exploring this dimension of self and experience (surely the modern equivalent of Rousseau's) leads into recesses as dark as any illuminated by the conscious identification with his father. For erotic love, as at once salvation and damnation, leads D. inexorably back into his Savannah past and into the presence of his dead mother. The "echo, the shadow, the influence, the sound of the vanishing nymph-cry" which is heard everywhere in *Ushant* represents both the plaintive voice of D.'s lovers and the fainter voice of "she now dead these fifty years!" (62).

Aiken acknowledges the ghostly maternal presence that awakens and murders love in the passage which most clearly asserts his need for love as artistic food. "From base and basic need to low-level self-esteem, and thus to the energy for the artifact, and the mercurial substance out of which it must be wrought" (314)—this is the writer's description of and rationale for sexual experience. His insatiable ego needs love and conquests as materials for art. Even the most sordid of affairs are turned into "parables of pity" (309). But behind and beyond the artificer's desire hovers a shadowy presence:

> the renewal of the sense of wholeness and unity; and that extraordinary residual and nostalgic ache, the haunting overtone of something like an inexpressible sorrow, which, although unhappy itself, seemed invariably to accompany even the serenest and sunniest of loves, and to give it its true character. Was it the element of *moritura* in it, the feeling of impermanence,

180

on the one hand, and of incompleteness on the other—the dazzle that was so perishable, the haloed sun-angel that was so momentary, the outline of magic that one instinctively knew was too beautiful to approach, and would vanish indeed, if one did? (314–15)

D. stops just short here of naming his mother as the ideal, inexpressible sorrow of his love life. But *"moritura,"* perishable beauty, nostalgic ache, and the image of the "haloed sun-angel" surely all point in her direction. One recalls, in the crucial description of his finding the parents' bodies, that their deaths committed him to the lifelong "search for an equivalent . . . that those two angelic people would have thought acceptable" (303). This suggests that a dual identification has taken place in Aiken's autobiographical consciousness: first with the father and art, then with the mother and sexual love. Since art and sex are as intimately linked as his parents were in life and death, his identification embraces all four. Just as the boy has grown into the poet his father was (only *better*), so the poet has become the passionately unstable lover he imagines his mother to be—only *more* passionate, *more* fickle. By loving, betraying, and then turning into fiction a succession of wives and mistresses, D. acts out his dual devotion to his dead mother as muse and love object and to his dead father as ideal (and hated) self. He has, in other words, identified with her, with him, and with them both. Aiken's psychic solution is expressed in the poetic language with which D. continues and concludes his soliloquy over "that nymph-cry in the forest" (315).

"I have not lost or destroyed my parent, he is inside of me." Thus T. L. Dorpat describes the identification with the suicide parent which surviving children frequently make.[23] Idealization, too, is another of the survivor's commonest defense mechanisms. Both psychic processes are openly and powerfully at work in *Ushant.* In a complex process extending over fifty years, he has internalized both the ethereal presence of his mother, which is projected onto or acted out in the idyllic affairs with Marian and Irene, and the aggressive, egotistic reality represented by her suicide. That act, as Freud points out, must be seen as a form of aggression—indeed, as a kind of murder; "probably no one finds the mental energy required to kill himself unless, in the first place, in doing so he is at the same time killing an object with whom he has identified himself, and, in the second place, is turning against himself a death-wish which had been directed against someone else."[24] Though Freud's dictum describes the father perhaps better than the mother, as a description of narcissistic aggression it clearly applies to both. Because Aiken has identified with both, he has internalized this unconscious enmity which must have existed between husband and wife in order for them to commit the double suicide. This fatal combination of romantic attachment and hostile aggression has been introjected and made a part of his own psyche.

Furthermore, this emotional complex is assigned a geographical location in Aiken's autobiographical imagination. It is formed first at the house of Savannah, where the idyll of childhood was so violently ended. Later it encompasses England, to which D. constantly travels to "rejoin the motherland" (142) and also to immerse himself in "the destructive element" (135). Thus "lodestar London," the place where his virginity is gently and romantically lost with Irene, is also (and increasingly as the narrative progresses) the spot for some brutal and cruel affairs. Of his capacity for inflicting pain D. speaks quite candidly: "Was it true, as some thought, that there was a streak of murderousness in him—a sadism, and cruelty, that made him capable of calculated murder?" (159). Often this destructive impulse dissolves in laughter, as in the case of the revolver acquired for his first European trip which terrifies the Italian chambermaid. Nothing lethal happens with this weapon except that it is once accidentally (and symbolically) discharged into a bed. Hence England is the locale for fully as much personal (and particularly marital) aggression as America is with D.'s ostensibly "wilder violences." After all, Ushant stands as England's lighthouse; its beacon is poised upon dangerous rocks "dedicated to blood and death" (327).

This confession of D. himself as a cruel lover living by betrayal of the other and loss to the self climaxes in the account of his attempted suicide at Saltinge. Like other significant scenes in *Ushant,* this episode unites love and death. In the very moment of losing consciousness in the gas-filled kitchen he thinks of a mistress's love letter which his wife will discover. So he staggers comically out to safety. Released by this ritual reenactment of parental history, D. expresses at first no remorse at having tried to betray his three small children exactly as he himself and his brothers were once betrayed; "for wasn't his life his own, to do with as he pleased?" (228). Soon, however, the deeper truth comes home:

> . . . how comprehensive had been his betrayal of all that he most profoundly and integrally set store by, the very light by which he had proposed to live. What sort of priest of consciousness was he who would himself be the first to take flight from it? and hadn't this been a double betrayal? For, quite apart

182

from the failure in his career, his work, wasn't there also that obligation, as pointed up by grandfather—both to the ancestors and the descendants—of transmitting the preciously learned inheritance? Weren't the three little D.'s, and his work, in this regard, practically synonymous? (240–41)

Here speaks the superego of his New England clerical grandfather. Unitarian admonitions often suppressed in a life spent in artistic and sensuous rebellion against religion and conscience return in the brave but slightly hollow words of his new wisdom. "Release, yes: for if the past had by no means been expunged—in fact, it was vivider than ever—just the same, it had been, in some uncanny fashion, finished. . . . And the pages to come, would they not now be richer than any hitherto, and more rewarding and surprising, if only because they were the pages he himself tried to tear from the book, the pages he had decided never to read? Grace abounding for the chief of sinners! no doubt about that" (228). "You shan't" at this point becomes the significant pun and ironic reminder of ineradicable Yankee origins and outlook. A post-Puritan ideology coexists with Aiken's "European" libertinism. Both, moreover, feed upon strong self-destructive urges.

This New England conscience helps as much as any other dimension of his psyche to define Aiken as an American artist. His moral identification with the New World is, I think, symbolically confirmed by the curious fact that, for all his love of Saltinge and the house there, he can never bring himself to dig an English garden; "the real truth was that to touch that earth was treason" (333). New Bedford, Cape Cod, and Savannah together form a spiritual landscape whose pull makes it impossible for him either to feel completely at home in England or to kill himself there. The invitation to destruction must therefore be refused. An essential American rootlessness is accepted as the only road for the "priest of consciousness" to travel. "Once one felt at home," he recognizes, "one would have no more to learn, or would have become so relaxed as to be no longer capable of learning; and one's very purpose for having come there at all, or a very important part of it, would be no longer valid" (334).

Hence *Ushant* closes neither with D. secure in a "finished" life after the attempted *felo de se* nor imaginatively returned to Savannah and the childhood tragedy which annihilated time for him in the first place. Instead of these two parentheses of timelessness and death, Aiken's narrative moves further up the spiral of actual experience. As D.'s history, it returns again to America for a long interlude in Mexico in which "the whole Hambo saga" is reenacted. Then the narrative circles back to its beginning, abandoning the waking world to resume the mood and metaphors of dream. But the dream is now of a real world. D. finds himself aboard a World War II troopship, just reconverted to civilian use. The time is 1945 and the *Gray Empress* is bringing "her cargo of uprooted and frightened people" (362) back to Britain. D. participates in this historical return but transforms its social significance into a private and universal meaning: "Well, they were all heroes, every one of them; they were all soldiers; as now, and always, all mankind were soldiers; all of them engaged in the endless and desperate war on the unconscious" (362). His wife Lorelei Three, old friends from before the war, and his three children all await the poet-pilgrim upon his return to Ariel's Island. So, too, does the house in Saltinge. As the dreamer imagines Ushant out there in the dangerous darkness, all the major metaphors of his tormented and creative self are reassembled.

At this point, certain lines of verse are remembered to complete the pattern of the voyager's recreated life and self. If the epigraph from Hughes' *Tom Brown's School Days* stands at the outset for a self already possessed of power to circumvent violence by becoming "the Poet of White Horse Vale," then the middle section of D.'s journey is exemplified in another set of lines:

> Was this the poet? It is man.
> A glass-cased watch, through which you scan
> The feverish fine small mechanism,
> And hear it ticking, while it sings:
> Behold, this delicate paroxysm
> Obedient to rebellious springs! (247)

These lines, we recall, had once been scrawled on the wall of the "Harvard Psychological Clinic Memorial Bathroom" of Aiken's farmhouse on Cape Cod. The inscriber was Lorelei Three, to whom *Ushant* is dedicated. The verse aptly summarizes Aiken's adult self who has indeed behaved like a "delicate paroxysm obedient to rebellious springs."

But the very last lines of verse quoted in *Ushant* discharge these tensions and terrors of the remote and the middle past by returning the reader to another, happier childhood. In the final paragraphs of his narrative, D. recalls a poem his little daughter Jean once wrote about a magical island with a magical mountain on it called Juhoohooa.

> And there was one montenn witch they called Juhoohooa
> Witch was larger than all the others

184

With lovely beards berds beairds in it
And buttful beasts that would come
When you called them
And buttful cats that would come in your window
And lovly froats and flowres flowrs
Witch would flowr all the year round (364)

His daughter's magical mountain becomes another and the final Ushant. Although the narrator hears the roar of real surf in the darkness
outside the ship and knows that real people are drowning in that
ocean, his imagination is rapt by the vision his little daughter has left
him. Another childhood, perhaps less tormented than his own, strikes
the last note in this remarkable narrative of a poet's intensely turbulent and violent life. That note makes "a divine harmony, a divine unison, which, as it had no beginning, can have no end—" (365). Art as
the delightfully misspelled creation of the next generation of family
poets remains Aiken's final and loyal ally in his "endless and desperate
war on the unconscious."

III

Contrasting two such powerfully evocative yet disparate stories as
Prison Memoirs of an Anarchist and *Ushant* illustrates some possibilities but also exposes the limitations of a thematic reading of life-history.
The chief danger is clear: selecting violence as a core experience is at
once too broad and too narrow a focus for interpreting an individual's
past. As everyone knows who is familiar with the growing literature on
violence in contemporary culture and in particular minds, the subject
is of bewildering intricacy and extent. Few of the historical, sociological, or psychological ramifications of American violence are eliminated
by concentrating upon autobiographies. Indeed, it is our argument that
these strands and pressures are all present in this mode of discourse history as in other kinds of historical and imaginative writing. The complex nature of autobiography as an overdetermined explanation of a
personal past makes it dangerous to emphasize even such an essential
aspect, forgetting other constituent elements of reinvented identity.
Thus, though Berkman and Aiken insist upon the primacy of political
and family violence in the evolution of their historic selves, the reader
must not forget another victim's cogent comment: "All of our experiences fuse into our personality," Malcolm X observes. "Everything that
ever happened to us is an ingredient" (150).
    Nonetheless, we have chosen to watch these men gazing into
Cato's mirror because we have been persuaded by their own accounts

that this aspect of the past organizes and focuses many, if not all, parts of their autobiographical identities. Malcolm X's life, as we shall see in Chapter Seven, was surely as violent as either of these men's; so also, in some respects, was Richard Wright's. Yet both these autobiographers subsume violent experiences and tormented relationships under a larger and different pattern. Consequently, the narrative momentum of each story leads through and beyond moments of great pain or shame. Religious conversion and political protest, like the growth of an artistic sensibility, finally overcome bitter memories within the ex-criminal and the novelist. By the end of *Black Boy*, therefore, the child's thoughtless act of arson has been transformed into a comprehensive symbol of his own creative imagination. Berkman and Aiken, on the other hand, though their narratives are highly imaginative acts of containment, keep circling back to violent points in their pasts. Narrative form, as a result, reveals a dual motion: forward into a changing network of new activities and relationships and backward to the traumatic moment of psychic arrest for a vital part of the same self. Both men's behavior and belief (political, aesthetic, and psychological) are bound inexorably to painful times and places.

To be sure, all ideologies contain secret sources of affect which contribute conscious and unconscious energies to the act of commitment. *Prison Memoirs* and *Ushant* are exemplary precisely because their authors articulate a wider range of relevant feelings and associations than most autobiographers are able to summon from "the foul unconscious" (*Ushant,* 242). I believe violence has had much to do with making these eloquent recoveries possible. Terrible memories of loss and suffering may, in certain talented imaginations like Aiken's and Berkman's, trigger massive (though sometimes long-suppressed) responses. One manifestation of this urge in Berkman's case is his impassioned ardor for the people, so similar in some respects to Sullivan's assertions about democratic architecture. That similar attitudes may lead in one instance to the *attentat* and in another to, say, the Owatonna Security Bank building is due to many factors. One autobiographical clue, however, is Berkman's Russian family. Young Sasha's violently conflicted feelings about his parents, which can be seen as oedipal in nature, are politicized at the time of his mother's death by her ambiguous sympathies for both the bourgeois and the nihilist factions within the household. This traumatic confluence causes in Sasha an emotional maelstrom, one of whose later effects is the journey to Pittsburgh. These anarchist beliefs and actions are, in ways Phyllis Greenacre might have explored had she considered politics a form of art, collective alternates, chosen yet predetermined. As we have seen in Chapter Four, a quite different set of social and historical circumstances help Louis Sullivan resolve analogous feelings toward certain of his own family in terms of quite different collective alternates. But we also recall that Sullivan's autobiographical consciousness suppresses other memories which, in the case of Aiken the poet, cannot be suppressed. To the aging author of *Ushant*, recollections of his father and mother remain so vividly attached to the brutal and compelling fact of death that a whole series of adult love affairs and marriages—precisely those relationships Sullivan omits—must be reenacted and linked to "those two angelic people" who are Aiken's equivalents of Sullivan's and Berkman's The People.

Examining and comparing such relationships between external circumstance and inner psychic forces, between ideology and autobiographical language, makes it possible to suggest the process by which originally intense but culturally valueless encounters with violence are endowed with social and moral significance. Each text, in this perspective, combines intractably private and readily sharable realms of reality. As an account of one person's history an autobiography risks being most singular, since it always records an unrepeatable sequence of events. No one's life ever duplicates another's. Hence Berkman's and Aiken's outward stories are as strange to one another and basically incomparable as Black Elk's and Thomas Merton's As literary discourse, however, *Prison Memoirs* and *Ushant* are somewhat closer and easier to compare. Gaps in experience are narrowed as the reader notes how two differently "circumstanced" persons employ similar narrative devices (like the *persona* and the flashback) for the same purpose of simultaneously heightening and distancing emotion. Berkman's Rakhmetov is a simpler political and literary *alter ego* than Aiken's D.; both, however, are appropriate bridges across which we can move into the strange worlds of each man's memory. Furthermore, the metaphors of self used to pattern these disparate pasts are, though not similar, relatively commonplace images. Berkman's American self as Aleck comes alive in the prison-yard tropes of bread, trees, flowers, the moon. Aiken the sophisticated poet also employs many everyday objects to make his historic particularity as a person available to the public. Even the father's scrapbook and typewriter are homely and specific tropes as compared to the more intricate imagery of much of Aiken's poetry.

The accessibility and very commonplaceness of these metaphors of the self underline the fact that these highly imaginative accounts are truly autobiographies. This is most clearly manifested in the case of the guns—the nexus, one can assume, of most American parables of violence. Berkman's pistol, which fails to fire in Frick's office, like Aiken's which does go off into a hotel bed, are after all recognizably historical objects; they are never purely dramatic or psychological symbols. By contrast with these recognizably actual weapons, Kit's lethal rifle in *Badlands* enjoys a far more mythic, even fictional status. This is because Malick seeks a universal statement about American violence and refuses to anchor his story to mere details of the Starkweather murders. He evokes some of that, but even more of the glamor and nostalgic appeal of the Western outlaw. Kit's rifle is thus largely freed from personal and public history to reenact *Civilization and Its Discontents* more nakedly and abstractly than Berkman's pistol.

Violence, then, as one consciously chosen identity theme, illustrates richly the multiple ways impulse and history can converge into an autobiographical occasion. Ancient (or recent) memories of overpowering pain form a highly charged and widely sharable ground on which author and audience meet. Language's infinite resources and the specific strategies of both fictional and journalistic narrative make possible this marriage of the strange and the familiar. Intense, deeply shared affects are as vital to autobiography as to fiction or film. Since sex as explicit personal experience is seldom recaptured in American autobiography (as will be seen in the next chapter), violence serves an important role here as in other areas of American culture.

Indeed, the "ideological problematic" of a still-shocking work like *Prison Memoirs of an Anarchist* is rendered more intelligible and (to a degree) more acceptable to American readers by the unconscious impulses and universal emotions embedded in its political statements. Moreover, subsequent history has made Berkman a prophetic anatomist of American violence, by no means as eccentric today as he was in 1912. His questioning of political legitimacy and his vivid demonstration of the various violences of the American system of justice are repeated in many later prison autobiographies. Even more fundamental, perhaps, is Berkman's illustration of the basic tension between all impersonal ideologies and the act of autobiography itself. George Jackson and Eldridge Cleaver also espouse selflessly (and passionately) the cause of the People in defending criminal acts of violence. Yet for many readers their autobiographical acts of declaring the self merely a cipher and instrument of a revolutionary cause serve to define and personalize each ideologue. Jackson voices the dilemma of many other radical autobiographers when he observes, "I've been asked to explain myself, 'briefly,' before the world has done with me. It is difficult because I don't recognize uniqueness, not as it's applied to individualism, because it is too tightly tied into decadent capitalist culture. . . . But then how can I explain the runaway slave in terms that do not imply uniqueness?" (10). Over half a century before, Berkman gave a trenchant reply to his fellow prisoner's dilemma, one which acknowledges the insidious power of American beliefs in personal uniqueness to undermine other systems. As Bruce Franklin demonstrates in *The Victim as Criminal and Artist,* some of the most eloquent voices from prison have, perhaps unwittingly or reluctantly, defined themselves in the act of denouncing official oppression and violence.[25]

What would impel a victim to risk making bitter memories of violence live forever as constituent elements in a perhaps unwelcomed individuality? Aiken, the poet whose elite, expatriate world seems light years away from Western Penitentiary or Soledad Prison, provides the enigmatic answer all autobiographers instinctively accept. As he looks back in memory at the bodies of his parents lying on the floor, and at himself the small boy gazing at the terrible sight, the aging autobiographer "knew he was irrevocably dedicated to a lifelong—if need be—search for an equivalent to it all . . ." (303). Personal history offers such an equivalent. Telling one's story provides an available antidote to the inescapable fact of death which is the human reality all violence and sudden pain point to. The impulse to find an assuaging order and meaning for the brutal legacy of the personal (and the cultural) past is of course as mysterious in this instance as in other life-stories. It is ultimately a creative response to life's destructiveness. Not everyone can afford to essay that answer, for the past's anguish is as likely to be reawakened as eased in the recreative act of writing one's history. Emma Goldman emphasizes this possibility in Berkman's case. In ensuing chapters we shall see how other exquisitely painful memories can be reexperienced as a result of an autobiographer's courage, memory, and imagination.

6

Becoming a Woman in Male America:
Margaret Mead and Anaïs Nin

IN 1869 JOHN STUART MILL wrote these prophetic words:"We may safely assert that the knowledge men acquire of women, even as they have been and are, without reference to what they might be, is wretchedly imperfect and superficial and will always be so until women themselves have told all they have to tell."[1] Listen to two American women's voices responding to Mill by reconstructing moments from their pasts. The first is that of an obscure Western wife who passed most of her life in Colorado mining towns nearly a century ago. There she knew men like Slippery Joe.

> Once Slippery Joe told me: "In the spring of 1876 I was workin' in Lake City; one day I saw all the boys gatherin' in front of a cabin. I figgered somebody had locked horns, so sauntered over, an' by gol! it was a woman talking politics, "Wimmins Rights," she called it. She said she was a schoolteacher somewhere back East an' she only got nine dollars a month an' men got twenty-four an' it riled her an' she hit the trail a-talkin'—an', kid, it don't look like a square deal, does it? . . . She was a good talker an' we all took in what she said, but I bet it'll be a cold day before I ever vote for a woman."
> "Was she married?"
> "She didn't look it. Her name was Susan B. Anthony. Another woman with her was called Elizabeth Cady Stanton. They was ridin' horseback from one camp to another."[2]

The second voice is that of Anaïs Nin recalling a conversation in Paris during the 1930s with Henry Miller and Lawrence Durrell.

190

"I know," I said, "that this is an important talk, and that it will be at this moment that we each go different ways. Perhaps Henry and Larry will go the same way, but I will have to go another, the woman's way."

At the end of the conversation they both said: "We have a real woman artist before us, the first one, and we ought not to put her down."

I know Henry is the artist because he does exactly what I do not do. . . . He gets outside himself. Until it becomes fiction. It is all fiction.

I am not interested in fiction. I want faithfulness.

All I know is that I am right, right for me. If today I can talk both woman's and man's language, if I can translate woman to man and man to woman, it is because I do not believe in man's objectivity. In all his ideas, systems, philosophies, arts come from a personal source he does not wish to admit. Henry and Larry are pretending to be impersonal. . . .

Poor woman, how difficult it is to make her instinctive knowledge clear!

"Shut up," says Larry to Nancy. She looks at me strangely, as if expecting me to defend her, explain her. Nancy, I won't shut up. I have a great deal to say, for June, for you, for other women.[3]

Though these are but two among thousands of women's voices from the past, Anne Ellis and Anaïs Nin help define the cultural boundaries within which autobiography in modern America has developed as a feminine art. In style, form, and content, *The Life of an Ordinary Woman* (1929) and *The Diary of Anaïs Nin* (1966–76) are radically different and yet secretly similar. Anne Ellis is so inconspicuously and humorously herself that she does not really represent the so-called average woman. Other vigorous expressions of personality also characterize works in the same vein, from *Autobiography of an Elderly Woman* (1911) and *The Autobiography of a Happy Woman* (1915) to *Ossie: The Autobiography of a Black Woman* (1971).[4] Each so-called ordinary individual seeks to escape that pigeonhole by reshaping common experiences and emotions in the necessarily uncommon act of telling her own life story. Ellis asserts:

I will try to write truthfully—why not? Not trying to dress it up or make it any better or in any way to change it. You know Herbert Quick said, "The life of the most ordinary man is interesting and priceless. The trouble is no one can write such a life." But I am going to try it! It will be the life of a very ordinary woman, hundreds just like it all around you, only mine happened to be lived for the most part in the excitements and hardships of mining camps. The record will be in pieces like a crazy quilt, as it comes back to me that way—all in bits. It is so hard to bring out of the garret of my memory things laid by thirty—yes, forty-five years ago (xi–xii).

What follows is a random (though chronological) account of happiness, hardship, and heartbreak—as plot, the very stuff of soap opera. This cheerful wife raised a family in one mountain shack after another and survived to bury two husbands and one child. The brute realities of frontier existence are, however, filtered through a pliable, even acquiescent, mind; she is no Rocky Mountain Susan B. Anthony. The substance of her remembered self is that of dutiful wife and mother within a rough-and-ready man's world. Hardly a milestone in literary history, *The Life of an Ordinary Woman* nonetheless serves as an early benchmark on the road to more imaginative works by more rebellious women writers.

Anaïs Nin is quintessentially one of these imaginative artists. She too inhabits a man's world and knows it. Neither Miller nor Durrell can put her down, however, despite the patent male condescension in their discovery in August 1937 of the first real woman artist. She touches such ironies lightly. More immediate concerns for her are the deeper issues of faithfulness to reality, belief in a personal source for all true knowledge. Nin identifies this mode of understanding with nonfiction, the appropriate mode of woman's intuitive expression. Therefore her *Diary* purportedly records real situations and experiences, actual conversations like this one. This international artist fluent in French, Spanish, and English claims also to understand the language of the sexes, in part because she is a creative writer who has also practiced psychoanalysis. She can speak *to* men, but both *to* and *for* women. The form of such faithful communication cannot be fiction—though Nin eventually wrote ten works of fiction—but rather a new kind of serial autobiography realized in the six volumes of her diary. That lifetime's labor, edited and published during the decade before her death in 1977, is no less unique and innovative an exploration of "the mystery of woman" (1:333) than *The Life of an Ordinary Woman* is typical and traditional.

A great deal had been written by modern American women autobiographers before the appearance of Anne Ellis's modest story in 1929. The names and personal narratives of Elizabeth Cady Stanton, Helen Keller, Jane Addams, Mary Antin, Ida B. Wells, Charlotte Perkins Gilman, and Isadora Duncan, for instance, are familiar to historians of our culture, if not always to literary critics.[5] Their stories afford intimate and irreplaceable accounts of political and social reforms, like the suffrage movement, as well as inside perspectives on more private battles against physical, sexual, racial, and cultural barriers. Thus they strengthen the twentieth-century tradition of women's autobiography, whether as the record of public or private experience, as essentially protest literature.

The half-century since Anne Ellis has been similar in some respects, vastly different in others. Though the number of women's lives written and published has skyrocketed, many such life-stories continue to record struggles against prejudice and oppression. But a notable enlargement in imaginative power and artistry also characterizes the nonfictional art to which Nin pledges her allegiance. In the sphere of public affairs, where women are often still treated as Slippery Joe treated Miss Anthony, important memoirs like those of Emma Goldman, Eleanor Roosevelt, Abigail McCarthy, Anne Moody, and Angela Davis, among numerous others, carry on the tradition of Addams and Stanton.[6] Another group of women with a wider audience are movie stars and entertainers who have sometimes employed (and been exploited by) ghostwriters to fabricate more or less slick imitations of an authentic life story. These latter-day successors to Isadora Duncan include Mae West, Billie Holiday, and Shirley MacLaine, who have either written their own authentic autobiographies or worked successfully with an amanuensis.[7] Still another group of women recreating new versions of old stories are the daughters of recent immigrants. Anzia Yezierska's *Red Ribbon on a White Horse* is a candid and moving narrative, less self-indulgent and in many respects more moving than its more famous ancestor, Mary Antin's *The Promised Land*.[8] Even more unusual is Maxine Hong Kingston's *The Woman Warrior*, an imaginative account of growing up as a Chinese-American woman in California.[9] Finally, the longest list of all is of women writers— novelists, poets, and dramatists—who have opened, closed, or punctuated their careers with a personal narrative. Edith Wharton and Ellen Glasgow, Gertrude Stein and Zora Neale Hurston, Lillian Hellman, Mary McCarthy and Maureen Howard, Gwendolyn Brooks, Maya Angelou and Nikki Giovanni are just a few of the notable women artists who have revealed their historic and creative selves through acts of memory as well as imagination.[10]

So much of this personal art and history is the product of the last two decades that Lillian Smith may be pardoned certain premature judgments in her pioneering essay "Autobiography as a Dialogue Between King and Corpse."[11] Speaking in 1962, the author of *Strange Fruit* notes the male domination of this as of most other fields of literature. She observes sadly "that women have not broken the million-year silence about *themselves*. Or, they are only beginning to." In trying to account for this reticence she cites deep-seated cultural attitudes toward autobiography as women see it.

> They know how *they* look in men's eyes. . . .
> But they dare not record how they looked to themselves. Why?
> There are reasons. One is: there are many women who have no awareness of themselves. They have never asked who they are and they don't care. . . . There are others, confused by what they have been told which is not in the least what they know about themselves, who have settled things by turning off the light in their interiors; they are different and they know it but these differences are easier to accept if unnamed.
> But there is a more cogent reason why women have kept their silence. They dare not tell the truth about themselves for it might radically change male psychology.
> So—playing it safe—women have conspired to keep their secrets. . . .
> But great autobiographies are not written by people who have conspired to keep silent, and we must face the fact that no woman has as yet written a great autobiography. (188–89)

Smith then offers her prescription for such an achievement. "To write the perfect autobiography," she asserts, "would of course require a man able to accept and bring all his selves together; . . . he would need to know the archaic depths of the unconscious and at the same time criticize these depths with a rational, logical mind; he would need to accept and understand his childhood as well as his present; and he would, finally, need to be a man who knows a great story never gives an answer to its listeners but instead asks a great question" (195). Her conclusion poses a challenge to all writers and readers of contemporary autobiography: "What a courageous and almost demi-urgic task to set out on the quest for the meaning of one's life, what stoical honesty is required in order to set it down! No wonder most of us settle for smaller matters. No wonder women for the most part have settled for notebooks and diaries and journals" (196).

Whether Smith's recourse to male adjectives and models in her prescription is ironic remains unclear. Nevertheless, her basic insight is unarguable: voluntarily turning off the light in one's interior indeed aborts any autobiographical impulse. But there are specific historical, social, and artistic circumstances affecting the nature and number, the forthrightness or timidity, of women's life stories. These circumstances are now being identified by historians and literary critics, feminist and otherwise.[12] One stimulus to such explorations is the remarkable outpouring of autobiographies by American women which have appeared since 1962. More than a few candidates for author of a "great" autobiography may be proposed and the choices defended in terms broader than Smith's. As the expression of what Adrienne Rich calls in *Of Woman Born* "the dim simmering voice of self," autobiography now forms an essential part of the network of feminine communication and cultural critique which blossomed in the 1960s and 1970s.[13] Internationally influential spokeswomen like Simone de Beauvoir, Margaret Mead, and Anaïs Nin have made their own life stories sounding boards for fresh social ideas, poetic images, historical visions and revisions, and psychological models. In doing so, they address both male and female readers. The conversations which Ellis and Nin initiated two or more generations ago have thus grown into a major cultural dialogue.

A perennial yet ever-changing aspect of the "woman question" in contemporary culture is highlighted through these acts of autobiography. That is the preoccupation—often more pressing than issues of work, political power, marriage, or leisure—with defining a female self in this culture. As Betty Friedan asserted in 1963, "the core of the problem for women today is not sexual but a problem of identity—a stunting or evasion of growth that is perpetuated by the feminine mystique . . .; our culture does not permit women to accept or gratify their basic need to grow and fulfill their potentialities as human beings, a need which is not solely defined by their sexual role."[14] Indeed, for readers attuned to the delicate interplay between literary text, social context, and the individual psyche, a woman's autobiography offers an incomparable means of "pick[ing] up the discord between the vitality of existence and the rigidity of social myth," as Barbara Watson puts the matter.[15] This discord, clearly present in the anecdotes of Ellis and Nin, becomes the major theme in many recent twentieth-century women's autobiographies. Personal histories indeed facilitate "exploring the female experience and moving debate into a realm that is real to the imagination."[16] The phrase, again Watson's, suggests the persistent formulas and stereotypes that have long shaped and impeded women's firsthand or "authentic" experience. Writing and reading personal history means unavoidably to confront and question such imposed definitions of self and experience. If the act of recreating one's past and discovering one's identity is a riskier enterprise for women than it is for men, that is because such an occasion is likely to challenge traditional beliefs (usually enunciated by men) about what it means to be an American female. We catch glimpses of these beliefs in and behind the comments by Slippery Joe, Henry Miller, Lawrence Durrell, and Lillian Smith.

The first myth often encountered in modern women's autobiographies affirms that a woman, far more than a man, must first be understood—indeed, must understand herself—biologically. She is defined culturally by her body and its sexual functions of reproduction and lactation. Women's ancient association with small children, so conventional wisdom continues to declare, accounts "naturally" for the sexual symmetry of society and its divisions into public and domestic realms. This traditional belief, given fresh impetus early in this century by orthodox Freudian thought, persists in the fact of anthropological evidence, asserted by Clifford Geertz and many others, that biological differences are everywhere interpreted and altered by cultural forms and expectations.[17] Another tenacious social myth holds that women are defined *relationally*—each is "naturally" or "essentially" a wife, mother, mistress, daughter, sister. As Nancy Chodorow puts it, the "feminine personality comes to define itself in relation and connection to other people more than masculine personality does."[18] Hence women's identities are considered to be less individual achievements than men's, more extensions of others' lives. Womanhood becomes, then, an ascribed status; a woman is "naturally" considered by others to be what she is. Still a third sexual stereotype encountered and struggled against is the conviction that women possess a special cast of mind. They are "constitutionally" emotional, subjective, concrete, unsystematic, intuitive, aesthetic. By nature, they are presumed to be weak in abstract powers of thought and so participate best in culture through the arts rather than the sciences. "Now, the way a woman feels is closer to three forms of life," Otto Rank declares to Nin; "the child, the artist, the primitive. They act by their instant vision, feeling, and instinct" (1:276).

Each of these familiar formulations functions both as myth and as ideology, for each asserts as timeless fact something which serves the immediate interests of particular groups, conspicuously men. Furthermore, each formula describes, however crudely, many actual expectations and reactions of the influential others among whom American women like Ellis and Nin play and replay their social parts. Since many of these others are male, such beliefs become part of the cultural context justifying women's subordination. Hence reading autobiographies which dramatize struggles with these cultural beliefs is likely to be an anxiety-inducing occasion—for women as well as men.

As cultural narratives, therefore, personal histories of modern women must be approached ideologically. Many are insider reports on life experiences in an oppressive culture. Women authors are not always explicit about the victimization embedded in their own stories. Indeed, I find Nin's conversation with her fellow writers ambiguous in precisely these terms. But as Sally Kempton remarks in "Cutting Loose," "it is hard to fight an enemy who has outposts in your head."[19] However, if readers (male and female) can reexperience vicariously the fight for an authentic feminine identity which autobiography affords, the scope and power of current social myths and stereotypes may be better understood and their coercive power to some degree contained. In the process, newer formulas and more flexible definitions of selfhood may be discovered. One succinct description to set beside the rigid myths already mentioned which may sensitize the reader of autobiography to such possibilities is Peter Filene's. "True feminism," he writes in *Him/Her/Self*, "meant that a woman was fully herself, worker and lover and mother if she wished, multiplying her roles beyond 'female' into the plenitude of her possibilities and also, thereby, into the anguish of ambivalence."[20] These are brave phrases in the abstract, but in particular cases describe a twilight zone into which the woman autobiographer often enters with mixed emotions and memories. Each attempt, moreover, constitutes a unique occasion, for as Sally Kempton again observes, "women's liberation is finally only personal."[21] Prescriptions and declarations must be tested in the individual life. "On the whole, feminist literary criticism and scholarship have been stubbornly empirical," Elaine Showalter also points out. "It seems unlikely that any theoretical manifesto could be both intellectually and politically adequate to describe the extreme diversity of the current approaches to literature which involve women, sex roles, the family, or sexual politics."[22]

Spurred by these suggestions to address the necessarily complex particular case, we shall here offer a comparative reading of two exemplary autobiographies published by American women within the past two turbulent decades. In focusing on Margaret Mead's *Blackberry Winter* and Anaïs Nin's opening volume of her *Diary*, we do not pretend to have chosen representative women's stories. Even if one supposed it possible to make a few works stand widely and accurately for contemporary women's experiences and modes of self-expression, these two might not be included. For Mead and Nin are transparently unique individuals. Yet paradoxically their special experiences and unusual achievements, although unduplicatable, happen to illuminate many dimensions of feminine identity as reconstructed in other autobiographies. This is true in part for cultural and historical reasons but more particularly because as autobiographers both women are creatively and critically self-conscious. Culturally, of course, Mead and Nin occupied polar positions and points of view: scientist and artist, native-born Easterner and cosmopolitan European emigrant, public spokeswoman and intensely private person. One recreates herself chronologically over many years as world-famous anthropologist and wife, mother, and grandmother. Her lifelong concerns as social scientist with culture and personality provide explicit links between these professional and domestic realms and roles. The other conceives herself almost stereotypically as the private female artist, intensely preoccupied with her own psychic processes and problems within a narrow orbit of family and friendships. Historically, the first volume of her *Diary* covers but three or four years of a young woman's Parisian experiences prior to her leaving for New York and a brief career as Rank's assistant. Nin is both confined and liberated in later publishing this record of young adulthood by the refusal of important family members (including her husband and brother) to be included. Mead, on the other hand, has been thrice married. She records this unconventional (for her generation) history with an unusually candid and dispassionate eye for the lessons it teaches about her present self. Nin's wholesale investment in articulate intimacy—in recording what she has called the social and emotional "ritual of one to one"[23]—in dramatizing the body, in speculating about feminine creativity, make her serial autobiography one of the most revealing explorations of social myths about women. The ambiguities in her enactment of these patterns are everywhere expressed in the *Diary*'s successive volumes. If, as certain of its devotees believe, *The Diary of Anaïs Nin* comes close to fulfilling Lillian Smith's prescription for "great" autobiography, that is partly because she has met head-on the challenge of stereotyped form: she transforms the journal or diary, in which women are supposed to take timid refuge, into a new and vital mode of self-construction.

Blackberry Winter and Volume 1 of the *Diary* make an instructive pair in this comparative study for other reasons as well. Though both women are old at the time of publication, they are chiefly young women within the space-time of their autobiographies. Hence both narratives afford parallels and contrasts to Sullivan's and Wright's histories and throw additional light on questions about childhood, creativity, and identity floated in Chapter Four. Moreover, their international and cross-cultural experiences as women competing in a man's world resonate in some respects with the perspectives eventually achieved by Du Bois and Malcolm X. Today, both American women and blacks are struggling to define and assert themselves. As individual accounts of widely shared encounters with received beliefs and stereotyped roles, *Blackberry Winter* and volume 1 of the *Diary* open up vistas upon other cultural milieux in which becoming a woman occurs differently than in the America of the early and mid-twentieth century. "We are all engaged in the task of peeling off the false selves," Nin once wrote in *Playgirl*, "the programmed selves, the selves created by our families, our culture, our religions. It is an enormous task because the history of women has been as incompletely told as the history of blacks."[24]

I

The initial query in all readers' minds—what do I know of this author as I begin this autobiography?—is often phrased with special force in the case of women's personal histories, for even today's women autobiographers are more likely than men to be unfamiliar subjects, coming as many of them now do out of obscurity (domestic or otherwise) into the spotlight of authorship. Such, however, was probably untrue in 1972 for the first readers of *Blackberry Winter*. Although they may not have personally encountered her books—*Coming of Age in Samoa, Growing Up in New Guinea, Sex and Temperament, Male and Female*—in a college course or Book-of-the-Month Club selection, they would probably recognize the author's face and figure in the dust-jacket photograph. Posed behind a museum model of a New Guinea or Trobriand Island village, Mead presents herself in her public role as ex-fieldworker and present anthropologist and culture critic. The face, figure, and haircut are in fact widely known to lecture and television audiences; only her walking staff is absent. Women readers particularly would be likely to greet this autobiographer familiarly. "The most powerful influence on modern women," Betty Friedan observed in 1963, "in terms both of functionalism and the feminine protest, was Margaret Mead. Her work on culture and personality—book after book, study after study—has had a profound effect on the women in my generation, the one before it, and the generation now growing up. She was, and still is, the symbol of the woman thinker in America."[25]

Well beyond the educated readership of *The Feminine Mystique*, however, Mead's place in American culture and her contributions to feminist thought and behavior were widely known by the time she turned, as an older but vigorous woman in her late sixties, to autobiography. Yet this public image and influence, as Friedan emphasizes, were complex, even paradoxical. Mead did more than any other to popularize a major discovery of twentieth-century anthropology—the extreme variety and flexibility of gender roles and sexual identities in different societies around the world. Male and female traits, Americans now realize, have developed and are displayed quite variously in the gentle Arapesh, the aggressive Mundugumor, and among the Tchambuli, where women are the business managers and men their emotionally dependent partners. This demonstrated plasticity in human nature led Mead to posit a complex interaction in each culture between biological or sex differences, cultural expectations, and innate temperamental types. Yet as Friedan also points out, Mead was early affected by psychoanalytic and functionalist concepts which encouraged an anatomy-is-destiny viewpoint that took women's social roles and identities as functional, culture-specific, not to be lightly challenged or changed. As a consequence, Mead's writings gave ambiguous support to the sexual stereotyping of the 1950s. "What the feminine mystique took from Margaret Mead was not her vision of woman's great untested human potential, but this glorification of the female sexual function that has indeed been tested, in every culture, but seldom, in civilized cultures, valued as highly as the unlimited potential of human creativity, so far mainly displayed by man."[26] This powerful but contradictory influence is significant first as mental furniture in the minds of readers of *Blackberry Winter* and then as both experience and argument within that life-history. "Those who found in her work confirmation of their own unadmitted prejudices and fears," Friedan warns, "ignored not only the complexity of her total work, but the example of her complex life."[27] Mead's own life, as her autobiography shows, has indeed been full of intellectual and emotional crosscurrents. These are reflected not only in the themes and structure but also in the very title of this unusual woman's history.

"*Blackberry Winter,* the time when the hoarfrost lies on the blackberry blossoms; without this frost the berries will not set. It is the forerunner of a rich harvest." This epigraph confronts the reader with an initial ambiguity: though the author is a scientist trained to make precise cultural observations and descriptions, she is also an amateur poet expressing herself through metaphor. What the "hoarfrost" is which has chilled but not killed her career or character is the first mystery of *Blackberry Winter: My Earlier Years.* Some will suppose it is simply the fact of being a woman competing as a pioneer in a man's cool world of science and education. More specifically, perhaps, the "frost" which insures the personal harvest of autobiography is her three husbands, from each of whom she is divorced by the midpoint in her career. That break falls about the close of World War II. Thus "hoarfrost" carries a third resonance; it refers historically to the beginning of the atomic era. "The atomic bomb exploded over Hiroshima in the summer of 1945," she writes. "At that point I tore up every page of a book I had nearly finished. Every sentence was out of date. We had entered a new age. My years as a collaborating wife, trying to combine intensive field work and an intense personal life also came to an end" (296). In actuality all three dimensions—the biosocial, the marital, and the historical—are intricately intertwined in her narrative, whose chronological momentum is abandoned at this point.

Historical chronology, in any case, is not the essential shape imposed upon her past. Mead's narrative structure is more subtle, proclaiming a different and specifically feminine continuity. Composed in three parts, the story consists of a pair of narrative parentheses enclosing the central, public account of her anthropological field work and its fruits in her earlier books and ideas. Part 1 establishes firm connections with family and the past. Part 3 brings these memories and relationships to bear upon Mead's recent roles as mother and grand mother and, in the person of her little granddaughter, projects her life on into the future. These private parentheses define as they embrace the public career, where personal ties and cultural problems always intertwine. Throughout, we observe an anthropologist's mind at work organizing private experience in terms of sexual, temperamental, and cultural differences. The result is a distinctly detached narrative whose subject's emotional complications and intimate revelations are usually identified but seldom exploited dramatically or analyzed at length. Compared to many other woman autobiographers, Mead is indeed a cool historian. She is very much the participant-observer of her own life but infrequently its inward-diving explorer and apologist. If emotional intensity and confessional candor are qualities expected of women autobiographers, Mead refuses from the outset to play the game.

Nevertheless, the careful historian does not distance herself emotionally from *all* portions of her past. Indeed, one reason she is able to analyze her own parents' strengths and shortcomings so sensitively is that, as she remarks at the outset, "I found no sharp break with the past" (5). From girlhood on, Mead's mind, temperament, and training teach her to build bridges across cultures and generations and between individuals. She is characteristically a *connector* before she becomes a *comparatist*. Hence as autobiographer she allows neither death, divorce, nor disagreements to sever once-vital relationships. She is able to view her own character and career as natural extensions of her cultivated Pennsylvania family, in which "I was a first child, wanted and loved" (17). In this family the women were for two generations college graduates. Though her father and brother were both professors, and her talented younger sisters married an artist and a writer, the tradition of genteel WASP intellectualism is not the crucial family fact. For her, "the most decisive influence in my life" (45) is her paternal grandmother. This beloved woman is the powerful force in her whole extended family, playing the role of wise adviser which Margaret herself later assumes within the same family circle—and beyond. "The content of my conscience," she remarks of this inheritance, "came from my mother's concern for other people and the state of the world and from my father's insistence that the only thing worth doing is to add to the store of exactly known facts. But the strength of my conscience came from Grandma, who meant what she said. Perhaps nothing is more valuable for a child than living with an adult who is firm and loving—and Grandma was loving. I loved the feel of her soft skin, but she would never let me give her an extra kiss when I said good night" (55–56).

Hence Mead defines herself initially, as Stephanie Demetrakopoulos has pointed out, in matrilineal terms.[28] She is the particular legatee of the females in her family, who are most positively the significant others of her growing-up. "I think it was my grandmother who gave me my ease in being a woman," she observes. "She was unquestionably feminine—small and dainty and pretty and wholly without masculine protest or feminist aggrievement. She had gone to college when this was a very unusual thing for a girl to do, she had a firm grasp of anything she paid attention to, she had married and had a child, and she had a career of her own. All this was true of my mother, as well" (55). Virtually every aspect of this atypical nineteenth-century pattern is repeated on a national and international scale in Margaret Mead's own life.

Experiences and ties with men, however, make a different story and constitute another emotional legacy. Beginning with her domineering, unimaginative, matter-of-fact father, she encounters male condescension and misunderstanding at nearly every stage of her growth from schoolgirl to world-famous anthropologist. "Look at those useless little hands!" remarks a friend of her father's. "Never did a day's work in their life and never will! You'd maybe make a good mistress, but a poor wife. You'd better study nursing!" (90). This was during World War I, at a time when Margaret was carrying an extra-heavy high school program in preparation for college, sewing all the costumes for a play, and single-handedly cooking and keeping house for a large family. "I exploded in one of the few fits of feminist rage I have ever had," she recalls. In later life, resentment of masculine condescension takes other forms. Once when Bronislaw Malinowski impugned her knowledge of kinship systems in the Admiralty Islands, she was so insulted that she postponed a field trip for three months in order to write a monograph on the subject.

Besides these inherited and experienced relationships with particular people, Mead's childhood and family past provide her also with a characteristic feeling for place. Here she seems to fit—but also to evade—the persistent stereotype that a woman's assumed attachment is to houses as the "natural" locus of her domestic identity. The Mead family moved so frequently—often four times a year—that no single sacred spot persists in her memory. Yet Margaret characteristically carved out her own niche in each new place. "As soon as we arrived," she recalls, "I ran ahead to find a room for myself as far away as possible from everyone else, preferably at the top of the house where I would always be warned by footsteps that someone was coming. After that, until we were settled in, I was busy exploring, making my own the new domain" (8). If inner domestic spaces help to define the girl and still appeal to the aging woman, this distinguishes her from both Louis Sullivan and Richard Wright, whose love of the outdoors and fiery rebellion against the family house may now be seen as perhaps gender-related as well as matters of genius and history. Later, when travel and impermanence became constants in her scientific career, she continued to stake out domains apart, as in her tower office at the American Museum of Natural History.

This act reflects larger patterns in her life and profession. "Going away, knowing I shall return to the same place and the same people— this is the way my life has always been" (12), she remarks of the anthropologist's practice of revisiting cultures and communities in order to record change and continuity. It is the same procedure W. E. B. Du Bois follows, as we have already noted in Chapter Two. Yet this social scientist—possibly because she is a woman anthropologist—makes much more of houses than Du Bois does. Field work, for instance, is presented in the photographs and text of *Blackberry Winter* as a series of huts, mosquito houses, and compounds in which a husband-and-wife team occupy a temporary center of observation and participation in others' lives. She illustrates the challenge of such work by an apt analogy. "For field work is a very difficult thing to do," she writes. "To do it well, one has to sweep one's mind clear of every presupposition, even those about other cultures in the same part of the world in which one is working. Ideally, even the appearance of a house should come to one as a new, fresh impression. In a sense it should come to one as a surprise that there are houses and that they are square or round or oval, that they do or do not have walls, that they let in the sun or keep out the wind or rain, that people do or do not cook or eat in a dwelling house. In the field one can take nothing for granted" (154). That this analogy is not accidental is underlined by the passage Mead chooses at the end of the narrative to characterize the thought of her first husband, Luther Cresswell. He writes of the House of Science in which there is always a New Room into which men from all fields and disciplines drift to share their discoveries and ideas. To be sure, this metaphor is not hers, but in choosing it to represent her husband's scientific sensibility she reveals much about her own.

Yet if one compares the huts and houses of *Blackberry Winter* with other locales in other women's pasts—with, for instance, Nin's villa at Louveciennes, or the midwestern places in Jane Addams's *Twenty Years at Hull House,* or the Store in Maya Angelou's *I Know Why the Caged Bird Sings,* or even with the all-white livingroom Mae West tells us about in *Goodness Had Nothing to Do with It!*—one is struck at once by how abstractly Mead thinks about houses. For the social worker of Chicago, Hull House is not simply a new locus of feminine activity in the world; it stands for Addams herself. Angelou, too, defines herself, at one phase at least of her development, in terms of the Store at Stamps. No such symbolic identification ever occurs in *Blackberry Winter.* In place of particular houses or rooms as expressions of the self, she speaks of small loved objects. "The need to define who you are by the place in which you live remains intact, even when that place is defined by a single object, like the small blue vase that used to mean home to one of my friends" (11). Yet it is surprising that no treasured objects are recalled by this inveterate traveler who depicts herself typically as an outside observer and temporary guest in the houses of others.

Far more significant than places and things, more important even than her own body in childbirth, are the ideas and personal connections in Margaret Mead's busy professional life. Yet people and concepts always intimately interrelate; this is the essence of her experience as female field-worker and theorizer. "Because of their age-long training in human relations," she writes, "for that is what feminine intuition really is—women have a special contribution to make to any group enterprise, and I feel it is up to them to contribute the kinds of awareness that relatively few men—except, for example, child analysts or men who have been intimately reared by women—have incorporated through their education" (205–6). Teamwork studying primitive cultures is the group enterprise she knows best and writes most frankly about. This career choice unites various earlier roles as freedom-loving college student and graduate student protégée, co-worker, wife, and critic of a succession of strong-minded men. She is as strong-minded as any masculine colleague and invariably more energetic. Though these attributes are put to cooperative purposes as often as to competitive ones, her relations with all three husbands, and especially with Reo Fortune and Gregory Bateson, are intense and short-lived partnerships, at once personal and professional.

"Contrast through comparison is necessary to complete a picture" (234) is the principle also governing the account of these marriages. Thus when she and Reo, her husband, and Bateson are together in New Guinea, working out in long conversations new theories of sex and temperament, she illustrates her own ideas in terms of their three contrasting personalities.

> Our ongoing discussions, of course, threw light upon each of us as a person. Both Gregory and I felt that we were, to some extent, deviants, each within our own culture. Many of the forms of aggressive male behavior that were standardized in English culture did not appeal to him. My own interest in children did not fit the stereotype of the American career woman or, for that matter, the stereotype of the possessive, managing American wife and mother. It was exciting to strip off the layers of culturally attributed expected behavior and to feel that one knew at last who one was. However, Reo did not have as great a sense of revelation about himself. Temperamentally, he fitted the expectations of his culture, even though New Zealand expectations about male behavior were milder and more pastoral and he himself was more concerned with the dangers of unbridled impulse. (240)

Yet different as they are, each of her husbands marries the same woman. She depicts herself as American "masculine" in drive, ambition, emotional reserve, and powers of abstract thought, yet "feminine" in her body size, gentleness, love of children, her concern to balance cooperation and rivalry, and her deference (up to a point) to male temperaments. But she makes clear that such a profile is far too simple a formula for her or any woman's identity. Equally important and revealing is *her* effect on co-workers who happen also to be her husbands. On this theme *Blackberry Winter* is more of an apology, for she seems sensitive to the accusation that she is a superhuman dynamo, almost heartlessly intense and intellectually competitive, incapable of sustained intimate relationships. "Yet people fail to see what should be attributed to me, that is, my capacity to enjoy and appreciate other people's work in a way that seems to give them something like a transfusion of extra energy to complete a piece of research or finish a book. But the fact is, they are happy under what is called my influence only as long as they are working at the top of their own capacity. When their own drive fails, so that they can no longer draw on my energy, they feel it to be a reproach or an unwelcome goad, and so repudiate it" (200). Too often, then, professional cooperation turns into personal competition, not so much through her own will as in the minds of the men with whom she works and lives. During their highly productive stay on Bali, however, Gregory Bateson coined the term *zygogenesis* to describe the acceleration of interaction between himself and his wife which led "not to a breaking point but to a harmonious equilibrium. Most of the time as we worked together far into the night—went to bed after washing our faces in the remaining pint of water when the last films had been developed, or after we had labeled the last film or had worked out a new theoretical point—we felt that we were working in harmony" (258).

Midnight moments like these are indeed a far cry from key scenes in many other women's autobiographies. The reader recalling Emma Goldman's or Anne Moody's arrests and imprisonments, Maya Angelou's rape, and Maxine Hong Kingston's explosion in the laundry will doubtless deem these far more dramatic events and metaphors of self. For this diminutive anthropologist, violence and high drama are simply not a fact of either professional or private life. Speaking of the real risks of field work in New Guinea, she notes that in addition to "the discomforts of high water, the torrents of the rainy season, and recurrent attacks of malaria, there never was any guarantee that one would in the end see the ceremony that might provide the key to an understanding of the culture. Perhaps in the whole of a field trip one would see no major ceremony, no important man would die, there would be no dramatic clash that would suddenly illuminate the plot of a people's lives" (247). In her own life's plot, the publication of a book, the elaboration of a scientific thesis, the birth of a daughter and granddaughter are the significant moments and turning points.

Only occasionally in her marital relations are there symbolic vignettes which strongly highlight character. One of these is her arrival in Europe after a long separation from Luther Cresswell. She recalls herself as the young anthropologist returning by P & O steamer from Samoa, starved for intellectual companionship and delighted to meet Reo Fortune on shipboard. Her husband awaits her in Marseilles, unaware of Reo's existence. "When the ship docked, we were still deep in debate and did not realize it," she remembers. "Finally, sensing that the ship was not moving, we walked around the deck and saw Luther standing on the dock, wondering what had happened to me. That is one of the moments I would take back and live differently, if I could" (175). A similar scene foreshadows the transition from Reo to Gregory Bateson. The three anthropologists slept once in a New Guinea village rumored to be under imminent attack from rival tribesmen. While Bateson stood in the plaza with some of the villagers,

> Reo covered the scene with a revolver from inside the guesthouse. That night we kept the lamp lit and took turns staying awake as we lay on the floor of our improvised mosquito room. No attack came, but Reo woke once to hear Gregory and me talking. There is much to be said for the suggestion that the true oedipal situation is not the primal scene but parents talking to each other in words the child does not understand. And by then Gregory and I had already established a kind of communication in which Reo did not share. (230)

The reader must make the most of such emotionally significant but undramatic moments, for in essential areas Mead's narrative is exasperatingly reticent. Her desire to understand and be understood is balanced by the need to guard relationships and areas of her inner life. In many ways, therefore, part 2 proves less informative than the twin enclosing parentheses of her narrative.

What connects Mead's relatively brief, intense career in the field (and her short, intense, professional marriages) with her earlier and later life are experiences with children. The Mundugumor's contempt for children so appalled the childless anthropologist that she returned to America determined to have one of her own. The arrival of her daughter via natural childbirth in 1939 and the birth of her granddaughter thirty years later are events crowding out many more public occasions. In thus choosing to emphasize herself as child-bearer and nurturer Mead willingly assumes a conventional role. "In fact," she points out, "the male invention of natural childbirth has had a magnificent emancipating effect on women, who for generations had been

207

muffled in male myths instead of learning about a carefully observed actuality" (277). With her own grandchild, too, the older woman not only plays a familiar cultural part but uses the occasion to restate a prime lesson of her scientific profession: the need to pay precise attention to individuals. "I visualize two-year-olds—all the two-year-olds I have ever known—with new comprehension," she observes. "I see their faces more clearly. I understand again, or anew, how they formed their first words. I grasp the meaning of puckered eyebrows, a tensed hand, or a light flick of the tongue. The known and loved particular child makes it possible for one to understand better and care more about all children" (310). Such remarks, along with the photographs accompanying them, reaffirm the dual identity Margaret Mead treasures and measures herself by. More vividly than in the three passages presented from her three husbands' writings—a remarkably gracious and candid way of letting them speak to the reader—the later pages of *Blackberry Winter* on her daughter and granddaughter reveal emotions only occasionally expressed earlier in this reserved recitation.

In fact, the idea of autobiography may have occurred to Mead, as perhaps it does to other women, while she speculated about (and re-saw herself in) her little child's trusting, responsive, outgoing nature. "How much was temperament?" she muses. "How much was felicitous accident? How much could be attributed to upbringing? We may never know. Certainly all a mother and father can claim credit for is that they have not marred a child in any recognizable way. For the total adult-child situation could be fully understood only if one also had the child's own interpretation of the parts adults played in its life" (292). However, *Blackberry Winter* does not turn into Cathy's story. It remains her mother's account of the parts adults and children have played in her life. As compared to Sullivan's or Wright's records of childhood and youth, Mead's is demonstrably more "other-directed," its author more attentive to other children's emerging identities as well as her own. Nevertheless, I disagree with Estelle Jelinek, who sees Mead's whole autobiographical intention "to outline the proper training of children."[29] What I find as Mead's larger aim is recording both a scientist's and a mother's understanding of childhood and family situations as well as a grandmother's reckoning of their cumulative impact upon her own personality and their meanings for the reader. That complex authorial self emerges as a consequence of carefully defined circumstances and conscious choices. By selecting a new twentieth-century career in the social sciences "in which personal relations and working relations are inseparable" (312), and yet insisting also upon traditional biological and marital rights and duties, Mead consciously assumed the burden of becoming one particular kind of modern American woman. Not *despite* but *because* of that public career, the intellectual content, tone, and even literary form of *Blackberry Winter* underline its author's identity as scientist-and-woman. If her personal history fails to raise the profound question Lillian Smith demands of "perfect" autobiography, perhaps that is because Margaret Mead clings too tightly to her anthropologist's identity with its cool observer stance. For a far more daring plunge into "the archaic depths of the unconscious" one has only to open Anaïs Nin's account of her "earlier years" as woman-artist.

II

To be poised continually between worlds, gripped in the "anguish of ambivalence," describes accurately the condition of the young Parisian whom we encounter through her older American self's editorial reconstruction. Though profound differences separate the *Diary* from *Blackberry Winter*—as indeed, from all other stories of publicly successful American women—her characteristic in-between state links Nin's exotic, international artist's life to others. Which self predominates at any given moment—the artificer of dreams, the bohemian café denizen, the bourgeoise wife and daughter, or the older reminiscent author—becomes the initial question about this experiment in autobiography. Nin continually makes passionate and explicit declarations about the several dimensions of her identity. One already seen is the 1937 conversation with Henry Miller and Lawrence Durrell. An even more emphatic assertion, because the product of reflection and not of an immediate occasion, occurs near the close of volume 1 of the *Diary*. "And what I have to say is really distinct from the artist and art," she concludes.

> *It is the woman who has to speak.* And it is not only the woman Anaïs who has to speak, but I who have to speak for many women. As I discover myself, I feel I am merely one of many, a symbol. I begin to understand June, Jeanne, and many others. George Sand, Georgette Leblanc, Eleanora Duse, women of yesterday and today. The mute ones of the past, the inarticulate, who took refuge behind wordless intuitions; and the women of today, all action, and copies of men. And I, in between. Here lies the personal overflow, the personal and feminine overfulness. Feelings that are not for books, not for

fiction, not for art. All that I want to enjoy, not transform. My life has been one long series of efforts, self-discipline, will. Here I can sketch, improvise, be free, and myself. (1:289)

This description of a book that is also a self, a personal overflowing, underscores an ambition as original as that animating *Leaves of Grass*. "I enlarge and expand my self," she cries at the outset of her monumental enterprise (1:29), and the Whitmanian language declares an intention to place a woman of the mid-twentieth century fully and completely on record. To do so entails inventing a special mode of discourse which transcends the usual forms of prose narrative. The paradox is that this on-the-spot replica of a woman's diverse reality is the result of a supremely artful act, for the core of both the living and remembering self is an artist, a writer. "And it is in our work, by our work, that we reassemble the fragments, re-create wholeness" (1:69). Reconstructing her split identity becomes a protracted, lifelong struggle, a "terrible algebra" (1:359) of imagination and memory. The process begun by the young girl of eleven on shipboard to America eventually stretches over half a century, fills several hundred notebooks, becomes the chief preoccupation of Nin's mature years. Finally, for over a decade before her death, the writer and her editor, Gunther Stuhlmann, worked at recreating this inscription of a woman's life. It was an achievement possible only for an older person, though one repeatedly urged upon her earlier by private readers of the notebooks as diverse as Miller, Rank, Edmund Wilson, Maxwell Geismar, Gore Vidal. "I am submerged by the enormity of my material," she exclaims in the sixth volume (6:192). In actuality, she did not sink under its weight. Over nineteen hundred pages of a sensitive woman's intimate thoughts, feelings, experiences, and relationships have been reassembled into one continuously flowing narrative. Before her death, her faith and her friends' faith were vindicated in the eyes of a growing circle of readers. Henry Miller's early prophecy in *The Cosmological Eye* ("a monumental confession which when given the world will take its place beside the revelations of St. Augustine, Petronius, Abélard, Rousseau, Proust, and others")[30] could now be considered in the public light which the autobiographer so long shunned.

The ordering and reordering of passing impressions and permanent memories make strenuous demands on Nin's readers and critics. Intuitive empathy and cool, intellectual judgment are equally required to embrace the surprising range of moods, ideas, personalities, ties, and social contexts recorded over thirty-five years of the writer's European and American experience. As the narrative of a richly private life, the *Diary*'s underlying rationale is as thoroughly psychological as Mead's is anthropological, for Nin deliberately organizes her life-story in line with Jung's injunction "proceed from the dream outward." Its keynote is taken from one of Calderon's titles, several times repeated: *La Vida Es Sueño*. Both phrases affirm the primacy not of external, everyday reality, but of the inner realm of dream and desire, idea and anxiety. Thus her principal task—a more ambitious one than Mead's—has been to find a language adequate to represent the intricate interplay of consciousness and the preconscious as she locates a woman's imagination within the society of men. Though timeless dream images provide the psychic foundation, a thread of historical continuity runs through this story of an unfolding self. Each of the six volumes takes a chronological slice through psychic and social experience. Furthermore, though recurring motifs unify the whole, there is also a perceptible movement in the *Diary* away from private dream toward history and social involvement. The engagement with the external world never overshadows the private agenda, however. This continues to include the development of the self in *all* its artful femininity, the problem of neurosis and the struggle for mental equipoise, intense relationships with a few individuals at a time, always the attempt to unite conscious art and spontaneous life.

Volume 1 opens in 1931, at the moment when the young woman is publishing her first book, a study of D. H. Lawrence. She lives with her family in a beautiful villa in Louveciennes, outside Paris, but her daily preoccupation is with avant-garde literary life in the city, especially with writers like Miller and Antonin Artaud. The tensions of this split existence lead to consultations with two famous psychoanalysts, René Allendy and Otto Rank. Though the book closes with the stillbirth of a daughter whose father is never identified, an even more significant crisis is the reunion with her father, Joaquin Nin, the celebrated Spanish musician who abandoned his family when Anaïs was a young girl. Volume 2 covers her departure for New York as Rank's lay assistant and her return to Paris when she decides on a writing career, not a career as a psychoanalyst. The Spanish civil war and World War II explode the artist's idyll on *La Belle Aurore,* a houseboat she rents in the Seine. "This volume will portray the end of our personal lives," she announces sadly (2:338). Volume 3 is therefore a wartime journal. As an unwilling exile now established for a third time in New York City, she struggles for acceptance of her intensely personal, poetic, associative, symbolist fiction. Failing to gain commercial publication, she establishes a handset press in Greenwich Village, from which *Under a Glass Bell* is issued in 1944. Edmund Wilson's *New*

Yorker review provides the tentative note on which the book closes. With volume 4, Nin surrounds herself with an admiring circle of talented, unknown, younger writers, of whom Gore Vidal is temporarily chief. Another act is to quit New York and discover California and Mexico. This western life continues in volume 5, which covers the years 1947–55. Here in the tropical setting which fits her romantic temperament an old theme is repeated: "America is cold and hard, and has treated me badly" (5:70). Being the perennial outsider becomes all the more trying as ties to the past are broken; both the father's and mother's deaths are recorded in this volume. With the sixth book, now explicitly a "Diary of Others" (6:319), Nin completes the circle of her life. Her novels at last win a measure of American acceptance, and she settles many past scores. The final note is one of quiet vindication:

> Volume 1 of the Diary is published!
>
> April, May, and June were months which erased all the past disappointments. I received wonderful reviews from Karl Shapiro, Jean Garrigue in *The New York Times,* Harry Moore, Marion Simon in the *National Observer,* Deena Metzger in *The Free Press,* and others.
>
> I gave a talk at Barnard College to an overflowing room.
>
> I appeared on Camera Three with lifesize sets of Louveciennes, reading from the diary. . . . My mail was described by one of my correspondents not as fan mail but as love letters. Suddenly there was joy, celebration, praise, invitations to lecture, flowers, interviews. In Berkeley at Cody's Book Shop, Ferlinghetti, one of my favorite poets, threw rose petals over my head. (6:396–97)

This long-delayed triumph underlines the fact that volume 1 occupies a special place in what James Leo Herlihy calls her "great saga of an individual" (6:44). The life-size sets of Louveciennes in the television studio emphasize the opening work as both separate story and synecdoche. Approaching the entire *Diary* through its beginning likewise offers instructive contrasts both to more traditional women's life-stories like Mead's and to experiments in multiple autobiography like Lillian Hellman's. Despite the fact that but three years of an exclusively European experience are recorded, volume 1 of the *Diary* traces a dramatic emergence into feminine maturity. This development extends backward deep into childhood, which is reentered more fully here than at any later point. Nin's preoccupation with her slim, girlish body, with a succession of intimate friendships and family relationships, and her apparently willing acceptance of traditional notions about feminine intuition and artistic creativity are major issues running through the later books. The fact that the aspiring young writer immersing herself in a daily bath of physical and social sensations is also undergoing analysis and studying its principles adds intellectual distance to emotional intensity. Years later Nin asserts that the male-female axis of human experience became actually less important to her than the continuing tension between art and psychoanalysis. Both problems, however, bedevil her here and fill the pages of her diary. The analyst's working principle richly and variously illustrated in volume 1 is her conviction "that it is in the moments of emotional crisis that human beings reveal themselves most accurately."[31] Thus for a variety of pertinent reasons the opening volume of Nin's serial autobiography invites analysis as an independent work, much as *Song of Myself* can stand apart from *Leaves of Grass*.

The editorial act reuniting the young writer in Paris and the older woman in California was a complex and emotional process. "I felt the need to publish the diary as strongly as the snake pushing out of its old skin," she recalls in volume 6. "All evolution had this impulse. The impulse to give and the impulse to hide fought a mighty battle in this quiet office overlooking a garden. I would call it a battle between the woman and the creator. The woman, protective, secretive, placing the needs of others before her own, accustomed to her mysteries which man has feared; and the creator, no longer able to contain her discoveries, her knowledge, her experiences, her lucidities, her compiling of the hidden aspects of people so ardently pursued" (6:380–81). Stuhlmann's objective sense of structure provides one external, sympathetic force assisting the autobiographer's struggle. Another essential presence is Dr. Bogner, the last of Nin's therapists, "so calm, so serene, so wise"; she quiets the diarist's doubts about privacy and publicity. The outcome of this cooperation between two women and a man is the autobiographer's decision to break her long silence. "The main, mature objective becomes clear. I believed every word I wrote. They were written by another self. So let this self, the creator, face the world" (6:380–81).

All autobiographies–Nin's no less than Antin's *The Promised Land*—which announce such a decisive split between past actor and present author are likely to arouse suspicions in readers who cannot fail to note the continuities. Nin's readers have additional grounds for doubting and reality-testing. There are, for instance, the questions of silences and signal omissions in this narrative of intimate relationships. These gaps, because they are so central to the autobiographer's announced concerns, are more palpably experienced as absences than is the case with either Louis Sullivan or Henry Adams. The most striking of these is the absence of Ian Hugo, Nin's husband, who like certain other relatives chose not to appear in volume 1 of the *Diary*. (He is passingly mentioned later, though never as her husband.) Nin's respect for others' wishes is explained in *The Novel of the Future* as well as in volume 6. "As a diarist I drew my own boundary lines indicating that a respect for the life of a human being is more important than satisfying the curiosity of invaders, violators of human rights. . . . I take delight in the creative possibilities of the intimate portrait, but it has to be with the collaboration of the sitter."[32] Mead, by contrast, assumes the easier task; she preserves the rights of others by refusing to probe or confess. Another of Nin's surprising suppressions, given her marriage and her friendship with Henry Miller, is the taboo about sensual experiences. "It was not in my nature to be explicit in sexual matters because for me they were welded to feeling, to love, to all other intimacies," she explained (6:379–80). Paradoxically, these very silences are meant to support the story's underlying psychological candor. "I had to act according to my own nature," she declares, "or else the diary itself would be destroyed" (6:380). To disappointed readers and suspicious critics she offers this excuse: "The fact remained that there was so much richness of experience that the excisions did not matter" (6:379). In *The Novel of the Future* she adds:

> To study a person in depth is more important than to catalogue his actions. If one is deaf to the vulnerability of a human being, it also means one has no ear for the more subtle recording of his sensitive wave lengths. Giving all the facts, all the incidents, all the anecdotes, rather than a meaningful selection of them in order of their importance and accompanied by clarification, very often leads to a shrunken portrait. If a full psychological portrait is given and if it is accurate enough, one can infer the rest, fill in, read between the lines, as with close friends or a member of one's family.[33]

Selective intimacies, then, are the presiding theme and action of volume 1. "Why are my devotions so concentrated on a few people?" (121), she characteristically asks Allendy. In search of an answer, her narrative reevokes, often in daily detail, certain friendships and family ties. These are the prime sources of her womanly and artistic self. Unlike the usual psychological novel or *bildungsroman,* however, there is no plot larger than Nin herself. Each of her six intimates—Miller and his wife June, Allendy, Artaud, Joaquin Nin, and Rank—is both a historical figure and a symbolic expression of the author's various sides or selves. Her social world, as a consequence, is radically restricted by both her autobiographical and psychological consciousness. Few uninteresting, ordinary, or untalented people appear in her pages, but those who are admitted within the portals of memory are sympathetically (and often exhaustively) dissected in their unique and universal humanity.

The gallery of psychological portraits is organized around the same occasion Nin later finds in many other women's lives, as revealed to her in fan letters from feminine readers. "It is always the relation of the younger woman to the interesting man," she remarks of this correspondence, "the same as in the Diary."[34] Here a striking difference appears between Nin and Mead. As one easily assumes the mantle of wise older woman (even when young), so the other continues, all her life, to depict male-female relations from the viewpoint of the ingenue. To be sure, June Miller is a major figure and early symbol in Nin's past. But it is significant that the narrative opens not with these two women getting to know each other intimately but with Nin and Henry Miller exploring the Parisian demimonde. In fact, Miller dominates the entire first half of the narrative. Through his energetic celebration of ugliness, eroticism, and explicitness, he represents for the young woman the artist as hard-boiled detective, someone archetypally masculine, assertive, critical. He attacks life's "vital center," while women like herself fill out the "circumference," that territory of women "untouched by the direct desire of man" (1:184). In his stimulating company, she experiences life and art in immediate, violent conjunction. Her mentor with the cold blue eyes, demonic curiosity, and underlying gentleness has "installed himself completely in the present" (1:9), secure in the conviction that life can be captured by the language of explicit realism. Henry Miller brings out both the "masculine" and "feminine" sides of Nin's still unformed nature, as she simultaneously imitates and rejects his virile values. At the same time, she remains a child while under his sway. "I am talking almost paternally to you," Miller once remarks, and this touches a tender spot. "At that moment I knew Henry had perceived the part of me that is half child, the part of me who likes to be amazed, to be taught, to be guided. . . . My childlike attitude toward older men. I can see nothing in it but immaturity, a need brought on by the absence of a father" (1:80). Therefore she is deeply disturbed when Miller advises her to stop keeping her diary. "He thinks it is a malady, an outgrowth of loneliness. I don't know. It has also become a notebook of my extroversion, a travel sketchbook: it is full of others" (1:158), she writes in self-defense.

If Henry Miller is both a historic figure and the archetypal novelist (for, as we have noted, Nin normally conceives of fiction as a male activity), his wife June is an even more mythic figure who swims into Nin's life. This aquatic metaphor is apt, for as Nin describes June in a letter: "she lives like a submarine, sunk always at the deepest level of instinct and intuition" (1:48). Beautiful, voluptuous, intensely nervous and insecure, June embodies Nin's notion of Woman as pure Id. She summons the infatuated younger woman into a chaos of anarchic emotion. "So June is BEING. . . . She does what others only do in their dreams. Mindless, the life of our unconscious without control. There is a fantastic courage in this, to live without laws, without fetters, without thought of consequences" (1:45). With June an imaginative love affair quickly develops—and as quickly subsides. Suppressed dreams of a feminine love both incestuous and lesbian rise to the surface. The emotional identification is as complete with June as is the intellectual tie with Henry. What stands between the two women preventing full intimacy is Nin's idealism and her devotion to beauty. Though June is a very beautiful woman—as the "Photographic Supplement" attests—her deranged life and tempestuous quarrels create forms of ugliness Nin cannot stomach. Attraction and repulsion are captured in one vivid scene in the Millers' Clichy apartment:

> June believes my seriousness is a reproach, a moral judgment. But it is not that. It is a repudiation of ugliness. Of June rolling in her vomit in her black satin dress. Ugliness and emptiness. The sorrow of emptiness. It is June who vomits, and I who feel I have vomited my whole life. The real wine, the real bodies, the real kisses, the real cafes, the real kitchen, external ecstasies. I yearn for the ecstasies of writing, reading, music, philosophy, contemplation; I yearn for that room I saw through an open window, lined with books, suspended over life, where nothing ever turns to dregs, where landings are not crash landings. . . . I place the cool towels over her forehead. I soothe her. I say, I am not cruel, I love you, June. June is snoring. I lie beside her, all dressed, coat and all. Henry brings coffee for both of us. June drinks it slowly. It is dawn. She asks me, "You will come back tonight?" (1:149)

The polarities in the author's mind between "real life" and aesthetic ecstasy are symbolized in Nin's Parisian surroundings. As the vision of the book-lined room suggests, her feeling for interior places

216

is even more acute than Mead's. The comfortable villa at Louveciennes, for instance, is a "beautiful prison" (1:7) set in its wild garden. Representing as well as containing her bourgeoise existence as dutiful daughter and wife, it stands in clear contrast to the amoral, raffish Clichy world of the Millers. The autobiographer shuttles by train and taxi between the two worlds as, in imagination, she oscillates between Henry's realistic order and June's myth-making destructiveness. Instead of producing creative excitement, however, this split existence soon brings loneliness and anxiety. "It is impossible for me to follow one direction," she cries, "to grow in only one direction" (1:51). Hence she enters treatment with Allendy. Through psychoanalysis she seeks the deep causes of her loneliness and urge to escape from present anxieties and phantoms of the past. The process, like several others in the *Diary,* is conceived as a journey into a labyrinth, one of Nin's favorite self-defining images. "Enter here," she invites the a-mazed reader, "where one discovers that destiny can be directed, that one does not need to remain in bondage to the first wax imprint made on childhood sensibilities. One need not be branded by the first pattern. Once the deforming mirror is smashed, there is a possibility of wholeness; there is a possibility of joy" (1:105).

Though Allendy proves to be himself a limited and lonely man and a doctor distrustful of the artistic imagination, he does initiate his patient's emotional escape from childhood. Together they discover what images the deforming mirror of memory contains. The lost image is the father's. Whereas Margaret Mead, even as a girl, handles her domineering father with a sort of exasperated adult directness, Nin's young self was shattered when Joaquin went away and the rest of the family moved to America. Here is the source of division: her deep need for intimacy as well as her fears about it, her motherly devotion to others and her "masculine" love of a free existence in which the very name of husband can be readily omitted. She has identified— somewhat like Conrad Aiken—both with her mother as the suffering nurturer, and with her father, the charming ladies' man and artist. Although she never uses psychoanalytic terms like "oedipal complex," one revealing scene which communicates her complex feelings about herself, father, mother, and women like June is the one in which, after voicing misgivings about her too-slender girlish figure, she shows Allendy her breasts. As an instance of immature exhibitionism, this moment merits the irony of Patricia Meyer Spacks.[35] But although the rational and fatherly scientist reassures her about her physical femininity, he cannot provide answers to her deeper questions. Because he stands for rational control over the unconscious rather than creative submission to it, Allendy's is a false and superficial wisdom. "I postpone death by living, by suffering, by error, by risking, by giving, by losing. Allendy has chosen to die quickly, early, for the sake of dominating life. The romantic submits to life, the classicist dominates it" (1:190). Nevertheless, she remains grateful to her first therapist, feeling "pride in his insight and his skill, for he recreated me" (1:191).

Whereas Allendy exemplifies the shortcomings of traditional psychoanalysis, Nin finds in Antonin Artaud, the Rumanian playwright of the absurd, Allendy's exact opposite: a mad poet whose masculine self-destructiveness matches June Miller's. His tormented outbursts and brooding silences arouse her womanly sympathy, and Artaud becomes one of the first of Nin's grown-up "children." When he begins to fall in love with her, she "invents" for him the quite accurate story of her split personality, "a divided being [who] could not love humanly and imaginatively both at the same time" (1:228). In one form or another, this is the game she plays with a succession of male protégés throughout the *Diary*.

With the introduction of Artaud, Nin completes the reconstruction of her arrival at maturity. Miller and Allendy on one side and June Miller and Artaud on the other are the four figures of merged fantasy and reality who outline her essential self. Now the second stage of a woman's maturation can begin with the simple yet portentous words "My father came" (1:206). It is a moment amply prepared for. "I find my father again when I am a woman," she writes. "When he comes to me, he who marked my childhood so deeply, I am a full-blown woman. I understand my father as a human being. He is again the man who is also a child" (1:202–3) She is, moreover, not merely a mature woman but the author of the ongoing diary whose various *raisons d'être* are now understood. "The diary began as a diary of a journey, to record everything for my father. It was written for him, and I had intended to send it to him. It was really a letter, so he could follow us into a strange land, know about us. It was also to be an island, in which I could take refuge in an alien land, write French, think my thoughts, hold on to my soul, to myself" (1:202). But whereas the diary once memorialized, punished, and pleaded with the absent parent in French (his adopted European tongue), soon it came to be written in English, that "rich, fertile, subtle, airy, fluid, all-sufficient" language of the foreign and unfriendly American culture (1:215). Just as the original diary allowed her to maintain a secret communion with the faithless father, so writing it in English allies her with her mother. English also signifies acceptance of the family's decision to come to the United States and confirms her commitment, however reluctant, to the world of outward circumstance. Hence, as with Alexander Berkman, the language in which this ex-European's autobiography is written communicates much more than information about the author.

Nin's understanding of these dimensions of her endless life-story has already unfolded by the time of the reconciliation. So the grown daughter possesses the instrument through which she can voice her independence while also acknowledging a continuing need of her father's love and approval. This balancing act always remains closely linked to her adult feminine beauty. "My father did not want a girl," she recalls. "My father was over-critical. He was never satisfied, never pleased. I never remember a compliment or a caress from him. At home, only scenes, quarrels, beatings. And his hard blue eyes on us, looking for the flaws. When I was ill with typhoid fever, almost dying, all he could say was: 'Now you are ugly, how ugly you are' " (1:76). Such painful memories help explain her lifelong love of beauty, decoration, and costumes, her desire, no less fierce than Mae West's, to defy the decades with her physical charm and beauty. Psychologically speaking, therefore, reentry into childhood can occur only after she has displayed her mature feminine charms. Then and only then is she free to reenter the cultivated but tempestuous atmosphere of the Nin household. Torn from this rich European environment, the young girl arrived with her family in New York clinging obstinately to her brother's violin case as they stepped on the dock; *"I wanted people to know I was an artist"* (1:218). What she did not then realize was her mother's part in planning the removal to America as a means of separating her children from their father and immersing them in a non-Latin culture. Hence Nin's later need to rewrite the account of her arrival in New York: *once* it expressed simply a girl's private world of illusion, an oedipal dream; *now* it must contain and connect other, intervening aspects of experience.

Above all, she must face her real father, not the idealized image from girlhood which she once confused with God and a lover. She discovers the truer, present parent by going away with him to the south of France on a short vacation. In several respects, this episode reverberates with oedipal overtones; it is a kind of honeymoon not unlike Maya Angelou's Mexican adventure with her father in *I Know Why the Caged Bird Sings*. In this case, however, Nin sees through her childish father and more deeply into her own nature. Also furthering this mature self-understanding is the gift of a photograph of himself by the supremely egocentric Joaquin. This reminds the reader, as it does the author, of Anaïs's own infatuation with photographs. In the

"Photographic Supplement" to the *Diary,* Nin has assembled a remarkable collection of family photographs, as well as many pictures of herself as dancer, costumed party-goer, indestructibly ageless poser and model. Like father, like daughter, one can say, recalling that in one session with her therapist Nin recalled "my father's passion for photography . . . ; he was always photographing me. He liked to take photos of me while I bathed. He always wanted me naked. All his admiration came by way of the camera" (1:87). Clearly, a continuing need to present herself in idealized poses before a succession of cameramen remains linked to still-powerful childhood memories and desires. The contrast here with Mead and her much more historical motives for the photographs in *Blackberry Winter* could scarcely be starker.

When the daughter sees—partly through a photograph—that her father has become a parody of the narcissistic artist, she realizes that she must abandon him, just as many years before he abandoned her. The "arithmetic of the unconscious," she calls this subtle revenge (1:313). Nevertheless, it is no easy decision. "I felt torn apart by my multiple relationships," she confesses, "and I would have been able to live fully in each one, had enough love and devotion for all of them, but they conflicted with each other. All of my father's values negated Henry's: all his exhortations and his influence were spent on eliminating from my life Artaud, Allendy, psychoanalysis" (1:269). Feeling like a shattered mirror, she again seeks refuge in an older man. Otto Rank, an analyst well-known in Paris in the 1930s for his work with artists, becomes Allendy's successor and opposite: "With Allendy, I was an ordinary woman, a full human being, a simple and naive one" (1:281). Rank too accepts her as a person, but he also perceives that "the core of this human being is an artist" (1:282). Therapy with him is aimed not at adaptation to ordinary life but to her individual world of creativity and the dream. "I tell him everything. He does not separate me from my work. He seizes me through my work. He has understood the role of the diary. Playing so many roles, dutiful daughter, devoted sister, mistress, protector, my father's new-found illusion, Henry's needed all-purpose friend, I had to find one place of truth, one dialogue without falsity" (1:286). Through Rank's vital personality, which transforms insecurity into self-confidence, Nin affirms her own uniqueness.

Otto Rank figures, then, as the final older man in Nin's coming of age. Intellectually at least, he is the vital link in the chain of intimacies composing her initial autobiographical identity. His ideas and personal presence allow her to define the developing pattern of her emotional life and seize control of its movement. By discovering in her art the vital core of a mature feminine identity, she is able to will her own rebirth. It is a fully original act, in Fromm's terms. "The real artist is never concerned with the fact that the story has been told, but in the experience of reliving it"; she writes, "and he cannot do this if he is not convinced of the opportunity for individual expression which it permits" (1:296–97) Autobiographical imagination, however, cannot ignore reality any more than the psychoanalyst can effect a cure without confronting the patient's actual past. The writer's passion for this kind of truth which fuses dream and reality is so strong that it brings about her decision to become a lay analyst under Rank. This represents an ideal compromise. "I want to earn my living by psycho-analysis, so that I may always write as I wish to, never make conces-sions" (1:328). At the same time—it is now the spring of 1934—through Rank she begins to recognize the oppressive presence of the everyday world. "I experienced my first knowledge of the monstrous reality *outside*," she writes. "Pessimism. Suicides. The concrete anxi-eties of men losing power and money. . . . Rank suddenly ruined finan-cially, losing his home, moving, forced to go to America." Against these ugly economic realities it is all the more necessary to oppose the private self and the diary: "with greater, more furious, more desperate stubbornness I continued to build my individual life, as if it were a Noah's Ark for the drowning" (1:331–32).

Nin's fight against life's *outside* climaxes not in episodes of social engagement like, for example, Gertrude Stein's involvement in World War I, but in a characteristically private and bodily crisis, one which dramatizes many dimensions of her newly achieved identity. Nin sud-denly announces her pregnancy. This act of autobiographical parthe-nogenesis is far more mysterious than Maya Angelou's, for no husband or lover has been mentioned. On one level, it represents a sort of suici-dal gesture, for according to her German doctor her girlish body is not made for maternity. In other respects, the fetus represents also the conscious conflict between her motherly and artistic natures, the one able to create life, the other dedicated to art. "It does not belong in my life," she exclaims, "for I have too many people to take care of. I have, already, too many children" (1:338). Moreover, becoming a mother reawakens the fears and desires she has labored hard to con-trol.

I sit in the dark studio and talk to the child: "You can see by what is happening in the world that there is no father taking care of us. We are all orphans. You will be a child without a father as I was a child without a father. That is why I did all the caring; I nursed the whole world. . . .

"It would be better to die than to be abandoned, for you would spend your life haunting the world for this lost father, this fragment of your body and soul, this lost fragment of your very self." (1:339)

This unborn child, of course, does have an actual father, though his name cannot be mentioned. Nin's willing suppression forces the reader to realize that the fetus represents not only the intrusion of male power into her womanly domain but also another fragmented image of her self. Yet when the girl child is stillborn, Nin is not heartbroken as most women would be. The mother's tears are shed in secret; in public she takes pains to keep her eyelash makeup on. "Nature connived to keep me a man's woman, and not a mother"; she concludes, "not a mother to children but to men. Nature shaping my body for the love of man, not of child" (1:346). This explanation (or rationalization) bridges the gap between dream and reality while dramatizing Nin's fundamental notion of her womanly identity.

Suffering and loss, and the reader's possible accusation of Nin's callousness and insincerity, are emotional problems which come together in her description of the stillbirth itself. She dramatizes the miraculous means by which she induced her girlish body, caught in protracted labor pains and unable to deliver the fetus, to complete the stillbirth. When the doctor and nurses cannot induce labor, she commands them: " 'Let me alone.' I place my two hands on my stomach and very slowly, very softly, with the tips of my fingers drum, drum, drum on my stomach, in circles. Round and round, softly, with eyes open in great serenity. The doctor comes near and looks with amazement. The nurses are silent. Drum drum drum drum drum in soft circles, in soft quiet circles. 'Like a savage,' they whisper. The mystery" (1:345).

The mystery has two parts. Next morning comes the spiritual completion of her physical ordeal which is the symbolic death of ordinary woman and rebirth of the artist. Anaïs, the little girl with Spanish Catholic scruples, still remains a part of the mature woman who now seeks her own kind of absolution. Just as no doctor could deliver the stillborn daughter, so no priest can pardon the sins (conscious or unconscious) associated with its coming. The writer performs both tasks for her womanly self in a mystical epiphany in the hospital room. Nin's mention of Saint Theresa in the prelude to this climax is one of the very few allusions in the *Diary* to other female autobiographers.

A blue sky and the sun on the wall. The nurse had raised me to see the new day. I lay there, feeling the sky, and myself one with the sky, feeling the sun and myself one with the sun, and abandoning myself to the immensity and to God. God penetrated my whole body. I trembled and shivered with an immense joy. Cold, and fever and light, an illumination, a visitation, through the whole body, the shiver of a presence. The light and the sky in the body, God in the body and I melting into God. I melted into God. No image, I felt space, gold, purity, ecstasy, immensity, a profound ineluctable communion. . . .

But from that moment on, I felt my connection with God, an isolated, wordless, individual, full connection which gives me an immense joy and a sense of the greatness of life, eternity. I was born. I was born woman. To love God and to love man, supremely and separately. Not to confuse them. (1:347–48)

Despite the mystical language, this moment is far easier to understand psychologically as crisis than as spiritual transformation or *metanoia*. To some readers, no doubt, the final disclaimer that she has learned not to confuse God and man has a hollow ring, for too many connections between the two have already been convincingly established with her own father as their ineradicable link. Both before and after this crisis, Nin remains a man's woman, at least as clearly as Lillian Hellman does. The notion of the artist absorbed from Rank coincides with her own predilections to give the definition of herself as artist a "masculine" orientation. Intuition is the "feminine" quality all artists must possess, but in her case intuition is incorporated into a personality whose models are virtually all men. Other aspects of femininity—including the nurturing instinct acquired by virtue of identification with her mother—are not denied but are to be subordinate. That is the symbolic meaning of the stillbirth: the woman has become the artist by means of a bodily process which underlines the continuing, yet transformed, presence of social stereotypes.

Psychoanalysis has taught Nin to accept her paradoxical identity as one bound to yet free of men. This woman was once a child whose father left her, but the void this created has been filled by the magic of words, whose creator will always be continuous (through memory) with that lonely, insecure child. Throughout the six volumes of her *Diary,* Nin remains that little girl yet continues to grow beyond her into creative maturity as a woman. This scene therefore symbolizes the *"exercise in creation"* which must occur if the neurotic is to overcome what she calls her "stuttering of the soul in life" (1:295). The scene in the hospital room therefore dramatizes the insight learned in the psychiatrist's office:

> My father left: love means abandonment and tragedy, either be abandoned or abandon first, etc. Not only the leap over the obstacle of fatality, but a complete artistic rehearsal of the creative instinct which is a leap beyond the human through a complete rebirth, or perhaps being born truly for the first time. To accomplish this it was not sufficient that I should relive the childhood which accustomed me to pain. I must find a realm as strong as the realm of my bondage to sorrow, by the discovery of my positive, active individuality. Such as my power to write, which Rank seized upon as the most vital core of my true maturity. (1:295)

That this power embraces imagination and dream even more than memory is attested to by the fact that this climax to volume 1 of the *Diary* forms also the climax of Nin's collection of short stories. "Birth" is the last and most powerful tale in *Under a Glass Bell;* it has been transferred to the realm of fiction from the realm of recreated reality with scarcely the change of a single comma.

Nin does not pretend, therefore, to imitate *The Autobiography of Saint Theresa* in this conclusion of her first volume. Her epiphany is not essentially religious; rather, it is an artistic and psychological metaphor. Moreover, the narrative does not end in the hospital room with the womanly writer melted (all too conveniently) into God the Father. Instead, Nin returns to the world, prepared to leave for New York and the adventure of a new career. Indeed, she calls herself an adventurer who has returned "with his arms full of gold." Her friends, happy at the discovery, now forget that they have tried to keep this adventurer from exploring. Though her pronouns here (like Lillian Smith's) are masculine, the meaning is clearly this woman's way of asserting a temporarily successful second birth.

> Psychoanalysis did save me because it allowed the birth of the real me, a most dangerous and painful one for a woman, filled with dangers; for no one has ever loved an adventurous woman as they have loved adventurous men. The birth of the real me might have ended like that of my unborn child. I may not become a saint, but I am very full and very rich. I cannot install myself anywhere yet; I must climb dizzier heights. But I still love the relative, not the absolute: the cabbage and the

warmth of a fire, Bach on the phonograph, and laughter, and talk in the cafes, and a trunk packed for departure, with copies of *Tropic of Cancer,* and Rank's last SOS and the telephone ringing all day, good-bye, good-bye, good-bye. . . . (1:359–60)

III

"To read books by women answers few questions, raises many. The books do not destroy or even seriously challenge the old, man-created myths about women, but they shift the point of view."[36] This cautious conclusion to Spacks's *The Female Imagination* follows her chapter entitled "Free Women." There, in discussing contemporary writers like Lillian Hellman and Anaïs Nin, Spacks traces the struggle for personal liberation which in centuries past characterized the memoirs and novels of Margaret Cavendish, Lady Mary Wortley Montagu, George Eliot, and others. Despite barriers of time and culture, there are significant continuities between these older English lives, historical and imaginary, and contemporary American life-stories. The most fundamental link is the effort, often bitter, silent, and protracted, to take control of one's own social identity by first imagining a new private self. To grow into new awareness of one's body and mind as parts of a distinct entity, to leave home and engage in independent occupations, are attitudes and actions answering the special, secret, often dimly perceived needs of a woman. This peeling away of layers of a false social identity (to adopt the metaphor both Mead and Nin employ) takes as many different forms in prose as there are feminine imaginations able to express themselves. Linking these particular texts to others is the simple but portentous decision to write. It is a more common (and easier) choice today than when Lillian Smith wrote. Though similar risky acts of self-exposure have recently been taken by younger women asserting a provisional self, I have opted to focus attention on these older, more experienced and final women autobiographers. I have done so in the belief that *Blackberry Winter* and volume 1 of the *Diary* are exemplary accounts of women finding themselves in the two activities many Americans consider crucial for women: career and childbirth.

Of the two, Margaret Mead offers the clearer, simpler instance of woman defining a self socially and historically through vocation. This usually masculine prerogative—for her generation, that is—was exercised by taking advantage of her privileged circumstances and making a brilliant entry into a new twentieth-century field which, like the movies, proved unusually receptive to women. The participant-observer science and art of anthropology provides her the appropriate channel into which she directs her formidable energies as woman, team member, and public intellectual. For Mead as for many other women (younger and older), autobiography becomes more of an historical account of past achievements than an imaginative enactment of identity. Yet the tripartite narrative structure (and letting her three husbands speak directly to the reader in characteristic quotations) are techniques of the memoirist we have not met in Du Bois, say, or Adams. In her case the public career is *enveloped,* literally and ideologically, by matriarchy as family lineage and natural childbirth and grandmotherhood as personal experiences and carefully observed actualities. By imaginatively articulating a woman's necessary role in field work and by taking childhood and gender as lifelong subjects for cross-cultural analysis, Mead fits others' expectations at the same time as she defines a unique place in a developing science. Marriages followed by divorces, like keeping her maiden name and choosing natural childbirth, are characteristic ways of both filling and breaking the mold of convention. The historic self reconstructed from such youthful choices and mid-career experiences becomes one model of the woman as thinker. No other American woman has enacted the role of coolly cerebral, morally sensitive public sage with more energy and self-confidence than Margaret Mead. It was a social function, as we have seen, foreshadowed and first imagined at her grandmother's side.

Many women, to be sure, have made their way onto the stage of history carrying a heavier burden of disadvantage and oppression than Margaret Mead. The autobiographies of Emma Goldman and Ida B. Wells, to mention only two obvious cases, are more passionate— though less self-conscious—accounts of becoming a woman in male capitalist white America. In the private realm, as well, there are numerous life-stories (Maya Angelou's again comes to mind, and Maxine Hong Kingston's) which record starker social circumstances and bitterer psychological pressures than Nin sought to contain in her *Diary.* Yet partly because of her experiment in serial autobiography extending over many decades, Nin demonstrates a radical commitment to autobiography as an imaginative and therapeutic act which these younger women have not, so far, matched. Over the years of mid-century, the *Diary* becomes an increasingly flexible instrument for the assertion of a romantic self. Nin illustrates, in a sustained way which can only be hinted at by my discussion of volume 1, woman's power to remake herself in the image of her dreams, without losing sight of the power (and secret appeal) of masculine myths influencing that development. Thus she brings into clear focus Spacks's question:

226

how exactly do women's autobiographical writings alter readers' perceptions of the presence and power of ancient, man-made myths operating in their lives?

To return to the biosocial stereotype, first, both Nin and Mead suggest ways of confronting an undeniable circumstance: women's bodies are culturally defined as an inescapable somatic condition which makes their lives variable and vulnerable. This imposed condition, even more starkly represented by Maya Angelou's rape than by Anaïs Nin's stillborn daughter, must at times quite simply be accepted. The candor and courage to expose and accept one's body, to assert at the same time its malleability and capacity for change, are qualities more convincingly expressed in these women's narratives than in many men's autobiographies. These women know and show that we are all physical beings.

The quest for a different, more graceful and ingratiating body takes different forms in contemporary women's autobiographies. It may originate in shameful moments like a little girl's stammering recitation in Stamps Colored Methodist Episcopal Church which opens *I Know Why the Caged Bird Sings,* or the case of typhoid fever which makes a fastidious father exclaim how ugly his daughter is. Or it may arise in less dramatic desires to become like a beautiful mother or competent grandmother. Whatever pasts have been confronted, the present and future need not find a woman caught in the same way within the cage of her body. Bearing children therefore need not define a self in social terms as a mother unless one so chooses. Conversely, accepting society's identification of women with children can, as in the case of Margaret Mead, keep one's mind and body youthful, sharp, adaptable. Thus change and continuity in one's self-concept are realistically and symbolically illustrated through preoccupation with the female body. The stereotype is altered and enlarged by being fully and consciously embraced.

Much the same can be said of the pressures on women to accept a relational status as inevitable if not natural. Both Mead and Nin are exemplary in accepting family ties and marital obligations as necessary elements of their historical selves. But Nin, the more intense celebrant and analyst of intimacy, willingly surrenders the role of wife. Other women's autobiographies—*The Woman Warrior,* for instance—also are narratives in which the very existence (not to mention importance) of a husband (and in Kingston's case, a child) is shrouded in silence. Women, no less than men like Sullivan and Adams, possess the freedom to pick and choose among such self-defining relationships. Their willingness to take intimacy as their theme but to treat it circumspectly represents another shift in perspective in women's autobiographies.

Another may be the fact that both Mead and Nin, in common with other women, present themselves as in-between persons, possessed of flexible ego boundaries and thus able to accept a thick skein of relationships *because* they are able to move in and out of such connections. They seem able to bridge traditional role expectations that characterize—and limit—the men and other women among whom they live. Often the roles of mother, wife, or daughter are played provisionally, with a strong sense of both their importance *and* their susceptibility to change. This in-between consciousness, often associated with the artist, is also linked, here as in other women's histories, to intimate experiences of different cultures and social groups.

Still another man-made myth whose persistence is acknowledged but whose significance is perceived unconventionally is the assumption that women are not by nature abstract thinkers. Intuitive, artistic, practical, personal are indeed ways of characterizing the mental outlooks of both the field worker and the writer–lay analyst. Neither woman, however, allows this to inhibit speculation and generalization. Indeed, *Blackberry Winter* is in some ways as ideologically explicit a life-history as *The Autobiography of W. E. B. Du Bois.* Nin, too, fills her *Diary* with reflections and hypotheses. Yet when she finds herself overwhelmed by an oppressive ring of relationships with men, it may seem all too "natural" for her to exclaim,

> I close my eyes to the immense web of ideologies. They weary me, this gigantic juggling of systems, orders, prophecies. I am a woman. I let my vision fall short. I understand everything, Spengler, Rank, Lawrence, Henry; but I get tired of those glacial regions. I feel their coldness, too high, too far from life. I am not happy there. I think of myself: I am tired of ideas. (1:304)

Yet in another mood equally frankly reported, she shows how much wider a range of experience, idea, and emotion her *Diary* contains than many male autobiographies. She can observe that her pleasure in intellectual discourse is "almost akin to the joys of love." "No matter what ideas, psychology, history, or art I learned from man," she explains later, "I learned to convert it into the affirmation of my own identity and my own beliefs."[37] In fact, Nin's practical psychoanalysis, like Mead's anthropological outlook, illustrates the non-Cartesian understanding of reality in which mind and matter, the self and the other, are fused. Acceptance of the necessary but principled subjectivity of all human thought is no longer the mark of an inferior, feminine mentality, but rather evidence of a highly sophisticated, modern understanding. Grasping together the phenomena of experience—subject, object, and their union in language—seems to be a capacity many women writers possess.

Filtering thought, experience, and emotion through the alembic of the author's retrospective consciousness is of course what occurs in all autobiography. Women do not essentially differ in their understanding of the art of personal narrative from men. But because their status has so often been defined as inferior and their freedom circumscribed by custom or law, women frequently are driven to treat personal history explicitly as an ideological instrument of liberation. Hence Margaret Mead and Anaïs Nin are appropriate authors to have treated here in exemplary terms. Though their social contexts are obviously unrepresentative, the very fact of education and class advantage serves to underline basic barriers women face in twentieth-century America. Nin took a while to see beyond the circle of intimacy which in volume 1 of the *Diary* seems to some readers to smack often of aestheticism. Yet to the end of her life she defended her plan to construct a new kind of autobiography out of a woman's understanding of society, art, and psychoanalysis. In "Notes on Feminism," she offers an eloquent late defense of the private cultivation of the self. "The nature of my contribution to the Women's Liberation Movement is not political but psychological," she writes.

> I get thousands of letters from women who have been liberated by the reading of my diaries, which are a long study of the psychological obstacles which have prevented woman from her fullest evolution and flowering. I studied the negative influence of religion, of racial and cultural patterns, which action alone and no political slogans can dissolve. I describe in the diaries the many restrictions confining woman. The diary itself was an escape from judgment, a place in which to analyze the truth of woman's situation. I believe that is where the sense of freedom has to begin. I said begin, not remain.[38]

It is in precisely these terms that Nin's *Diary* and Mead's *Blackberry Winter* are offered here as exemplary women's autobiographies. They should be considered important, imaginative, but not indispensable beginning points in an exploration which must range beyond, before, and behind. Peeling off layers of an inherited social self, to discover in the act of autobiography a more satisfactory—because less myth-ridden, less man-made—identity, makes these two women exemplars. But one should not forget that quests like theirs began at the century's beginning in life-stories like Jane Addams's and Mary Antin's. Similar struggles continue to be recorded today. Moreover, in autobiographies of the 1970s like *I Know Why the Caged Bird Sings, Pentimento,* and *The Woman Warrior,* the adequacy of nonfictional prose to contain the complexities of women's private experiences is questioned. In Chapter Eight we will see Lillian Hellman as another exemplary woman autobiographer tackling again and again the formal problem of reinventing her self in a man's world.

7

Two Recreate One: The Act of Collaboration in Recent Black Autobiography—Ossie Guffy, Nate Shaw, Malcolm X

As READERS HAVE REALIZED since at least 1945, autobiography is among black Americans one of the richest, most varied, and most revealing modes of personal expression. The date refers not only to the end of World War II and the beginning of the atomic era but also to the publication of *Black Boy*. The distribution of Wright's autobiography to over 325,000 members of the Book-of-the-Month Club and its enthusiastic reception was a landmark in American literary history. One of his severer critics, however, was W. E. B. Du Bois, whose very different notions of autobiography as history had most recently found expression in *Dusk of Dawn*, published in 1940.[1] Both books reveal their differences in the subtitles: *An Essay Toward an Autobiography of a Race Concept* reflects Du Bois's denial of the luxury of a purely personal chronicle; *A Record of Childhood and Youth* reminds Wright's readers that *Black Boy* is not, after all, a novel but a version of actual events in the author's own experience. By example and precept, the historian-sociologist and the novelist and short-story writer helped to define the nature and scope of black autobiography which in the succeeding generation came to mirror wider and wider areas of black life in America. In the decades since these epochal works, nearly every segment of the black experience has found a voice through the art of personal history. Male and female, young and very old, the Harvard-educated scholar and the Alabama tenant farmer, the revolutionary prisoner and the Hollywood actress, the expatriate novelist and the Watts housewife—these and others have tried, like Du Bois, to repossess historical selves in a straightforward memoir or, like Wright, to dramatize by various fictional techniques the often bitter truths of their private experience.

231

As both history and literature, autobiography has indeed proved capacious and flexible enough to satisfy the expressive needs of diverse talents and careers. The result is a cultural achievement vastly extending the tradition Wright and Du Bois themselves inherited from Langston Hughes, Zora Neale Hurston, and Claude McKay, from Ida B. Wells, James Weldon Johnson, and Booker T. Washington. If the works of these earlier writers—*Up from Slavery, Along This Way, Crusade for Justice, I Wonder as I Wander, A Long Way from Home,* and *Dusttracks on a Road*—originally attracted fewer readers than *Black Boy,* all have since profited from the paperback revolution, which has made *Roots* and *Up from Slavery* almost as readily available as *True Confessions.* Haley's best-seller, aided enormously by television, is but one of several recent experiments in black autobiography. More conventional narratives by James Baldwin, Claude Brown, Malcolm X, Eldridge Cleaver, Maya Angelou, Dick Gregory, George Jackson, and Anne Moody have also found readers who discover in them compelling visions of what it means to be black in white America. For their part, black autobiographers now play a major role in the struggle for cultural independence within the black community. Paradoxically, this move helps to widen communication with white readers as well as black.

Because contemporary black autobiography is such a characteristic and influential form of cultural expression, it has attracted critics, historians, and commentators in growing numbers. It is the only subdivision of American autobiography to have in print four full-length studies devoted to it. The descendants of Du Bois and Wright are thus beginning to receive the careful appreciation their works demand.[2]

One aspect of this rich subject noted by nearly every commentator but little discussed in detail is the fact that many recent black autobiographies are not written by their subjects alone but are the result of collaboration. This practice has characterized American autobiography since antebellum times, when some slave narratives appeared (either openly or secretly) as the work of a ghostwriter or amanuensis. Collaboration is of course by no means confined to black autobiography but has been practiced by all sorts of persons willing to satisfy the curiosity of their fellows about the lives of the inarticulate, uneducated, or the preoccupied. By this device readers have recently been given the autobiographies of many different black Americans: Muhammad Ali, Arthur Ashe, Pearl Bailey, Sammy Davis, Jr., Althea Gibson, Dick Gregory, Billie Holiday, Mahalia Jackson, Joe Louis, Willie Mays, Archie Moore, Floyd Patterson, Jackie Robinson, and Nate Shaw. "Edited by Ed Fitzgerald," "As Told to Charles Einstein," "with

Evan McLeod Wylie," "Billie Holiday with William Dufty," *The Auto-biography of Malcolm X* with the assistance of Alex Haley, *All God's Dangers: The Life of Nate Shaw* by Theodore Rosengarten, *Ossie: The Autobiography of a Black Woman,* "As Told to Caryl Ledner by Ossie Guffy"—these and similar title-page notations draw attention to an increasingly prevalent autobiographical occasion in contemporary America. Indeed, if *nigger:* "An Autobiography by Dick Gregory with Robert Lipsyte," is at all representative, the ersatz life-story may often outsell conventional autobiographies; "Over One Million Copies Sold!" is the publisher's boast printed directly beneath the two names responsible for *nigger.* However, as has already been seen in the case of *Black Elk Speaks,* collaboration can prove not merely amenable but, in fact, essential to powerful artistic narratives which possess great historical significance as well. It would be wrong to consign collaborative autobiographies exclusively to the realm of either popular or black culture.

Nevertheless, black autobiography offers a convenient and appropriate context for considering collaboration as a distinctive occasion of contemporary literary culture. Not only are there many examples to choose from, but their imaginative range is surprisingly wide. Measured by historical significance as well as audience appeal, a great gap yawns between a merely topical success like *Yes I Can, The Story of Sammy Davis, Jr.* and the contemporary masterpiece *The Autobiography of Malcolm X.* To explore and compare some representative texts across this spectrum is the aim of this chapter. In doing so, we will raise general issues about this special form of autobiographical discourse which, though arising within the framework of race and oppression, poverty and success, comedy and tragedy in various black lives, go beyond even these important themes. Given such vital cultural concerns, how may the historian of culture use ambiguous personal documents like these, which are neither true autobiographies nor biographies but an intermediate mode? Must (or can) one read collaborations in the same way one reads and reality-tests conventional life-histories? How are details of the collaborative process itself communicated, if at all, and where does this occur in the text? Is such "background" information important? Can one come to trust a collaborative work as one trusts (or distrusts) a traditional narrative? How is that trust earned or forfeited? Though such questions will necessarily bring different, even contradictory, answers depending upon the texts addressed, this whole phenomenon is significant enough to take seriously. At one level, comparison and contrast serve to define and heighten the artistry of individual achievements. More broadly, to look at the practice of collaboration between a literate and an illiterate person raises issues of exploitation. Although the vitality and flexibility of contemporary autobiographies are enhanced when collaborations are included in the discussion, their presence has perplexing ideological and moral implications. More starkly than elsewhere in this book, the ensuing pages on Dick Gregory and Ossie Guffy and Nate Shaw and Malcolm X drive home the fact that autobiography is often not a nicely delimited literary activity; it can be created out of frankly commercial motives as its practitioners recover and celebrate new areas of human experience.

I

That many recent life-stories of black Americans are variations on the collaboration occasion suggests initially a look at signals—at the intentions of makers and the expectations of consumers of this novel literary product. These frequently converge, as one might expect, in the uncomplicated desire to share the story of a life in as simply vivid and appropriate language as possible. History, understood as the narrative unfolding of social relationships and temporal changes within an individual existence, remains basic to the intentions of most black autobiographers. Roger Rosenblatt notes the prevalence of historical autobiographies among black writers and succinctly accounts for it: "No black American author has ever felt the need to invent a nightmare to make his point."[3] Given this overriding ideological motive, there is a tendency, as Du Bois once confessed, to treat niceties of style and inventive techniques of narration as minor matters. Drawing attention to the creative self at the typewriter or tape recorder is often not very important, since there are two persons in that situation and neither subject nor scribe is famous in that particular role. (One notes how few well-known writers appear as partners in autobiographical collaborations.) *What* has happened in this life is more immediately compelling than *how* it is being communicated or *by whom*. Hence the line between autobiography and biography is sometimes deliberately vague.

Yet style and language are decisive in at least one respect: most collaborative autobiographies deliberately simulate an oral performance by the subject. The reader almost always *hears* a voice. If that subject is well known, the process of reality-testing begins (perhaps unconsciously) by comparing this recreated voice with the one heard on other occasions—on the screen, record, television set, or in public appearances. Collaborating authors often anticipate this elementary historical response in a prefatory note or introduction. A typical example is found in *The Raw Pearl.*

> Most autobiographical books by people whom we frequently refer to as celebrities, [writes Hiram Hayden the editor] including actors, entertainers, etc., are either actually written by someone else, though attributed to the celebrity, or are published "as told to" someone else.
>
> This is not the case with Pearl Bailey's book. Another editor, Wendell Shackelford (who worked on the book prior to coming to work for Harcourt Brace & World), and I have worked editorially from the transcript of many tape-recorded conversations with Miss Bailey. We have been at some pains in helping to give the book its final shape to retain not only her own words but, as we think of it, her distinctive voice. We hope that the legion of her admirers will find that voice to be the same in this book as it is when she talks to an audience—vivid, spontaneous, natural.[4]

Because Hayden is more careful than most to distinguish between "words" and "voice" and locates himself and Shackelford in between the reader and Pearl Bailey, his description applies widely to other collaborations. Elsewhere, however, such explanations are often missing or relegated to the back of the book. The latter is the case with the afterword to Mahalia Jackson's autobiography. "*Movin' on Up* is the result of a collaboration which carried Mr. Wylie across the continent, to Miss Jackson's Chicago home and New Orleans birthplace, to Music Inn in the Berkshires and to concert halls and recording studios. A song by Mahalia Jackson, can still send shivers down his spine, Mr. Wylie says."[5] Because Evan McLeod Wylie doesn't himself speak here, the final impression is of an impartially sympathetic, and hence trustworthy, recorder. Such modesty, essentially that of the anonymous ghostwriter, is underlined by the location of the afterword.

A somewhat subtler way of apprising the reader of the presence of two authors and winning assent to their activity is to be found in *nigger.* Though Robert Lipsyte's name is on the cover, his precise role is never explained. Instead, the book begins with a series of prefatory notes, two of which sound very much like Gregory's own voice. But the third is printed in italics, as if to leave in doubt who speaks:

Richard Claxton Gregory was born on Columbus Day, 1932. A welfare case. You've seen him on every street corner in Amer-

ica. You knew he had rhythm by the way he snapped his cloth while he shined your shoes. Happy little black boy, the way he grinned and picked your quarter out of the air. Then he ran off and bought himself a Twinkie Cupcake, a bottle of Pepsi-Cola, and a pocketful of caramels.

You didn't know that was his dinner. And you never followed him home. [6]

The ensuing narrative does follow young Richard home, in order to recapture the bittersweet realities of Gregory's childhood and youth in a family tenuously held together by Momma's loving sacrifices and periodically torn apart by an absent father's drunken return. In the recital, which continues to the book's close, we presumably hear Gregory's own intonations, rhythms, and comic style of storytelling, as captured by Lipsyte. Though the narrator begins as a St. Louis slum kid and grows by pluck and perseverance into a collegiate track star, the presiding presence is that of the present nightclub entertainer and well-known civil rights activist. A sheaf of photographs documents this transformation from obscurity and oppression to fame and self-assertion. Though Gregory laces the anecdotes with sharp jibes at injustice and racism, his message is upbeat. "When we came back to Chicago," he remarks of one civil rights trip to the South, "there was a letter waiting for me that brought tears to my eyes. I had made *Who's Who in America.*

> That's why so many people are willing to lay down their lives to save this great country from the cancer of hate that is destroying it. Where else in the world could a Negro, born and raised on relief, make *Who's Who?* In 1952 I was a welfare case, and in 1963 I was on a list of famous men. In America, with all of its evils and faults, you can still reach through the forest and see the sun. But we don't know yet whether that sun is rising or setting for our country. (193)

Through Gregory's final Franklinian metaphor, one is reminded that the authors may be aware of a familiar autobiographical model in recounting another poor boy's rise to fame through hard work, independence, and ingratiating tact. Though Gregory's humor differs from the Doctor's, both men learn early how to manipulate men and words in order to assert and advance themselves without provoking violent opposition. Both are didactic storytellers. Once, for instance, Gregory recalls his first high school prom. The social tensions between himself as a poor boy and his snobbish middle-class date are repeated in the midnight fight which ends the dance. A crowd of hoodlums—poorer boys who cannot afford to rent a tuxedo or buy a gardenia—greet the departing dancers with sticks and blows. But Gregory's wisecracks and his reputation as a track star save him from humiliation. The lesson of that night is driven home in a brief conclusion:

> There were other proms after that, and I learned what to do to have fun, to take girls who wanted to be with me, who wanted to dance to funky songs. I learned to slip out of the dance two hours early and buy some wine for the meanest cat standing outside. . . . I opened the windows so the cats outside could peep right in. . . . The guys on the outside were in on the party, too. And they acted nice because they didn't want those windows pulled to shut them out. (65)

As narrative-*cum*-sermon, *nigger* consists of a string of such symbolic episodes in which violence (though an ever-present danger and often a reality) is turned aside by jokes. Humor cajoles hostile nightclub hecklers or late-night hate-callers to "act nice." Bigots are beguiled into acknowledging their shared humanity with this black storyteller who mixes satire and sentiment so adroitly.

Building bridges across the footlights, or from the inner city to the comfortable suburbs, is likewise message and motive in other collaborative acts in recent black autobiography. For Gregory or Mahalia Jackson this objective is facilitated by the subject's standing as public figure. Occasionally, however, something has happened to the public image which turns a success story into an apology. Such is the case with *Lady Sings the Blues*. Billie Holiday's well-publicized drug habit and frequent arrests provide a very different theme and conclusion to her rags-to-riches story. "A habit is hell for those you love," she explains. "And in this country it's the worst kind of hell for those who love you."[7] The bitter irony is that neither fame nor her attempts to reform save her from persecution by the police. "I've had my troubles with the habit for fifteen years, on and off," she confesses. "I've spent a small fortune on stuff. I've kicked and stayed clean; and I've had my setbacks and had to fight all over again to get straight" (187). This double fight with herself and the law is connected to the act of writing her autobiography when she remarks, "But I'm not crazy. I knew when I started to work on this book that I couldn't expect to tell the truth in it unless I was straight when it came out" (187). Perhaps because *Lady Sings the Blues* claims to be "straight" autobiography, William Dufty is prevented from writing the last chapter. Unlike Haley, perhaps he has no contract allowing him the biographer's last word. Only on the back cover is the reader reminded of Billie Holiday's tragic defeat by drugs, in a blurb which calls her "the greatest blues woman to live—and die—in black America."

If works like *Movin' on Up* and *nigger* are representative success stories, *Lady Sings the Blues* is the variation which demonstrates that many collaborations are essentially historical fables. Facts like drug addiction, while not ignored, must be fitted into the hallowed success formula: from the farm or slum to Carnegie Hall or Yankee Stadium. Often part of the package is a glossy insert of photographs, intended to lend visual proof of the fable's truthfulness. Words, voice, and pictures are, then, the grounds on which the reader is asked to rest his faith. Words relate the subject's chronological story. Voice recreates the self's style. Together, words and voice underline widely shared American beliefs in tolerance, hard work, talent, and money. Though a black audience is sometimes specifically addressed, the usual readership is assumed (often tacitly) to be middle-class, white, and as unfamiliar with a black ghetto as with the Brown Derby. The collaborators' ploy is to dramatize the subject's familiarity with both worlds and his or her right to criticize as well as praise America on grounds of experience with both extremes. That this social critique often employs a vocabulary and rhetoric reminiscent of the black pulpit is nicely illustrated by *nigger*. "You didn't die a slave for nothing, Momma," Gregory exclaims. "You brought us up. You and all those Negro mothers who gave their kids the strength to go on, to take that thimble to the well while the whites were taking buckets. Those of us who weren't destroyed got stronger, got calluses on our souls. And now we're ready to change a system, a system where a white man can destroy a black man with a single word, Nigger. When we're through, Momma, there won't be any niggers any more" (209).

II

When, however, the subject/author of an autobiography is unfamous and presumably untalented, this formula for successful collaboration doesn't work. To such life-stories the average reader brings initially little more than curiosity—sometimes, in fact, skepticism or outright hostility. Consequently the creators of books like *Ossie* or *All God's Dangers* face a different task: to locate an unknown life within an acceptable framework of the known and the socially significant (history) and to tell an appealing, convincing story (discourse). In recent years this challenge has attracted many writers as popular interest in the lives of less visible Americans has grown, encouraged by the social ferment of the civil rights movement, by new techniques in oral history, and by new sociological models for the life study, such as the work of Oscar Lewis. Two striking products of this cultural situation are *Ossie: The Autobiography of a Black Woman* (1971) and *All God's Dangers: The Life of Nate Shaw* (1974). Both introduce readers to the lower reaches of American society—one urban, the other rural—from which their subjects, unlike Gregory or even Holiday, have not been able to escape. Here speak black voices a middle-class reader may never have heard before, telling of a world glimpsed perhaps only through car windows and even more remote than the exotic venues of the boxer or entertainer. If we can generalize from these instances, this remoteness stimulates the authors to describe with some care the participants and the circumstances of their collaboration. Unlike paperback productions written to capitalize on the more or less ephemeral fame of a black subject, these two autobiographies make more serious claims on our attention as historical documents.

"I'm a woman, I'm black, I'm a little under forty," Ossie Guffy announces, "and I'm more of black America than Ralph Bunche or Rap Brown or Harry Belafonte, because I'm one of the millions who ain't bright, militant, or talented."[8] However, these downright words are not the book's opening note; they are preceded by a preface by the actual writer, Caryl Ledner, who as a concluding note *About the Author* points out, is a television writer living in Beverly Hills with her husband and two children. Thus a middle-class, presumably white person presents Ossie, tells how they came to collaborate, and even what her life means. "During this turbulent time of the emergence of the black American from the shadow world into which he has been pushed by white society," Ledner writes, comes this "personal history of one black woman, growing up in the less dramatic but more usual world of lower-middle-class America, in the period from 1931 to the present." Then she continues:

> I was introduced to Ossie Cuffy in the fall of 1967 by a social worker who recognized in Ossie the real spirit of the black woman in America. . . . When we met, we liked each other immediately, and we both felt that we would like to spend a little time together getting to know each other and that, if at the end of that time we both wanted it, I would try to get Ossie's story down on paper. We both wanted it, and this is the result. Ossie talked and I wrote, and I've tried to keep to her words and her thoughts. I've added continuity and some organization; but the thoughts and the feelings and the reactions are Ossie—a woman who is black. (vii–viii)

239

By being so explicit, Ledner promises the reader a more faithful record of a more representative black life than is true of most collaborations. She seeks to accomplish this, first of all, like the others, by creating a voice of vernacular vigor and apparent candor. Her Ossie is a woman educated by bitter experiences but sustained by innate optimism—in several ways a younger version of Dick Gregory's Momma. "I've been on welfare, but I ain't never been on dope. I got more children than I can rightly take care of, but I ain't got more than I can love; I've worked until I fell over and then got up and worked again—and I ain't one whit different than most of my neighbors" (ix). Then she addresses the question of the stereotypes prevalent in the mass media. "Your TV screens are showing more black faces," she observes, "and you're reading about us in your papers, but you ain't getting any picture of what we're really like, 'cause most of us ain't got any voices speaking for us. I don't think most whites are like Richard Nixon or Lucy or George Wallace, and most blacks ain't like Dick Gregory or Julia or Muhammad Ali. Most whites are like you, and most blacks are like me" (ix–x).

Such disarming forthrightness is of course a calculated rhetorical strategy. It is one which covers up some real problems. Though Ledner herself distinguishes between Ossie's actual words and her private thoughts and feelings, the reader has no way of doing so within the text or of checking any part of the story against external evidence. Although stereotypes about black life, the ADC family, and the welfare mother are criticized, some still remain. They probably persist because of the social gap between the collaborators and their temporary alliance under the aegis of a social worker confident enough to declare that Ossie Guffy represents that dubious abstraction "the spirit of the black woman in America." Like other slick and popular studies of "the black experience" aimed at capitalizing upon the events of the recent past, *Ossie* proves to be a puzzling mixture of glib Madison Avenue sociology and genuine self-presentation. Though perhaps sincere and often accurate, it strikes a convenient ideological compromise between "white man, listen" and "what's done is done." Though this may reflect the early 1970s outlook of many blacks, it may more accurately reflect the wish of both authors to appeal to a distant, potentially disapproving, and predominantly white public. Neither Ossie Guffy nor Caryl Ledner is explicit enough in confronting such questions. Neither seems to know how difficult it is to establish an authentic self through the words and assumptions of another who, though a woman like herself, comes from a very different world.

If *nigger* illustrates the formula success story at its best and *Lady Sings the Blues* is a confessional or apologetic variant, *Ossie* suggests another impulse behind collaborative autobiographies during the past decade or more: to capture a mass audience by blending popular sociology and journalism in the manufacture of a plausible, affecting, but dubious version of an obscure life. All three works affirm the basically historical consciousness of black autobiographers and their collaborators; all three simulate oral performances as the natural narrative entry into the self and its past. But to turn from these representative works to *All God's Dangers* is to enter virtually a different cultural realm, one in which history is defined far more precisely and the act of oral performance refined into something approaching genuine folk art. Nate Shaw and Theodore Rosengarten cooperate so well in this achievement because they share the same autobiographical assumptions. That is, both the illiterate farmer and the Harvard historian are attuned to the varied possibilities in storytelling for self-location, self-disclosure, and self-definition. Moreover, they see this history-making activity extending always beyond the self to embrace time, nature, and society. Consequently Shaw's autobiography stands demonstrably closer to *The Autobiography of Malcolm X* than it does to more topical successes like *nigger* or *Ossie*. Only a close and critical scrutiny of Rosengarten's techniques and assumptions as historian-scribe suggests the work's limitations as measured by the masterpiece published nine years before.

As with other works already discussed, *All God's Dangers* puts the issue of collaboration right up front, first by modestly refusing to claim the term "autobiography" for its title and then through Rosengarten's long, prefatory address to the reader. While this letter establishes Rosengarten's *modus operandi,* it also continues the practice of having a white spokesman introduce and in effect sponsor a black man's story. This perpetuates the cultural manipulation Frederick Crews suggests when he notes in "Do Literary Studies Have an Ideology?" how often in our capitalist culture "the oppressor researches the oppressed."[9] Nevertheless, the preface at least spells out how and why this has been done. Moreover, in explaining his editorial role Rosengarten also emphasizes the shape of the subsequent long recitation and the explicit notions about history, autobiography, and personal identity behind it. Thereby the editor also acknowledges the roles he has played as literary and cultural critic.

"Nate Shaw belongs to the tradition of farmer-storytellers," he begins.

These people appear in all civilizations and are only beginning to disappear in the most advanced ones. Their survival is bound up with the fate of communities of small farmers. When these communities disperse and farms become larger, fewer in number, and owned more and more by absentee investors, the sources of story material and audiences dry up.

But the decline of storytelling is more complicated than this. It has to do with the passing of craft activities, like basket-making, which generate the rhythms at which stories flow; with the appeal of competing voices of culture, such as television; and with the unfortunate popular assumption that history is something that takes place in books and books are to be read in school.[10]

This comment not only locates Shaw in a broad historical process, it deemphasizes race while stressing the significance of farming, crafts, and place as central elements in his identity. That self has been recreated during long sessions of storytelling before Rosengarten's tape recorder, stretching to more than 120 hours in all. The writer freely admits that his translation does not do full justice to Shaw's virtuoso performance, which sometimes has created special problems for the editor. "In editing the transcripts of our recordings I sometimes had to choose among multiple versions of the same story," he writes; "other times, I combined parts of one version with another for the sake of clarity and completeness. Stories that seemed remote from Shaw's personal development I left out entirely. By giving precedence to stories with historical interest or literary merit I trust I haven't misrepresented him" (xxiv). Finally Rosengarten confesses to a very personal relationship with his eighty-six-year-old subject. "Here, I want to make my sympathies clear. Nate Shaw was—and is—a hero to me. I think he did the right thing when he joined the Sharecroppers Union and fought off the deputy sheriffs, though, of course, I had nothing to lose by his actions. My questions must unavoidably have expressed this judgment but they did not, I believe, change the substance of his responses" (xix).

One editorial decision, however, which does influence the manner if not the matter of this story as autobiography is Rosengarten's use of pseudonyms. Except for a few public figures like Booker T. Washington, the characters in *All God's Dangers* live under aliases. This tampering with the subject's historical identity transforms him into something of a type or even literary character. The writer defends his editorial decision "as a measure of protection and privacy" for the old black man and his extensive family. He also specifies exactly how names have been changed: "I have had to change the names of all the people and most of the places in the narrative," he explains. "In devising aliases I tried to be faithful to the sources, sounds, and meanings of the original names. Generally, where blacks and whites shared the same surnames or first names, they share aliases here" (xxiv). Nonetheless, one wonders about Rosengarten's undeclared motives. For one thing, Nate Shaw's true identity as Ned Cobb was apparently pretty widely known in Alabama, partly as a result of his act of defiance in 1932 when he came to the assistance of a fellow black farmer whose mules were being seized by a grasping landlord. Cobb was wounded in this unprecedented refusal to accept the inequities of the sharecropping system. He served twelve years in prison. As a minor episode in Southern labor history, Ned Cobb's deed is part of history. As "Nate Shaw" he is slightly displaced from this position and put more firmly under the manipulative control of the writer-editor. Furthermore, as Rosengarten admits, Ned Cobb has a place in literary history as well. Among the acknowledgments in the first edition is a cryptic bow to "John Beecher for leading the way almost forty years ago" (xxv). What this remark fails to specify is the existence of "In Egypt Land, A Narrative Poem, 1940."[11] Though this poetic version of Cobb's stand may not be as familiar to readers as Faulkner's Yoknapatawpha tales (which are mentioned in relation to Nate Shaw's storytelling artistry), nevertheless Beecher, the liberal white poet, long ago placed this particular black man in our literary annals. Writing much closer to the historical event, he felt no need to cloak Cobb's identity. Thus when, in the later paperback edition, Rosengarten inserts an announcement of Ned Cobb's true identity and names Beecher's poem, he is in effect admitting something that should have been spelled out from the outset. Nate Shaw's name, like the alias "Tukabahchee County, Alabama," and the book's metaphoric title, testifies not only to Rosengarten's urge toward the mythic and fictional elements in the story and life he has recorded but also to a proprietary impulse which smacks of exploitation.

Nonetheless, when one begins Nate Shaw's own account of that life, such doubts about the collaboration process are almost swept away by the vernacular poetry and dramatic presence of the old tale-teller and folk historian. Shaw's understanding of historical autobiography is so intuitively accurate and complete that there is no question of wholesale manipulation by the educated questioner from Cambridge. "Them secrets I know—I got by history," he observes of his decades-long experience as cotton-farmer, basket-maker, and penitentiary prisoner. "You ought to look back at it as well as forwards" (512). Quite clearly, he has made this repossession of the past himself. "As the years come and go it leaves me with a better understandin of history," he declares (37). Though Rosengarten has ar-

ranged and pared Shaw's recollections in order to create a more coherent narrative, this is probably no more an intervention (that is, no
more of a reinvention) than what Lipsyte or Wylie have done with
their subjects' words. Shaw demands respect and credence not only
for the astonishing richness and precision of his remarkable memory—it is "as though he had kept a mental journal," Rosengarten mar-
vels (xix)—but also by his keen insights into his own and others'
identity and location in social time and space. He possesses an unusual
sensitivity to the individual natures of the people he has known, black
and white, over the generations. He supplies each one's characteristic
combination of speech, gesture, and action. Shaw evinces still another
autobiographical attribute which links him to Malcolm X: he can sus-
pend present feelings, often bitter and frustrated, to recapture afresh
the attitudes and emotions of his younger self. Again like both Malcolm X and Black Elk, he has no trouble stamping his ever-developing
personality upon the narrative through the imaginative precision of
his vigorous Alabama idiom. Finally, the inveterate tale-spinner knows
the difference between stories told to entertain and those told "for
the truth" (4). Both by words and voice, then, Nate Shaw displays the
consciousness of the true autobiographer. This Theodore Rosengarten
could scarcely have simulated.

Always Shaw's imagination is a historical one, anchoring himself
in particular times and places and within specified social networks.
Everywhere the "rock bottom" reality of his existence is expressed in
work. Unremitting labor during seventy years, a span nearly equal to
Du Bois's, defines his outlook, imagination, vocabulary, and his capacity to stand on his own feet in the face of all God's dangers. "I come
here to work out. I didn't come in this world to rust out" he once reminds his improvident, domineering father (139). Circumstances
which prove oppressive fate for the average black sharecropper
become in Shaw's case opportunities to "come up from the bottom" (124), to become a renter and gradually accumulate the mules
and Model T's which earn him the envy of his less energetic neighbors.
He observes with quiet pride, "This whole country knowed me for my
work" (184). By skill and sweat he relates to his local world—to nature
and animals, tools and guns, to members of his family and to fellow
blacks, and to the whites who "work" sharecroppers and keep them
tied to the land in peonage. Nate too remains tied to the land, but by
his own choice and in his own way. His steady industry affords him
the means to follow his relatives to the North, but except for one brief
trip to Philadelphia, he remains in Alabama. "I don't wash my feet
with city water," he declares (521).

Shaw's consciousness of his life's historical significance extends also to politics and public events. A fierce pride of race and property rights leads him into the Alabama Tenant Farmers Union, which is the decisive act of his life, as he now sees it, for it puts him in opposition to white society and so eventually lands him in prison. Both in rebelling and by serving time as a good prisoner he behaves consistently. When he emerges from prison his career as a mule farmer has been virtually ended by the advent of the tractor and large-scale farming. Nonetheless, he remains proud of his defiance. Though his own sons cannot see the necessity of their father's foolhardy action, that is because "they don't see that deep in regards to their own selves." He himself has never been "natured" to submission. "But if you don't like what I have done, then you are against the man I am today," he remarks in a characteristic linkage of past and present. "I ain't goin' to take no backwater about it. . . . Don't nobody try to tell me to keep quiet and undo my history" (573–74). Racism and capitalism—"this old 'ism' that's been plunderin me and plunderin the colored race of people" (574)—are the institutional forces he sees whites using against poor blacks; "work em to death or don't work em enough, that's how they do around here" (563). His grasp of economics and politics is different from Du Bois's or Angela Davis's, but his ideological sense of having participated in and made history is as firm as theirs. "I wish my children peace and good will," he concludes. "I wish the way will be clearer for em than ever in history and to know that I had a part in makin it clear—that's the grandest of all" (577).

All God's Dangers is thus a doubly rich historical document. Its subject's historical vision is displayed by his professional historian collaborator in order to reveal both the character of Nate Shaw himself and the nature of Alabama rural life in this century. Both man and world are recreated through an idiomatic language which unites both—but not in any imitated Southern or black dialect, for as Rosengarten asserts flatly, "I did not hear it" (xxiv). The authors' control of specific detail is impressively broad yet precise. No ordinary historical work can duplicate, for example, Shaw's description of Mr. Henry Chase's hardware store and the catalog of gear and goods bought there over the years. Even a reporter as sympathetic and observant as James Agee at the Gudger farm does not catch so nicely the rhythms of the rural voice and the intuitive awareness of country people in their place. Quite unlike Agee, Rosengarten effaces himself entirely from the surface of the narrative as soon as the preface is finished, allowing Shaw a more complete dominance of the narrative than even Black Elk asserts in his book. Yet Shaw's is not simply a virtuoso display of vernacular vigor, on the pattern of *nigger* or *Ossie*. Larger ideological and psychological issues and insights quite naturally emerge, and Rosengarten's claim that the old farmer possesses an "awesome intellectual life" (xxiii) is scarcely an exaggeration. Mythic overtones also resonate through the story's religious language and in the descriptions, at once concrete and metaphoric, of mules, horses, foxes, and the cycle of the seasons. All these contribute to, as they emanate from, the self of the speaker. They cannot be abstracted without seriously damaging the imaginative unity and integrity of the book. *All God's Dangers*, despite Rosengarten's unnecessary use of aliases, is truly a personal history, for two men have perceived that Nate Shaw himself stands at the center of every asserted truth in his story. "But I have had my eyes open too long to the facts," he concludes, "and my ears, what I've heard; and what I have touched with my hands and what have touched me is a fact" (581).

III

Though Rosengarten and Shaw never refer to it, a model existed in 1974 for their cooperative venture. In the eyes of many, the high watermark of postwar black autobiography—whether collaborations or conventional narratives—came with the publication of *The Autobiography of Malcolm X* in November 1965, twenty years after *Black Boy* and only a few months after Malcolm X's assassination at the Audubon Ballroom in Harlem. The dates are significant both in locating the work historically and in underlining the tragic shape of the life recreated therein. "It has always been my belief that I, too, will die by violence," Malcolm X observes at the outset, speaking of his father's death and the violent lives of his Southern uncles. "I have done all that I can to be prepared."[12] Because the autobiographical act is part of that preparation, it is appropriate that his story opens and closes on the same note. "Anything I do today, I regard as urgent. No man is given but so much time to accomplish whatever is his life's work. My life in particular never has stayed fixed in one position for very long. You have seen how throughout my life, I have often known unexpected drastic changes" (378). Change and mortality are indeed interlocking motifs of this absorbing account of a tempestuous career, characteristic concerns which, paradoxically, underscore significant continuities in the personal identity of a protean American. How such a complex public personality could have been captured on the run by Alex Haley and his past patterned so coherently into narrative is part of the mystery of this remarkable collaborative act. Given the many talented black writers of the postwar generation with a feel for autobiography—poets like Gwendolyn Brooks, who celebrated Malcolm X's life and death, and novelists like James Baldwin, who has written a scenario of *The Autobiography*—it is intriguing that this particular pair happened to meet and cooperate. An ex-hustler, pimp, prisoner, and streetcorner preacher and an ex-Coast Guardsman and journeyman writer for popular magazines make an unlikely team indeed. As the opening and closing comments confirm, and Haley's epilogue documents with chilling effect, they brought off this feat in the nick of time. In doing so they answered Malcolm X's own question: "How is it possible to write one's autobiography in a world so fast-changing as this?" (408). One simple yet profound answer is: through collaboration.

Indeed, no contemporary life-history I know, black or white, expresses with greater passion and power the experience of living at breakneck speed in twentieth-century urban America. Furthermore, no recent autobiography exerts a stronger moral leverage upon its readers, black and white. Listening to Malcolm X telling his story, as Larry Neal has written, is both a painful and a beautiful experience.[13] To set this against other collaborations brings out the extraordinary intensity of idea and emotion of this story of a driven man who, in the words of Robert Hayden, "became much more than there was time for him to be."[14]

In retrospect, one of the black leader's most historical acts was to respond as he did to the overture Haley made in 1959. At the time it was a difficult decision for the young, very busy preacher for the Nation of Islam. Not only was he preoccupied with and tightly controlled by his sect's leader, the Honorable Elijah Muhammad (who had to consent to the collaboration), but he had to accept a man coming under the dubious auspices of *Playboy* and the *Reader's Digest*. Hence the gingerly attempts to get acquainted and the care with which the two reached a working agreement. In the epilogue Haley records this process. Since his version follows rather than precedes Malcolm X's story (which itself comes after an introduction by the white journalist M. S. Handler), Haley does not preempt the reader's attention as Rosengarten does with his preface. On the other hand, the epilogue is a far fuller rounding-out of a dramatic narrative than Neihardt's explanation of the making of *Black Elk Speaks*. Of these three works, this one achieves the best balance of autobiographical and biographical viewpoints and therefore realizes most fully the possibilities inherent in the collaborative act.

If sound, this judgment rests partly on the precise agreement made and partly on the actual process of the two men's cooperation.

To begin with, Malcolm X insisted, "Nothing can be in this book's manuscript that I didn't say, and nothing can be left out that I want in it." In accepting this stipulation, Haley won an equally important concession. "I asked for—and he gave—his permission that at the end of the book I could write comments of my own about him which would not be subject to his review" (387). Malcolm X pointed out, "A writer is what I want, not an interpreter" (456). But by the time the epilogue was written and the book published, Malcolm X was dead. As biography, therefore, a major burden of Haley's section is to record the tragic last months of the black leader's life. Nearly as absorbing and essential, however, is the story of their collaboration, which is traced from earliest overtures and beginnings in notes jotted down on paper napkins by the busy Minister Malcolm while he and Haley talked. Later, in midnight sessions in Greenwich Village, Haley's adroit questioning encouraged Malcolm X to probe deeper into his past actions, relationships, and motives. All the while the black leader was living through the agony of his break with Elijah Muhammad, a split with portentous consequences for both the public and private self. The temptation was therefore extreme to revise the past already revisited, including his conversion in prison. Haley saw this as a great danger. "Telephoning Malcolm X, I reminded him of his previous decision, and I stressed that if those chapters contained such telegraphing to readers of what would lie ahead, then the book would automatically be robbed of some of its building suspense and drama. Malcolm X said, gruffly, 'Whose book is this?' I told him, 'Yours, of course' and that I only made the objection in my position as a writer" (414). Though Haley's suggestion was finally accepted, the narrative does signal future changes in Malcolm X's viewpoint and values. Yet these announcements are not intrusive enough to disturb the vivid sense of a self living and moving fully in each moment and milieu of the past. Here, as elsewhere, compromise between competing impulses in the two collaborators reflects the dual perspective—*then* seen from *now*—of all autobiography.

Although Haley and Malcolm X agreed they would try to be historically and ideologically faithful to the changing circumstances of his life, they also recognized that this aim had to be balanced against literary claims of the writer, the collaborative occasion, and the audience. This dual commitment aroused in Malcolm X strong emotional resistance, reflecting only dimly perceived psychic imperatives pressing for expression. When, for instance, Haley succeeded in getting him to talk about the women in his past, deep-seated fears rose to the surface. " 'I don't *completely* trust anyone,' " he told Haley candidly, " 'not even myself. I have seen too many men destroy themselves.

Other people I trust from not at all to highly, like The Honorable Elijah Muhammad.' Malcolm X looked squarely at me. 'You I trust about twenty-five percent' " (389). The full significance of this remark emerges later when, in a late-night phone call, Malcolm X blurts out abruptly, "Alex Haley?. . . . I trust you seventy per cent" (400). Clearly a dramatic shift in relationship has taken place, one with deep significance for the entire story. Trust and distrust are the central psychological motifs running throughout the narrative. They might never have been dramatized so effectively—or even represented at all—had the writer, as the second consciousness in this creative process, not kept asking questions like "I wonder if you'd tell me something about your mother?" (390). Like other great autobiographies, this one enacts an often unpleasant exploration within. As both the means by which this was accomplished and the dramatic record of its results, *The Autobiography of Malcolm X* illustrates the truth-telling possibilities of the collaborative activity.

Where the two men agreed wholeheartedly was with Malcolm X's passionate desire to historicize his own existence as he seeks to change American history. "I'm telling it like it *is!*" he exclaims. "You *never* have to worry about me biting my tongue if something I know as truth is on my mind. Raw, naked truth exchanged between the black man and the white man is what a whole lot more of is needed in this country—to clear the air of the racial mirages, clichés, and lies that this country's very atmosphere has been filled with for four hundred years" (273). Though he survived only thirty-nine years, less than half Du Bois's span, he shares with the austere scholar the conviction that man realizes himself in history. Therefore his story, as the matter-of-fact title promises, is a memoir in the tradition of Douglass, Ida B. Wells, and Du Bois. He and Haley place on record the "life of only one ghetto-created Negro" (379) by means of a convincingly concrete chronicle. Persons, places, dates, song titles, as well as larger social forces and historic events give a sense of both ideological specificity and mythic resonance to the striking episodes and turning-points of his life. These are patterned coherently by the traditional but appropriate image of the journey or quest. Unlike Nate Shaw, who carefully anchors his identity in one Alabama locale, Malcolm X's characterizing metaphor is the traveler who symbolically moves *counter* to the traditional movement of American and European history: not east to west, but from Mason, Michigan, back to Boston and New York, then finally all the way east to Mecca and Africa. Paralleling this spatial and spiritual movement toward a source of power and meaning is Malcolm Little's descent into a life of crime and self-degradation. As with many other spiritual accounts—and one of the signal achievements of *The Autobiography* is its blending of social and spiritual levels of experience—this fall is a rise in false social prestige and standing within the community of criminals. Rising and falling, soaring sunward and plummeting to the ground (like "the reefer-smoking Negro in the second balcony" [74] of the Savoy Ballroom) is the complementary pattern of this peripatetic life. This motif Haley expresses imagistically in terms of the Icarus myth.

As a unique blend of oral social history and spiritual confession, Malcolm X's story cannot be contained by the category of memoir; it becomes as well a testament, polemic, apology, and eventually a searingly honest baring of the inner self. Midway through the narrative, he pauses to recognize all these emerging, interlocking intentions. "I want to say before I go on that I have never previously told anyone my sordid past in detail," he remarks at the moment of his arrest and imprisonment.

> I haven't done it now to sound as though I might be proud of how bad, how evil I was.
>
> But people are always speculating—why am I as I am? To understand that of any person, his whole life, from birth, must be reviewed. All our experiences fuse into our personality. Everything that ever happened to us is an ingredient.
>
> Today, when everything I do has an urgency, I would not spend one hour in the preparation of a book which had the ambition to perhaps titillate some readers. But I am spending many hours because the full story is the best way I know to have it seen, and understood, that I had sunk to the very bottom of the American white man's society when—soon now, in prison—I found Allah and the religion of Islam and it completely transformed my life. (150)

Such a statement can be read on several levels at once: as his recognition and repudiation of the "bad nigger" stereotype and the crass commercial motives of its exploiters, and as a rejoinder to those whose knowledge of Malcolm X was in 1964 and 1965 so incomplete and inaccurate. His appeal is to skeptical but fair-minded readers, both white and black, willing to test the half-truths and outright lies of the mass media against the evidence of this personal account. The same wager is made, three years later and under very different circumstances, when Norman Mailer writes *The Armies of the Night*. To poor blacks in Northern ghettoes, of course, Malcolm X is no apostle of racial hatred or victim of television stereotyping. He is their fearless partisan and straight-talking hero. Having experienced every oppression and degradation they had known, having transformed himself from hoodlum into world-renowned leader, he speaks to and for them. Thus by recording with candor and completeness all his social and religious experiences, Malcolm X hopes to convert these disparate, even antagonistic, audiences into the "objective reader" addressed at the end. With the same mixture of fervor and distaste of an ex-slave narrator, therefore, he reenters the "sordid past," confident that his own sins will be outweighed by evidence of society's systemic evils.

In doing so, the storyteller, like Nate Shaw, is armed by a powerful memory for meaningful details. Whether recalling the obscure youth Malcolm Little arriving in Roxbury dressed in ill-fitting hick clothes, or the public orator gazing from the window of the Harvard Law School and recalling scenes of his gangster exploits only a few miles and years away, he demonstrates a thoroughly historical consciousness of self. His voice re-endows the actors of the past with their onetime reality, even though he always brackets them within the perspective of the older narrator who has been twice saved. As historian, he evokes the Depression succinctly from the bitter viewpoint of a fatherless welfare family living perilously on pride and day-old bread. Wartime Harlem is recaptured in all its frenzy and frustration. The famous names and faces of its nightlife and musical scene are evoked through the eyes, but no longer the moral innocence, of the young newcomer entering that glittering Mecca and embracing its false values.

Stitching together this parable of small-town boy in the city are three ballrooms—Roseland, Savoy, and Audubon. Each is vividly recaptured, though the last only in Haley's epilogue. Thereby the basic tensions of black urban life are dramatized from *within, below,* and *outside,* for these are Malcolm X's moral perspectives on American social experience. Each new situation and role—the hungry welfare child mooching a meal from neighbors, the single black boy in a Midwestern school, the shoeshine kid snapping his rag over Johnny Hodges's shoes, the hustler, the draft-dodger, the prisoner known as Satan—is rendered precisely but unsentimentally. White institutions like the school and church readily exhibit their members' racial biases. Thus Mr. Ostrowski, the teacher who advises Malcolm Little to abandon unrealistic dreams of becoming a lawyer, symbolizes a whole system. He also sharpens for the alert reader contrasts between this Michigan boyhood and Du Bois's Massachusetts upbringing, in which Frank Hosmer plays a quite different role. Though his white schoolmates patronize Little as their mascot or "pink poodle," the adult who remembers leaving school for the street now values a true education as sincerely as Du Bois. And he has obtained one by his own efforts; Norfolk Prison Colony has become his Fisk and Harvard. "I'd put prison second to college," he remarks to Haley, "as the best place for a man to go if he needs to do some thinking. If he's *motivated,* in prison he can change his life" (391–92).

Conventional religion, too, seems hostile or irrelevant to the adolescent, though to the man now looking back after two spiritual conversions some significant prophecies and vital patterns are descried. His mother's visions and dietary practices, for instance, are on one level simply Seventh-Day Adventist delusions, but on another level they foretell the son's final Islamic allegiance, as A. L. Elmessiri has pointed out.[15] His father's Southern Baptist religion and Garveyite politics are similarly sorted out: one is irrelevant, the other an invaluable legacy. The explicit theological proclamations by the later Nation of Islam convert read less convincingly than the often anguished memories of childhood and youth. Yet even Minister Malcolm is a necessary stage in the evolution of this strong black identity. Though some of his historical and social statements as a Muslim sound biased or even absurd, these must be understood, like the beliefs and speculations of the older Henry Adams, as in part dramatic recoveries of the intellectual life of a changing mind.

At every stage of his story, then, the autobiographer grounds his moral and social criticism in historical circumstance and personal experience. "I believe my own life *mirrors* this hypocrisy," he observes characteristically. "I know nothing about the South. I am a creation of the Northern white man and of his hypocritical attitude toward the Negro" (271). Everywhere he proclaims his opposition to American history as racial oppression. "Human rights! Respect as *human beings!* That's what America's black masses want. That's the true problem. The black masses want not to be shrunk from as though they are plague-ridden. They want not to be walled up in slums, in the ghettoes, like animals. They want to live in an open, free society where they can walk with their heads up like men, and women!" (272). Such ideals, similar in language to those of immigrants like Mary Antin and Alexander Berkman, are to be realized in a particular time and place, just as Malcolm X's manhood has been achieved in and through the gritty circumstances of contemporary life. Like Nate Shaw, therefore, he insists on the right to become an American *here,* not in exile abroad. Thus it is appropriate that the story closes with his return from Mecca, the establishment of the Organization for Afro-American Unity, and his symbolic encounter with the white man at the traffic light. "I don't mind shaking hands with human beings. Are you one?" (363), he remarks to the motorist whose outstretched hand symbolizes the reader's recognition of the autobiographer's right to put the question. From innocent black boy to criminal, through proud black manhood to a larger humanity above race and nationality—this is the trajectory of Malcolm X's historic journey into the self. It is a story finally anchored in the year 1965, the year, of "the conscience-salving Civil Rights Bill," as he calls it (379). At the same time, it is a cultural parable of a "black man who has lived further down in the mud of human society" (379) than most. "But it is only after the deepest darkness that the greatest joy can come," he concludes, and the preacher's idiom carries more authority here than Dick Gregory's: "it is only after slavery and prison that the sweetest appreciation of freedom can come" (379).

The Autobiography of Malcolm X expresses on several levels, then, a time-obsessed vision of an individual's and a group's twentieth-century experience. Conceived even more than *All God's Dangers* as an ideological story with mythic resonances, it produces an even more dramatic and emotional effect upon a wider audience than Rosengarten and Shaw have found. Like other collaborations, Haley's achievement as the writer rests upon successfully recreating another's voice as well as words. (There are, oddly enough, no photographs except the arresting one on the paperback's cover.) Several reasons exist why the mature Malcolm's presence is so vital to the impact and meaning of his autobiography as history *and* discourse. In the first place, oral verisimilitude here reflects, as elsewhere, the actual process of composition, for despite the vividly evoked presences of earlier selves, the book is dominated by the midnight monologist pacing Haley's flat and talking specters of his haunted past into reappearance. This present speaker is shown to be a natural outgrowth of earlier articulate selves: the youth in Boston avidly soaking up street slang; the prisoner copying the first page of the dictionary in preparation for a debate; the Nation of Islam preacher fishing for converts on a Harlem street. Even a small error like printing Fanny Kemble's name as "Kimball" (176) underlines the spoken quality and sincerity of the narrator. A closer look at this familiar literary device confirms the subtlety of Haley's manipulation of Malcolm X's voice. For one thing, the reader's assumption that memory works spontaneously and accurately as a kind of blurting-out is exploited. "They had a white cook-helper, I recall—Lucille Lathrop. (It amazes me how these names come back, from a time I haven't thought about for more than twenty years)" (26), he remarks of his stay in the juvenile detention home. As memory's gates open, the actual lingo of past individuals, groups, and locales reappears with astonishing freshness. Then, as Minister Malcolm replaces Detroit Red, the narrator quotes from his own speeches to illustrate a different vocabulary and outlook from that of the reefer salesman. Each idiom and stage of life bequeath something to the present speaker's vernacular style, which has more variety enriching it than Nate Shaw's experience can provide.

One striking continuity is the narrator's penchant, early developed, for catchy phrases, aphorisms, and metaphors. These are the hallmark of the mature public orator and storyteller. "We didn't land on Plymouth Rock, my brothers and sisters—Plymouth Rock landed on *us!*" (201) typifies the ready-tongued debater who once scored with streetcorner crowds and now does so with liberal white readers. "I was sold forever on credit" (52) describes the purchase of his first zoot suit and succinctly excoriates white economic exploitation and the mental bondage of many blacks. "You would have thought God had lowered some of his angels" (50), he observes wryly of the black dancers scrambling for white partners at Roseland, and this jibe at sexual motives includes himself and Sophia, as well as readers of both races and sexes. Such apt phrase-making of the successful hustings performer also reminds present listeners of bitter social and racial realities he has personally lived through. There is, moreover, little difference in the style or content of the politician-preacher and the figurative language used to reveal more private realms. Inner and outer experience are neatly connected by remarks like "I worked out at Ella's kitchen table like there was no tomorrow" (39) and, later, "I wore my guns as today I wear my neckties" (138). Though these homely aphorisms recall specific moments, they also keep reminding the reader of Malcolm X's persistent preoccupations with time and violence, with falling while apparently rising. In the imaginative encounter with memory, past and present are linked through the speech of one partner as arranged by the other, whose claim to be the "dispassionate chronicler" (456) is continually vindicated by the aural evidence of Malcolm X's presence. Even more effectively than through the many dramatic episodes which punctuate the narrative, the simulated words and voice create the characteristic texture and tone of *The Autobiography*.

Nonetheless, Haley's success in replicating an oral presence and power does not explain all the book's moral intensity and emotional density. Neither the narrative pace of Malcolm X's nineteen chapters nor the fated climax in Haley's epilogue can fully account for the tense urgency of this recitation. Quite aside from being a sustained dramatic monologue, *The Autobiography* is a multilayered story—simultaneously an inverted success myth, a spiritual quest for utopia, and a psychological search for the father lost on the bloody streetcar tracks of Lansing. These interlaced elements are displayed not only through event and character but also through metaphors binding his historical experiences and emotional states together. The most common of these unifying tropes, as has already been noted, is the actual yet symbolic journey: from west to east, from sin to salvation, from blindness to sight and insight, from distrust to the beginnings of trust, from false social selves to a more authentic identity. Several other metaphoric motifs interlock and widen this pilgrimage pattern. One is the names and nicknames which mark successive stages in the transformation of young Malcolm Little into El Hajj Malik El Shabazz. Another, even richer group of actual yet emblematic images describes the clothes and personal belongings Malcolm X puts on or takes off during his brief lifetime. Even more vividly than Gandhi's hats or Adams's manikin or Sullivan's pantalettes, clothing emphasizes the social roles and temporary identities imposed upon Malcolm X by others. But, for the narrator, this traditional trope carries private spiritual significance as well. To change clothes and adopt thereby a different *persona* always works in the direction of a more authentic self. Thus, though these garments and objects reflect social reality, they also manifest Allah's plan. The zoot suit and stolen clothes of Homeboy and Detroit Red represent his deluded state and debased values as hipster and hoodlum. But the Lil Abner suit worn out of the prison gate, like the suitcase, glasses, and wristwatch he buys, announce a new self, a different kind of traveling man. Taking off clothes is also a symbolic act. His life as a pimp produces no graphic images dramatizing the white man's "cesspool morals" (91), for this is in several respects a decidedly puritanical salvation story. Imagination is not necessary, however, to complete the meaning of the scene when Sandwich Red gets the drunken "red-faced cracker soldier" (77) on the Yankee Clipper to strip in preparation for a fight, which dissolves in laughter and ridicule at the white man's expense. This wartime moment contrasts with a later disrobing when the Mecca pilgrim doffs his own American garments and puts on a pair of white towels as the visible sign of rebirth. Though a political parallel to Gandhi (whom he read about in prison) may be intended here, more significant is the image of a grown man willingly becoming a baby again.

As revealing as all these metaphorical motifs are, none is more vividly a reflection of the inner self than the repeated pattern in Malcolm X's life of two persons face-to-face—one a dark-skinned Negro, the other a light-skinned or white partner or opponent. The variations of this dramatic pairing are numerous: Malcolm Little's father and mother arguing and fighting; his mother and Ella Collins embracing at the insane asylum; Malcolm himself dancing with Laura and then, on the same evening, with Sophia; his last handshake at the traffic light. All these contrasting figures with dark and light skins or identities are actual persons from the past of a black man with a "mariny" complexion. But they also represent forces and feelings struggling for balance within his own psyche. They are metaphors, that is, of the ceaseless struggle between trust and suspicion, between love and domination, in all personal relationships, first with parents, then with women as diverse as Sophia, Ella, and Betty Shabazz; and with men like Elijah Muhammad, Alex Haley, and M. S. Handler. Ideological differences are often depicted in these confrontations and temporary unions between dark and light. Once, at least, the two forces are combined in the visionary figure of the man in Satan's prison cell who "wasn't black, and he wasn't white" (186). This "non-European" presence ostensibly signifies W. D. Fard, founder of the Nation of Islam, but likewise foreshadows Elijah Muhammad as well as symbolizes the universal, raceless identity Malcolm X later discovers at Mecca.

Because these paired figures represent—among other realities—impulses within Malcolm X himself, they are an important means of expressing psychic dimensions of the autobiographical act. As the younger, light-skinned son of a very black father and "near-white" mother (whose respective fates are violent death and insanity), he remembers feeling continually split apart, lost, and betrayed by his quarreling parents whose skins are reminders of his mixed racial inheritance and social environment. Such suppressed resentments coexist, of course, alongside conscious recognition of hatred, prejudice, poverty, ignorance, and state bureaucracy as actual causes of the Little family's breakup. In a sense, Malcolm X's life, like Conrad Aiken's in a very different sphere, represents a search for the meaning of his parents' lives and deaths—a meaning, in terms of his own career and character. As a child, Malcolm Little is caught between his Georgia-born preacher-father, who openly favors his light-skinned son, and his West Indian mother, a Seventh-Day Adventist mystic who, just as openly, criticizes him because his skin color resembles hers. These differences become inevitably associated with the arguments and blows the parents often exchange—blows from the rough father who cannot stand the "smooth words" used by the better educated mother. Their son grows up to become Minister Malcolm X, thus reenacting his father's activism, right down to the violent end. Conscious and unconscious emulation of and need for a father are major motives in the son's career, leading him to a series of father-substitutes, of whom Elijah Muhammad is clearly the most significant. Anyone who wonders why this ex-hustler from Harlem can become so genuinely distraught over the discovery of Elijah Muhammad's several adulteries must admit that a symbolic but equally wounding family betrayal has taken place in Malcolm X's psyche. To see the oedipal implications of his tie and his ultimate break with the leader of the Nation of Islam is not, however, to deny other grounds for the obedience and the rivalry between the passive leader and his aggressively active lieutenant.

These implications of the dark-light pairings depicted in *The Autobiography* reinforce a truth Haley carefully prepares us to see— namely, that Malcolm X's mother is just as vital a presence in his memory as the dead father. From his earliest years, the child imitates his verbally adept mother, turning her own weapons against her, when necessary; "for if she even acted as though she was about to raise her hand to me, I would open my mouth and let the world know about it. . . . I learned early that crying out in protest could accomplish things" (7–8). This strategy of substituting verbal for physical violence in response to danger or discrimination becomes the pattern of his later behavior. Thus in a work filled with the threat and presence of pain and death, there is recorded but a single act of direct assault by the narrator. That occurs, significantly, when Detroit Red strikes Sammie's girlfriend. Elsewhere actual violence by Malcolm X himself is only hinted at, threatened, or treated ironically, as in the accounts of his first and last boxing matches and of his palming the bullet when playing Russian roulette with his gang. Words, not knives or pistols, are the chosen instrument this black man employs in resisting attack or racial oppression and in defining the self. Though his vocabulary and motivation differ sharply from Wright's or Gregory's, all three men share this mode of self-assertion. To note this maternal legacy is not, of course, to account for it wholly in such terms, nor is it to deny the physical courage manifested throughout his life and death. Indeed, one mark of his manhood is his continual risking of his standing with the reader by confessing such ignominious episodes as being caught under the bed by Sophia's husband or conking his head in the toilet.

"Raw, naked truth" is indeed the dangerous motto adopted for this public and private history. It is a sword which threatens to wound both narrator and conscientious reader. Once cajoled into facing memories of his mother and Laura, Malcolm X does not shrink from other painful confrontations. When, for instance, he describes the embrace between his insane mother and his half-sister Ella Collins, it is not merely to dramatize a meeting between the weakest and strongest—and the lightest and darkest—women in his family. The tableau also depicts his own mixed feelings about vulnerability and the necessity of force in male-female relationships. His mother, by proving a weak reed, has dramatized the insufficiency of maternal love and protection, hence the inevitability of her son's distrust. Ella, on the contrary, replicates the masculine force of their dead father. Therefore the fact that this *"strong,* big, black, Georgia-born woman" has broken the spirits of three husbands by her "domineering ways" (319) matters less than the fact that she had the courage to break with Elijah Muhammad and find the true Islamic faith. Ella Collins points her younger half-brother toward an independence defined as activity, aggression, male chauvinism, just as his mother's negative example points him, less consciously, in the same direction. Having experienced the destruction and failure of a mother's love, he is prepared to see all relationships in power terms. "All women, by their nature, are fragile and weak: they are attracted to the male in whom they see strength," he observes (93). This attitude is never fully relinquished, though he does come to see (at least rationally) its moral and emotional inadequacy.

The depths of Malcolm X's complex relationship with his mother are unforgettably evoked in a remark made in reference to his last visit to her in the Kalamazoo asylum. "I can't describe how I felt," he says. "The woman who had brought me into the world, and nursed me, and advised me, and chastized me, and loved me, didn't know me. It was as if I was trying to walk up the side of a hill of feathers" (21). Compressed into this simple simile is a weight of emotional meaning comparable to that which Richard Wright expresses through memories of the nightmare following the fire and beating in the opening of *Black Boy.* Here, helplessness as well as the softness and comfort of a mother's breast, a whiteness at once pure and threatening, a son's sense of a slippery footing in the uphill struggle for her love are implied by the arresting phrase. Like the opening scene of *The Autobiography,* which graphically depicts the violent world into which the child in the mother's womb will be born, it pictures the warring extremes of Malcolm X's inner and outer worlds. Almost to the end, he continues to regard love as a mixture of aggression, lust, and weakness. Only after his marriage to Betty Shabazz and the late, tentative friendship with Haley does he begin to overcome a lifetime's penchant for distrustful dominance.

Mecca, with its memory of a roomful of pilgrims from various nations and races all snoring in one universal language, marks the decisive turning-point in this tentative transformation. Though not a complete about-face, his final Islamic identity embodies new convictions not only about race and religion but also about power as personal domination. "Mankind's history has proved from one era to another that the true criterion of leadership is spiritual," he concludes. "Men are attracted by spirit. By power men are *forced*. Love is engendered by spirit. By power, anxieties are created" (368). Such new awareness allows him not only to extend his hand to the white man at the traffic light but also to trust his own followers during the dangerous, hectic weeks just before his assassination. "If I can't be safe among my own kind, where can I be?" (432) is not only a statement of racial solidarity which turned to bitter historical irony; it is also a personal affirmation dearly bought by a lifetime's struggle against suspicion and anxiety. Thus the tragedy of Malcolm X's early death is more than the profoundly pitiful waste which everyone feels at the death of a young hero. To readers of *The Autobiography* his death is particularly poignant because it terminates a vital psychological development beyond what Erikson calls the most basic psychic conflict: the conflict all humans feel between basic trust and mistrust. Just before the end, this wary and wounded man began really to change and mend. By winning a partial but memorable victory over his own bitter past and the oppressive circumstances shaping it, Malcolm X speaks to and for all people—but especially to and for black Americans, for whom trust in themselves and in others, as well as in a hostile, changing world, is often a difficult emotional achievement, as it clearly was for Malcolm X. White readers, too, need the same lesson, though this may come harder, since to accept this insight into another's life and death means also accepting many bitter truths about themselves and their violent racist culture.

As the language of this complex book keeps suggesting, the trajectory of Malcolm X's recreated life leads through and beyond history and social experience. As the expression of a powerful autobiographical vision, the narrative dramatizes a deeper urge than even a proud man's will to live, learn, and change on his own terms. That underlying impulse, telegraphed first in the opening prophecies about his father's and his own fate, has been identified by Roger Rosenblatt, who notes the calm, celebratory attitude toward death in many black autobiographies. Like others, Rosenblatt argues, Malcolm X has in fact dictated an extended suicide note. As a success story about achieved black manhood, *The Autobiography* records an astonishing series of historical selves and social masks. Moving from one identity to another is this man's version of what Stephen Henderson calls "survival motion."[16]

But in the process of coming to terms with his impending murder, Malcolm X communicates a vision of his life as something larger than "survival." Because the self who speaks is in fact dead, his story communicates the possibility of an ideal self beyond blackness, beyond the definitions of Roxbury or Harlem or Madison Avenue. The conscious imitation of his father's career is one clue to this self's desire to move beyond history; another is the Icarus myth with its promise of a fall outside time. "One writes autobiography not because one seeks art or safety," Rosenblatt remarks, "but out of a desire to see both a shape and end to one's life, to seek the end of everything which has been in flux and process, and at the same time to understand it all."[17] Even more explicitly than *Black Boy* or *I Know Why the Caged Bird Sings, The Autobiography of Malcolm X* exemplifies the "life as the death weapon." Only George Jackson's *Soledad Brother* comes close to its vision of a completed life—completed both by the biographical act of Haley's epilogue and the autobiographical consciousness of Malcolm X himself. "If I'm alive when this book comes out, it will be a miracle," Haley recalls him saying at one of their last sessions. 'I'm not saying it distressingly.' He leaned forward and touched the buff gold bedspread. 'I'm saying it like I say that's a bedspread' " (410).

IV

On July 2, 1979, NBC television covered a news conference called to announce publication of baseball superstar Rod Carew's autobiography. Standing in the back of the room and ignored by virtually everyone was Ira Berkow, the writer actually responsible for writing this latest example of "celebrity autobiography." Because of the novel yet growing familiarity of this occasion, the television reporter focused on the white writer rather than on the black athlete's childhood in Panama or his spectacular career on the diamond. When interviewed, the writer voiced no disappointment at not also being up in front of the microphone. The double satisfaction, he said, of producing a readable, accurate, and salable story *and* receiving 50 percent of its royalties was sufficient. Writing was his trade and he made a good living at it. Also present at the media event was John Leonard, book reviewer of the *New York Times,* who commented with icy disapproval, "The American public wants the hot stuff." A book like this, though giving readers what they want when they want it, is a "fraud," he said. "Some are more interesting than others," Leonard admitted, but "it's still a fraud."[18] Clearly he had no intention of reviewing it in his column. The unspoken assumption was that a *sine qua non* of autobiography is the single literate author.

Leonard's and Carew's audiences represent important but often opposed influences on the literary and commercial activity we have been examining in this chapter. Though the almost ghostwritten lives of a Rod Carew or a Judge John Sirica are not exactly identical to *nigger* or *Ossie*, there are significant overlaps in content, style, and reader expectation. But perhaps because I share some of Leonard's reservations, this discussion of collaboration has not included any true ghostwritten autobiographies. A desire to test these autobiographical acts as history and, in their own way, as conscious art, has led me to consider only works by declared, self-conscious authors. That is, I have been particularly attentive to collaborations in which the authorial enterprise is not only openly admitted on the title page but also described in some detail and defended. Such explicit awareness creates grounds for defining what is "autobiographical" within this hybrid form. In responding to evidences of self-consciousness within, before, after, and outside the subject's story, we start with the tentative assumption that a trustworthy version of personal history or memoir has been intended. The works chosen here are representative in inviting such a preliminary response. That is, *nigger, Ossie, All God's Dangers,* and *The Autobiography of Malcolm X* are all re-creations of social experience; their subjects achieve personal identity within a set of historical circumstances about which the subjects themselves—and not just their hired writers—are explicitly and continuously aware. Such a stance toward the self already assumes a certain detachment, a willingness to stand outside and typify one's existence for others; it emphasizes one's experiences as social member over private and psychic activities. Thus the presence of the collaborating writer (even if he or she is white and perhaps of a different social background) makes less of an intrusion than it would in a more novelistic narrative like *Black Boy*, since in a memoir attention is, at least to begin with, directed outward from the self on to the world of others and backward in time.

Therefore the argument here is that Lipsyte, Ledner, Rosengarten, and Haley play essential roles in helping to recover the historical identities of their several subjects. The cultural critic should therefore examine collaborations not simply with a skeptical awareness of their difference and inferiority, but also looking for all cues to the cultural context within which the work has been created, the actual interplay of personality and outlook between the two collaborators, the nature of the audiences openly or covertly addressed, and the achieved balance between autobiographical and biographical elements. One should be alert also to indications of recoveries and discoveries of the subject's past as *facilitated* but not *invented* by another. The writer's influence will be recognized in the common features mentioned above: style as the simulated oral performance, a legendary success plot, traditional metaphors of the self like the journey or clothes. Both the writer's attempts to efface himself and any direct references or dramatic enactments of his or her presence should be noted. Constantly it must be borne in mind that though a subject self is always at the center of any truly autobiographical narrative, in the case of a collaborative work, *this self is never alone.* Whether his or her role in the earlier process of creation was a dominant one like Malcolm X's or gives evidence of being a more passive one like Ossie Guffy's, the spotlight must somehow play on this self in the finished text. Through *words* (what the subject actually says about the past) and *voice* (how that information reflects individual style, tone, and characteristic values and attitudes), the writer presents the subject in the act of presenting the self. The most successful and trustworthy autobiographies are those which find ways to draw attention to this intricate dramatic situation. Sometimes still another dimension and set of perspectives are provided by photographic images, ostensibly objective evidence of historicity but actually someone else's selective and subjective view of that self and past.

As a complex literary occasion, therefore, the collaboration must be carefully scrutinized not as a solo but a tandem or group performance, essentially dramatic and historical in nature. It must be read somewhat as Freud read Michelangelo's statue of Moses: as the end product of a prior process or set of gestures partly hidden and partly known.[19] Though a writer's skill and imagination have combined words and voice into a more or less coherent and convincing narrative, the actual writer had no large fund of memories to draw upon; the subject's memory and imagination are the original sources of the arranged story and have also come into play critically as the text takes final shape. Thus *where* material comes from and *what* has been done to shape it are separable and of equal significance in collaborations. The simulated oral performance is common precisely because it readily recalls that connection. In the case of black autobiographies, the use of this device may also be related to literary tradition, for in black culture the preacher, orator, novelist, dozens-player, and poet have often dramatized themselves as speakers bending the standard white language into a personal and communal idiom.

Thus the text of a collaborative autobiography can and must be examined as closely as other texts, even when it is seen to be one person's attempt to communicate another's inner states and spiritual experiences through his or her own words. Though this is admittedly a murky area, some of its mystery is dispelled when understood by analogy to the psychological case-history. Though a case-history is written about one psyche's past and present by another person, it is commonly treated as the reasonably trustworthy record and evaluation of that patient. It is not normally read as the confession of the psychiatrist, even though he or she is the author.[20] This is so despite the additional fact that the information contained therein has been collected through the same kind of leading questions Rosengarten mentions as possibly eliciting and directing Nate Shaw's political memories. The same correctives need to be applied in both cases: a collaboration must be critically examined as a whole. Any single item stands or falls as a trustworthy and significant bit of evidence in relation to the broad patterns of behavior and motivation discerned in the entire record. Thus Malcolm X's striking simile about visiting his insane mother—"It was as if I was trying to walk up the side of a hill of feathers"—can be accepted as the authentic language of his psyche (and not Haley's) only after relating the phrase to the whole pattern of words and emotional attitudes toward the mother (and other significant ones) in *The Autobiography*. As the ramifying links between one part and another of a longish narrative are traced, the role of the writer necessarily expands as the subject emerges as a believable self. Though Haley calls himself Malcolm X's "dispassionate chronicler," he is in fact not only his subject's historian and literary critic but his psychiatrist and spiritual confessor as well. That is why a crucial sentence in *The Autobiography* is "Alex Haley? . . . I trust you seventy percent," for it underscores Haley's reliability as it connects the central psychological drama of the life itself to the collaborative act recreating that life.

As important as writers like Haley and Rosengarten are, however, it is unlikely that there exists any collaborative autobiography which can successfully survive the kind of multifaceted analysis here suggested without a subject possessed of a powerful memory and imagination. These qualities cannot be supplied by the writer, although that collaborator must also possess them. More important for the successful writer of a collaboration is the ability to submerge himself in another's life without losing critical perspective on that life and personality. Thus contemporary achievements like *All God's Dangers* and *The Autobiography of Malcolm X* depend upon both the force and integrity of the self who is their subject and the special qualities of autobiographical and historical consciousness expressed in the words supplied by the *second* name on the cover, by the writer who often has to stand at the back of the room when praise is handed out. Occasionally, however, a Theodore Rosengarten will win the National Book Award and an Alex Haley will win even wider recognition as the author of two notable works in the richly varied field of contemporary American autobiography. Given the perhaps disproportionate rewards to the writer, we need to know more about the circumstances, social and legal, attending the creation of a prize-winning collaboration. Nevertheless, if in the light of history *The Autobiography of Malcolm X* proves, as is likely, the more lasting of Haley's achievements to date, the chief reason is recorded on its last page: "he was the most electric personality I have ever met, and I still can't quite conceive him dead" (456).

8

Factual Fictions: Experiments in Autobiography by Norman Mailer, Frank Conroy, Lillian Hellman

BEGINNINGS AND ENDINGS, as we have already seen, are crucial components of many autobiographical acts. The opening scene of *Black Boy*, like the first sentence of *The Education of Henry Adams*, communicates by synecdoche a sense of the ensuing narrative's shape and self. Anaïs Nin's volume 1 of the *Diary* concludes with the announcement "I cannot install myself anywhere yet" (360), and this confession imitates Henry Miller by emphasizing the author's still-fluid identity. The final paragraph of *The Autobiography of Alice B. Toklas* brings Gertrude Stein's game to a close by returning the reader to the opening, a circularity emphasized in the original edition by the photograph on the last page of the manuscript's first page. Similar imaginative births, deaths, and rebirths occur in other American autobiographies, each of which displays its own strategy for bridging the gap between the finality of formal art and the ongoing, often messy life of the historian. Often these opening and closing movements serve to introduce the past actor and then merge that tentative identity with the present narrator's firmer one. An artful split in the time-bound self may be announced and then, perhaps a whole book later, healed. As always intricate combinations of history and discourse, autobiographies often dramatize their deepest divisions and tensions in the first and final pages, paragraphs, and chapters. Middles are sometimes less significant than they are in novels.

Yet as we have seen in the last chapter, autobiographers commonly commence not with chapter 1 but with an introduction or preface. Together with the author's name (or names), the title, and, in this paperback era, cover blurbs and photographs, these set initial terms of the autobiographical contract. Traditionally, such prefaces announce, apologize, and explain; they are relatively straightforward statements inviting in advance a trustworthy relation with the reader.

Today, however, overtures are often quite different, and have been so for at least a generation. Prefaces and introductions to recent books about the self frequently signal very different impressions of what is to follow. Consider the following as by no means unusual cues to some changing aspects of the basic autobiographical occasion:

> If the reader prefers, this book may be regarded as fiction. But there is always the chance that such a book of fiction may throw some light on what has been written as fact.
> Ernest Hemingway, *A Moveable Feast*[1]

> Many a time, in the course of doing these memoirs, I have wished that I were writing fiction. The temptation to invent has been very strong, particularly where recollection is hazy and I remember the substance of an event but not the details—the color of a dress, the pattern of a carpet, the placing of a picture. Sometimes I have yielded, as in the case of the conversations. My memory is good, but obviously I cannot recall whole passages of dialogue that took place years ago. Only a few single sentences stand out: *"They'*d make you toe the chalk line," "Perseverance wins the crown," "My child, you must have faith." The conversations, as given, are mostly fictional. Quotation marks indicate that a conversation to this general effect took place, but I do not vouch for the exact words or the exact order of the speeches.
> Mary McCarthy, *Memories of a Catholic Girlhood*[2]

> What follows is based on actual occurrences. Although much has been changed for rhetorical purposes, it must be regarded in its essence as fact. However, it should in no way be associated with that great body of factual information relating to orthodox Zen Buddhist practice. It's not very factual on motorcycles, either.
> Robert Pirsig, *Zen and the Art of Motorcycle Maintenance*[3]

> Old paint on canvas, as it ages, sometimes becomes transparent. When that happens it is possible, in some pictures, to see the original lines: a tree will show through a woman's dress, a child makes way for a dog, a large boat is no longer on an open sea. That is called pentimento because the painter "repented," changed his mind. Perhaps it would be as well to say that the old conception, replaced by a later choice, is a way of seeing and then seeing again.
> That is all I mean about the people in this book. The paint

has aged now and I wanted to see what was there for me once, what is there for me now.

Lillian Hellman, *Pentimento: A Book of Portraits*[4]

Though the events of this book bear similarity to those of that long malaise, my life, many of the characters and happenings are creations solely of the imagination. In such cases, I of course disclaim any responsibility for their resemblance to real people or events, which would be coincidental. The character "Patience," for example, who is herein depicted as my "wife," is a fictionalized character bearing no similarity to anyone living or dead. In creating such characters, I have drawn freely from the imagination and adhered only loosely to the pattern of my past life. To this extent, and for this reason, I ask to be judged as a writer of fantasy.

Frederick Exley, *A Fan's Notes: A Fictional Memoir*[5]

Warnings and confessions like these would be unnecessary or out of place if these books were *simply* fiction; novelists don't normally bother to write introductions. But for the authors quoted here, the question of what a fiction is, and therefore what is a factual story, is cast into doubt from the first page. Unequivocal assertions, like M. S. Handler's introduction to *The Autobiography of Malcolm X*, no longer work. Either to remain silent or to reaffirm a verifiable, historical discourse seems equally false to now-altered perceptions of the nature of autobiography. Definitions and boundaries once shared between writer and reader are growing hazier. In the case of Exley, they seem to be disappearing before our eyes.

Moreover, as one moves deeper inside other contemporary works, beyond the preface to the text itself, the same blurring of distinctions can often be seen. Nin calls her twilight zone "the dream," as in this typical comment near the end of volume 1 of her *Diary:* "This diary is my kief, hashish, and opium pipe. This is my drug and my vice. Instead of writing a novel, I lie back with this book and a pen, and dream, and indulge in refractions and defractions. I can turn away from reality into the reflections and dreams it projects, and this driving, impelling fever which keeps me tense and wide-awake during the day is dissolved in improvisations, in contemplations. I must relive my life in the dream" (1:333–34). Another artist seemingly caught in this confusion of realms is Vladimir Nabokov. *Speak, Memory* has been derisively labeled by one reviewer as a "fairy tale" about a "sugar-plum life in a sugar-plum kingdom."[6] The magical artificer provides, however, not only a map and photographs of his childhood domain but a six-page preface as well, documenting the circumstances of its creation. Then in the opening paragraph of a central chapter Nabokov restates his position as novelist-autobiographer. "I have often noticed that after I had bestowed on the characters of my novels some treasured item of my past," he observes, "it would pine away in the artificial world where I had so abruptly placed it." He continues,

> Although it lingered on in my mind, its personal warmth, its retrospective appeal had gone and, presently, it became more closely identified with my novel than with my former self, where it had seemed to be so safe from the intrusion of the artist. Houses have crumbled in my memory as soundlessly as they did in the mute films of yore, and the portrait of my old French governess, whom I once lent to a boy in one of my books, is fading fast, now that it is engulfed in the description of a childhood entirely unrelated to my own. The man in me revolts against the fictionist, and here is my desperate attempt to save what is left of poor Mademoiselle.[7]

Though the man seeks to separate himself and his memory from the fictionist, there are certain readers of *Speak, Memory* who, like James Rother, cannot distinguish this "desperate attempt" at personal history from *Ada,* say, or *Lolita.* Rother has a plausible explanation: the whole of Nabokov's ironic, fantastic, parodic work is, no matter what he himself says about it, of a piece. It is purely imaginative. None of Nabokov's books should be read as authentic recapturings of the past, for like everyone else only more so, his memory can never escape his present imagination, which is a novelist's. "To demand that memory speak beyond earshot of the present," Rother asserts, "is to make of memory a ventriloquist's dummy which, being unable to speak for itself, must be spoken for just as characters in novels are spoken for. And what this dummy inevitably articulates are facts," he continues, "facts delivered in the wooden prose of history and which, by their rich profusion in text after text, disguise the ongoing impersonation of truth, deny that what is being said yields no recapturable past. The parafictionist, regardless of who he is *not* being from moment to moment, can only speak in the language shared by his created selves—those autobiodegradable doubles who, by some magic of dissimulation, give his world resonance within the voice-box of a book."[8] Struggle as he may, Rother argues, Nabokov remains the hostage of his multilingual imagination. Hence *Speak, Memory,* despite preface or protests by the author, is properly parafiction, not at all historical autobiography. Rother's description of parafiction as an artist's "ongoing impersonation of truth" is echoed by other contemporary critics, many of whom share his thinly veiled contempt for facts and history's "wooden prose." No matter how hard the writer tries, "life and fiction bleed together," as Doris Eder succinctly puts it.[9] Thus an aspiring autobiographer like Nabokov finds himself caught in the postmodernist dilemma: "how to escape self-fictionalization in a narrational free-fire zone that has lost all its hold on reality."[10] The solipsism of much contemporary literature and philosophy threatens now to embrace personal history as well.

Exley's preface suggests that writers themselves often accept this radical diagnosis. Many refuse to announce themselves as conventional autobiographers. "Transfiction," "parafiction," "surfiction" are safer umbrellas under which to pretend to repossess one's past. Consequently a new mode of autobiographical writing has emerged, to which these terms (and also the term "mock autobiography") are applied. Frank Conroy's *Stop-time,* Gore Vidal's *Two Sisters,* George Cain's *Blueschild Baby,* Herbert Gold's *Fathers,* and Ronald Sukenick's *Up* are some of the better-known books frequently called parafictions, and thus placed somewhere beyond the borders of autobiography.[11] These works employ a variety of devices for undermining the reader's normal assumptions about "fact" and "fiction." *Blueschild Baby,* for instance, is announced as a novel about Harlem and heroin addiction, but its protagonist is "George Cain," whose life bears a close resemblance to that of the man described on the dust jacket as the author. *Two Sisters* likewise presents "Gore Vidal" as one character among others presumably more fictitious. *Up* is even more ingenious. The chief character is at least three persons at once: Ron Sukenick, Strop Banally, Roland Sycamore. After a series of comic encounters among these "characters," Ron Sukenick and his (real-life) wife Lynn give a party to celebrate the completion of "my novel." An "author's dedication" is read which thanks actual persons from an ostensibly real past. Then one of the fictional characters enters.

> "Who's that?" asks Lynn.
> "Nancy."
> "So that's the one," she says.
> "It's only a novel don't forget."
> "I understand that very well, but don't say only. It's been three years of our lives. Anyway I thought she'd be prettier." (327)

Clearly we are in a different and murkier realm here than while reading a conventional autobiographical novel like *Look Homeward, Angel*. Both the name and rules of the game have changed between 1929 and 1968.

Up and its ilk exhibit (and often mock) the features of prose writing usually associated with realistic fiction, including chronological narration and scenic structure, dialogue and fully rounded characters, symbolic detail, a point of view wider than that of the narrator. Yet these works also suggest, however ironically, that real or historic selves and verifiable stories may still exist—if only somewhere else. As pseudoautobiographies (if this is an accurate term), these works thrust the reader squarely into the "narrational free-fire zone" of which Rother speaks. One of two things has occurred. Either autobiographers have altered their aims and assumptions by the wholesale borrowing of techniques from postrealist novelists, or else novelists, sensing the popularity and vitality of autobiography and buttressed by a belief in solipsism, are encroaching more and more upon the domain of personal history. Both developments are bound to disorient readers clinging to conventional distinctions between "history" and "literature" and still convinced that personal identity remains the aim of the autobiographical act. These new narrative modes challenge not simply the possibility of a verifiable narrative but also the very persistence of a coherent self as well. On this point Sukenick, though writing through a "character," summarizes the philosophy of much parafiction:

> Realistic fiction presupposed chronological time as the medium of a plotted narrative, an irreducible individual psyche as the subject of its characterization, and, above all, the ultimate, concrete reality of things as the object and rationale of its description. . . .
>
> Reality doesn't exist, time doesn't exist, personality doesn't exist. God was the omniscient author but he died; now no one knows the plot, and since our reality lacks the sanction of a creator, there's no guarantee as to the authenticity of the received version. Time is reduced to presence, the content of a series of discontinuous moments. Time is no longer purposive, and so there is no destiny, only chance. Reality is, simply, our experience, and objectivity is, of course, an illusion. Personality, after passing through a phase of awkward self-consciousness, has become, quite minimally, a mere locus for our experience. In view of these annihilations, it should be no surprise that literature, also, does not exist—how could it? There is only reading and writing, which are things we do, like

eating and making love, to pass the time, ways of maintaining a considered boredom in face of the abyss.

Not to mention a series of overwhelming social dislocations.[12]

Perhaps only by confronting such a declaration of radical relativism can one appreciate fully the closeness of the traditional ties between realistic fiction and the conventional modes of autobiography— memoir, confession, and apology. "Too late!" the parafictionist remarks; both fiction and its fellow forms from the eighteenth century have become free-floating projections of the imagination, loosed totally from time and social reality.

Although Sukenick's spokesman is a comic posturer and not to be taken at face value, he raises questions which others entertain more seriously. One such is Ma'sud Zavarzadeh, who in *The Mythopoeic Reality* argues that contemporary experience within our "technetronic culture" has totally transformed the novel by obliterating distinctions between fact and fiction on which it has rested for two centuries. "The literal," Zavarzadeh believes, "has been heavily invested with fictivity, both inwardly under the pressures of new forces created by various technologies and outwardly through such new communications media as television, which uncovers the dramatic texture and quality of the events constituting our perceptual environment."[13] The result is the emergence of "a dramatized society in which events have the substance of actuality and the shape of fiction." One response to this altered sense of reality is the nonfiction novel, which deliberately incorporates "the centrifugal energies of reality and the centripetal forces of fiction" (226) into a new "bi-referential narrative" capable of comprehending contemporary chaos. Though Zavarzadeh does not discuss autobiography as a possible mode of such bi-referential stories, he might well have done so, particularly in his enthusiastic analysis of Mailer's *The Armies of the Night,* for it is a historical fact that autobiographers have lived with all kinds of cultural tensions in the past and have managed to find new forms for expressing and containing them. Placing the self at the center of social chaos may indeed be more difficult in a post-Hiroshima world than it was for Whitman or Alexander Berkman, but it is possible that the contrast between present and past is quantitative and not, as Zavarzadeh argues, qualitative.

In exploring such hypotheses, we should remind ourselves again that autobiography is a content, not any particular form. Therefore, as Georg Misch some years ago pointed out, autobiography is free to borrow fresh vigor from all of life's changing experiences and from the other cultural forces and artifacts of its age. If on this point Misch is as sound a guide as Sukenick and Zavarzadeh, it should be useful to look for other contemporary developments besides parafiction or the nonfiction novel. A beginning might be made through a rapid content survey of the personal narratives published in such numbers in the last decade or so by authors as diverse as Norman Mailer, Carlos Castaneda, Andy Warhol, Julius Lester, Gary Snyder, Lillian Hellman, Robert Lowell, Robert Pirsig, and many others. This remarkable literature of personal experience lends ample support to Sukenick's assessment of life "as a series of overwhelming social dislocations." Violence; ghetto oppression and despair; drug addiction and years in insane asylums and prisons; mental breakdown; psychedelic or mystical alterations in consciousness; alienation from job, spouse, sexual role, or social milieu; disenchantment with public morality and policy—all of these and still other themes of personal fragmentation are dramatically reenacted in such recent books as *The Armies of the Night,* Lester's *Search for the New Land, A Fan's Notes, Zen and the Art of Motorcycle Maintenance,* Snyder's *Earth House Hold,* and Lowell's *Life Studies.* Indeed, perhaps the only common bond among these works is the energetic search for an appropriate language and form for representing private discontinuity amid public disorder. Moreover, the fact that several of these confessional books are by previously unpublished writers from many walks of life indicates that the struggle to impose order upon a radically confused past and present goes on almost everywhere.

One model for these surreal versions and visions of contemporary history is certainly parafiction, which as we have seen offers the reader the option of refusing to read them as history at all. Parafictionists contend that narratives which frankly embrace fantasy are actually truer to social reality. They are, in fact, the histories of our day, more faithful to reality than traditional chronological stories reconstructed from memories, old letters, diaries, and other *simulacra.* If an authentic personal identity is possible at all, it must emerge in language reflecting the patterns of present chaos. Autobiography, then, becomes something different; "not simply an attempt to retell one's past life on a linear scale," as Burton Pike argues, "but rather in effect a novel written in the present, with one's past life as its subject." Pike goes on to describe this redefinition:

> Not all fiction is autobiographical but, on this deeper level, all autobiography is fiction. The past does not exist. There are memories of it—scattered shards of events and feelings—but

they are re-created within a later context. There is no way to retrieve the original fact of experience. The only way of giving the illusion of doing so is to reinvent the past in the present. Writing autobiographically is a way of making this process systematic; the act of writing fixes the pseudopast and the present in relation to each other, and lends to both the appearance of permanence.[14]

Collapsing all narrative modes into "fiction" provides, however, no answer to Sukenick's assertion about fiction's own loss of credibility. Why bother with either mode if not only the self but also society, time, and reality itself have become unbelievable absurdities? Yet as Alfred Kazin points out in "Autobiography as Narrative," one of the earliest descriptions of parafiction, certain contemporary writers cling to the conviction that *something* still separates autobiography from fiction. Otherwise, why would Hemingway bother to compose *A Moveable Feast* after already writing *The Sun Also Rises?* Kazin, himself an accomplished autobiographer in *A Walker in the City* and *Starting Out in the Thirties,* believes that Hemingway—like Nabokov, Dahlberg, and others—rewrites his Parisian past out of contradictory impulses. On one level, all these authors realize everything they write is fiction; therefore, each of their so-called autobiographies is a "narrative which has no purpose other than to tell a story, to create the effect of a story, which above all asks (as the books by St. Augustine, Rousseau, Thoreau, and Henry Adams do not) to be read for its value as narrative."[15] In these terms, then, Kazin's "narrative" becomes a synonym for pure invention. The reader of *Speak, Memory* or *Because I Was Flesh* should therefore discount all authorial gestures toward the retrieval of an actual, verifiable past. These are nothing more than literary ploys. "Obviously, autobiography does not appeal to us as readers because it is more true to the facts than is fiction"; Kazin declares, "it is just another way of telling a story, it tells another kind of story, and it uses facts as a strategy" (213). Nonetheless, Kazin acknowledges the nagging pressure of another aim: the need of these same storytellers to try to recapture (by whatever artifice) some shred of a separate, nonfictional, and historical self. There is, he seems to say, a genuine urge toward history in Nabokov's comments about man, fictionist, and poor Mademoiselle. "When a good novelist relates as fact what he has already used as fiction," Kazin admits, "it is obvious that he turns to autobiography out of some creative longing that fiction has not satisfied" (212). He nowhere defines this longing, however, nor does he indicate how the present-day reader may distinguish "creative" from "recreative" acts of the imagination. The same dilemma confronts other parafictionists, as we have seen in the case of Sukenick. How else may one explain Lynn's retort at the end of *Up*? Her warning "don't say only" about a book which purports to be a novel echoes Hemingway's preface by reminding us that one person's fiction is another's fact. Reader expectation, then, remains a strong force pressing upon even the most unconventional autobiographers of today.

Some of these inner doubts and desires and similar public assumptions and pressures affect the work of another group of writers currently experimenting with new autobiographical forms: the New Journalists of the 1960s and early 1970s. In the remarkably varied work of Norman Mailer, Tom Wolfe, Hunter Thompson, Joan Didion, Truman Capote, Studs Terkel, and others, one encounters versions of contemporary history which are often so "fictional" and personal in style, tone, and structure that conventional distinctions between reportage, the novel, history, and autobiography seem to disappear. Acting on the principle that only by centering on the self can social and historical reality be adequately presented, these writers engage in wholesale raids on other media for narrative devices to put at the service of the reporting self. Personal journalism, as Tom Wolfe has jocosely put it, is a "low rent form"; as compared to the novel, the magazine and newspaper are socially and artistically inferior. On this point, the New Journalists and parafictionists agree: the novel is their norm against which other narratives are still measured. All admire fiction's flexibility, its capacity to reproduce at the same time the surfaces of experience and subtle, surreal depths of consciousness, its appeal to both popular and elite audiences. At the same time, less prestigious media like autobiography, film, television, and even the comic strip also contribute techniques and inspiration to the imaginative reporter. Operating eclectically and opportunistically to exploit new fads and old forms, the New Journalist often creates a vivid sense of self and style. At the same time that the journalist satisfies the reader's need for novelty he or she must continue to feed an equal appetite for information and pleasure. So, unlike parafictionists, these writers are practicing empiricists. Most would probably reject Sukenick's metaphysics even though, as Tom Wolfe admits, they might find such "intracranial exercises" fascinating. But a philosophy of the absurd is often out of place in a popular medium like magazine or book journalism. Ordinary readers crave recognizable representations of life and chronological and referential realities of time and place. "The externals are the same for everybody," Wolfe argues. "The audience desperately wants to be able to make a pattern out of what it really is they're looking

274

at." The personal journalist's role is to give the common reader the self *and* the subject. "The best thing is to have both," Wolfe declares, "to have both someone who will bring you bigger and more exciting chunks of the outside world *plus* a unique sensibility, or rather a unique way of looking at the world, a unique fantasy life, even, to use the way Freud explains it, a unique emotional reality of his own that somehow echoes or vibrates with the emotional states of the reader. So that you get both the external reality and the subjective reality."[16] Wolfe's motto for subjective reportage is "Take, use, improvise." Eclecticism authorizes all sorts of novelistic devices—scenic structure with climaxes and surprises galore; literal and surreal speech; interior monologues; a wealth of symbolic descriptions and details. Everything is grist for the journalist in seeking to reproduce the ambiguous, zany, irrational world of the self and the Merry Pranksters, Las Vegas, or a Washington Peace March.

Particularly as practiced by highly self-conscious and experimental writers like Mailer, New Journalism emerged in the 1960s as a variant form of autobiographical discourse. For even the most surreal narratives of Wolfe and Thompson are not intended to be taken as fictional. "I would not put myself next to him," Wolfe remarks of one of his subjects, "if I had not been there. No, I'm expecting the reader to allow me a certain leeway *if* it leads towards a better grasp of what actually took place. . . . I don't expect him, however, to grant me the right to make up anything. I think it kind of kills the whole thing." To which Wolfe's interlocutor replied, "That's fiction, I guess." Wolfe agreed: "Because part of the impact is the fact that you're telling the reader *this* happened. This is not a short story. This is not a novel. This is not fiction."[17] Though of course he does not speak for all New Journalists, Wolfe's claim for the essential historicity of his idiosyncratic art is widely shared. However preoccupied with exploiting a personal vision and style, popular journalists operate within conventions. One of these which limits their works as autobiography is the narrowly contemporary time-frame of their highly topical subject-matter. Yet even in this case the public present and a personal past may often be mixed in surprising proportions. Ranging far into the past and deep within his own mind and memory, Studs Terkel, for example, adopts an essentially autobiographical perspective in *Talking to Myself.*[18] *The Armies of the Night,* on the other hand, though even more subjective, focuses almost exclusively upon Mailer's still warm experiences during the 1967 Peace March. The surprising rapidity with which Mailer recaptures this portion of his own and the nation's past is another hallmark of the journalist, but it is one which autobiographers too have sometimes shared; Mailer's book, serialized first in *Harper's*, was written scarcely more quickly than Gertrude Stein composed *The Autobiography of Alice B. Toklas*. Like her, Mailer exploits the expressive possibilities of instant history, instant art, instant autobiography.

Terkel and Mailer provide an instructive contrast in another respect. Both utilize the latest technical modes of recording personal experience. Terkel's instrument is the tape recorder. The peripatetic interviewer has as constant companion his Uher, which ultimately becomes the presiding symbol of the narrative self created in *Talking to Myself*. Mailer's favorite media, on the other hand, are cinematography and television. One of the calculated shocks to the reader of *The Armies of the Night* is the revelation on page 152 that "The Participant" has all along been photographed by a team of British documentary filmmakers. This surprise underscores the issues of truth and deception with which he struggles throughout the book. Mailer's confession also invites the reader to imagine the story itself as a kind of film documentary in prose. Mailer's subsequent experiments in filmmaking, like *Maidstone*, continue to display (and dissect) the self who stands before and behind the camera lens. Other recent autobiographers are also aware of possible parallels between their prose works and motion-picture narratives. It is no coincidence that Hellman's *Pentimento* was so readily converted into a prize-winning film or that *Stop-time* (though of course powerfully influenced by jazz), also reinvents Conroy's life as a sequence of film clips. The actual obstacles to this transfer of autobiographical image and identity from words into film have been brilliantly examined by Elizabeth Bruss.[19] But simply as literary metaphor, the motion picture has proved an important stimulus to much recent autobiographical experimentation.

Many of the most popular and innovative forms of autobiographical literature today are, then, attempts to recreate a self amid and against a variety of cultural cross currents and forces which limit or deny that possibility. These circumstances form a complex network, only a few of whose strands have been suggested here. As Misch might have predicted, the situation cannot be reduced to the single phenomenon of parafiction. Yet despite critical announcements of the death of autobiography, authors and audiences continue to act on its possibility. Many readers resist or simply ignore the proclamations of Kazin and the others which collapse conventional distinctions between history and fiction. Furthermore, what audiences believe and ask for makes a palpable difference to certain writers, if not to all critics. The force of this truth is underscored by Barrett Mandel, who asserts that "autobiographies and novels are finally totally distinct and this simple fact *every reader knows.*" The reader almost never mistakes the two. "It is academic sleight-of-hand to say that books which stand perfectly well on their own as paragons of style and form are not what they appear to be."[20]

Though I agree with Mandel's commonsensical emphasis upon audience expectation as basic to all autobiography, nonetheless certain contemporary autobiographies do emit highly ambiguous signals. The prefaces quoted at the beginning of this chapter indicate that not all books are what they appear to be. Some are deliberately *not* what they seem. Further exploration of this foggy terrain between so-called factual accounts of personal experience and outright fantasies is therefore in order. As we have argued throughout this book, an appropriate way to proceed is to examine and compare particular texts which not only illustrate but whose authors also theorize about these issues of fact and fiction in contemporary autobiography.

We begin with *The Armies of the Night* as an exemplary expression of autobiography emerging from New Journalism. Not that it is a more unequivocal account than *Pentimento* or *Stop-time,* but it is in several respects the most public of contemporary personal narratives. Mailer seizes the events of October 1967 almost as they happen and are being transferred from television screen and newspaper to the history books. Furthermore, the writer through whose sizable ego political events are filtered is very much a public man and literary legend. "The Historian" and "Novelist" melt into "the Participant," while the private self, as most readers realize before finishing the book, is surprisingly silent. Like Whitman—Mailer's fellow Brooklynite who came to Washington in an earlier national crisis and stayed a good deal longer—the autobiographer defines himself chiefly in the present historic moment and through a self-appointed role. Much more than *Specimen Days, The Armies of the Night* is reticent about the personal past—about childhood, the family, and even the early career. Thus Mailer appears to confirm Russell Hart's contention that one hallmark of contemporary memoirs is their *personal* but not *private* involvement with public events.[21]

A polar opposite to Mailer is Frank Conroy, whose *Stop-time* is as conspicuously private a story as Aiken's *Ushant.* World War II and the atomic bomb might as well have taken place on another planet for all the recorded impact they seem to have had on this ordinary and wholly unhistoric existence. Often termed a novel by careless readers, *Stop-time* seems to fit perfectly Sukenick's and Rother's assumptions about parafiction. If Mailer's book distills personal truths from a single, highly publicized historical event, Conroy's narrative commits itself to the mystery at the core of an almost anonymous existence, stretching over some fifteen years. As Mailer brings to present autobiographical consciousness the historical tradition of Whitman and Henry Adams, Conroy realizes better than most contemporary autobiographers the artistic impulse, shared with novelists and short-story writers, to repossess the childhood and youth of a hidden life.

Mystery, too, is the ultimate lesson of Lillian Hellman's recollections of her long and creative life in *Pentimento.* The mysteries of motive and temperament in the self and in seven or eight important others are woven into a tight tissue of recreated relationships. These are deployed in a long temporal perspective. Through this act of the memory a comprehensive sense of the mystery of life itself is generated. At the story's center sits the author, an aging, almost solitary survivor whose social identity stands midway between Mailer's middle-aged notoriety and Conroy's inconspicuous youth.

In dramatizing their unique versions of participation, isolation, and opposition in relation to contemporary society, these three autobiographers wrestle also with different private demons. Mailer's is chiefly the ego; Conroy's is time; and Hellman's death. Finally all three narratives exploit in revealing counterpoint the resources of fiction and other arts—though each work remains, as I hope to suggest, authentic autobiography. Like other contemporary works (including those with the perplexing prefaces) which demonstrate the difficulties of defining oneself in a time of "overwhelming social dislocations," Mailer, Conroy, and Hellman articulate many of the fundamental issues faced by autobiographers in the turbulent decade from the mid-1960s to the mid-1970s. These issues will doubtless continue to perplex personal historians of the future.

I

In *The Armies of the Night,* Mailer places himself squarely in the Adams-Du Bois lineage of those proclaiming the public self in the social arena as the proper subject for memoir. Hence "History" takes precedence over "The Novel" in the subtitle: "History as a Novel; The Novel as History."[22] This priority prevails throughout, despite the novelistic devices and literary theories later employed. All personal experience and one's identity, he asserts, are fundamentally conditioned by external circumstances, epitomized for him by the Vietnam War and the institution of the Pentagon. In 1967, Washington becomes the locus for a symbolic struggle between these potent forces and the dissenting individual citizen. Despite its manifest absurdities, the Peace March of that year demonstrates an indisputably historical fact—America was then (and may well remain) a deeply divided culture and polity. Mailer first defines and then embraces the occasion's polarities: hawks vs. doves; urban hippies vs. small-town straight Americans; the mass vs. the single self; social involvement vs. passivity; technology vs. mystery. As representative Ego caught in cultural crisis, he feels himself similarly divided: he is both member of the march and the writer who stands outside in order to comment accurately and honestly upon its multiple meanings.

The most immediately palpable of these is that American public life is a vast arena for egotistical display and histrionics, an insight equally well exemplified by the demonstrators, government officials, and Mailer himself. Throughout the first book he displays himself comically and mercilessly as the most outrageous of American swellheads. His theatrical manners annoy and sometimes offend even his closest friends and admirers. Slowly, however, another side emerges. Mailer the gross and drunken egomaniac—as many readers find him—is also a modest son and the scion of hallowed ancestors. The show-off claims descent from culture-heroes like Whitman, Hemingway, and Henry Adams. These presences—and others equally august—hover in the atmosphere of his allusive prose. Yet this appropriated elite heritage never gentles the barroom Mailer, who offers himself, with all his accumulated contradictions and pretensions on display, as a proper guide through the "crazy house of history" (68). Since he has found the Peace March a supremely ambiguous experience, Mailer cheerfully nominates himself as historian with special qualifications: someone "ambiguous in his own proportions, a comic hero" with an imagination already trained "to recapture the precise feel of the ambiguity of the event and its monumental disproportions" (67–68). In short, a Novelist offers himself in service to History.

His dual role as participant and observer sensitizes Mailer to both the substance of public action and the style of official utterance. Thus though the prime target of his personal polemics is American imperialist technology and its ideology, equally deadly enemies are the writers and photographers of the mass media. Their accounts of the march, like the press's coverage of Vietnam, provoke this corrective account, which opens with the promise, "Now we may leave *Time* in order to find out what happened" (14). Against the professional prevaricators of Madison Avenue he pits his own historical memory and artistic vision. "One could not communicate the horror to anyone who did not write well" (80), he remarks with some smugness about these other clumsy, meretricious journalists. Unlike theirs, his story will be authenticated not only by an appropriate idiom but also by imaginative penetration into the secret recesses of history; he will go where mere journalists dare not go. This movement within events by way of the self establishes the principal autobiographical dimension of *The Armies of the Night,* which as a mixed narrative—part history, part testament, part confession—recalls similar American books with very different subject matters: books like *Walden, The Souls of Black Folk,* and *Let Us Now Praise Famous Men.* Mailer, too, aims to write a prose classic, and there are readers like Warner Berthoff who believe he has done it.[23]

Because he genuinely desires to fill the shoes of Thoreau and Agee, Mailer cannot play the literary role of the detached and omniscient author, any more than he can or will imitate the newspaperman whose daily duty is to mask the self. Thus New Journalists like John Hersey and Capote—creators of modest, relatively impersonal prose in *Hiroshima* and *In Cold Blood*—are no fit models for Mailer. The American military behemoth of the 1960s presents a threat which Mailer believes is so malign, self-satisfied, and ultimately so "obscene" that it can only be described and defied by an equally assertive individual voice. Ego has become, he declares, a national disease; ego endowed with moral sensibility must be the social cure. This is the plain—yet plainly ambiguous—rationale for the book. The writer feels acutely the obligation to put his self on the line (literally and figuratively) as neither Hersey nor Capote were impelled to do by their violent subjects.

Furthermore, Mailer's own past makes authorial reticence impossible as it renders passive conformity unthinkable in the realm of action. For more than two decades, this narrative keeps reminding us, Mailer has collected within himself the most explosively creative forces in contemporary culture manifesting them forth as personal energy, imagination, experimentation, passion, *chutzpah.* Brooklyn, Harvard College, and the army during World War II ushered him into a career organized around the claim to be the representative spokesman of his generation. This youthful voice, first heard in 1948 in *The Naked and the Dead,* echoes here in muted but unmistakable accents. He invokes the military past (without, however, returning to it) as he enters the minds of the marshals and soldiers guarding the Pentagon. Another underscoring of his own cultural presence is revealed in the name of the musical group which performs at the Pentagon, for Mailer has given the Fugs their politely obscene name. In this way his present battle to make obscenity a legitimate mode of social criticism is linked to the earlier revolt in *The Naked and the Dead* against respectable literary language.

Connections like these emphasize Mailer's self-appointed role in American culture as Romantic artist and social critic. Through the title *The Armies of the Night* he adds to the image of himself as a *Village Voice* Byron the Victorian moral authority of a Matthew Arnold. Like his American literary ancestors, Englishmen are appropriate, too, in suggesting the scale of his ambition. That in actuality he has earned more notoriety than true fame is a fact he wryly admits, for Mailer knows and plays off the fact that he is the average American reader's archetypal male and aggressive Jew as Intellectual, Activist, Innovator, Iconoclast. Like Freud in John Cuddihy's *The Ordeal of Civility*, he is a bull in his culture's china shop, smashing old forms and challenging accepted beliefs, just as, in his latest novel *Why Are We in Viet Nam?* he has deliberately "kicked goodbye . . . to the old literary corset of good taste" (62). One "civility" long since discarded is authorial detachment, for in Mailer's previous works he has usually identified intimately with his creatures and their fantasies. Furthermore, Mailer's long-standing ambition to write the Great American Novel is another dimension of his historic and histrionic career about which, like Franklin in his plan for moral perfection, he is ironic and serious.

These reminders of a personal past and stake in the present reach the reader through many direct and indirect references. Each contributes to the picture of a powerful authorial identity with a usable past who is managing this literary performance and playing the leading role. Even more immediately significant than his past, however, is Mailer's present mood and situation as participant and author. Mailer begins by acknowledging himself at a crossroads in his private life. Confessing to the suspicion "that he was getting a little soft, a hint curdled, perhaps an almost invisible rim of corruption was growing around the edges" (73), Mailer carries to Washington some middle-aged doubts about "career, his legend, his idea of himself" (73). These too are soon employed to characterize the corrupt culture symbolically revealed on the steps of the Pentagon.

Personal doubts never undermine Mailer's conviction that he is prepared by his total past for this symbolic showdown between two parts of America's collective ego, typified by the soldiery and the peaceniks. As this public confrontation takes place, an inner confrontation also occurs between Mailer and an alter ego encountered in Washington. This split authorial self is perhaps prophesied in Mailer's choice—a surprising one to many readers—of third-person narrative. Instead of the intimate and insistent "I," he employs other terms—

"your protagonist," "Mailer," "the Historian," "the Novelist," "the Participant." This device, which recalls both the aristocratic detachment of Adams and the archness of Gertrude Stein, works particularly well in many passages to separate and connect the author and actor.

One side of the self is displayed at the crucial opening episode at the Ambassador Theatre, where Mailer reinvents himself as the Wild Man who first performs an "unscheduled scatological solo" in the men's room and then happily broadcasts the fact in a drunkenly obscene speech to the assembled marchers. As a demonstration of a New Journalist's inventiveness, the scene is a *tour de force*. It ushers the reader into Mailer's "Theatre of Ideas" while also announcing a major metaphor of self in this experimental autobiography. For the Ambassador Theatre, with its pitch-black men's room, brilliantly lit stage, cast of mildly disapproving supporting characters, and divided audience out front, is offered as a convincing image of Norman Mailer himself. As the story unfolds, the theater neatly contrasts with the other symbolic building, the Pentagon, that "blind, five-sided eye of a subtle oppression" (132), "undifferentiated as a jellyfish or a cluster of barnacles; . . . anonymous, monotonous, massive, interchangeable" (254–55). Through these two edifices, at once actual and symbolic, *The Armies of the Night* asserts its claim as personal and public history.

Mailer's unsparingly comic display of his uncouth self at the Ambassador also serves to introduce the book's central issues and moral values. The drunken master of ceremonies acts out, however ironically, his passionate belief in ego moving spontaneously in the grace of the existential moment. Yet he knows afterward he has made a fool of himself, and this sense of shame escalates into an assertion later that a strong sense of guilt is essential to one's sharpest social insights. Also part of a familiar Mailerian ideology is the old conviction about the social value of obscenity in language. "There was no villainy in obscenity for him," he declares, "just—paradoxically, characteristically—his love for America . . . " (60). So Mailer never felt more like an American than when he was naturally obscene—"all the gifts of the American language came out in the happy play of obscenity upon concept, which enabled one to go back to concept again. What was magnificent about the word shit is that it enabled you to use the word noble . . . " (61).

Scatological fireworks do work effectively to illustrate Mailer's ideology and exhibit an inner (and somewhat different) self. That *The Armies of the Night* is apology as well as memoir and confession is seen in Mailer's unspoken rejoinder to Robert Lowell, whose "one withering glance" backstage bespeaks that patrician poet's distaste for Mailer's public manners:

You, Lowell, beloved poet of many, what do you know of the
dirt and the dark deliveries of the necessary? What do you
know of dignity hard-achieved, and dignity lost through innocence, and dignity lost by sacrifice for a cause one cannot
name? What do you know about getting fat against your will,
and turning into a clown of an arriviste baron when you would
rather be an eagle or a count, or rarest of all, some natural aris-
tocrat from these damned democratic states. No, the only subject we share, you and I, is that species of perception which
shows that if we are not very loyal to our unendurable and
most exigent inner light, then some day we may burn. (54)

What makes this soliloquy at once sincere, flatulent, and genuinely
moving is not its self-pitying opening but the sudden intimation at the
close of the ideal from which Mailer knows he is diverging in this very
performance.

With many of his well-known eccentricities underlined (if not explained), Mailer carries the reader dramatically back into the recent
past. At the same time that he shows up the foolish, obscene, brilliant,
honest adult, he drops a few well-chosen hints about the younger man
and boy who is also Norman Mailer. Childhood and youth are, however, gingerly handled by this author who otherwise prides himself on
the range of his imagination. Any reader who insists upon epigenetic
consciousness as the *sine qua non* of autobiography will certainly un-
derrate *The Armies of the Night,* for compared to two other Brooklyn
celebrants of the self, Mailer shows far less interest in beginnings than
either Walt Whitman or Ron Sukenick. He offers a characteristically
political and social excuse: "the evils of the present not only exploited
the present, but consumed the past, and gave every promise of demol-
ishing whole territories of the future" (110). If, as Sukenick asserts, history is a destructive nightmare, then a meaningful past is not merely
irrelevant and inaccessible, it is positively dangerous. But Mailer's am-
nesia has additional implications. He prefers the present because his
aim is not reminiscence but seizing the "feel of the phenomenon,"
finding words for the grace and shame of the immediate moment.
Though written almost entirely in the past tense as befits its claim to
History, *The Armies of the Night* strives insistently to dramatize perceptions, ideas, and memories as if they were as immediate as scenes
in Anaïs Nin's *Diary.* Both conscious and preconscious processes are
served by this preference. "Consciousness, that blunt tool," he explains, "bucks in the general direction of the truth: instinct plucks the
feather. Cheers!" (40). But what is most significant about Mailer's consciousness (History) and instinct (Novel) is their availability only to the

mature man. Childhood provides no reservoir of significant truths to be tapped. Maturity—*manhood* in his case—is paramount, for "you earned manhood provided you were good enough, bold enough" (36). In the present social crisis only a fully mature person can see and act.

Fidelity to historical and psychic imperatives, then, led Mailer to turn his back on childhood with its lesser virtues, innocence and modesty. Yet this decision contains a paradox, one Mailer acknowledges when he watches a group of young protesters turn in their draft cards at the Justice Department. Standing there, nursing his hangover,

> a deep gloom began to work on Mailer, because a deep modesty was on its way to him, he could feel himself becoming more and more of a modest man . . . and he hated this because modesty was an old family relative, he had been born to a modest family, had been a modest boy, a modest young man, and he hated that, he loved the pride and the arrogance and the confidence and the egocentricity he had acquired over the years, that was his force and his luxury and the iron in his greed, the richest sugar of his pleasure, the strength of his competitive force. . . . (93)

Though less dramatic than the earlier scene in the theater, this is an equally meaningful autobiographical moment. In the immediate "feel" of the experience Mailer is struck by how different he is from his own youthful self and how far he stands from the true modesty of these young men. Last night's showboating at the Ambassador was, for all its excess, a man's act with social implications to be winnowed from the waste by mature reflection. If it was also boyish exhibition, now is the time to repudiate that dimension of his identity. Standing on the sidewalk and looking at these young men who are *not* playing games, he experiences a flash of genuine self-recognition. "As if some final cherished rare innocence of childhood still preserved intact in him was brought finally to the surface and there expired, so he lost at that instant the last secret delight he retained in life as a game where finally you never got hurt if you played the game well enough" (94). Nevertheless, many readers will find it hard to accept the fact Mailer has suddenly become an adult in this epiphanic moment at the Justice Department. Rather, the autobiographical truth is that he genuinely wishes us to honor his boyish need to deny his boyishness.

However, after this ambiguous confession Mailer begins to relate to others with a somewhat different mixture of his usual strident competitiveness and sensitive empathy. Feeling like "a damn Quaker" (71) gentles and sharpens him and permits the modest man he's so ambivalent about to reappear in book 2. Thus in the very act of repudiating innocence and modesty Mailer renews and repossesses them. Even in book 1 there are several fleeting views of the rejected youthful Mailer. One occurs in "The Armies of the Dead," a brief gem of cinematographic description of the marchers "prancing" past the reflecting pool toward the Lincoln Memorial. "Going to battle! He realized that he had not taken in precisely this thin high sensuous breath of pleasure in close to twenty-four years, not since the first time he had gone into combat, and found to his surprise that the walk toward the fire fight was one of the more agreeable—if stricken—moments of his life" (106–7).

The youthful marchers "streaming to battle" wear weird and comic costumes. They are like actors from a movie-set America, illustrating its past (Daniel Boone, Wyatt Earp, Confederate gray) and present (Sgt. Pepper's Band, Martians and Moon-men); "the aesthetic at last was in the politics—the dress ball was going to battle" (109). Yet despite his own acknowledged weakness for theatricality, Mailer perceives a grim reality behind the gay parade: "the history of the past was being exploded right into the present" (110). He perceives that these middle-class "Crusaders" possess only a fractured sense of the cultural past their costumes are meant to evoke, for the "tissue" connecting them to an earlier America has been torn—literally and figuratively bombed away by Eniwetok, Hiroshima, Nagasaki, and Vietnam. War is not the only explosive; LSD too has helped destroy many personal and collective pasts. Mailer thus matches two "villains" against each other at the Pentagon: militarism and counterculture self-indulgence. His insight emerges from the sympathetic double-consciousness of the middle-aged reporter who secretly cherishes, as he formally denies, the boy within.

Temperament and technique, personal presence and the ironic absence of the past are, then, inextricably connected aspects of reality brought to a pitch of intensity and symbolic resonance in the book's later chapters. Even as this heightening takes place, the author springs his surprise of the cameraman who has all along been recording The Participant for British television. This mild shock is immediately converted into significant self-revelation. Mailer contrasts the image of his present self with an earlier record also made for television. "Watching himself talk on camera for this earlier documentary," he notes,

He was not pleased with himself as a subject. For a warrior, presumptive general, ex-political candidate, embattled aging enfant terrible of the literary world, wise father of six children, radical intellectual, existential philosopher, hardworking author, champion of obscenity, husband of four battling sweet wives, amiable bar drinker, and much exaggerated street fighter, party giver, hostess insulter—he had on screen in this first documentary a faint taint, a last remaining speck of the one personality he found absolutely insupportable—the nice Jewish boy from Brooklyn. Something in his adenoids gave it away—he had the softness of a man early accustomed to mother-love. (153)

From the ironic perspective of his present public identity, this youthful, anonymous self is indeed an "insupportable" role. Nonetheless, Mailer reminds us in several oblique ways of the son of Mrs. I. B. Mailer and the grandson of modest immigrants. First, there is his ambiguous yet genuine patriotism, for *The Armies of the Night* is surely as "American" an autobiography as *The Promised Land.* Another legacy is his empathy and understanding for others as ordinary and undistinguished as his once-adenoidal self. Still another reminder of the "nice Jewish boy from Brooklyn" is the running game of emulation with his fellow marchers, particularly with Lowell, Macdonald, Coffin, Nichols, and the other liberals whose eyes always glint with "that old-fashioned Wasp integrity" (201). These embodiments of "everything principled and austere in the American character" (84) are treated with more respect and less irony than any other social group. There is wistfulness in Mailer's description of Lowell marching as if at "a damn Ivy League convocation . . . ; he looked for the moment like one Harvard dean talking to another, that same genteel confidential gracious hunch of the shoulder toward each other. No dean at Harvard ever talked to *him* that way, Mailer now decided bitterly" (83).

"Mailer is a Jew" (240). This abrupt and not irrelevant explanation occurs at the end of a *Washington Post* account of Mailer's speech upon his release from Occoquan jail. It underlines another of the paradoxical autobiographical features of *The Armies of the Night.* The sentence is a newspaperman's ironic addendum to Mailer's widely quoted remark: "Today is Sunday . . . and while I am not a Christian, I happen to be married to one. And there are times when I think the loveliest thing about my dear wife is her unspoken love for Jesus Christ" (240). Mailer turns a journalist's jibe at his contradictions and rhetorical excesses into a major cultural statement. By the book's close, the assertion of a person's (or a nation's) unspoken love for Jesus Christ, even though issuing from the mouth of a supposedly secular-minded Jew not noted for his piety, proves more trenchant than Mailer's Left Conservative preachments in the sermon chapter "Why Are We in Viet Nam?" Beverly's dubious Christianity, the unacknowledged spirituality of a television commercial actress, affords her husband a profoundly serious comment on American culture.

> He had come to decide that the center of America might be insane. The country had been living with a controlled, even fiercely controlled, schizophrenia which had been deepening with the years. Perhaps the point had now been passed. Any man or woman who was devoutly Christian and worked for the American Corporation, had been caught in an unseen vise whose pressure could split their mind from their soul. For the center of Christianity was a mystery, a son of God, and the center of the corporation was a detestation of mystery, a worship of technology. Nothing was more intrinsically opposed to technology than the bleeding heart of Christ. (211–12)

In common with the peaceniks, hippies, marshals, Jews, Marxists, and WASP academics allied in this bizarre affair, Beverly exhibits the "mysterious character of that quintessentially American event" (241). Like the Crusaders streaming into battle and the soldiers defending the Pentagon, she too is separated from her own soul. As another representative American, she wears her social self as they wear costumes and uniforms. In order to reveal what lies hidden, paradoxical, and priceless within the person, the event, and the culture, Mailer deliberately courts disbelief by making outrageous statements which even his own wife will not understand or accept.

This bold spiritual diagnosis is made possible by the collaboration between "The Historian" and "The Novelist." At this point near the close of book 1, Mailer explains and justifies the strategies of his autobiographical testament. Instead of beginning with an explanatory preface, he has like a novelist plunged the reader into the subjective wash of vividly evoked events. Now is the time for explanations and signposts. "It insisted on becoming a history of himself over four days, and therefore was history in the costume of a novel." The protagonist's contradictions and unique qualifications are reiterated; he is "a simple of a hero and a marvel of a fool, with more than average gifts of objectivity." Working with "unprotective haste" (241), he has created a double-barreled narrative—a personal history exhibiting the features of a novel (book 1) and a "collective novel" or "Short History" (241) (book 2). In short, *The Armies of the Night* is self-consciously an experiment in factual fiction.

Mailer's metaphor for this collaboration between himself as participant and observer evokes still another edifice. As the "journeyman artist" of book 1, he has erected a watchtower from which the reader in book 2 may survey the political horizon and scrutinize the forest of history, a "forest of inaccuracy," he reminds us, fabricated by mass media. Though jerry-built, Mailer's lookout is fully equipped with telescopes by the master builder. "Of course, the tower is crooked, and the telescopes warped," he admits, "but the instruments of all sciences—history so much as physics—are always constructed in small or large error; what supports the use of them now is that our intimacy with the master builder of the tower, and the lens grinder of the telescopes (yes, even the machinist of the barrels) has given some advantage for correcting the error of the instruments and the imbalance of his tower. May that be claimed of many histories?" (245).

Such explanations (whose cogency and originality will not convince all readers) underscore Mailer's conviction that he has written both a personal *history* and *personal* history. Yet in the briefer second book he appears to abandon the novelistic techniques employed earlier to construct his tower, including the omnipresent commentary in a narrator-actor's voice, the cast of real figures and eponymous characters like the Grandma with Orange Hair, the fully developed scenes and descriptions with their dialogues, imaginary conversations, and interior monologues. Nevertheless, the final seventy-five pages of ostensibly objective narrative are fully as "fictional" as the opening section. Mailer emphasizes this when describing the climactic nighttime confrontation of the marchers with the army on the Pentagon steps. In creating this journalistic, emotional, and moral climax, he insists he has been as faithful to his own memory and to recorded facts as he was from the first. By remaining "dutiful to all newspaper accounts, eyewitness reports, and historic inductions available" (284), he reminds the reader that he was not present at the vigil; he was then in Occoquan Jail. Nevertheless, the historian still writes as the novelist; he has created "some sort of condensation of a collective novel." In explaining his phrase Mailer draws distinctions between "history" and "fiction," which are very close to Tom Wolfe's: "an explanation of the mystery of the events at the Pentagon cannot be developed by the methods of history," he writes, "only by the instincts of the novelist."

No, the difficulty is that the history is interior—no documents can give sufficient intimation: the novel must replace history at precisely that point where experience is sufficiently emotional, spiritual, psychical, moral, existential, or supernatural to expose the fact that the historian in pursuing the experience would be obliged to quit the clearly demarcated limits of historic inquiry. The collective novel which follows, while still written in the cloak of an historic style, and, therefore, continuously attempting to be scrupulous to the welter of a hundred confusing and opposed facts, will now unashamedly enter that world of strange lights and intuitive speculation which is the novel. (284)

Faithful to his promise, the novelist-historian transforms himself into the Modest Man whose shadowy presence appears in book 1. The experimental narrative abandons overt celebration of self (through personal judgments and opinions continue to abound) in order to simulate a kind of documentary film, with Mailer as cameraman but no longer chief actor. His prose-camera focuses both on behavior and inner emotional states as the seated demonstrators are threatened and brutally treated by the equally threatened soldiers and marshals. The book's pervasive metaphors of theater and costume return, ironically united and completed in the aftermath of this dramatic climax, when Mailer's impassioned imagination penetrates the last mystery of the historic event: the Quaker pacifists who, stripped of their clothing, lie naked in the Hole of the D.C. Jail. In a peroration worthy of *Specimen Days* (and far more eloquent than the actual peroration, "The Metaphor Delivered," which closes the book), Mailer crystallizes the spiritual vision at the core of his story. Of these naked protestors, he reports, "For many days they did not eat nor drink water. Dehydration brought them near to madness."

> Here was the last of the rite of passage, "the chinook salmon ... nosing up the impossible stone," here was the thin source of the stream—these naked Quakers on the cold floor of a dark isolation cell in D.C. jail, wandering down the hours in the fever of dehydration, the cells of the brain contracting to the crystals of their thought, essence of one thought so close to the essence of another—all separations of water gone—that madness is near, madness can now be no more than the acceleration of thought.
>
> Did they pray, these Quakers, for forgiveness of the nation? Did they pray with tears in their eyes in those blind cells with visions of a long column of Vietnamese dead, Vietnamese walking a column of flame. . . .

The prayers are as Catholic as they are Quaker, and no one will know if they were ever made, for the men who might have made them were perhaps too far out on fever and shivering and thirst to recollect, and there are places no history can reach. (318–19)

On this egoless and mysterious note *The Armies of the Night* ends its highly personal exploration of the American Ego. As private and cultural theme, ego first authorizes and justifies an authorial identity, then defines the cultural contradictions experienced by that self at a symbolic historical moment. Mailer's language locates this central consciousness in an actual Washington setting of 1967, peopled by other historic selves as well as a few imagined types and groups. Thus on one level Mailer's account can be reality-tested as a version of history. He deliberately encourages us to do so by comparing his story with accounts in *Time,* the *Washington Post,* and on the six o'clock news. Thereby he asserts that the Ambassador Theatre, the Pentagon, and the Occoquan and D.C. jails are as "real" as Whitman's hospitals and battlefields (specific historic localities he wishes us to recall). Yet the theatrical display of private ego which takes place at one historic site, and the polar vision of the anonymous, selfless Quakers at the other historic site, are ultimately imaginative performances whose significance as cultural data can be determined only in relation to their creator, Norman Mailer. Through—and in spite of—the Novelist's bag of tricks, the Historian's goals have been realized. An ambiguous—in fact, unknowable—event has been rendered at once more comprehensible *and* more mysterious. Furthermore, this complex, quick-order artifact succeeds in making a dual claim on the reader as personal document and political directive. As in the exemplary case of Henry Adams, Mailer's experience is now available for future use as "the personification of a vision which will enable one to comprehend other visions better" (245). With Dilthey, Mailer asserts that only as experience *is* personalized—that is, made an original act in the Frommian sense—can any sort of trustworthy historical knowledge be created. In the process, the book touches briefly on the personal past and even more lightly on the growth of Mrs. I. B. Mailer's son into the present historian/novelist/cameraman/participant. Nevertheless, a significant portion of the narrator's public and private life has been evoked in an inimitable idiom. Consequently for the common reader, if not to Rother or Zavarzadeh, *The Armies of the Night* seems as close to autobiography as Norman Mailer has yet come in his rich, varied career.

II

Although *Stop-time* appeared only a year before *The Armies of the Night* and thus emerges from virtually the same cultural moment, the two autobiographies are strikingly different in nearly every respect except their deliberate exploitation of the resources of fiction. Mailer suggests some of these differences and the deeper similarity in his enthusiastic blurb on the back of Conroy's book. It is, he writes, "an autobiography with the intimate unprotected candor of a novel." Then he adds: "What makes it special, however, is the style, dry as an etching, sparse, elegant, modest, cheerful. Conroy has that subtle sense of the proportion of things which one usually finds only in established writers just after the mellowing of their careers." Coming from a famous novelist whose own middle-aged, modest(?) and mellow(??) personal history lay only a year in the future, this praise is doubly revealing in defining Mailer's own criteria for a younger man's achievement. The older writer deftly puts a finger on features of *Stop-time* that made it, if not an immediate best-seller like Mailer's, at least an important contribution to the remarkable literature of the self published in the 1960s.

The portrait figure staring from the paperback cover lends substance to Mailer's encomium. Conroy's mature autobiographical perspective is predicted in the calm, watchful features of the gangling youth whose eyes are compelling in their direct gaze. One is ready before the first page for detachment and "unprotected candor." *Stop-time* indeed displays the confessional honesty found in much fiction, especially in the *bildungsroman*. Yet the back cover reminds the reader that this is no novel. "Painting of Frank Conroy by John Rich, Paris, 1953" is a factual statement reinforced in the penultimate chapter, when Frank and his young English painter friend John get drunk on *vin chaud* at the Select Cafe on the day Frank is admitted to Haverford College.

To be sure, Kazin or Rother might argue that such superficial evidences of historicity are mere literary deception. *Stop-time* may simply be exploiting actual details of its author's experience to create another kind of narrative resembling, to recall a common Parisian setting, *A Moveable Feast.* Plausible evidence can be marshaled to support such a parafictionist explanation. Besides presenting an unknown young writer as hero, the story possesses a plot appropriate to a *bildungsroman:* the growing up of Frank Conroy from the age of three or four until his moment of escape from the family when he arrives at college. "I've won, I made it. I'm starting a new life," he exults.

Although tone and setting are quite different, there is much to remind the reader of Eugene Gant or Holden Caulfield.

Equally novelistic is the framework of prologue and epilogue bracketing the narrative and establishing its emotional and temporal setting. The author introduces himself living in England, married, a father, and presumably composing this very book. Periodically, "in a wild, escalating passion of frustration, blinded by some mysterious mixture of guilt, moroseness, and desire" (3), he drives up to London to play the piano and get drunk. But "the drive home was the point of it all." In his Jaguar at three in the morning he races through towns and lanes, deliberately courting accident and death. In the epilogue this almost happens. Miraculously, however, as the car skids toward a village fountain, the front wheel catches the curb. "The side of the car bumped very gently against the fountain, inches away from my face. . . . A window was raised, and after a moment a man's voice called out, 'Here. What's all this?' My throat burning with bile, I started to laugh" (304). These are the final lines of a book which, while seldom as "cheerful" as Mailer asserts, certainly reads suspiciously like a first novel.

In between these dramatic bookends, still other fictional features are present to disconcert readers who would take seriously the publisher's "autobiography" classification on the back cover. The narrative is divided into twenty short chapters or vignettes. These bear titles like "Please Don't Take My Sunshine Away" and "Losing My Cherry." Several first appeared in *The New Yorker* or *Paris Review,* a fact which recalls Mary McCarthy and the autobiographical ambiguities of *Memories of a Catholic Girlhood.* Finally, external evidence (not easy to come by, since this is indeed Conroy's first published book) is available to inform us that certain of the names, like that of his stepfather, have been altered. Surely Rother has reasons for placing *Stoptime* squarely within the "narrational free-fire zone" of parafiction.

Nevertheless, I am convinced this work is essentially autobiography. As Mailer asserts, it is a fiction of fact, not of fantasy. No more an "impersonation" of past reality than *Black Boy*—and less so than *A Fan's Notes,* with which it is frequently lumped—Conroy's story, like them, utilizes fictional techniques in service of a highly tuned autobiographical consciousness. Though much less concerned with historical movements and social issues than Mailer, Conroy reinvents a very particular past. The scenes of childhood and youth—New York, Florida, and the highways in between; P.S. 6 and Stuyvesant High, the Folk High School of Elsinore in Denmark, and Paris—are evoked in concrete and convincing detail; the reader never doubts the reality of his Chula Vista and Lexington Avenue. But the boy who rides his bicycle and learns the yo-yo in that Florida ghost town of the 1930s has an inner consciousness which fascinates and compels Conroy's attention much more than his American environment. The older writer, though sensitive to much that has since happened to him, skips over a decade of time in order to fix attention on that boy's mind and to describe the special kind of social spacelessness he endured. It was the particular fate of Frank Conroy to grow up virtually in a historical void, in a family without normal institutional ties or social relationships, a situation which distinguishes this candid account from other writers' autobiographies like Wright's or Aiken's. Yet Conroy's very success in evoking a past spent in the social interstices of America in the 1930s and 1940s marks a special kind of historical awareness.

Repossessing such a suspended past is made even more problematic by Conroy's acute awareness of himself as connected to and yet radically cut off from his free-floating boyish self. In seeking to reenter his past, Conroy is often repulsed less by the social isolation of a peripatetic and disorganized family than by the hazards and hiatuses of memory. More than once he carefully investigates moments that dramatize this fact. "A few minutes' walk from school there was a building on the south side of the street I always looked up at," he recalls of himself as a Manhattan teenager:

> A brownstone, four stories high, with a stoop and garbage out front. I never knew I was going to look at it. Something would trip me off—perhaps the act of stepping up on the curb and turning to avoid the mailbox, or the quality of the surface of the sidewalk, or the sound of children's voices from the small park nearby. My head would turn automatically, before I had time to think, and I would find myself staring up at that particular building. Because I'd been told, I knew I'd lived there for many years as a child. Passing it my mind became still. All the noises of the world stopped abruptly, like a movie running on without a sound track. I had lived in the building until I was eight years old and yet I lacked memories of it. No image of the apartment, no image of having lived there, no image of myself. It was spooky. Walking by, I watched the entrance as if expecting someone to emerge. (225)

This passage aptly typifies *Stop-time*'s reflective tone and deliberately mundane atmosphere—the "sparse" and "modest" (if not "elegant") style Mailer admires. Though the eight-year-old never emerges from the brownstone, Conroy recaptures several older selves in similar stances of curious expectation. The teenager and the present writer are alike in their involuntary, almost dreamlike response to the city scene; walking, looking, listening are almost automatic acts for both. Yet neither self experiences an epiphany or significant symbolic memory, such as would likely be the case in an autobiographical novel like, say, Henry Roth's *Call It Sleep.* Instead of nostalgia or pain, there is merely the laconic admission "my mind became still." Nothing testifies to possible meaning except "spooky" silence. The adult writer carefully distances himself from earlier selves by using the metaphor of the movie with the silent sound track. Yet Conroy's cinematographic imagery differs from Mailer's precisely in dramatizing such thoroughly undramatic interruptions in the temporal flow of everyday experience. An incident as spare as this, then, differs both from realistic fiction, which usually cannot afford such "empty" moments, and from sur- or parafiction, which would not treat the author's reflections about himself quite as scrupulously as Conroy does. Instead, Conroy engages in what Barrett Mandel asserts is the distinctive autobiographical act. "What defictionalizes autobiography," Mandel writes, along with "readers' powers of cocreation," is "the author's animation in the present of his or her past. The author, it may be said, is always present in autobiography."[24] Though *Stop-time* contains vivid episodes which if taken separately might be read as typical *New Yorker* short stories about childhood, it is always unified by this brooding curiosity about the mysteries of recollection. For Conroy, the past is something "which actually happened" though never fully recoverable. His precise prose, therefore, reflects a consciousness constantly at work weaving moments and thoughts into a pattern of bewildered understanding. Such creative interplay provides the principal drama and interest of this quietly compelling evocation of an anonymous past.

These autobiographical assumptions about a book sometimes read as fiction or parafiction can be assessed by a closer look at Conroy's narrative strategies and psychological preoccupations. In place of Mailer's concern to penetrate the mysteries of highly publicized events, Conroy shows a characteristic preoccupation with the problem of incoherence deriving from the barriers separating the author from his unspectacular past. How to impose a semblance of order upon the mysterious, incomplete operations of memory is a prime issue energized also by powerful psychic pressures. At virtually every point in this compressed narrative, Conroy reveals himself acting out ancient fears and desires. The particular psychic legacies of childhood which are transformed into effective words and images are his complex feelings about solitude, madness, and death.

As is the case with *The Armies of the Night,* what comes first and last in *Stop-time* carries special significance. The picture in the prologue of an author driven by a "mysterious mixture of guilt, moroseness, and desire" is fleshed out at once in "Savages," the short opening chapter. Indeed, the first laconic sentence—"My father stopped living with us when I was three or four" (5)—makes a portentous note of introduction for the chief ghost from Conroy's past. It establishes *absence* as a major motif and characteristic family situation. Absence also begins to define the title's several meanings. Time stops in various ways in the ensuing dozen pages. By the second page, for example, the absent father is dead of cancer. Looking back on this event and earlier schoolboy moments, the narrator remarks, "My faith in the firmness of time slips away gradually. I begin to believe that chronological time is an illusion and that some other principle organizes existence" (16). Yet he can never articulate another principle operating in his life. Time slows and stops back there in the past; the self is likewise accelerated or suspended as present imagination engages that cloudy past. "I get so uncomfortable floating around like this," he remarks, "that I almost gratefully accept the delusion that I've lived another life, remote from me now, and completely forgotten about it. Somewhere in the nooks and crannies of memory there are clues. As I chase them down a kind of understanding comes" (16).

The first clue to Conroy's particular understanding is contained in one vividly remembered experience at school:

> I remember waking up in the infirmary at Freemont. I had been sick, unconscious for at least a day. Remembering it I rediscover the exact, spatial center of my life, the one still point. The incident stands like an open window looking out to another existence.
>
> Waking in a white room filled with sunshine. The breeze pushes a curtain gently and I hear the voices of children outside, far away. There's no one in the room. I don't know where I am or how long I've been there. It seems to be afternoon but it could be morning. I don't know who I am, but it doesn't bother me. The white walls, the sunlight, the voices all exist in absolute purity. (16)

Though some might call this moment a spiritual epiphany, it is closer in tone and language to the memory of the brownstone building than to similar "spots of time" in a religious autobiography like *The Seven Storey Mountain.* Moreover, this timeless moment differs from Nin's hospital visitation at the close of volume 1 of her *Diary.* No melting

295

into God occurs, no miraculous restoration of health and wholeness. There is no joyful return to life after the vision of absolute purity, certainly no "Fruit. Flowers. Visitors" (1:348). Instead, Conroy isolates a solitary and enigmatic experience which has become the "spatial center of my life" and sets it against other frenetic, even violent scenes at Freemont School which form the rest of the chapter. He thereby locates this hospital scene amid others dealing with his unstable and dying father.

Connecting these sharper and hazier recollections is another major motif of *Stop-time:* "fun and games." Conroy reports that his father, in a fit of either playfulness or madness, once pretended (or actually attempted) to push his mother over the railing of an ocean liner. This "game" led to still another confinement in "the ubiquitous rest home he was never to escape" (6). Freemont School, too, possesses a similar playful madness. Under its liberal, incompetent, and alcoholic headmaster, Freemont "was a perpetual semihysterical holiday. We knew there were almost no limits in any direction." This pseudo-freedom evoked in him "that peculiar floating sensation of not knowing what's going to happen next" (7). Once this situation is dramatized unforgettably in a game when the schoolchildren stage a revolt by running away into the night, pursued by the entire faculty. "On that warm night," he recalls, "I touched heights I will never reach again—baiting a thirty-year-old man, getting him to chase me over my own ground in the darkness, . . . (ah, the *wordlessness* of the chase, no words, just action)" (7–8). Running wild and lying alone in an infirmary bed "looking out to another existence" make, then, a powerful pair of childhood recollections. Compared to these, other memories of Freemont are of less consequence, although more patently "fictional," as in the beating of Ligget, a schoolboy display of ignorant cruelty which Conroy records with unsparing candor.

"Fun and games" therefore becomes a deadly serious theme and metaphor of self whose enlarging significance leads past the simple scene of schoolboy brutality, past even the wordlessness of the midnight chase, into the remembered presence of the unbalanced father and the time-stopped moment in the infirmary. The center of these images and moments is Conroy himself, who is at once that unthinkingly cruel boy, the midnight runner savoring his "victory over authority" as perhaps one way of unconsciously imitating a madcap father, and the adult Jaguar driver still savagely playing games of violence, insanity, and death. Conroy's brooding autobiographical presence exhibits nearly all its characteristic qualities very early, then, in these first pages. Running *wild* and running *away* become repeated responses to the formlessness and emptiness of Conroy's environment, exemplified later in other relations in the family—"if family is the proper word" (65)—with the mother, stepfather, and sisters. As a way of expressing and controlling deep-seated fears, resentments, and needs, the boy early develops a passion for all sorts of games. This need to organize his life is seen at a supreme pitch in his mastery of the yo-yo. The opposite impulse toward disorder appears in the game of Hysteria invented by the students at the Folk High School in Denmark. Even people are occasionally depicted as games, as when he describes his stepfather Jean as "a sort of emotional pinball machine" (30). All these pastimes and tropes in *Stop-time* acquire a personal urgency quite different from Mailer's playfully serious notion of war games in the Amazon, his proposed alternative to war. Never does Conroy seem to share Mailer's "cherished rare innocence of childhood" or his secret conviction that one would never get hurt "if you played the game well enough." Instead, the peculiar intensity of games-playing for Conroy is reflected in the *tempo* of each game. Play for this boy becomes a way of arbitrarily quickening or slowing time, a ritualized realization, at best, of the center of existence, at worst, of manic randomness. Given this fascination with tempo, it is hardly surprising that Frank Conroy grows up to become a jazz pianist and a writer whose book's title is also a jazz term.

What makes *Stop-time* more obviously autobiographical than *The Armies of the Night* are the adult writer's constant ruminations as he dramatizes the actions and motives of his younger self. As with the brownstone soliloquy, one is never sure which of these reflections are to be ascribed to the young boy and which are later interpretations. Conroy's delicate strategy convinces us that both selves, though separated by the mists of memory, are similarly self-aware. While his sister responded to the chaos of family life by turning outward to the world, Frank becomes a boy skeptic. "Like most children I was antisentimental and quick to hear false notes," he observes. "I waited, more than anything else, waited for something momentous to happen. Keeping a firm grip on reality was of immense importance. My vision had to be clear so that when 'it' happened I would know. The momentous event would clear away the trivia and throw my life into proper perspective. As soon as it happened I would understand what was going on, and until then it was useless to try. (A spectacularly unsuccessful philosophy since nothing ever happened.)" (19)

Once the young philosopher approaches "it" when, with his friend Tobey, he finds a dead mule in the Florida pinewoods. "The stench was too much for us and after poking the corpse we ran away, gasping for breath," he remembers. "We talked about that mule for weeks. What was its fascination? Death dramatized, something of unbelievable importance being revealed right in front of us. But something else too. We rambled over a tremendous amount of space every day, over vast areas of silent, empty woods (a pine woods on sandy ground is more like a desert than anything else), rambled over miles of wasteland trying to find the center of it, the heart, the place to *know* it" (24–25). Who could be more strikingly different from a nineteenth-century boy like Louis Sullivan than this young questioner rambling the Florida woods of the 1930s in search of "the place to *know* it"? Characteristic of Conroy and perhaps typically contemporary is the very fact that "it" is never defined or discovered.

As young Frank gropes toward an adult self, he becomes hopelessly entangled with a neurotic stepfather and an unresponsive mother. Gradually, the tenor of his ruminations on the past change, become more emotionally charged. The mask of intellectual detachment is abandoned as the boy struggles to locate himself between the poles of madness—represented variously by his father, stepfather, Uncle Victor, the inmates at the Southbury Training School, Nell Smith, and his sister Alison—and the utterly unimaginative self-sufficiency of people like his mother, Dagmar. How to become a perceptive and independent person without being insane or dangerously unstable is a crucial challenge for this sensitive youth. Just as the narrative is neatly bracketed by recollections first of his father and then of his sister as mental patients, so it is punctuated throughout by comments about the problem of acquiring a stable identity adequate to cope with such threats. "I stood balanced on the pinpoint of my own sanity, a small, cracked tile on the floor" (54), he recalls of the traumatic winter in the Connecticut countryside. In the hopelessly retarded or insane inmates of the Training School he sees one limit of human identity. "Searching for the limit" (84) is, in fact, Conroy's characteristic response to all fresh experience, one he shares with Mailer and Hellman. But, unlike theirs, his daring openness to experience exists alongside (and against) intimate and still-active family memories of the limits of sanity. Far from evading these specters, Conroy weaves them thickly into the fabric of his narrative.

As a consequence, the continual risks and tentative achievements of growing up in twentieth-century America are recorded more graphically in *Stop-time* than in *The Armies of the Night* and more continuously than in *Pentimento*. As the title keeps reiterating, a changing sense of time and tempo is the metaphoric key to Conroy's developing identity. Thus the whole story is carefully constructed around a series of social encounters and solitary moments which—like the empty days at Southbury—play off against that opening experience of timelessness in the Freemont infirmary. This, in retrospect, is the self's temporal, imaginative, and psychic starting-point. "I don't know who I am, but it doesn't bother me" forms an autobiographical benchmark against which are measured other moments and stages on his way toward the adult writer at the wheel of the Jaguar.

This narrative movement is both linear and associational. Its oscillations between the poles of "normalcy" and "insanity" are graphically described in two crucial boyhood episodes. The first vision of ordinary time is located at a Fort Lauderdale filling station. "At the first gas station I stopped for a Coke and checked the tire pressure. I liked gas stations. You could hang around as long as you wanted and no one took any notice. Sitting on the ground in a shady corner with my back against the wall, I took small sips at the Coke and made it last. . . . The delicious smell of gasoline, the cars coming and going, the free air hose, the half-heard voices buzzing in the background—these things hung musically in the air, filling me with a sense of well-being. In ten minutes my psyche would be topped up like the tanks of the automobiles" (110). This is normal childhood time, slowed almost to a stop for retrospective adult savoring. Within its range fall other memories nearly as comforting—whole days passed in the dog kennel at Chula Vista, droning hours of school boredom, listening to records with his ear only a few inches from the speaker, gazing down from a New York fire escape and losing, like Melville's Ishmael, "all sense of time and direction" (141).

The second Florida memory is more dramatic and locates Conroy's life at the other pole—at a manic pitch of frenzied motion and emotion. Early in the second chapter he relates the frightening experience of once awakening on his Uncle Victor's living-room couch. Still "drifting between the half-light of dreams and the reality of morning sun" (28), he watches his uncle seated at a desk suddenly collapse in a nervous breakdown. Terrified, he leaps from the house "away in one continuous fluid streak of speed, arms and legs pumping like the shafts of an engine."

> Rushing from the house in my underwear, I streaked around a palm tree and ran full tilt into the back of a parked car. It was the primitive symbolism of the comic strips come to life. My head hit the trunk with a tremendous CLONG while stars and colored lights swirled in profusion. For one silly instant, listening to the huge sound reverberating down my entire life

299

span, it seemed I *was* a comic strip character in a cartoon somehow living out the plot and reading it simultaneously. Spread-eagled over the deck of the car, sinking back into a sleep from which no more than sixty seconds ago I had awakened, sinking as well from the trunk to the ground, slipping slowly off the hot metal, limp as a dishrag, it came to me that the world was insane. Not just people. The world. (29)

This event, treated almost comically at first, is an initiation whose implications reverberate "down my entire life span." One notes, for instance, how this episode is linked to the other, happier moment at the filling station and both are connected to the prologue and epilogue. Their common tie is the automobile, which throughout Conroy's story serves as the vehicle, at once commonplace and mysterious, for a cluster of feelings connected with the past, flight, danger, adventure, and self-destruction. Running *away*, running *toward*, and running *into* (as almost occurs in the village fountain in the epilogue) are recurring acts often associated with automobiles. I think they are also associated with "the stillness inside me, the thanatoid silence" (178) which overwhelms the New York teenager as he runs away from the family apartment. That flight occurs when he finally feels his life and soul to be at a complete standstill—a social and psychic paralysis and isolation symbolized also by the Yale lock his stepfather turns on the bedroom door to keep Frank out of his life.

Stop-time, then, unfolds linearly as a historical narrative suspended between the psychic realities of arrested and madly syncopated time. Both extremes touch "another existence"; both metaphorically evoke the realms of dream, desire, the timeless unconscious, and death. Even when Conroy recalls himself as an adolescent coming into the "normal" tempo of adult social relationships, he continues to link his characteristic sense of time to a consciousness of death. This occurs most explicitly on shipboard as he travels to Denmark. "Sitting at the bar," he recollects,

I slipped effortlessly from one moment to the next, each perception dying gradually like a slow movie fade-out while the next built up underneath it. I got up from the stool and crossed the empty room, surprised to find myself in motion. Outside, on deck in the darkness, a cool wind made my jacket billow around my body. I went to the rail and stared down at the water. I imagined jumping. The ship would keep going, eventually disappear, and there would be only the sea, me, and the sky—nothing else. For a moment the purity of it overwhelmed

me. I felt I had to jump, not just to die, but to experience the
moments of total solitude as I waited. From another deck I
could hear the music of a small orchestra. Someone passed behind me. I turned and walked along the deck, my fingers trail-
ing along the surface of the rail. (254–55)

Here, in deliberate counterpoint to memories of his father's mad antic
at another ship's rail, and his own precarious moment at Southbury
balanced "on the pinpoint of my own sanity," Conroy sees himself
poised on a seesaw between adult consciousness (symbolized by the
ship's orchestra) and a child's unconscious pull toward timelessness,
purity, oblivion (all represented by the sea). The narrative momentum
of the passage subtly and unhurriedly tips the youth forward into maturity and "normal" time.

To authenticate this mature identity, Conroy must find a way to
unite the present writer (who we know from the prologue is making
this story) with his recaptured family past. In the final brief chapters
of *Stop-time* this is deftly done through several significant contrasts.
First Conroy casually describes his desk at the Folk High School on
which stands a typewriter "surrounded by the pages of a short story
I was writing" (266). He has begun to see an end to amorphousness
through learning to arrange words more precisely than, for instance,
his matter-of-fact mother is able to do. On the same desk lies her letter
from New York. "Thousands of miles away from her I discovered she
unconsciously accepted her limitations, confining her written statements to a level of almost childish simplicity. She stated facts, nothing
more. Her letters were peculiarly dead—dead with all the outward
signs of life, like stillborn infants. I later learned that she wrote them
at top speed, without reflection, and could not remember what she'd
written from one letter to the next" (278). Though less scathing than
other comments about Dagmar, this is clearly a son's artistic declaration of independence.

How to wring something more than mere "facts" from words is
the final challenge Frank learns in Paris from his painter friend, John
Rich. One afternoon John hands him a small drawing, asking him what
object in reality it represents. "It appeared to be a machine of some
sort, various cogs, levers, and bars against a flat surface" (293). When
Frank fails to see, the artist identifies the subject as the lock on the
Metro door. "I looked again and recognized it instantly. In a single
moment I understood distortion in art. The drawing was highly complex, much more elaborate than the simple bar and catch I had
watched interacting countless times on the Metro doors. What he had

drawn was the *process,* the way the bar approaches the catch, slides up the angled metal, and drops into the locked position. He had captured movement in a static drawing" (294). *Stop-time* is itself proof that Conroy has indeed understood. In translating Rich's drawing into a narrative depicting the process of his own life, he signals the release writing provides not only from the "stillborn" past—symbolized by his mother's unreflectively factual letters—but also from certain tormenting memories of that isolated past like the Yale lock his stepfather once turned in his face.

Writing is, then, simultaneously a means of emerging from and embracing the amorphous and mysterious past. This discovery is heralded by the title of the final chapter, "Unambiguous Events." By balancing the opening chapter, this ending also reproduces the envelope pattern of prologue and epilogue. Yet the closure of fiction is balanced against the openness of autobiography, as Frank, the high school graduate, walks the New York streets of his childhood with a new secret in his heart.

> "I've won. I made it. I'm starting a new life." And it was true. Haverford College would give me the chance to start with a clean slate, and that was all I'd ever wanted. My acceptance into a good college meant that I could destroy my past. It seemed to me to amount to an *order* to destroy my past, a past I didn't understand, a past I feared, and a past with which I had expected to be forever encumbered. In the face of this incredible good fortune life took on a hallucinatory brightness. It was like a religious conversion. (295)

This final reflection puts the autobiographer's stamp on the story. The youth on Lexington Avenue is caught up in a reflective moment that instantly and ironically summons up whole sections of the past— including the moment years before in the Freemont infirmary. Like that one, this superficially resembles a religious conversion, but is not. It differs, however, in signaling an escape *through* rather than *from* time. As a qualified conclusion to a growing up, the moment possesses the deceptive clarity of an adolescent's mood; in the phrase "hallucinatory brightness" one detects the ironic presence of the older writer in England who both believes in, yet has grounds, to doubt the finality of Frank's escape from his family past.

Although in certain respects the intellectual climax of this real-life *bildungsroman,* this is not the closing moment of *Stop-time.* Sandwiched between it and its fulfillment—the halcyon moment of his arrival at Haverford in a taxi—is the touching episode of his sister's mental collapse. Alison's strategy of assertive independence from family chaos proves a miserable failure. She returns from Europe in an opposite state from Frank's: she has suddenly regressed to early childhood while he has matured. "The responsible, self-sufficient Alison was gone. The new Alison was an infant—love-starved, grasping every available scrap of attention, physically passive as if her very bones and muscle had gone back to childhood softness, and utterly blind to everything but her own needs" (299). Blindness to all but the needs of the self has indeed proved a family curse. More than once, he has seen self-awareness turn into insanity, a form of commitment to a fictitious existence. Ego therefore possesses a very different resonance for Conroy than for Mailer. Though it heralds an integrated self and mature identity, ego also describes the last desperate "game" adults can play. In making the reader realize that "fiction" and "game" are dangerously appropriate psychological categories for parts of his past Conroy also reminds us that he is the same person who once struggled in Florida to "keep a firm grip on reality" and in Connecticut learned to face the "overbearing, undeniable reality of those empty days." Playing games was once that boy's characteristic strategy for coping with the "paralyzing sloppiness of life in general" (115). The same impulse later meant driving a Jaguar and writing a book which, unlike the first novel Conroy composed but never published, is a "true" autobiography about various "fictional" worlds. Stop-time's author discharges his debt to that first literary effort by appropriating fictional techniques as he explores "fiction" as one dimension of a real and threatening world.

Three years after Stop-time, Conroy reemphasized these autobiographical aims in a foreword to Autobiography of a Schizophrenic Girl, a remarkable psychoanalytic and literary document of mental illness. Renée's successful recreation of her distorted mental states, he writes, "reinforced my belief that almost anything was possible through language. She had gone back to another world with words, showing us its shape, all the while speaking in the most straightforward voice imaginable. . . ." Her achievement directly inspired him.

> My own fears of reliving what had been a chaotic, frightening, and confusing childhood seemed, after her example, fears I could not allow myself. She had faced her large demons; I would face my small ones. During four-and-a-half years of work on Stop-time, years in which there were many violent and unexplained emotional storms battering me about, arising

303

presumably from the solo (I was not in analysis) rediscovery of my childhood, I invoked Renée often, holding her in my mind as a nervous traveler might hold a St. Christopher medal in his hand.[25]

Though Conroy also acknowledges the heartening example of Mary McCarthy's *Memoirs of a Catholic Girlhood* ("It proved that even a dull childhood can make fascinating reading") his foreword properly underlines the deeper debt to the anonymous French girl, who may have reminded him in some ways of his own sister. As another young and inexperienced writer, Renée showed Frank Conroy how—by means of autobiography, a more challenging medium than fiction—one may surround and shape the invisible, dangerous world with words, while speaking in "the most straightforward voice imaginable."

III

In distinctively different directions, then, Mailer and Conroy explore the historical, imaginative, and psychological limits within which contemporary autobiographies may be read as factual fictions. Burton Pike, though without mentioning Conroy's name, sharply defines their divergent viewpoints and objectives. "For Norman Mailer," he writes, "the social stance takes precedence over the attempt to define a personal identity in terms of a reinvented past. Such writers of the self take their present experiences and attitudes as representative of certain forces at work in their culture. The present divorced from the past means everything to them."[26] In fact, as we have sought to show, Mailer connects somewhat more of his personal past to present experiences and attitudes than Pike recognizes. But Pike would be closer to the mark in contrasting Mailer with a childhood-explorer like Conroy. "For the adult autobiographer, childhood may offer models for these metaphors of timelessness, which cannot be brought into adult life in any other way. The device of dwelling on childhood," he continues, "may also serve two other functions: It may be a way of blocking the ticking of the clock toward death, of which the adult is acutely aware, and it may also represent a deep fascination with death itself, the ultimate timeless state."[27]

If these are indeed polar attitudes toward time and history, then no contemporary writer has made a more concerted effort to bridge Pike's gap—to combine Mailer's presentist and social definition of the self and Conroy's brooding fascination with childhood—than their mutual friend Lillian Hellman. Her extraordinary efforts to comprehend the past are underlined by the fact that she has written three or four quite different autobiographies. This unusual feat necessarily affects the reading of *Pentimento* as it conditions comparisons between it and *The Armies of the Night* and *Stop-time*.

Most autobiographers write one personal history. As John Sturrock declares, it is an "unrepeatable event; not even Rousseau made autobiography his profession."[28] Yet after a long and distinguished career in the theatre, Lillian Hellman abandoned writing in that form and took up directly the subject of the self. Within eight years she published *An Unfinished Woman* (1968), *Pentimento: A Book of Portraits* (1973), and *Scoundrel Time* (1976).[29] Moreover, in that last volume she vows she "must write again about Dashiell Hammett" (43), the person who figures in all three as "my closest, my most beloved friend" (*UW*, 224). Evidently experimenting with various forms of memoirs no more forecloses the future than it has completed her past.

Nonetheless, a second or third autobiography—particularly one not part of a chronological series like, say, Dreiser's or Angelou's—poses special problems. Why is another narrative necessary? What new or nagging motives prompt the return? Will a second or a third look at one's life correct memory's *errata*, as Franklin imagines for himself after death? Or does it encourage increasingly "fictitious" versions of the self? There are doubtless as many answers to these queries as there are cases to consider for other reasons. Du Bois's belated conversion to communism bears small resemblance to Gertrude Stein's late-coming fame, yet both are occasions for writing another autobiography. All multiple autobiographers struggle in one way or another with changing identities. At the same time, however, a second or third history affords readers opportunity to ascertain or confirm an author's "identity theme" or "personal myth," that assumed core of being and behaving which persists through all stages and changes of the life cycle. Thus the possibility of late (or middle-aged or even youthful) transformations need not deny persistences. Nor should either of these preoccupations blind us to the fact that each autobiographical act which deals with change and continuity is itself a unique world of words. Each emerges from its own historic moment and epigenetic stage; each is the product of an imagination continuously recreating its past.

Seeing *again* and seeing *afresh* are distinguishing, perhaps contradictory, features of a second or third autobiography. Both are powerfully exemplified in *Pentimento*. From its title and epigraph to the final word, Hellman's second book about herself explores the question: What changes and what persists in human thought, memory, and imagination? Recollections of others and reconceptions of herself combine in the metaphor of pentimento, the painter's practice of painting over a canvas and thus changing one's mind without discarding anything. This technical term puzzles Jimsie, the young Harvard student and dropout who figures in the seventh and final chapter, though it is one which Bethe, the quite unintellectual subject of the opening chapter, would not even have bothered to grasp. Yet these disparate figures from the recent and the remote past are both crucial to Hellman's recreation. In exploring these first and final stories as complementary microcosms of *Pentimento,* we shall, however, need to emphasize an obvious aspect of this autobiographical occasion: the reader already knows Lillian Hellman from *An Unfinished Woman* as one cannot know Frank Conroy and as one doesn't quite know Mailer from his previous books. After 1976, Hellman's reader will have three distinct, or at least overlapping, images superimposed in the mind. In fact, after 1980, there is the fourth personal volume, *Maybe: A Story.* So in order to appreciate the "fictional" features of the autobiographical achievement of *Pentimento,* it is desirable to see it from multiple temporal and imaginative perspectives. But in line with the retrospective stance taken by all personal historians, it is most essential to place the Hellman of *Pentimento* in relation to the earlier, more traditional autobiographical self.

Hellman invites this contrast not only by *Pentimento*'s title but also by the last word of *An Unfinished Woman.* That book is deliberately left hanging by its last, one-word sentence. This signals the author's dissatisfaction as well as sense of achievement: "I do regret that I have spent too much of my life trying to find what I called 'truth,' trying to find what I called 'sense.' I never knew what I meant by truth, never made the sense I hoped for. All I mean is that I left too much of me unfinished because I wasted too much time. However" (244). Among other confessional possibilities, this is an admission that a traditional chronological narrative—one which moves from "I was born in New Orleans to Julia Newhouse from Demopolis, Alabama" (1), to Dashiell Hammett's death in January 1961—has proved in important respects a waste of time. Obeying historical convention has somehow obscured too many truths about the self. Now, for the second time, she retraverses some of the same ground, while making significant shifts. One noticeable change is the stronger authorial voice; in *Pentimento* we sense the older woman's reflective presence even more clearly than we do Frank Conroy's English self in *Stop-time.* Still more important is her decision also to play around with time, to subordinate chronology to the portraits of seven or eight crucial persons out of her past. Each figure in her portrait gallery stands in a distinct spot of time. None of the portraits is of her father or mother or Hammett, the three most important persons in her life. This achronic design and oblique approach probably result from the failure of *An Unfinished Woman* to complete itself as a linear narrative, for the first autobiography turns in the last part into three portraits of Dorothy Parker, Helen Jackson, and Dashiell Hammett. Here, however, the significant others in Hellman's past are less central, and thus available as more transparent reflections of herself. Vivid and idiosyncratic as they are, the characters in *Pentimento* all face in the direction of the author, thus illustrating the epigraph while justifying the subtitle. Beneath each set of features, that is, emerges the shadowy but unmistakable outline of Hellman's own face. Bethe and Willy, Julia and Arthur W. A. Cowan, Jimsie and Helen, even Hammett himself, play dual roles. They are themselves and act out their own natures until the bitter end. But they also dramatize projections of the author as she imagines herself to have been, to be still. Therefore *Pentimento* both continues and intensifies the experimental form of its admittedly less successful predecessor.

Personal identity becomes even more clearly the preoccupation of the aging woman who returns to her life for a second, more "fictional" look. A deep and serious curiosity about her own character as the nexus of past relationships and present reflections connects Lillian Hellman to younger contemporaries like Conroy as to older autobiographers like Gertrude Stein. This traditional impulse embodied in a new form helps explain the photographs on the covers of her autobiographies. These introduce the reader not to the beautiful, young playwright of *The Children's Hour* (whose picture heads the sheaf of photographs inside *Scoundrel Time*) but to that "fine, craggy face filled with life that was and life that is."[30] Though this phrase from *An Unfinished Woman* ostensibly describes Elena, her Russian friend from World War II days, it aptly characterizes the author's own image in the other two books as well.

"The paint has aged now," the epigraph concludes, "and I wanted to see what was there for me once, what is there for me now" (vii). This sense of the crumbling past as constantly responsive to pressures of the present is a motif in both books. Here, however, time is arrested rather than set in motion by the first words of the story. "The letter said, says now," she begins, that "Bethe will be sailing between November 3rd and November 6th . . ." (5). Her German grandfather's letter, delivering their handsome but poor and ill-educated relative to the American branch of the family for an arranged marriage, represents established historical fact. Because it has not disappeared or changed, the old family letter symbolizes one part of the truth Hellman sought but could not quite seize in *An Unfinished Woman*. Placed at the head of Bethe's portrait, it signals Hellman's historical imagination and ambition. Trustworthy documents may sometimes be found to connect past and present. Whenever possible, she will use them in this book of portraits, thereby affirming that an informed memory and not just a playwright's imagination is at work.

Hence the opening scenes properly introduce a sixteen-year-old girl who is not only fascinated by her cousin Bethe and her lover but also fascinated by the past itself and with writing about it. She is a girl already "wanting to fill in missing parts of myself" (70) and discovering what she really sprang from. This sense of family history is carefully differentiated from her aunts' "fancies or regrets" (8). Instead, she admires the historical and literary sensibility expressed in her grandfather's letters and notebooks preserved in an old valise. That valise, first claimed as her own and then lost under mysterious circumstances during Bethe's involvement with the New Orleans mafia, is the first metaphor of self in *Pentimento*. It testifies to lifelong interests and commitments as unmistakably as does the young girl's "writer's book" from which Hellman frequently quotes. Together they proclaim her preoccupation with the family past to be the central thread in her evolving identity and career as a playwright. The choice of "Bethe" as the opening episode underlines the dual significance of her sixteenth year: she first sees then what passionate love can mean in a woman's life and she begins a lifelong struggle to represent that fact in appropriately dramatic language. Further, "Bethe" declares that the warfare between love and family, between the independent woman and a society built on the deceptions of marriage, money, and masculine authority, will be Lillian Hellman's psychic and artistic legacy from the recovered past.

As one symbol of that past waiting to be repossessed, the grandfather's letter, while only part of the truth, makes a solid beginning point around which Hellman builds the picture of Bethe and herself as champions of free love. Much else about the past, however, remains mystery. Part of its elusiveness—even as a collection of "facts" in letters and diaries—is the apparent absence of pattern or meaning. This is true especially of family memories. "I am all out of order here—as most memories are," she remarks as she begins to relate Bethe's love affair with the mafia mobster, "and even when I read my own childhood diaries, the notes about Bethe make no pattern, or they make a pattern in terms of years and seasons. But I cannot separate now what I heard described from what I saw or heard for myself" (13). So the reminiscing self struggles toward an explanatory design for the slippery facts of memory and of historical records. She is aided, but also inhibited, by her conviction that the sixteen-year-old girl and the seventy-year-old woman are actually much more alike than they are different. "It is, indeed, strange to write of your own past," she observes. " 'In those days' I have written, and will leave here, but I am not at all sure that those days have been changed by time. All my life I believed in the changes I could, and sometimes did, make in a nature I so often didn't like, but it now seems to me that time made alterations and mutations rather than true reforms; and so I am left with so much of the past that I have no right to think it very different from the present." (21) This confidence in an essential continuity of character, so different from Conroy's or Mailer's, is complicated, however, by the fact that neither the girl nor the older woman possesses an orderly or logical mind. Both are intensely sensitive; *Pentimento*, even more than *An Unfinished Woman*, is punctuated with moments of violent anger, vomiting, and gagging. Such characteristically extreme responses to people and situations begin in "Bethe." Clearly Hellman is often bewildered as well as outraged by the past and by herself. Once, for instance, she recalls sitting on a New Orleans bench with Bethe: "I went into an incoherent out-loud communication with myself, a habit people complain about to this day, trying to tell her what was the truth in what I had just said and what wasn't" (18–19). *Pentimento* itself fits this description. One reason for its focus upon the portraits of others is to control the potential incoherence of the painter in words. Bethe, the silent listener on the streetcar bench, provides the necessary structure for this tempestuous self-history, just as in Lillian's writer's book Bethe once served as the secret "code" for a girl's observations and confessions.

Because she is, more than many of the later characters, so much a projection of her passionate young cousin, Bethe lacks sharp outlines and inner motivations which a character in fiction or drama normally possesses. She is at the service of her recreator, who as a properly autobiographical artist cannot help manipulating her in order to delineate herself. Since Hellman is an accomplished playwright and screenwriter, Bethe's portrait is dramatic and pictorial. The overdetermined richness of reference of its metaphoric language is nicely captured in an early scene in an Italian restaurant—one which serves as a striking synecdoche of Hellman's artistry:

> The man turned from the wall, the eyes dropped to the table, and then the head went up suddenly and stared at Bethe until the lips took on the look of her lips and the shoul-

309

ders went back against the chair with the same sharp intake of muscles. Before any gesture was made, I knew I was seeing what I had never seen before and, since like most only children, all that I saw related to me, I felt a sharp pain as if I were alone in the world and always would be. As she raised her hand to her mouth and then turned the palm toward him, I pushed the heavy paste stuff in front of me so far across the table that it turned and was on the tablecloth. She did not see what I had done because she was waiting for him as he rose from his chair. She went to meet him. When they reached each other, his hand went down her arm and she closed her eyes. As I ran out of the restaurant, I saw her go back to our table. (22)

Here, compressed into a dozen lines, is a small epiphany as characteristic of Hellman's life and imagination as those bigger (more masculine?) events which help to open Mailer's and Conroy's works. As the dramatization of a vivid memory, the scene simultaneously communicates the present writer's sense of her former girlish self, that girl's perceptions of herself and others, and the mysterious nature of passionate love both are destined to share with Bethe. It resonates with later moments in *Pentimento* while recalling (and confirming) earlier states and situations in *An Unfinished Woman*. Its emotional clarity derives initially from the presentation of passion as an impersonal force dominating Bethe and ready to do the same for young Lillie. "The eyes," "the head," "the lips," "the same sharp intake of muscles" are anatomical details which temporarily divest the man and the woman of individuality and control. Their bodies move by the same hidden strings which topple the paste under the watching girl's hand. At the same time these taut, highly charged phrases call attention to the artistry of the authorial presence restaging this tableau and endowing it with an intensity derived not only from that particular memory but from other, later ones over a lifetime. Yet the young girl's individuality stands out against the lovers' unselfconsciousness and the writer's spare style. Two comments emphasize this already achieved self-consciousness. The first is "since like most only children, all that I saw related to me"; this seems to be an early statement of an essential and continuous identity, one which might have emerged during the scene itself. Equally revealing, however, is the second, more visceral outburst: "I felt a sharp pain as if I were alone in the world and always would be." Both confessions recall a remark near the close of *An Unfinished Woman:* "what interested me as a child still does" (202). The Lillian of that story likewise experiences many of the wracking emotions dramatized in "Bethe." Once, hiding high up in her fig tree, that early Lillian "was first puzzled by the conflict which would haunt me, harm me, and benefit me the rest of my life: simply, the stubborn, relentless, driving desire to be alone as it came into conflict with the desire not to be alone when I wanted not to be" (9). The pull toward people—often, as here in "Bethe," explained as sexual attraction of the woman for the man—parallels an equally mysterious and imperious impulse to run away, to seek solitude. Young Lillian's flight from the restaurant is thus typical of contradictory feelings often overpowering her and not to be fully explained. Similar moments in later experience are usually precipitated by charmingly unfaithful men: her own father getting into the taxi with Fizzy; Uncle Willy with the Cajun woman at the bayou; Hammett and her frequent rages at his infidelities. Each is a version of the scene in the Italian restaurant, for in each she is powerfully attracted but recoils or is forced into separation. Even the "Julia" episode, which dramatizes her involvement with the political passion of her "beloved friend," ends with Hellman's angry withdrawal from the Long Island picnic.

This cluster of emotions and characteristic responses is everywhere associated with the pervasive fact of death, which renders all separations final and all unions traps. As she keeps reminding the reader, this is a survivor's story, one of whose coherences is the fact that all but one of its actors are dead. Bethe too dies, though her story (like the whole narrative) does not close on an elegiac note. Instead, Bethe's symbolic power lives on in Hellman's imagination and living relationships. As the archetypal rebel, she occupies the first frame in Hellman's picture gallery. Her declaration "Now I am woman and woman does not need help" (18) sweeps Germany, the Bowman family, marriage, and many other social shibboleths away under the wind of a woman's will and passion. Bethe is the bittersweet reminder of love's primacy and price; that is why Hellman first tries to tell Hammett about her as they are going to bed for the first time. She repeats the attempt in the chapter's last lines, after Bethe's death, with the usual results: "I never went back to Germany because now it was the time of Hitler, and I don't even remember talking again about Bethe with my aunts, although one drunken night I did try to tell Hammett about Bethe, and got angry when he said he didn't understand what I meant when I kept repeating that Bethe had had a lot to do with him and me. I got so angry that I left the apartment, drove to Montauk on a snowy day, and came back two days later with the grippe" (39).

"It was you who did it," Lillie exclaims to Bethe after she herself has grown up, married and divorced. "I would not have found it without you. Now what good is it, tell me that?" (37). As in most addresses to her dead family, there is loving irony in this outburst. Part of its bite reflects the persistence here of a child's rage at the adult world for being built on such a dangerous emotional foundation. Present too is an older woman's veiled rage at Bethe's German (or is it her feminine?) simplicity for accepting life on these terms. If Patricia Meyer Spacks is right in criticizing *An Unfinished Woman* for its author's surrender to masculine values, *Pentimento*'s anger may mark a later realization of the cost of thus surrendering to love and to men.[31] Julia is assuredly right when she remarks in the Berlin restaurant that anger is as vital to Lillian Hellman's character (girl and woman) as devotion is. Their connection is more clearly identified, dramatized, and firmly located in family history in the opening portrait/self-portrait of *Pentimento* than anywhere in the earlier autobiography.

But though it is a rich orchestration of personal motifs and metaphors, "Bethe" is no more a complete microcosm of this book than Mailer's opening scene at the Ambassador Theatre or young Conroy's days and nights at Freemont School. Synecdoche never embraces *everything*. This is especially true of autobiography, which because it is a kind of history has more loose ends to be loyal to than poetry, fiction, film, or drama. In various ways, most autobiographies, though they may open with richly symbolic statements like "Bethe" or "Toward a Theatre of Ideas," at the close usually open outward into the ongoing life of the autobiographer *as well as* return to the characterizing themes and metaphors announced earlier. The reader of *Pentimento*, like the moviegoer who has seen *Julia*, recognizes that other sections of this complex narrative contribute essential touches to the self-portrait, just as they memorialize unique individuals Hellman has known, loved, and been angry with. Nonetheless, without dismissing these chapters, the final twenty-five pages (embracing the closely linked chapters "Turtle" and "Pentimento") serve the special artistic function of bringing us back to the opening forty pages already discussed.

Two vital aspects of the writer's experience and character hardly touched on in "Bethe" are politics and her intimate friendships with black women. These themes are most fully treated in "Willy" and "Julia." As abidingly ambiguous concerns—one social and public, the other private and familial—they reappear at the book's end in the characters of Jimsie and Helen. Neither person is as striking as the earlier figures they in part represent; Jimsie possesses little of Julia's passionate and fatal dedication to a cause; Helen seldom rises to the rhetorical and moral heights of irony reached by Sophronia and Caroline Ducky. But though less dramatic—less "fictional" in ways the film *Julia* illustrates—Helen and Jimsie preside over the ending because they *are* the recent past as well as types and successors. Jimsie, in fact, is more: he speaks not only for Hellman's present but also for the future, and thus adumbrates that prophetic dimension all major autobiographies possess.

Another presence in these final pages is not less but more flamboyant than its predecessors. "Turtle," the Pleasantville animal who teaches "Miss Religious L. H." an important lesson about life and death and another exasperating truth about Hammett, is one of the snapping turtles first mentioned in *An Unfinished Woman*. There, however, the turtle enters only to provide a comic touch to the portrait of Dorothy Parker. Once on a spring walk the two friends pull a turtle from the trap in the lake. When the animal's penis extends in fear, Dorothy Parker remarks, "It must be pleasant to have sex appeal for turtles. Shall I leave you alone together?" (192). Recalling that pleasantry, one understands better this richer, more somber reminiscence. Though this turtle's head is nearly severed by Hammett's rifle bullet and axe, it lives on for several days, awing Hellman, horrifying Helen, and apparently boring Hammett. Life at a level even deeper than sex is a mystery equal to the mystery of death, one which books and phone calls to the New York Zoological Society cannot fathom. Hellman struggles with the mystery, which Hammett's seeming indifference shows must be a solitary experience.

The resolution of this struggle takes several forms. One is her conscious acceptance of death as necessary and desirable. This possibility appears in the first action of the closing pages, when she gets caught in the rip-tide off Martha's Vineyard. "I went down, and when I came up again I didn't care that I couldn't see the shore, thinking that water had been me, all my life, and this wasn't a bad way to die if only I had sense enough to go quietly and not make myself miserable with struggle" (220). But Lillian Hellman's character as unfolded in her autobiographies is one which can never accept sensible surrender. As the survivor of Hammett's death she must stand all night in a snowy Cambridge street in front of the nursing home he was to have lived in while she taught at Harvard. "Death ain't what you think," Helen tells her then, speaking out of a feminine, black, and Catholic perspective Hellman respects but cannot share; "A rest. Not for us to understand" (238). Her own fierce denial of this view remains. It must find expression, for it is the residue of that rage—against injustice, infidelity, men, sexuality, herself, *life*—already revealed as basic to her character. Through Helen and then later through Jimsie, this anger is once again vented, controlled, and eventually directed back toward the political world where in earlier experiences of Spain, Germany, and the McCarthy period it had previously gone. Rage and love emerging together under the precarious control of words—this is surely Lillian Hellman's identity theme.

In order to accomplish this, Hellman again presumes, as she has done before in relations with black women, to explain another's mind. Helen Jackson's passive acceptance of American racism, like her acceptance of death, is a fact neither she nor Jimsie—two white liberals—can comprehend or tolerate. Hellman characteristically insists that it must mask an "anger [which] was so great, hidden so deep for so long, that it frightened her and she couldn't face it" (241). This reading of a black woman's motives—a dangerous, perhaps condescending act for a white Southern woman—is at least understandable when one recalls Helen's predecessors, for it was from Sophronia, her wet nurse in *An Unfinished Woman*, that the little girl first felt the reality of an abiding love somehow more trustworthy than her own mother's, trustworthy precisely because the black woman's love coexisted with "a kind of contempt for the world she lived in and for almost everybody, black or white. . . ." (*UW*, 211) From Caroline Ducky, too, the child heard the bleak, consoling truth about her own family which was to energize her entire life and imagination: "Part what you born from is good, part a mess of shit" (69).

Though she is a fainter echo of these bitter truth-sayers, Helen Jackson maintains her separate identity. Her folk wisdom coexists alongside ignorance and indifference regarding political realities. On the other side, Jimsie's civil rights activism serves to locate *Pentimento* in the historic present of the 1960s and early 1970s. When he drops out of political society, the brilliant young scientist reenacts the drama of commitment and detachment which has been a major personal struggle in all three of Hellman's histories. The fact that Jimsie, once beaten about the kidneys on a Mississippi freedom ride, now carves *rosettes de bois* for an interior decorator is a succinct statement about the world Hellman is left in as a political survivor. Nevertheless, he also reminds us of her own penchant for walking away in anger. More poignant and revealing, however, is the emotional tenor of Jimsie's new life in Oregon. Discussing his girl friend, the older woman asks,

"You like Carrie?"
"She's O.K."

"That's all?"
"Isn't that enough?"
"No," I said, "I don't think so."
"Not for you," he said. "For me." (244)

Though this dialogue could as easily come from the conclusion of a short story as any in *Stop-time*, it isn't fiction. Though Mary McCarthy would remind us that the reader has no way of knowing how accurately the exchange has been remembered, what makes it autobiographical is the way it resonates with earlier episodes and relationships—including the central thirty-year relationship with Dashiell Hammett. Her passionate feelings about fidelity strike here against a young man's laconic and wary reserves, which reveal Jimsie's own character and echo that of others, including Hammett's. But they are Lillian Hellman's too, for through Jimsie's voice her own ambivalent feelings about close personal attachments can still be heard. In yet another way, Jimsie speaks both for himself and for his fellow survivor in their last talk about Helen, the latest of the dead.

"You once told me you didn't understand about like or dislike."
He said, "I loved Helen."
"Too bad you never told her so. Too late now."
"I told it to her," he said, "the night I looked up your word, pentimento." (245)

Jimsie and Helen thus together conclude the narrative in ways that confirm yet change the opening. Like Bethe, they are ordinary people, as unknown to history as many of the personages in the middle of the story are famous. Despite striking differences in age, temperament, race, and vocabulary, they have partially succeeded in defeating death by declaring their love for one another in time. Lillian Hellman must do so in words. When still a sixteen-year-old girl she learned that "love, I think, but I'm not sure" (32) was to be the priceless gift from her poor German cousin. But ego and an only child's ineradicable suspicions of love often prevent her from fully acknowledging attachments or repairing the frequent (and deeply necessary) separations. Some relationships, however, were (and are) so intense, complex, and long-lasting that words cannot possibly express or preserve them. There is therefore an implied superficiality about Jimsie's "love" for Helen and Carrie which contrasts with

315

Hellman's own feelings about her mother, her father, and Hammett. These emotional ties represent the deepest layers of paint in the self-portrait. They are never to be clearly revealed, no matter how often attempted. Though there are some shadows in his picture too, Jimsie represents the surface reality of the recent past, the living present. If through him Hellman appears to be condemning the emotional detachment of Sixties youth, we should also recognize her own deep reserves of solitude. Writing even a fourth autobiography could not uncover all the mysteries and contradictions of her personality or historical past—which is why metaphor and synecdoche must suffice.

It is in this arena of personal attachments and detachments, in the insistent yet mysterious marriage of love and rage, rather than in the philosophical questionings of "Miss Religious L. H.," that *Pentimento* is most convincing as a second look into the mirror of autobiography. More successfully than in *An Unfinished Woman,* the author integrates the claims of her public and historic identity with the imperatives of a private, confessing, ultimately asocial self. In striking a balance neither of her other memoirs achieves, Hellman employs many fictional techniques as necessary means of articulating her temporal vision. As a symbolic opening, "The letter said, says now," announces her autobiographical consciousness, her sense of the past in the present, the present determining the past. Synecdoche, too, seems to be another of Lillian Hellman's favorite devices for dramatizing this consciousness. If "the part for the whole" works even better for her than it does for Mailer or Conroy, this may be one happy consequence of her choice of the picture gallery. As the experimental form discovered at the end of *An Unfinished Woman,* the "book of portraits" manages to combine Conroy's short-story compression and psychological intensity with Mailer's broader narrative thick with social, political, and literary references and resonances. Hellman's conviction that so much of the past survives in her present helps her to penetrate the mysterious facade of memory which so often baffles Conroy. This belief in the continuities of personal identity also distinguishes her from Mailer, whose presentist orientation, much more than mere journalistic necessity, is the deliberate preference of a flamboyant public man who has largely turned his back on the family past. Lillian Hellman never turns the back on hers—indeed, she is held in the grip of family history and early relationships much more tightly than either of the younger men. Writing several autobiographies rather than just one is therefore both testimony to a playful control of the past and evidence of her entrapment by it.

316

Though these comments fit *The Armies of the Night, Stop-time,* and *Pentimento* into Mandel's aesthetic category of autobiographical "paragons of style and form," their broader purpose has been to raise some cultural issues about recent experiments in (and changing expectations of) autobiography in America. Two facts have served as our starting point: the current popularity of autobiographical writing in a variety of new forms and modes, and attempts by literary critics and journalists to define these new shapes and predict future forms. Yet as a map of a big, changing, and still somewhat unexplored territory, these pages leave many areas blank. For instance, we have said nothing about the confessional poetry of Robert Lowell, Allen Ginsberg, Adrienne Rich, Anne Sexton, and others, which has exerted a marked influence on some prose autobiographies. Nor have we mentioned, even in passing, mixed media works like Lowell's *Life Studies*, Gary Snyder's *Earth House Hold*, and Rich's *Of Woman Born*, which are complexly but recognizably autobiographical experiments. In choosing to focus upon recent prose autobiography which lies along and athwart the traditional borders between "fact" and "fiction," we have ignored important works lying between prose and poetry (Lowell and Snyder) or between personal and institutional history (Rich). Doubtless there are significant experiments also going on in film, painting, music, drama, and other arts—including possibly architecture—which might be studied as autobiography. Perhaps the metaphors and techniques borrowed from fiction, film, and painting by Mailer, Conroy, and Hellman can be matched by autobiographical purposes and devices in the sister arts. (One instance of what I have in mind is Robert Russell Bennett's "Autobiography," written when the composer was 87.[32]) If so, such connections will need to be established through imaginative translation of the categories of autobiography into other media and forms—a challenge to future critics of American culture.

Inescapably a part of this challenge will be the fact that autobiography originates as a verbal artifact; its historical, psychological, and philosophical reconstructions are accomplished only by means of words. Though personal identity has until recently been the accepted locus of these aspects of self-consciousness, the self thus simulated has no recoverable existence apart from language. Words in traditional autobiographical texts are arranged in two principal ways—as *narrative* (to represent the temporal sequence of one's historic experience) and as *metaphor* (to suggest in images the simultaneous existence of parts of the self and soul). As we have emphasized, narrative and metaphor are frequently combined, as they are in prose fiction and other imaginative modes, in the rhetorical device of synecdoche or microcosm, the part of an action which stands for the whole. Often synecdoche is most successfully employed autobiographically in opening scenes or chapters and, less often but still significantly, in closing episodes or images. Though the three texts approached in this way are all contemporary, they have many parallels and precedents; Mailer, Conroy, and Hellman share their predilection for this strategy of self-presentation with Richard Wright, Claude Brown, and Maya Angelou, Emma Goldman and Jane Addams, Vladimir Nabokov and Alexander Berkman. Synecdoche, it may seem at first glance, is a sophisticated narrative device used by experienced writers like novelists or poets, but not necessarily by the neophytes and amateur writers who have composed many notable American autobiographies. This proves, upon examination, to be a false assumption. For many writers today, particularly in a climate of self-awareness where both public and private experience enforce repeatedly the lesson of fragmentation and dissociation, the symbolic opening scene may provide the only glimpse of a whole self which then disappears into the separate actions which follow. Historical and psychological definitions of the contours of an essential and continuous personality are first attempted but later lost under the pressures of social incoherence or failures of memory. The imagination is fired to make an initial definition of the self's social location and psychological state in language which proves to be broadly characteristic. A similar situation often exists, so psychologists report, in the psychiatric interview, where frequently the very first remark provides the key to the whole analysis. (This analogue suggests that if "synecdoche" or "microcosm" are too grandiose terms for this phenomenon, "key" will serve as well.)

Conclusions, too, as each of these exemplary autobiographies demonstrates, may compress the self into final words which combine the author's mixed sense of mystery and understanding at having repossessed a past. By reconfronting the reader with imaginative and emotional echoes of the beginning, an effect of artful closure is suggested, even though as historical narrative the ending may not tie up loose ends or plausibly unite the self on the page to the one writing. By thus asserting for the last time one's literary and historical imagination the autobiographer may reveal her or his deepest attitudes toward time and change. As is variously and vividly the case with Mailer, Conroy, and Hellman—none of whom is particularly known as a religious writer—such closing symbolic moments paradoxically express one's spiritual vision and fierce denial of death, thus intimating the "death" dimensions of an otherwise secular, time-bound identity.

Synecdoche, then, like dialogue, is one of the common fictional techniques currently employed by autobiographers in their attempts to deal with the postmodernist dilemma Rother describes: "how to escape self-fictionalization in a narrational free-fire zone that has lost all hold on reality." Paradoxically, such techniques borrowed from novels and plays can serve to *rescue* the autobiographer from self-fictionalization and *connect* the self to reality. I have already noted some of the ways this paradox works: in the prefaces or introductions which alert readers to ambiguities about to be encountered; through biographical foreknowledge which tells the reader that, in certain cases, the user of a fictional technique has been or is actually a novelist; and by the historical and social specificity of the synecdochal situation. If they are true microcosms, opening and closing episodes alert readers to the complex nature of autobiography as history, art, and psychic statement. Though the three we have examined happen to be known as professional and "creative" writers, other autobiographers examined earlier in this book have successfully appropriated the same techniques. Alexander Berkman and Dick Gregory, for example, employ dialogue, dramatic and symbolic opening scenes, metaphoric imagery and description. Of these, dialogue is the oldest and commonest narrative device. It early crept into American autobiography in Franklin's *Autobiography* (though without the usual punctuation) and is today used by nearly everyone. Mary McCarthy is unusual only in warning us so carefully about her use of it. Thus for two centuries all sorts of American writers have exploited fictional devices without misleading readers about their autobiographical aims. Kazin's claim, therefore, that "autobiography as narrative obviously seeks the effect of fiction, and cannot use basic resources of fiction, like dialogue, without becoming fiction" (212) seems to me a dubious generalization. Much more plausible is Mandel's counter-statement: "autobiographers use techniques of fiction, but such usage does not turn an autobiography into a fiction any more than Dvořak's use of folk motifs turns the *New World Symphony* into a folk song. At every moment of every true autobiography (I do not speak here of autobiographical novels) the author's intention is to convey the sense that 'this happened to me,' and it is this intention that is always carried through in a way which, I believe, makes the result different from fiction."[33]

Mandel here refutes Kazin's right to define certain narratives as fictions *without considering the claims of both author and audience.* While the one position seeks to contain the meanings of autobiography within the text itself and treat its language and structure as elements of an autonomous fable, the other view insists that authorial intentions and reader expectations always tend to remove autobiography from the self-contained universe of fantasy. Completeness in autobiography, Mandel declares, exists beyond the text in readers who "turn to autobiography to satisfy a need for verifying a fellow human being's experience of reality. They achieve satisfaction when they feel strongly that the book is true to the experience of the author and when they are aware, to a lesser degree, that the book is an achievement of literary construction, making use of pretense as a way of highlighting its opposite, reality."[34] This too is the response expected of (and achieved by) personal journalists like Wolfe and Mailer.

One of the shrewdest evaluations of this disagreement over the admittedly paradoxical nature of autobiography remains that of Norman Holland. Agreeing with Mandel, he first grounds all distinctions in the experience of the reader; "the basic difference between our experience of fiction and our experience of nonfiction," he observes,

> stems from the difference in the amount of reality-testing each asks from us. . . . It is our different expectations from fiction and non-fiction rather than the texts as such that differentiate our degrees of involvement. Non-fiction usually asks us to do more reality-testing than fiction. The more we reality-test a work of literature, the more we become aware of the reality of ourselves as separate beings, and the less, therefore, we take the literary work into ourselves (introject it) and feel the psychological process it embodies as though it were happening in us.[35]

Detachment rather than suspension of disbelief, then, is the normal reading stance toward nonfiction—and therefore toward most autobiography. However, from Holland's psychoanalytic outlook, *all* writing contains unconscious fantasies which it is the purpose of language to express and manage. These are the psychic residues of old fears and repressed desires which surface in dreams as in other kinds of stories. In this respect Kazin is correct in his impulse to include fantasy in his definition of autobiographical narrative. "Both fiction and non-fiction rework unconscious fantasies or issues into meaning," Holland believes. "Fiction, though, usually pulls us toward feeling that transformation as though it were our own, while nonfiction tends to put us off into spectatorship."[36]

Experiencing autobiographical prose, then, which is both fictional and nonfictional, requires two distinct responses, either simultaneously or in alternation.[37] If reality-testing and spectatorship are intellectual and emotional signposts of a nonfictional or historical narrative, then willing suspension of disbelief and a blurring of the self's imaginative borders are the experiential signs of fictional discourse. When one response succeeds another—as should occur, for instance, when Mailer's imagination places the Grandma with Orange Hair alongside Walter Teague at the Pentagon—then, Holland would say, our response immediately changes, or should change; we do not expect Grandma to behave or be like Teague or Judge Scaife. Or, to take a more extreme instance, the reader's response to *A Fan's Notes* will oscillate even more wildly when, warned by Exley's *Note to the Reader* and the subtitle, *A Fictional Memoir*, one realizes that Patience, the roan-haired wife, occupies a reality different from that of Exley's father, mother, or Frank Gifford. "I was much given to fantasy" (80), the narrator remarks of his former self, the inmate of mental institutions. This confession warns us to be careful reality-testers. Hence, as Exley reaches for surreal fictional effects to confirm his real penchant for fantasy (as in his description of the death of Mr. Blue, the mad traveling salesman), he feels impelled to stop and explain his double-dealing:

> And though Mr. Blue's way of death was fitting, I never tell anybody the way it really happened; any more than in a hundred places in these pages I have told what "really" happened. I can't tell the mode of Mr. Blue's death because in actuality it was so right as to force the reader's credulity to the breaking point. Attempting to make Mr. Blue's death more believable, I considered a number of possibilities. . . .
> Yet the endings, both the "real" and the imagined ones, I now know lack something for me, somehow don't surfeit the romantic man, the hopeful creature, within me. (296–7)

The differing realities of Patience and Frank Gifford are thus aspects of the psychological identity of the narrator, who openly requests the freedom to speak with one voice about his father and with another about his wife. Fantasy is therefore a dimension of the real world which, Norman Holland argues, exists in the minds of all readers, writers, and characters. No story or self-portrait can exist without this element.

What Exley's book demonstrates even more clearly than Mailer's, Conroy's, or Hellman's is the possibility of a narrative filled "in a hundred places" with imaginary details being read as authentic autobiography. The category "fictional memoir" puts a heavy strain upon the average reader's reality-testing and introjecting capacities. That is one of the facts of contemporary experience, Zavarzadeh might say, but no stranger than many other circumstances. Guiding the reader in this taxing affective and intellectual enterprise is the narrator's voice cuing us to transformations of "fact" into "fiction" and warning us over and over how hard she or he has found it to distinguish between the two. Hence one may still decide to call *A Fan's Notes* autobiography if there is sufficient evidence of a consciousness at work repossessing— or, in Pike's phrase, reinventing—a past, even when that same consciousness engages in explicitly fantastic alterations of the historical past. Psychological consistency across time, and a kind of moral honesty in naming the game and announcing the rules, are attributes of traditional autobiography which continue to connect the often widely separated realms of fact and fantasy.

Witnessing a memory at work, watching it wrestle for testable truth about the self and its past, and accepting a writer's need for and use of fantasy as a valid expression of psychic and social reality—these, it seems to me, persist as hallmarks of autobiographical consciousness and achievement. They may be united, as this chapter has indicated, in many different combinations of narrative form and language. But when that third faculty, the impulse toward fantasy (what *could* have happened rather than what one believes *did* happen) outweighs the wrestle with memory in a given reader's perception of a text, then the shadowy line between autobiography and fiction has been crossed. This will always be a subjective judgment, like my personal conviction that Mailer, Conroy, and Hellman have not crossed that line, that Exley crosses and recrosses it constantly, that Sukenick's ideology makes him a resident, most of the time, of the province of fantasy.

Yet for autobiography it is never a simple dichotomy between nonfiction and fiction; rather, it is a question of language being used to recreate self-consciousness, to simulate on the page the psychic patterns and preoccupations which, as *both* memory and dream, are most "I." Similarly, it will always remain a matter of opinion whether a given narrative embraces enough of the author's entire experience, public and private, to support plausibly the identity asserted or implied. Moreover, since autobiography, even in its most experimental contemporary forms, is both art and history, it will be up to the reader to evaluate the purpose and success of each combination of the two, for as Fred Chappell suggests, there will always be some tension between the aims and attributes of history and fictional discourse. As it is the intent of the literary artist to create in the reader a sensation of ultimate mystery or "bewilderment"—about the self, the past, about life and death—it is the historian's aim to induce the opposite sensation of comprehension, of understanding more clearly the sources and course of a time-bound event or life.[38]

We have seen how three exemplary autobiographies dramatize this tension and express versions of this vision. Metaphor, synecdoche, and the associational logic of images (rather than mere chronology) are three techniques, at once literary and psychological, which Mailer, Conroy, and Hellman employ to articulate mystery. The very same techniques, they have decided, also illuminate the social and historical experience of fragmentation, alienation, and isolation which in quite different ways are significant parts of their personal pasts. There is, then, as J. H. Hexter might say, *noetic* value in the rhetorical strategy of Mailer's theatrical opening and imagery; we simply cannot understand the Peace March as a historical event recreated by this writer without first seeing him on the Ambassador stage.[39] The same is true of the boy at Freemont School and the young girl at the New Orleans restaurant with her cousin. All three symbolic openings establish the self as the particular locus of meaning in each narrative. This tenacious desire to declare the individual self the necessary center and source of social reality persists today despite powerful opposing pressures. One of the cultural functions of autobiography continues to be to demonstrate viable ways of reasserting personal identity in the face of social chaos and spiritual meaninglessness. I am convinced that the present popularity of autobiography is closely linked to this cultural role, as it has since the time of Franklin, Woolman, and Olaudah Equiano.

At the opening of this century, Wilhelm Dilthey could confidently assert that social and historical experience helped the autobiographer perform this self-construction by presenting the memory with significant moments possessing a "special dignity." The "intimacy of understanding" which resulted enabled the autobiographer to create a coherent personal history, "by experiencing values and realizing purposes in his life, making plans for it, seeing his past in terms of development and his future as the shaping of his life and of whatever he values most."[40] Many Americans today cannot share this nineteenth-century confidence in the meaningfulness and malleability of history or in the powers of human memory, imagination, and language to shape and value. Yet moments of "special dignity" and sharable significance may still be recovered in personal narratives, three of which we have examined and compared. At the beginning and end of each story the author creates what one could call moments of Diltheyan dignity as a way of ordering the chaos of the past. Though it is a contemporary irony that Norman Mailer's moment of "special dignity" is a drunken display of ego on a theatrical stage, his is in some respects the most traditional declaration of confidence in the social uses of personal history. In *The Armies of the Night* the Novelist and the Historian are co-creators, in what we have taken to be legitimate autobiography of an experimental kind, of "the personification of a vision which will enable one to comprehend other visions better" (245). By thus echoing Henry Adams, Mailer means to teach us how to read not merely other autobiographies like Malcolm X's or Margaret Mead's but future kinds of historical narratives—all of which are at base personal visions.

Frank Conroy is exemplary in another respect. *Stop-time* suggests the more therapeutic and spiritual (though not necessarily religious) function of the autobiographical act: "to surround the invisible world with words, showing us its shape." Both these aspects of autobiography—the social/historical/didactic and the imaginative/psychological/spiritual—are, however, strategies in the more inclusive enterprise of self-presentation. Although all autobiography displays human knowledge as it issues from its source in personal experience, each autobiography remains a picture in words of the author/narrator. Freed of many of the physical constraints of the painter, and responsive to time and history in ways Rembrandt, Van Gogh, or Eakins cannot be, the autobiographer as self-portraitist tries in many different ways to duplicate Lillian Hellman's achievement: limning with words the mysterious nature and temporal existence of the "fine craggy face filled with life that was and life that is." Through this "original act" she becomes one of the latest in the long line which began in 1646 with Thomas Shepard—of Americans who by means of autobiography have organized the world around the self.

Notes

1. See Norman R. Yetman, "The Background of the Slave Narrative Collection," *American Quarterly* 19 (Fall 1967): 534–53; Nancy Lurie, *Mountain Wolf Woman, Sister of Crashing Thunder: The Autobiography of a Winnebago Indian* (Ann Arbor: University of Michigan Press, 1961); Theodore Rosengarten, *All God's Dangers: The Life of Nate Shaw* (New York: Avon, 1974).

2. William Dean Howells, "Autobiography, A New Form of Literature," *Harper's Monthly* 119 (October 1909): 798.

3. Alfred Kazin, "The Self as History: Reflections on Autobiography," in *Telling Lives: The Biographer's Art,* ed. M. Pachter (Washington, D.C.: New Republic Books, 1979), p. 76.

4. See Louis Kaplan et al., eds., *A Bibliography of American Autobiographies* (Madison: University of Wisconsin Press, 1961); Richard G. Lillard, *American Life in Autobiography: A Descriptive Guide* (Stanford: Stanford University Press, 1956); Russell C. Brignano, *Black Americans in Autobiography: An Annotated Bibliography of Autobiographies and Autobiographical Books Written Since the Civil War* (Durham: Duke University Press, 1974).

5. Bibliographies in preparation include Patricia K. Addis, *Her Story: An Annotated Bibliography of Autobiographical Writings by American Women* (Metuchen, N.J.: Scarecrow Press); Mary L. Briscoe, *A Bibliography of American Autobiography, 1946–1976;* Delores K. Gros-Louis, *Autobiographies of American Women: An Annotated Bibliography;* Carolyn Rhodes, *First Person Female American.*

6. Howells, "Autobiography, A New Form of Literature," p. 796.

7. Jean Starobinski, "The Style of Autobiography," in *Autobiography:*

Essays Theoretical and Critical, ed. James Olney (Princeton: Princeton University Press, 1980), pp. 73–83.

8. See Philippe Lejeune, *Le Pacte autobiographique* (Paris: Éditions du Seuil, 1975).

9. See Jack H. Hexter, "The Rhetoric of History," in *Doing History* (Bloomington: Indiana University Press, 1971), pp. 15–76, esp. pp. 24, 31.

10. Lillard, *American Life in Autobiography,* p. 1.

11. The phrase is Robert Hartl's and is quoted in Paul Hernadi, *Beyond Genre: New Directions in Literary Classification* (Ithaca: Cornell University Press, 1972), p. 18.

12. See, e.g., Roy Pascal, *Design and Truth in Autobiography* (Cambridge: Harvard University Press, 1960), esp. chap. 5; Barrett J. Mandel, "Full of Life Now," in Olney, ed., *Autobiography,* pp. 49–72; and Darrel Mansell, "Unsettling the Colonel's Hash: 'Fact' in Autobiography," *Modern Language Quarterly* 37 (June 1976): 115–32, reprinted in *The American Autobiography: A Collection of Critical Essays,* ed. Albert E. Stone (Englewood Cliffs, N.J.: Prentice-Hall, 1981), pp. 61–79.

13. Howells, "Autobiography, A New Form of Literature," p. 797.

14. Francis Russell Hart, "Notes for an Anatomy of Modern Autobiography," *New Literary History* 1 (Spring 1970): 488, reprinted in *New Directions in Literary History,* ed. Ralph Cohen (Baltimore: Johns Hopkins University Press, 1974), pp. 221–47.

15. See Gordon Allport, *The Use of Personal Documents in Psychological Science* (New York: Social Science Research Council, 1942), pp. 125–42.

16. Ibid., p. 185.

17. Georges Gusdorf, "Conditions and Limits of Autobiography," in Olney, ed., *Autobiography,* p. 38.

18. Paul Diesing, *Patterns of Discovery in the Social Sciences* (Chicago: Aldine-Atherton, 1971), part 2.

19. Margaret Mead, *Blackberry Winter: My Earlier Years* (New York: Simon & Schuster, 1972), pp. 236, 214. All subsequent references, cited parenthetically in the main text are to this edition.

20. Allport, *Use of Personal Documents,* p. 186.

21. Ibid., p. 190.

22. Karl J. Weintraub, "Autobiography and Historical Consciousness," *Critical Inquiry* 1 (June 1975): 838.

23. Peter Glassman, "Acts of Enclosure," *Hudson Review* 30 (Spring 1977): 141.

24. Erich Fromm, "The Creative Attitude," in *Creativity and Its Cultivation,* ed. H. H. Anderson (New York: Harper, 1959), p. 50.

25. Wilhelm Dilthey, *Pattern and Meaning in History,* ed. H. Rickman (New York: Harper & Row, 1960), pp. 85–86. Parenthetical references in the main text will be to this Torchbook edition.

26. Gertrude Stein, *Everybody's Autobiography* (New York: Vintage, 1973), p. 64.

27. Hart, "Notes for an Anatomy of Modern Autobiography," pp. 490–91.

28. Pascal, *Design and Truth in Autobiography*, pp. 82–83.

29. Kazin, "The Self as History," p. 81.

30. Henry Adams to Mrs. Edward Fell, June 27, 1908, quoted in "Introduction," *The Education of Henry Adams*, ed. Ernest Samuels (Boston: Houghton Mifflin, 1974), p. ix.

31. Alex Haley, *The Autobiography of Malcolm X* (New York: Grove Press, 1965), p. 408. This will be the edition cited in all parenthetical references in the main text.

32. Starobinski, "The Style of Autobiography," p. 78.

33. Paul de Man," "Autobiography as De-Facement," *Modern Language Notes* 94 (December 1979): 920.

34. See Jeffrey Mehlman, *A Structural Study of Autobiography: Proust, Leiris, Sartre, Lévi-Strauss* (Ithaca: Cornell University Press, 1974); Ronald Sukenick, *Death of the Novel and Other Stories* (New York: Dial Press, 1969).

35. Mutlu Konuk Blasing, *The Art of Life: Studies in American Autobiographical Literature* (Austin: University of Texas Press, 1977), p. 67.

36. See Erik Erikson, *Life History and the Historical Moment* (New York: W. W. Norton, 1975), p. 113.

37. John Sturrock, "The New Model Autobiographer," *New Literary History* 9 (Autumn 1977): 59.

38. Thomas Merton, *The Sign of Jonas* (New York: Harcourt Brace, 1953), p. 153. Parenthetical references in the main text are to this edition.

39. See Barrett J. Mandel, "Autobiography-Reflection Trained on Mystery," *Prairie Schooner* 46 (Winter 1972–73): 323–28.

40. Ronald Grele, "Movement Without Aim: Methodological and Theoretical Problems in Oral History," in *Envelopes of Sound: Six Practitioners Discuss the Method, Theory, and Practice of Oral History and Oral Testimony*, ed. Ronald J. Grele (Chicago: Precedent Publishing, 1975), p. 142.

41. William C. Spengemann and L. R. Lundquist, "Autobiography and the American Myth," *American Quarterly* 17 (Fall 1965): 501–19.

42. See Warren I. Susman, "History and the American Intellectual: Uses of a Usable Past," *American Quarterly* 16 (Summer 1964): 243–63.

43. See James M. Cox, "Autobiography and America," in *Aspects of Narrative*, ed. J. Hillis Miller (New York: Columbia University Press, 1971), pp. 143–72. For a feminist rejoinder, see Estelle Jelinek, "Introduction: Women's Autobiography and the Male Tradition," *Women's Autobiography: Essays in Criticism* (Bloomington: Indiana University Press, 1980), pp. 1–20.

44. See Georg Misch, *The History of Autobiography in Antiquity* (Cambridge: Harvard University Press, 1951), vol. 1, chap. 1; Anna R. Burr, *The Autobiography: A Critical and Comparative Study* (Boston: Houghton, 1909).

45. Anaïs Nin, *The Diary of Anaïs Nin, Vol. I, 1931–34* (New York: Swallow Press and Harcourt Brace, 1966), p. 119. Parenthetical references in the main text will be to this Harvest Book edition.

46. See Rebecca C. Barton, *Witnesses for Freedom: Negro Americans in*

Autobiography (Oakdale, N.Y.: Dowling College Press, 1976); Sidonie Smith, *Where I'm Bound: Patterns of Slavery and Freedom in Black American Autobiography* (Westport, Conn.: Greenwood Press, 1974); Stephen Butterfield, *Black Autobiography in America* (Amherst: University of Massachusetts Press, 1974); Robert B. Stepto, *From Behind the Veil: A Study of Afro-American Narrative* (Urbana: University of Illinois Press, 1979).

47. Blasing, *The Art of Life;* Thomas Cooley, *Educated Lives: The Rise of Modern Autobiography in America* (Columbus: Ohio State University Press, 1976); G. Thomas Couser, *American Autobiography: The Prophetic Mode* (Amherst: University of Massachusetts Press, 1979).

48. See Robert F. Sayre, *The Examined Self: Benjamin Franklin, Henry Adams, Henry James* (Princeton: Princeton University Press, 1964), and Cox, "Autobiography and America."

49. The phrase is quoted in Frederick C. Crews, "Do Literary Studies Have an Ideology?" *PMLA* 85 (May 1970): 428.

50. See Gene Wise, "Paradigm Dramas in American Studies: A Cultural and Institutional History of the Movement," *American Quarterly* 31 (1979): 293–337, esp. 332.

51. See Richard Sennett, *The Fall of Public Man* (New York: Knopf, 1976), and Peter Berger, B. Berger, and H. Kellner, *The Homeless Mind: Modernization and Consciousness* (New York: Vintage Books, 1973).

52. Elizabeth Schultz, "To Be Black and Blue: The Blues Genre in Black American Autobiography," *Kansas Quarterly* 7 (Summer 1975): 81–96; reprinted in Stone, ed., *The American Autobiography,* pp. 109–132.

53. See Olney, ed., *Autobiography,* pp. 296–320.

54. See Robert F. Sayre, "The Proper Study—Autobiographies in American Studies," *American Quarterly* 29 (1977): 241–62.

55. H. Stuart Hughes, *History as Art and as Science: Twin Vistas on the Past* (New York: Harper & Row, 1964), p. 54.

56. Clifford Geertz, "Thick Description: Towards an Interpretive Theory of Culture," *The Interpretation of Cultures* (New York: Basic Books, 1973), pp. 3–30.

57. Michael Agar, "Stories, Background Knowledge and Themes: Problems in the Analysis of Life History Narrative," *American Ethnologist* 7 (May 1980): 234.

CHAPTER TWO.
HISTORY AND A FINAL SELF:
W. E. B. DU BOIS AND HENRY ADAMS

1. Philippe Lejeune, *L'autobiographie en France* (Paris: Éditions du Seuil, 1971), p. 52.

2. Henry Adams, *The Education of Henry Adams,* ed. Ernest Samuels (Boston: Houghton Mifflin, 1974), p. 38. Parenthetical references in the main text are to this Riverside edition.

3. Karl J. Weintraub, "Autobiography and Historical Consciousness," *Critical Inquiry* 1 (June 1975): 823.

4. Erik Erikson, *Life History and the Historical Moment* (New York: W. W. Norton, 1975), p. 125.

5. Parenthetical references in the main text are to the New World paperback edition of *The Autobiography of W. E. B. Du Bois: A Soliloquy on Viewing My Life from the Last Decade of Its First Century* (New York: International Publishers, 1968).

6. See Houston A. Baker, Jr., *Long Black Song: Essays in Black American Literature and Culture* (Charlottesville: University Press of Virginia, 1972), pp. 96–108, and Stephen Butterfield, *Black Autobiography in America* (Amherst: University of Massachusettes Press, 1974), pp. 133–40.

7. W. E. B. Du Bois, *The Souls of Black Folk* in *Three Negro Classics*, ed. John Hope Franklin (New York: Avon Books, 1965), p. 209.

8. See Harold Cruse, *The Crisis of the Negro Intellectual* (New York: William Morrow, 1967), p. 564.

9. Claude McKay, *A Long Way from Home* (New York: Harcourt, Brace & World, 1970), pp. 110.

10. Truman Nelson, "W. E. B. Du Bois: Prophet in Limbo," *The Nation*, 186, January 25, 1958, p. 79.

11. See Ernest Samuels, *Henry Adams: The Major Phase*, (Cambridge: Harvard University Press, 1964), pp. 337–45.

12. Quoted in ibid., p 332.

13. Quoted in *Education*, ed. Samuels, appendix A, p. 515.

14. David Minter, *The Interpreted Design as a Structural Principle in American Prose* (New Haven: Yale University Press, 1969), p. 105.

15. Ernest Samuels, *The Young Henry Adams* (Cambridge: Harvard University Press, 1948), pp. 51–52. See also Elisabeth Stevenson, *Henry Adams, a Biography* (New York: Collier Books, 1961), pp. 321–30.

16. See ibid.

17. See Richard Bridgman, *Gertrude Stein in Pieces* (New York: Oxford University Press, 1970), pp. 20–34.

18. Richard P. Blackmur, *Henry Adams*, ed. V. A. Makowsky (New York and London: Harcourt Brace Jovanovich, 1980), p. 4.

19. William Jordy, *Henry Adams, Scientific Historian* (New Haven: Yale University Press, 1952), p. 275.

20. Quoted in Samuels, *Henry Adams: The Major Phase*, p. 250.

21. Quoted in ibid., p. 334.

22. Charles Francis Adams, Jr., *Charles Francis Adams, 1835–1915: An Autobiography* (Boston: Houghton Mifflin, 1916), p. 4. Parenthetical references in the main text are to this edition.

23. Vern Wagner, *The Suspension of Henry Adams: A Study of Manner and Matter* (Detroit: Wayne State University Press, 1969), p. 91.

24. Quoted in *The Education of Henry Adams*, ed. Samuels, p. 513.

25. Ibid., p. 511.

26. Quoted in Samuels, *Henry Adams: The Major Phase,* p. 340.

27. Ibid., p. 341.

28. Patricia Meyer Spacks, "Stages of Self: Notes on Autobiography and the Life Cycle," *Boston University Journal* 25 (1977): 7, reprinted in *The American Autobiography: A Collection of Critical Essays,* ed. Albert E. Stone (Englewood Cliffs, N.J.: Prentice-Hall, 1981), pp. 44–60.

29. See Richard B. Hauck, *A Cheerful Nihilism: Confidence and "The Absurd" in American Humorous Fiction* (Bloomington: Indiana University Press, 1971).

30. Quoted in Samuels, *Henry Adams: The Major Phase,* p. 559.

31. Francis Russell Hart, "History Talking to Itself: Public Personality in Recent Memoir," *New Literary History* 11 (Autumn 1979): 204.

CHAPTER THREE.
THE SOUL AND THE SELF:
BLACK ELK AND THOMAS MERTON

1. John S. Dunne, *A Search for God in Time and Memory* (Notre Dame: University of Notre Dame Press, 1977).

2. See ibid., p. 205, and William C. Spengemann and L. R. Lundquist, "Autobiography and the American Myth," *American Quarterly* 17 (Fall 1965): 501–19.

3. Henry D. Thoreau, *Walden* (Princeton: Princeton University Press, 1971), p. 90.

4. The edition of *The Seven Storey Mountain* to be cited parenthetically in the main text is the Signet edition (New York: New American Library, 1948).

5. Annie Dillard, *Pilgrim at Tinker Creek* (New York: Bantam Books, 1974), p. 2. Parenthetical references in the main text are to this edition.

6. Dunne, *A Search for God,* p. 169.

7. John G. Neihardt, *Black Elk Speaks: Being the Life of a Holy Man of the Oglala Sioux* (Lincoln: University of Nebraska Press, 1961). Parenthetical references in the main text are to this Bison edition.

8. Quoted in Sally McCluskey, "Black Elk Speaks—And so Does John Neihardt," *Western American Literature* 6 (Winter 1972): 238.

9. See Robert F. Sayre, "Vision and Experience in *Black Elk Speaks,*" *College English* 32, no. 5 (February 1971): 513.

10. Ibid., p. 512.

11. See Carl G. Jung, *Collected Works of C. G. Jung* (New York: Pantheon Books, 1963), p. 206.

12. *The Journal and Major Essays of John Woolman,* ed. Phillips P. Moulton (New York: Oxford University Press, 1971), pp. 24–25. Parenthetical references in the main text are to this edition.

13. John G. Neihardt, *A Cycle of the West* (Lincoln: University of Nebraska Press, 1949), pp. 109–10.

14. Thomas Merton, *The Sign of Jonas* (New York: Harcourt Brace, 1953), p. 89.

15. Thomas Merton, "Notes on the Future of Monasticism," quoted in Sister Theresa Lentfoehr, "Thomas Merton: The Dimensions of Solitude," *American Benedictine Review* 23 (September 1972): 339.

16. Dennis McInerny, *Thomas Merton: The Man and His Work* (Washington D.C.: Cistercian Publications, 1974), p. 2.

17. Ibid., p. 69.

18. Gabriel Moran, "People, Places and Metaphors," in *Journeys: The Impact of Personal Experience in Religious Thought,* ed. Gregory Baum (New York: Paulist Press, 1975), p. 236.

19. A perceptive discussion of Thoreau and depth experience is found in Janet Varner Gunn, *"Walden* and the Temporal Mode of Autobiographical Narrative," in Stone, ed., *The American Autobiography,* pp, 80–94. See also her recent *Autobiography: Toward a Poetics of Experience* (Philadelphia: University of Pennsylvania Press, 1982).

20. See "Kith of Infinity," by Sonitow P. Sucharitkul, epigraph to *"Don't Fall Off the Mountain"* (New York: Bantam Books, 1970).

CHAPTER FOUR.
THE CHILDHOOD OF THE ARTIST:
LOUIS SULLIVAN AND RICHARD WRIGHT

1. Patricia Meyer Spacks, "Stages of Self: Notes on Autobiography and the Life Cycle," *Boston University Journal* 25 (1977): 7, reprinted in *The American Autobiography: A Collection of Critical Essays,* ed. Albert E. Stone (Englewood Cliffs, N.J.: Prentice-Hall, 1981), p. 8.

2. Phyllis Greenacre, "Early Physical Determinants in the Development of the Sense of Identity," in *Emotional Growth: Psychoanalytic Studies of the Gifted and a Great Variety of Other Individuals* (New York: International Universities Press, 1971), 1, p. 144. Parenthetical references to Greenacre in the main text are to this work, unless otherwise specified.

3. *Daedalus* 88 (Summer 1959): 537–48. Parenthetical references in the main text are to this source, though the reader's attention is called to a longer book version published posthumously as *The Ecology of Imagination in Childhood* (New York: Columbia University Press, 1977).

4. Louis H. Sullivan, *The Autobiography of an Idea* (New York: Dover Publications, 1956). Parenthetical references in the main text are to this paperback edition; Richard Wright, *Black Boy: A Record of Childhood and Youth* (New York: Perennial Classic, 1966). Parenthetical references in the main text are to this edition.

5. See G. Thomas Couser, *American Autobiography: The Prophetic Mode* (Amherst: University of Massachusetts Press, 1979), chap. 9.

6. Willard Connely, *Louis Sullivan as He Lived: The Shaping of American Architecture* (New York: Horizon Press, 1960); Sherman Paul, *Louis Sullivan:*

An Architect in American Thought (Englewood Cliffs, N.J.: Prentice-Hall, 1962).

7. Connely, *Louis Sullivan as He Lived,* p. 294.

8. Quoted in ibid., p. 295.

9. See Frank Lloyd Wright, *A Testament* (New York: Horizon Press, 1957), especially book 1—Autobiographical, and *An Autobiography* (New York: Duell, Sloane & Pierce, 1957).

10. Sherman Paul, *Louis Sullivan: An Architect in American Thought,* p. 5.

11. Reprinted in ibid., pp. 1–3.

12. Walt Whitman, *Complete Poetry and Selected Prose and Letters,* ed. Emory Holloway (London: Nonesuch Press, 1967), pp. 332–34.

13. See illustrations in *The Autobiography of an Idea,* opposite pp. 218, 219, and inside back cover.

14. See, e.g., plate 16, Impromptu, of *A System of Architectural Ornament According with a Philosophy of Man's Powers* (New York: Press of the American Institute of Architects, 1924).

15. Edith Cobb, "The Ecology of Imagination in Childhood," *Daedalus* 88 (Summer 1959): 540.

16. Greenacre's somewhat obscure language occasionally necessitates paraphrase or interpretation. In a later essay, "The Family Romance of the Artist," she explains thus: "The artist has an inborn heightened perceptiveness of the outer world (including intensified and precocious awareness of form and rhythm) . . . ; this leads to the development of the background of 'collective alternates' (ultimately cosmic emotional conceptions) which invest the main personal relationships of life," 2, p. 507.

17. "It is possible that in children of potential genius this inner state of awareness of tumescent feeling may be especially strongly pervasive. Combining with the sensitive perception of external objects, it may give rise to sensations of invigoration, inspiration, and awe. These depend not so much on the actual sight of the penis as on a communion with outer forms which reflect inner feelings in a way which I have tried to describe under the title *Collective Alternates.* It seems to me also that under such conditions the development of the family romance in especially strong form is inevitable." Phyllis Greenacre, "The Childhood of the Artist: Libidinal Phase Development and Giftedness," *Emotional Growth,* 2, p. 494.

18. This explanation deepens but does not deny Cesar Graña's evaluation of Sullivan's democratic rhetoric. "Sullivan's pronouncements speak for a profoundly arrogant and profoundly naïve intellectual tradition. As [Hugh Dalziel] Duncan himself admits, Sullivan was an autocratic aesthetician quite free of the common touch. . . . I suspect that his near-religious democratic tone was one way of investing his own gifts with the blessings of historical necessity." *Fact and Symbol: Essays in the Sociology of Art and Literature* (New York: Oxford University Press, 1971), p. 134.

19. See Norman N. Holland, *Poems in Persons: An Introduction to the Psychoanalysis of Literature* (New York: W. W. Norton, 1975), pp. 45–49.

20. Paul, *Louis Sullivan: An Architect in American Thought*, p. 12.

21. "Fortunate is such a child," Greenacre writes, "if the own father fulfills the need for the model with which then to identify. It is my suspicion, however, that in some instances where this is not true, the child carries the ideal with him as though it were the real father, and that subsequent identification may be made and the development of direction of talent determined in part at least by the chance encounter with some individual or even some experience which strikes a decisive harmonizing note with part of the hidden image of the father belonging to the original experience of infantile inspiration." "The Childhood of the Artist," 2, p. 494.

22. Connely, *Louis Sullivan as He Lived*, p. 295.

23. In *Annual Report of the Smithsonian Institution* (1958), pp. 527–42.

24. Connely, *Louis Sullivan as He Lived*, p. 32.

25. Michel Fabre, *The Unfinished Quest of Richard Wright* (New York: Morrow, 1973), p. 249.

26. See Ralph Ellison, *Shadow and Act* (New York: Random House, 1964), p. 77.

27. Quoted in Fabre, *The Unfinished Quest of Richard Wright*, pp. 251–52.

28. See Sidonie Smith, *Where I'm Bound: Patterns of Slavery and Freedom in Black American Autobiography* (Westport, Conn.: Greenwood Press, 1974), pp. 49–50.

29. See Robert Bone, *Richard Wright* (Minneapolis: University of Minnesota Press, 1969).

30. See W. E. B. Du Bois, "Richard Wright Looks Back," *New York Herald Tribune Weekly Book Review*, 21, March 4, 1945, p. vi; George Kent, *Blackness and the Adventure of Western Culture* (Chicago: Third World Press, 1972), pp. 77–78.

31. R. K. White, "*Black Boy*: A Value Analysis," *Journal of Abnormal and Social Psychology* 42 (October 1947): 444.

32. See Constance Webb, *Richard Wright: A Biography* (New York: Putnam, 1968), pp. 20–23, and Fabre, *The Unfinished Quest of Richard Wright*, pp. 9–10. Webb asserts that this memory was "confirmed in conversation with Richard Wright," p. 20.

33. Fabre, *The Unfinished Quest of Richard Wright*, pp. 7–8.

34. Ibid., p. 10.

35. Ibid.

36. Ellison, *Shadow and Act*, p. 85.

37. See Webb, *Richard Wright: A Biography*, p. 409.

38. Gaston Bachelard, *The Psychoanalysis of Fire* (Boston: Beacon Press, 1968), p. 73. He observes: "The problem of the knowledge of fire is a true problem of *Psychological Structure*," pp. 101–2. Nearly every complex Bachelard discusses is present in *Black Boy*: fire as the symbol of love and sexual desire; of hunger and its imagined gratification; the wish for change; the passage of time and an end to human processes; a vital intensity of being, substantial richness, and permanence. See esp. pp. 16, 111. Moreover, opposite

emotions and sensations are often symbolized: "To be aware that one is burning is to grow cold; to feel an intensity is to diminish it," p. 112. The ambiguous power of fire to focus and intensify the imagination with both creative and destructive energy. "The result is that in the last analysis all the complexes attached to fire are painful complexes. Complexes both conducive to the acquiring of a neurosis and the writing of poetry," p. 112.

39. Cobb, "The Ecology of Imagination in Childhood," p. 540.

40. Ellison, *Shadow and Act,* p. 79.

CHAPTER FIVE.
CATO'S MIRROR: THE FACE OF VIOLENCE IN THE AUTOBIOGRAPHIES OF
ALEXANDER BERKMAN AND CONRAD AIKEN

1. Rollo May, *Power and Innocence: A Search for the Sources of Violence* (New York: W. W. Norton, 1972), p. 65.

2. Jacob Bronowski, *The Face of Violence: An Essay with a Play* (Cleveland and New York: Meridian, 1968), p. 112.

3. Erik Erikson, *Life History and the Historical Moment* (New York: W. W. Norton, 1975), p. 124.

4. See Roger J. Porter, "Unspeakable Practices, Writable Acts: Franklin's *Autobiography,*" *Hudson Review* 32 (Summer 1979): 224–38, and Richard Bushman, "On the Uses of Psychology: Conflict and Conciliation in Benjamin Franklin," *History and Theory* 5 (1966): 225–40. See also H. St. John Crèvecoeur, *Letters from an American Farmer & Sketches of XVIII-Century America,* ed. Albert E. Stone (New York: Penguin Books, 1981).

5. See Albert E. Stone, "Cato's Mirror: The Face of Violence in American Autobiography," in *Prospects: An Annual of American Cultural Studies,* vol. 3, ed. Jack Salzman (New York: Burt Franklin, 1977), pp. 331–69.

6. *Personal Memoirs of U. S. Grant* (Cleveland and New York: World Publishing, 1952), p. 556.

7. Alexander Berkman, *Prison Memoirs of an Anarchist* (New York: Schocken Books, 1970), p. x. parenthetical references in the main text are to this paperback edition.

8. Quoted in Emma Goldman, *Living My Life* (New York: Dover Publications, 1970), 2, p. 506.

9. George Jackson, *Soledad Brother: The Prison Letters of George Jackson* (New York: Bantam, 1970), p. 158. Parenthetical references in the main text are to this paperback edition.

10. John William Ward, "Violence, Anarchy, and Alexander Berkman," *New York Review of Books,* 15, November 5, 1970, p. 28.

11. Goldman, *Living My Life,* 1, p. 483.

12. Ibid., p. 471.

13. Ibid., p. 484.

14. See Frederick Douglass, *Narrative of the Life of Frederick Douglass,*

An American Slave, Written by Himself, ed. Benjamin Quarles (Cambridge: Harvard University Press, 1960), pp. 143–44.

15. Erik Erikson, *Life History and the Historical Moment* (New York: W.W. Norton, 1975), p. 123.

16. Sigmund Freud, *The Origin and Development of Psychoanalysis* (Chicago: Henry Regnery, 1965), pp. 60–61.

17. Quoted in Introduction, Jackson, *Soledad Brother,* pp. 2–3.

18. Conrad Aiken, *Ushant: An Essay* (Cleveland and New York: Meridian, 1962), p. 197. Parenthetical references in the main text are to this paperback reissue of the original 1952 edition.

19. Henry A. Murray, "Poet of Creative Dissolution," *Wake* 11 (1952): 100–101.

20. Albert C. Cain and Irene Fast, "Children's Disturbed Reactions to Parent Suicide: Distortions of Guilt, Communication, and Identification," in *Survivors of Suicide,* ed. Albert C. Cain (Springfield, Ill.: Thomas Pubs., 1972), p. 94.

21. Murray, "Poet of Creative Dissolution," pp. 101–2.

22. Murray (p. 102) mentions the fact that Freud himself found *Great Circle* such a successful demonstration of his basic concepts that he invited Aiken to Vienna for a three-month experimental analysis. Aiken comments in *Ushant:* "One would oneself come very close, one day, to going to Vienna to work with that genius of explorers," p. 248.

23. See T. L. Dorpat, "Psychological Effects of Parental Suicide on Surviving Children," in Cain, ed., *Survivors of Suicide,* p. 134.

24. Sigmund Freud, "The Psychogenesis of a Case of Homosexuality in a Woman," *Standard Edition,* vol. 18 (London: Hogarth Press, 1958), 162; quoted in Dorpat, "Psychological Effects," p. 130.

25. See H. Bruce Franklin, *The Victim as Criminal and Artist: Literature from the American Prison* (New York: Oxford University Press, 1978). Franklin's comments on Berkman are found on pp. 147–48, those on Malcolm X on pp. 236–41.

CHAPTER SIX.
BECOMING A WOMAN IN MALE AMERICA:
MARGARET MEAD AND ANAÏS NIN

1. John Stuart Mill, "The Subjection of Women," *John Stuart Mill: A Selection of His Works,* ed. John M. Robson (New York: St. Martin's Press, 1966), p. 372.

2. Anne Ellis, *The Autobiography of an Ordinary Woman* (Boston: Houghton Mifflin, 1929), pp. 36–37. Parenthetical references in the main text are to this edition.

3. Anaïs Nin, *The Diary of Anaïs Nin, Vol. II, 1934–1939* (New York: Harcourt Brace Jovanovich, 1966), pp. 232–33. Parenthetical references in the main text are to this Harvest Book edition.

4. Mary H. Vorse, *Autobiography of an Elderly Woman* (New York: Arno Press, 1974); *The Autobiography of a Happy Woman* (New York: Moffat, 1915); *Ossie: The Autobiography of a Black Woman,* Ossie Guffy as told to Caryl Ledner (New York: Bantam Books, 1971).

5. Elizabeth Cady Stanton, *Eighty Years and More: Reminiscences, 1815–1897* (New York: Schocken Books, 1971); Helen Keller, *The Story of My Life* (New York: Dell Publishers, 1961); Jane Addams, *Twenty Years at Hull House with Autobiographical Notes* (New York: New American Library, 1960); Mary Antin, *The Promised Land* (Boston: Houghton Mifflin, 1969); Ida B. Wells, *Crusade for Justice: The Autobiography of Ida B. Wells* (Chicago: University of Chicago Press, 1970); Charlotte Perkins Gilman, *The Living of Charlotte Perkins Gilman, An Autobiography* (New York: Appleton-Century, 1935); Isadora Duncan, *My Life* (New York: Liveright, 1955).

6. Emma Goldman, *Living My Life* (New York: Dover Publications, 1970); Eleanor Roosevelt, *This Is My Story* (New York: Harper & Brothers, 1937); Abigail McCarthy, *Private Faces/Public Places* (Garden City: Doubleday, 1972); Anne Moody, *Coming of Age in Mississippi, An Autobiography* (New York: Dell Delta Book, 1968); Angela Davis, *With My Mind on Freedom, An Autobiography* (New York: Bantam Books, 1974).

7. Mae West, *Goodness Had Nothing to Do With It!* (New York: Manor Books, 1976); Billie Holiday with W. Dufty, *Lady Sings the Blues* (New York: Lancer Books, 1956); Shirley MacLaine, *"Don't Fall Off the Mountain"* (New York: Bantam Books, 1970).

8. Anzia Yezierska, *Red Ribbon on a White Horse* (New York: Scribners, 1950).

9. Maxine Hong Kingston, *The Woman Warrior: Memoirs of a Girlhood Among Ghosts* (New York: Vintage Books, 1977).

10. Edith Wharton, *A Backward Glance* (New York: Scribners, 1964); Ellen Glasgow, *The Woman Within* (New York: Harcourt Brace, 1954); Gertrude Stein, *The Autobiography of Alice B. Toklas* (New York: Vintage, 1960); *Everybody's Autobiography* (New York: Random House, 1937); Zora Neale Hurston, *Dust Tracks on a Road, An Autobiography* (Philadelphia: J. B. Lippincott, 1942); Lillian Hellman, *An Unfinished Woman, A Memoir* (New York: Bantam Books, 1970); *Pentimento: A Book of Portraits* (New York: New American Library, 1973); *Scoundrel Time* (Boston: Little Brown, 1976); Mary McCarthy, *Memories of a Catholic Girlhood* (New York: Berkley Pub., 1963); Maureen Howard, *Facts of Life* (New York: Penguin Books, 1978); Gwendolyn Brooks, *Report from Part One* (Detroit: Broadside Press, 1972); Maya Angelou, *I Know Why the Caged Bird Sings* (New York: Bantam Books, 1970); *Gather Together in My Name* (New York: Bantam Books, 1975); *Singin' and Swingin' and Gettin' Merry Like Christmas* (New York: Bantam Books, 1977); Nikki Giovanni, *Gemini: An Extended Autobiographical Statement on My First Twenty-one Years of Being a Black Poet* (Indianapolis: Bobbs-Merrill, 1971).

11. In Lillian Smith, *The Winner Names the Age: A Collection of Writings*

(New York: W. W. Norton, 1978), pp. 187–98. Parenthetical references in the main text are to this edition.

12. See, e.g., reference in footnote 35 to Patricia Meyer Spacks; also Suzanne Juhasz, "Some Deep Old Desk and Capacious Hold-all: Form and Women's Autobiography," *College English* 39 (February 1978): 663–68; Mary G. Mason, "The Other Voice: Autobiographies of Women Writers," in *Autobiography: Essays Theoretical and Critical,* ed. J. Olney (Princeton: Princeton University Press, 1980), pp. 207–35; *Women's Autobiography: Essays in Criticism,* ed. Estelle C. Jelinek (Bloomington: Indiana University Press, 1980); Lillian Schlissel, "Women's Diaries on the Western Frontier," *American Studies* 19 (Spring 1977): 87–100.

13. Adrienne Rich, *Of Woman Born: Motherhood as Experience and Institution* (New York: W. W. Norton, 1976), p. 41.

14. Betty Friedan, *The Feminine Mystique* (New York: Dell Publishers, 1974), p. 69.

15. Barbara Watson, "On Power and the Literary Text," *Signs: Journal of Women in Culture and Society,* 1 (Autumn 1975): 112.

16. Ibid., p. 113.

17. See Clifford Geertz, "The Growth of Culture and the Evolution of Mind," in *Theories of Mind,* ed. J. Scher (Glencoe, Ill.: Free Press of Glencoe, 1962), p. 729.

18. Nancy Chodorow, "Family Structure and Feminine Personality," in *Woman, Culture, and Society,* ed. Michelle Z. Rosaldo and Louise Lamphere (Stanford: Stanford University Press, 1074), p. 44.

19. Sally Kempton, "Cutting Loose: A Private View of the Women's Uprising," *Esquire* 74 (July 1970); reprinted in *The American Sisterhood,* ed. Wendy Martin (New York: Harper & Row, 1972), p. 352.

20. Peter Filene, *Him/Her/Self: Sex Roles in Modern America* (New York: Harcourt Brace Jovanovich, 1974), pp. 233–34.

21. Kempton, "Cutting Loose," p. 352.

22. Elaine Showalter, "Literary Criticism," *Signs* 1 (Winter 1975): 436.

23. Anaïs Nin, "Eroticism in Women," in *In Favor of the Sensitive Man and Other Essays* (New York: Harcourt Brace Jovanovich, 1976), p. 11.

24. Ibid., p. 4.

25. Friedan, *The Feminine Mystique,* p. 126.

26. Ibid., p. 134.

27. Ibid., p. 139.

28. Stephanie A. Demetrakopoulos, "The Metaphysics of Matrilinearism in Women's Autobiography: Studies of Mead's *Blackberry Winter,* Hellman's *Pentimento,* Angelou's *I Know Why the Caged Bird Sings,* and Kingston's *The Woman Warrior,*" in Jelinek, ed., *Women's Autobiography,* pp. 180–205, esp. pp. 184–91.

29. Jelinek, ed., *Women's Autobiography,* p. 10.

30. Henry Miller, "Un Être Étoilique," in *The Cosmological Eye* (Norfolk, Conn.: New Directions, 1939), p. 269.

31. Anaïs Nin, *The Novel of the Future* (New York: Collier Books, 1968), p. 159.

32. Ibid., p. 149. Stuhlmann further explains some of these problems: "In preparing this volume for publication, Miss Nin, and the editor, still faced certain personal and legal considerations inherent in the nature of the Diary. Several persons, when faced with the question of whether they wanted to remain in the Diary 'as is'—since Miss Nin did not want to change the essential nature of the presentation—chose to be deleted altogether from the manuscript (including her husband and some members of her family). The names of some incidental figures have been omitted or changed, since as any reader will soon see, the factual identity of a person is basically unimportant within the context of the Diary. Miss Nin's truth, as we have seen, is psychological" (1, p. xi).

33. Ibid., p. 152.

34. Duane Schneider, *An Interview with Anaïs Nin* (London: Village Press, 1973), p. 9.

35. See Patricia Meyer Spacks, *The Female Imagination* (New York: Alfred A. Knopf, 1976), pp. 390–91.

36. Ibid., p. 405.

37. Nin, "Notes on Feminism," in *In Favor of the Sensitive Man,* p. 28.

38. Ibid., p. 27.

CHAPTER SEVEN.
TWO RECREATE ONE: THE ACT OF COLLABORATION IN RECENT BLACK
AUTOBIOGRAPHY—OSSIE GUFFY, NATE SHAW, MALCOLM X

1. See Du Bois's review, *New York Herald Tribune Weekly Book Review,* March 4, 1945, p. 2.

2. See, e.g., Rebecca C. Barton, *Witnesses for Freedom: Negro Americans in Autobiography* (Oakdale, N.Y.: Dowling College Press, 1976); Sidonie Smith, *Where I'm Bound: Patterns of Slavery and Freedom in Black American Autobiography* (Westport, Conn.: Greenwood Press, 1974); Russell Brignano, *Black Americans in Autobiography: An Annotated Bibliography of Autobiographies and Autobiographical Books Written Since the Civil War* (Durham, N.C.: Duke University Press, 1974); Stephen Butterfield, *Black Autobiography in America* (Amherst: University of Massachusetts Press, 1974); Michael G. Cooke, "Modern Black Autobiography in the Tradition," in *Romanticism, Vistas, Instances, Continuities,* ed. David Thornburn and Geoffrey Hartman (Ithaca: Cornell University Press, 1973), pp. 255–80; John M. Blassingame, "Black Autobiographies as History and Literature," *Black Scholar* 5 (December 1973–January 1974): 2–9; Roger Rosenblatt, "Black Autobiography: Life as the Death Weapon," *Yale Review* 65 (Summer 1976): 515–27; and the Summer 1975 issue of *Kansas Quarterly;* Elizabeth Schultz, "To Be Black and Blue: The Blues Genre in Black American Autobiography," *Kansas Quarterly* 7 (Summer 1975): 81–96; reprinted in *The American Autobiography: A Collec-*

tion of Critical Essays, ed. Albert E. Stone (Englewood Cliffs, N.J.: Prentice-Hall, 1981), pp. 109–32.

3. Rosenblatt, "Black Autobiography: Life as the Death Weapon," p. 517.

4. Preface, Pearl Bailey, *The Raw Pearl* (New York: Harcourt, Brace & World, 1968), p. vii.

5. "The Co-Author and the Book," Mahalia Jackson with Evan McLeod Wylie, *Movin' on Up* (New York: Hawthorn Books, 1966), p. 221.

6. *nigger* by Dick Gregory with Robert Lipsyte (New York: Pocketbooks, 1965), p. xi. Parenthetical references in the main text are to this edition.

7. *Lady Sings the Blues,* Billie Holiday with William Dufty (New York: Doubleday, 1956), p. 186. Parenthetical references in the main text are to this Lancer edition.

8. *Ossie: The Autobiography of a Black Woman,* Ossie Guffy as told to Caryl Ledner (New York: Bantam Books, 1971), p. ix. Parenthetical references in the main text are to this Bantam edition.

9. Frederick C. Crews, "Do Literary Studies Have an Ideology?" *PMLA* 85 (May 1970): 425, quoting Martin Nicolaus, "The Professional Organization of Sociology: A View from Below," *Antioch Review* 29 (Fall 1969): 381.

10. Theodore Rosengarten, *All God's Dangers: The Life of Nate Shaw* (New York: Avon, 1974), pp. xxii–xxiii. Parenthetical references in the main text are to this edition.

11. See John Beecher, *Collected Poems, 1924–1974* (New York: Macmillan, 1974), pp. 33–48.

12. Alex Haley, *The Autobiography of Malcolm X* (New York: Grove Press, 1965), p. 2. Parenthetical references in the main text are to this edition.

13. Larry Neal, "And Shine Swam On," *Black Fire: An Anthology of Afro-American Writing,* ed. LeRoi Jones and Roy Neal (New York: Morrow, 1968), pp. 644–45.

14. Robert E. Hayden, "El Hajj Malik El-Shabazz," in *Angle of Ascent: New and Selected Poems* (New York: Liveright, 1975), p. 58.

15. A. L. Elmessiri, "Islam as Pastoral in the Life of Malcolm X," *Malcolm X: The Man and His Times,* ed. J. H. Clarke (New York: Macmillan, 1969), pp. 69–78.

16. See Stephen Henderson, *The Militant Black Writer in Africa and the United States* (with M. Cook) (Madison: University of Wisconsin Press, 1969).

17. Rosenblatt, "Black Autobiography: Life as the Death Weapon," p. 525.

18. NBC Evening News, July 2, 1979. The quotations represent my notes taken at the time.

19. See Sigmund Freud, "The Moses of Michelangelo" (1914), in *Character and Culture* (New York: Collier Books, 1963), pp. 80–106.

20. But see James Hillman, "The Fiction of Case History: A Round," in *Religion as Story,* ed. James B. Wiggins (New York: Harper & Row, 1975), pp. 123–73. Hillman emphasizes that the psychoanalytic case history "is not autobiography; nor is it biography" (p. 134)—since the "plot" of a case history is a mental condition. Nevertheless, he points out other similarities. Besides "the

modesty of the humble narrator in the background" (p. 127), there are the complex interactions of writer and subject including "the analysis of one persons' story by the other, . . . the critic working over an embodied history, . . . the talk between two partners in a dialectic, . . . a contest between singers" (p. 139).

CHAPTER EIGHT.
FACTUAL FICTIONS: EXPERIMENTS IN AUTOBIOGRAPHY BY
NORMAN MAILER, FRANK CONROY, LILLIAN HELLMAN

1. Ernest Hemingway, *A Moveable Feast* (New York: Bantam Books, 1965), preface.

2. Mary McCarthy, "To the Reader," *Memories of a Catholic Girlhood* (New York: Berkley, 1963), pp. 9–10.

3. Robert Pirsig, "Author's Note," *Zen and the Art of Motorcycle Maintenance* (New York: Morrow, 1974).

4. Lillian Hellman, *Pentimento: A Book of Portraits* (New York: New American Library, 1973). Parenthetical references in the main text are to this Signet edition.

5. Frederick Exley, "A Note to the Reader," *A Fan's Notes: A Fictional Memoir* (New York: Random House, 1968).

6. N. Berberova, *Russian Review* 26 (October 1967): 406.

7. Vladimir Nabokov, *Speak, Memory* (New York: Putnam, 1966), p. 70.

8. James Rother, "Para-Fiction: The Adjacent Universe of Barth, Barthelme, Pynchon, and Nabokov," *boundaries 2,* 5 (Fall 1976): 42–43.

9. Doris Eder, in *Surfiction: Fiction Now and Tomorrow,* ed. Raymond Federman (Chicago: Swallow Press, 1975), p. 12.

10. Rother, "Para-Fiction," p. 22.

11. Frank Conroy, *Stop-time* (New York: Viking Press, 1967) (parenthetical references in the main text are to this Compass edition); Gore Vidal, *Two Sisters: A Memoir in the Form of a Novel* (Boston: Little, Brown, 1970); George Cain, *Blueschild Baby* (New York: McGraw-Hill, 1970); Herbert Gold, *Fathers: A Novel in the Form of a Memoir* (New York: Random House, 1967); Ronald Sukenick, *Up* (New York: Dial Press, 1968). Parenthetical references in the main text are to this edition.

12. Ronald Sukenick, "The Death of the Novel," in *The Death of the Novel and Other Stories* (New York: Dial Press, 1969), p. 41.

13. Ma'sud Zavarzadeh, *The Mythopoeic Reality: The Postwar American Nonfiction Novel* (Urbana: University of Illinois Press, 1976), p. 226. Parenthetical references in the main text are to this edition.

14. Burton Pike, "Time in Autobiography," *Comparative Literature* 28 (Fall 1976): 337–38.

15. Alfred Kazin, "Autobiography as Narrative," *Michigan Quarterly Review* 3 (Fall 1964): 211. Parenthetical references in the text are to this source.

16. Interview in Joe D. Bellamy, *The New Fiction: Interviews with Innovative American Writers* (Urbana: University of Illinois Press, 1974), p. 90.

17. Ibid., p. 95.

18. Studs Terkel, *Talking to Myself: A Memoir of My Times* (New York: Pantheon Books, 1977).

19. Elizabeth Bruss, "Eye for I: Making and Unmaking Autobiography in Film," *Autobiography: Essays Theoretical and Critical,* ed. J. Olney (Princeton: Princeton University Press, 1980), pp. 296–310.

20. Barrett J. Mandel, "Full of Life Now," in Olney, ed., *Autobiography,* p. 54.

21. F. Russell Hart, "History Talking to Itself: Public Personality in Recent Memoir," *New Literary History* 11 (Autumn 1979): 193–210.

22. The edition of *The Armies of the Night* henceforth cited parenthetically is the Signet Edition (New York: New American Library, 1968).

23. See Warner Berthoff, "Witness and Testament: Two Contemporary Classics," in *Aspects of Narrative,* ed. J. H. Miller (New York: Columbia University Press, 1971), pp. 188–98.

24. Mandel, "Full of Life Now," p. 64.

25. Foreword, *Autobiography of a Schizophrenic Girl,* an Analytic Interpretation by Marguerite Sechehaye (New York: New American Library, 1970), p. viii.

26. Pike, "Time in Autobiography," p. 342.

27. Ibid., p. 335.

28. John Sturrock, "The New Model Autobiographer," *New Literary History* 9 (Autumn 1977): 51.

29. Lillian Hellman, *An Unfinished Woman, A Memoir* (New York: Bantam Books, 1970) (parenthetical references in the main text are to this edition); *Scoundrel Time* (Boston: Little Brown, 1976) (parenthetical references in the main text are to this first edition). See also, however, *Three/By Lillian Hellman* (Boston: Little, Brown, 1979), and *Maybe: A Story* (Boston: Little, Brown, 1980).

30. *An Unfinished Woman,* p. 174.

31. Patricia Meyer Spacks, *The Female Imagination* (New York: Alfred A. Knopf, 1976), pp. 382–83.

32. I am grateful to Catherine Bruch for drawing Bennett's programmatic piece to my attention.

33. Mandel, "Full of Life Now," p. 53.

34. Ibid., p. 58.

35. Norman Holland, "Prose and Minds: A Psychoanalytic Approach to Non-Fiction," in *The Art of Victorian Prose,* ed. George Levine and William Madden (New York: Oxford University Press, 1968), pp. 332–33.

36. Ibid., p. 322.

37. See also Darrel Mansell, "Unsettling the Colonel's Hash: 'Fact' in Autobiography," *Modern Language Quarterly* 37 (June 1976): 115–32, reprinted in *The American Autobiography: A Collection of Critical Essays,* ed. Albert E. Stone (Englewood Cliffs, N.J.: Prentice-Hall, 1981), pp. 61–79.

38. Fred Chappell, "Six Propositions About Literature and History," *New Literary History* 1 (Spring 1970): 521–22.

39. See, again, Jack H. Hexter, "The Rhetoric of History," in *Doing History* (Bloomington: Indiana University Press, 1971), pp. 15–76.

40. Wilhelm Dilthey, *Pattern and Meaning in History,* ed. H. Rickman (New York: Harper & Row, 1960), pp. 85–86.

Index